TOMARE!

止まれ
[STOP!]

D1483832

You're going the wrong way!

Manga is a completely different type of reading experience.

To start at the *beginning*, go to the *end*!

That's right! Authentic manga is read the traditional Japanese way—from right to left, exactly the *opposite* of how American books are read. It's easy to follow: Just go to the other end of the book, and read each page—and each panel—from right side to lett side, starting at the top right. Now you're experiencing manga as it was meant to be!

Pumpkin Scissors

Imperial Army State Section III

by
Ryotaro Iwanaga

Translated and adapted by
Ikoi Hiroe

Lettering and retouch by
North Market Street Graphics

Ballantine Books • New York

Pumpkin Scissors volume 4 is a work of fiction. Names, characters, places, and incidents are the products of the author's imagination or are used fictitiously. Any resemblance to actual events, locales, or persons, living or dead, is entirely coincidental.

A Del Rey Manga/Kodansha Trade Paperback Original

Published in the United States by Del Rey, an imprint of The Random House Publishing Group, a division of Random House, Inc., New York.

Publication rights arranged through Kodansha Ltd.

First published in Japan in 2005 by Kodansha Ltd., Tokyo

ISBN 978-0-345-50334-3

Printed in the United States of America

www.delreymanga.com

1 3 5 7 9 8 6 4 2

Translator/adapter: Ikoi Hiroe
Lettering: NMSG

Contents

Noblemen also
have families and
loved ones!

—Ryotaro Iwanaga

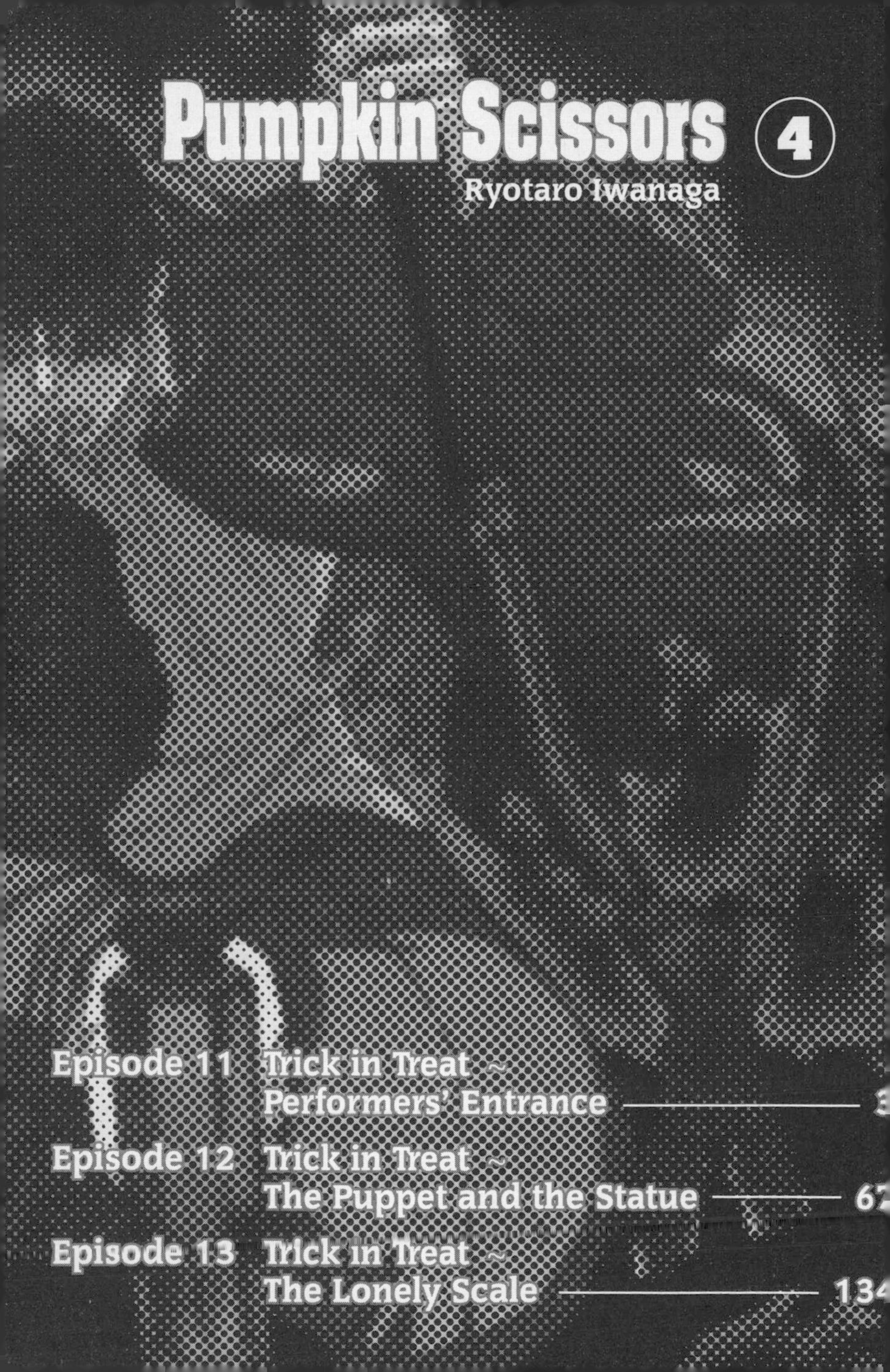

Pumpkin Scissors 4

Ryotaro Iwanaga

About This Story

The bloody war between the Empire and the Republic of Frost left a deep wound throughout the Empire.

Three years have passed since the cease-fire, now known as the Thin Ice Treaty. The Empire is still plagued with starvation and disease while gangs of former soldiers terrorize the populace. The Empire is now fighting another battle to repair the destruction of war. Imperial Army State Section III was established as a "propaganda" tool to placate the masses. However, the members of Imperial Army State Section III, known as "Pumpkin Scissors," are committed to cutting through the thick skin of corruption and crime to bring justice to the people...

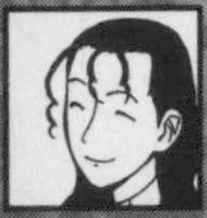

Solice

Alice's older sister and the oldest daughter of the Malvin family. Married. She has nerves of steel underneath her gentle and relaxed demeanor.

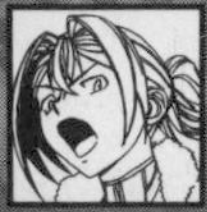

Elis

Alice's older sister and the second oldest daughter of the Malvin family. Married. Her dynamic and passionate personality combines well with her sharp intuition. She cares for Alice deeply.

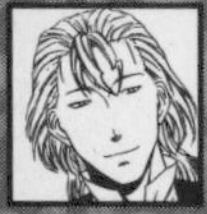

Lionel

Alice's fiancee. He's not a high-ranking nobleman, but his talent and charisma have made him the toast of high society. He's known as the young "Lion" of the financial world.

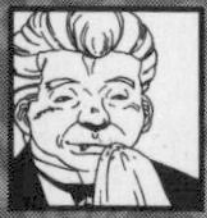

Lord Paulo

The economic director of the Empire. A brutal, arrogant man. A treacherous nobleman who willingly abuses his power. He's misappropriating public funds in secret.

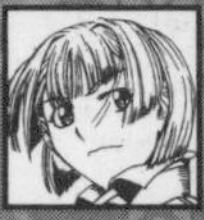

Lieutenant Alice Malvin

Born into nobility, she's a straightforward and kind soul. The 2nd lieutenant for Pumpkin Scissors, she works hard to advance the cause of reconstruction and war relief for the people.

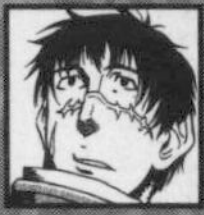

Corporal Oland

A towering giant, he was a scarred-up veteran who reenlisted into Section III. During the war, he was one of the Invisible Nine unit members.

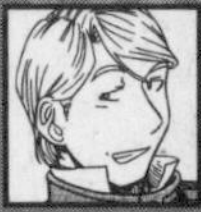

Warrant Officer Oreldo

An officer in Pumpkin Scissors, aka "Stockade Houdini." He comes across as a mellow, light-hearted guy, but he also seems to have a serious side.

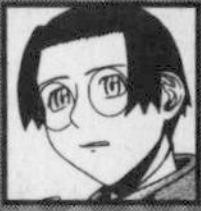

Warrant Officer Machs

He seems to be the most sensible of all the Pumpkin Scissors members. Yet, he's friends with Oreldo, so there may be more than meets the eye...

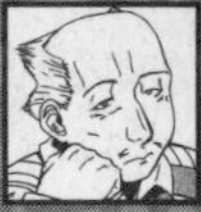

Captain Hunks

The leader of Section III, his razor-sharp mind is hidden underneath his leisurely, low-key exterior.

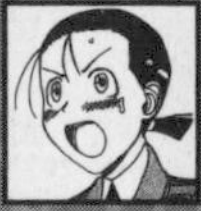

Sergeant Major Stecchin

A clumsy young girl, she's the paper pusher for Section III. She doesn't resemble a soldier, nor does she consider herself to be one.

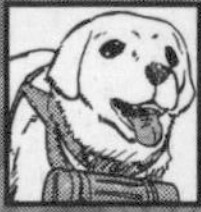

Mercury

Section III Courier Private First Class Messenger Dog. He's a lovable male with a goofy face. He hasn't been seen recently...

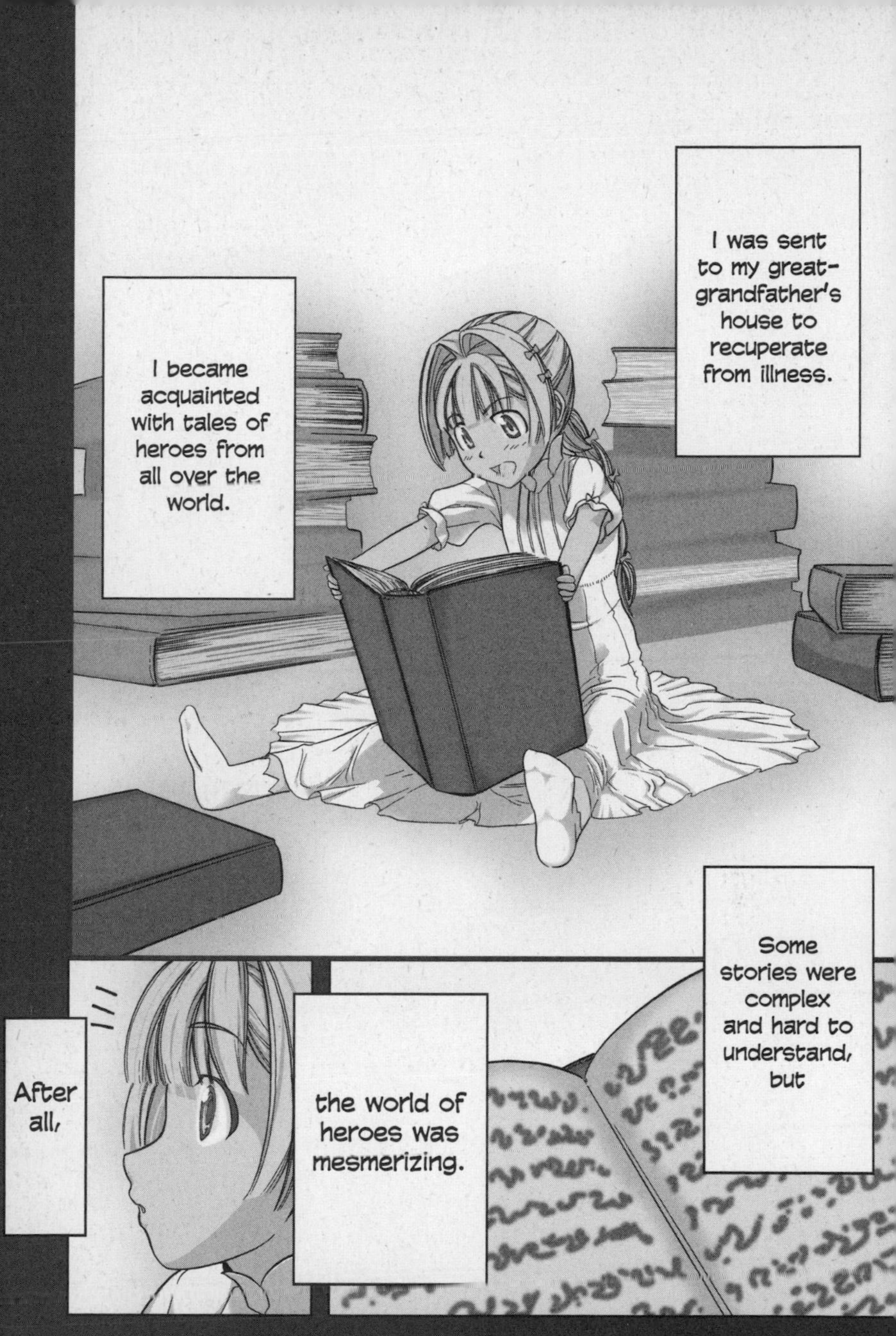
I was sent to my great-grandfather's house to recuperate from illness.
I became acquainted with tales of heroes from all over the world.
Some stories were complex and hard to understand, but
the world of heroes was mesmerizing.
After all,

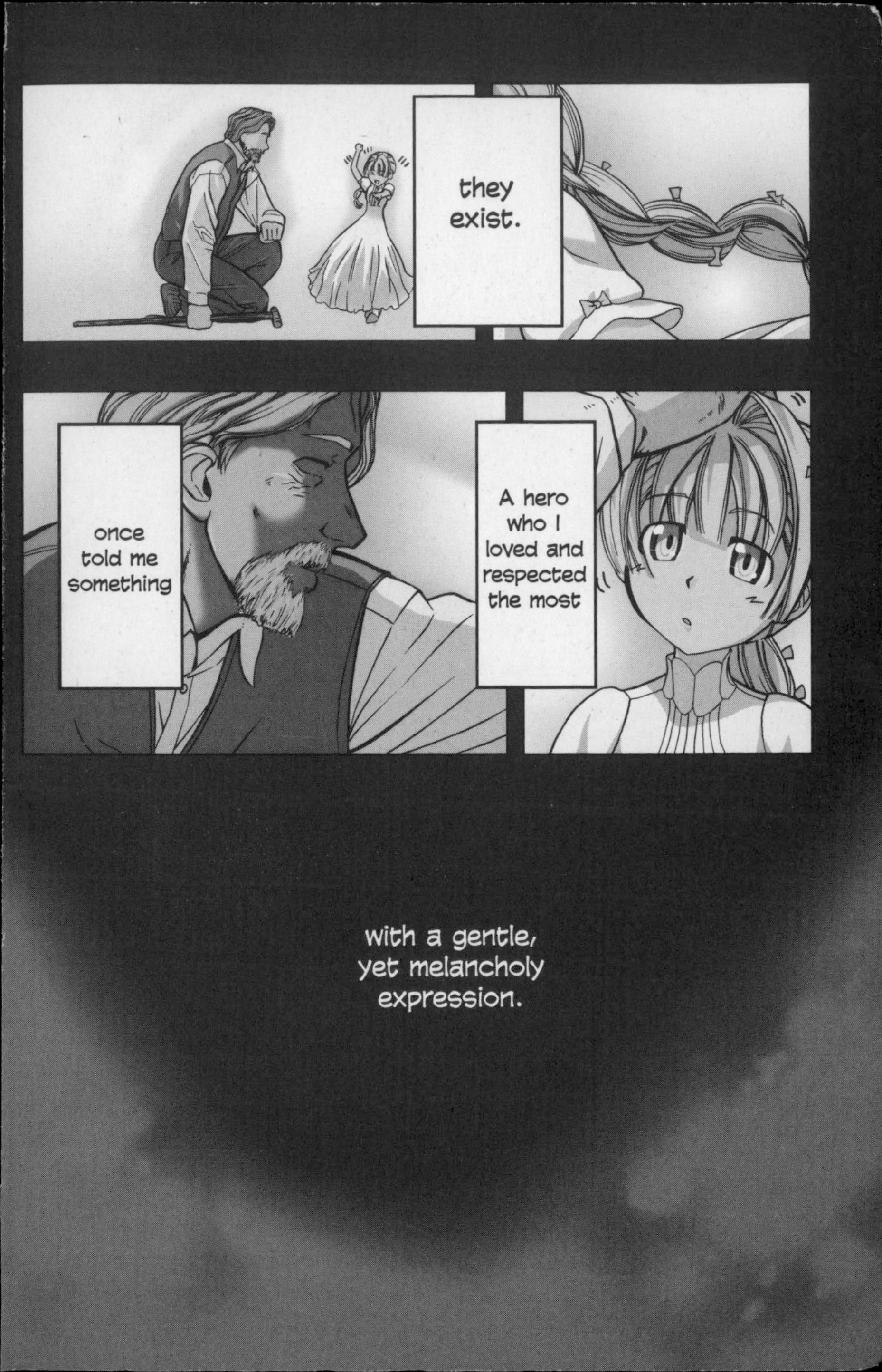
they exist.
A hero who I loved and respected the most
once told me something
with a gentle, yet melancholy expression.

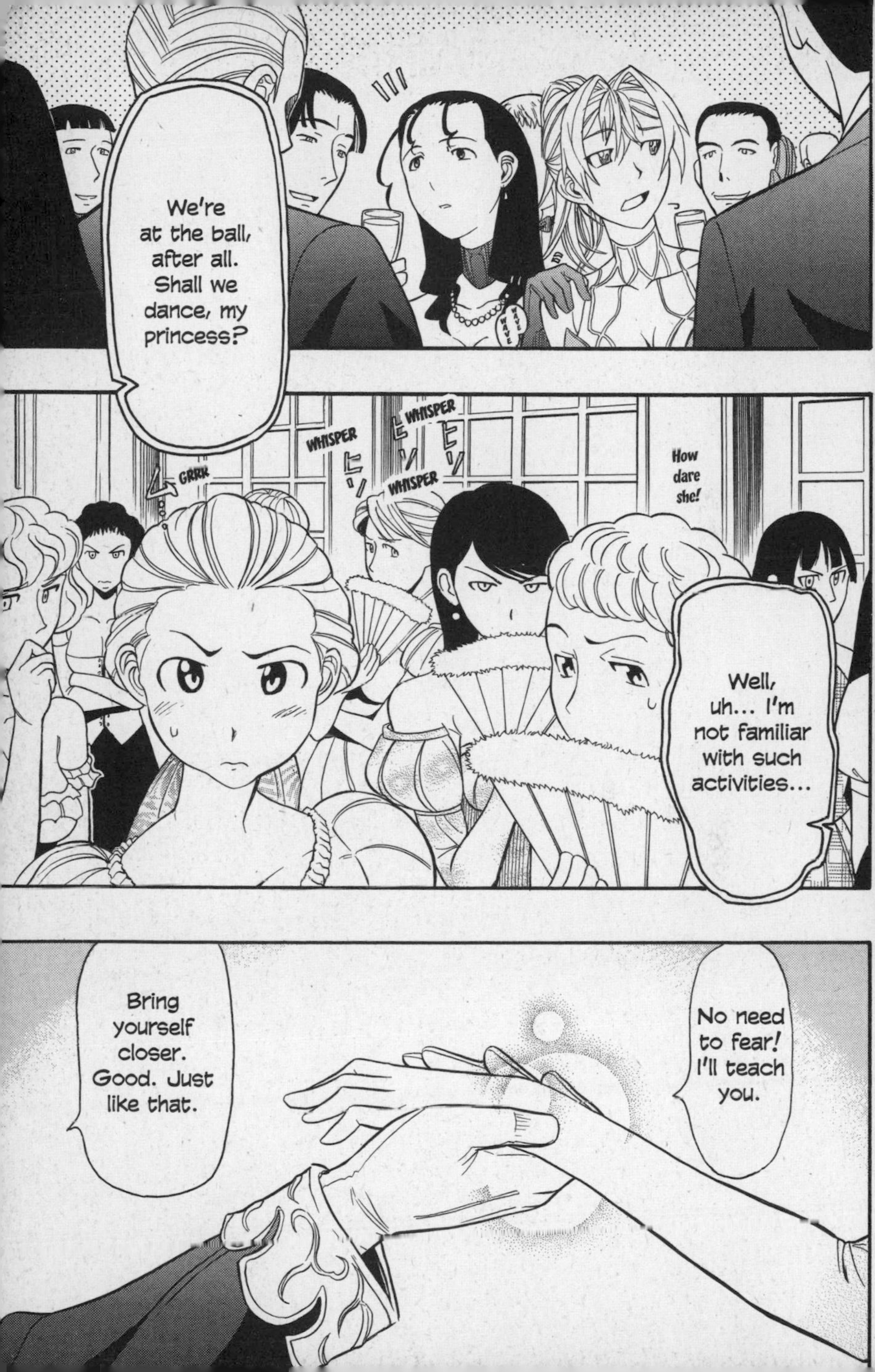
WAVE WAVE
We're at the ball, after all. Shall we dance, my princess?
How dare she!
Well, uh... I'm not familiar with such activities...
WHISPER
WHISPER
WHISPER
GRRK
No need to fear! I'll teach you.
Bring yourself closer. Good. Just like that.

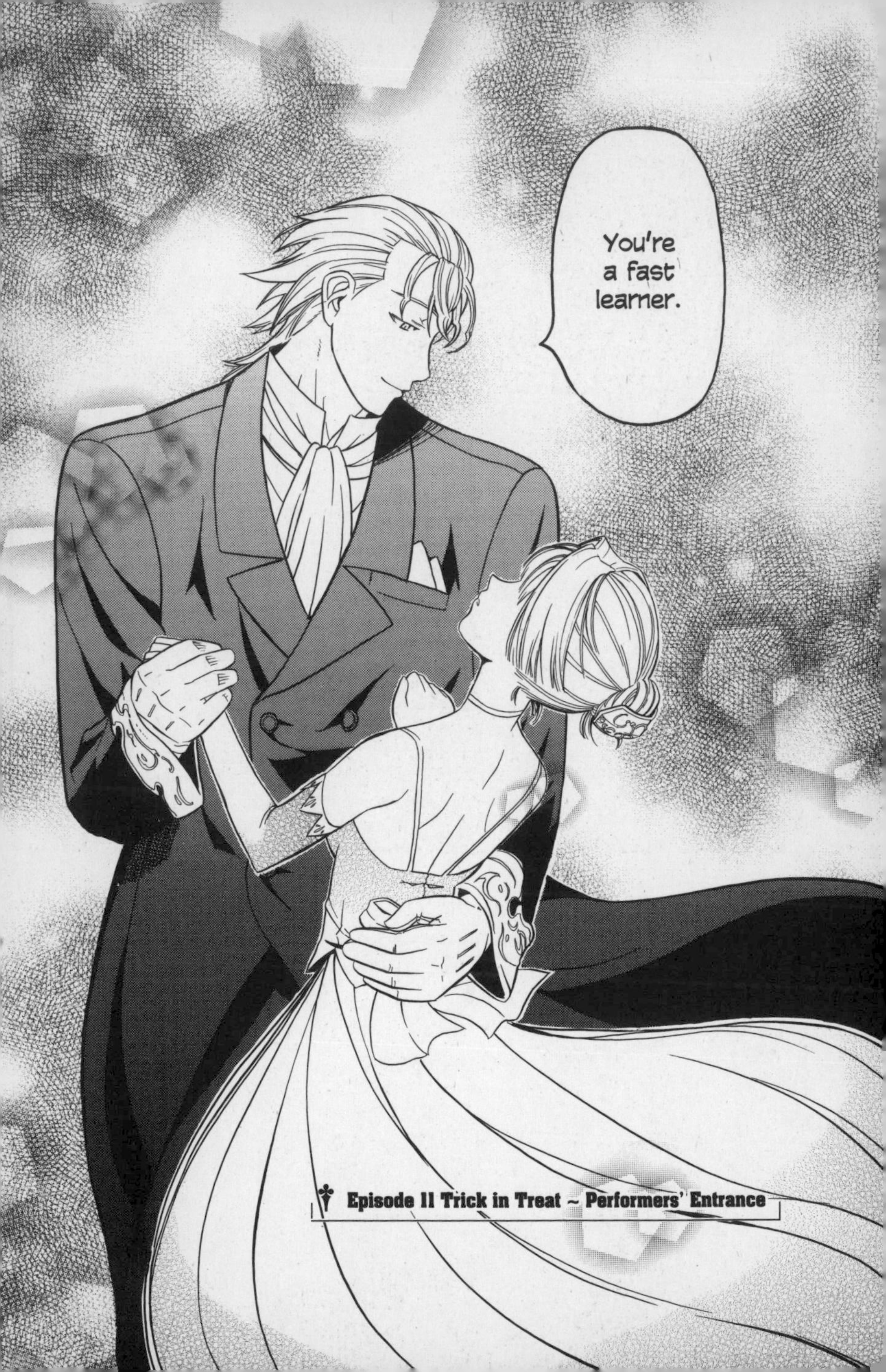
You're a fast learner.
Episode 11 Trick in Treat ~ Performers' Entrance

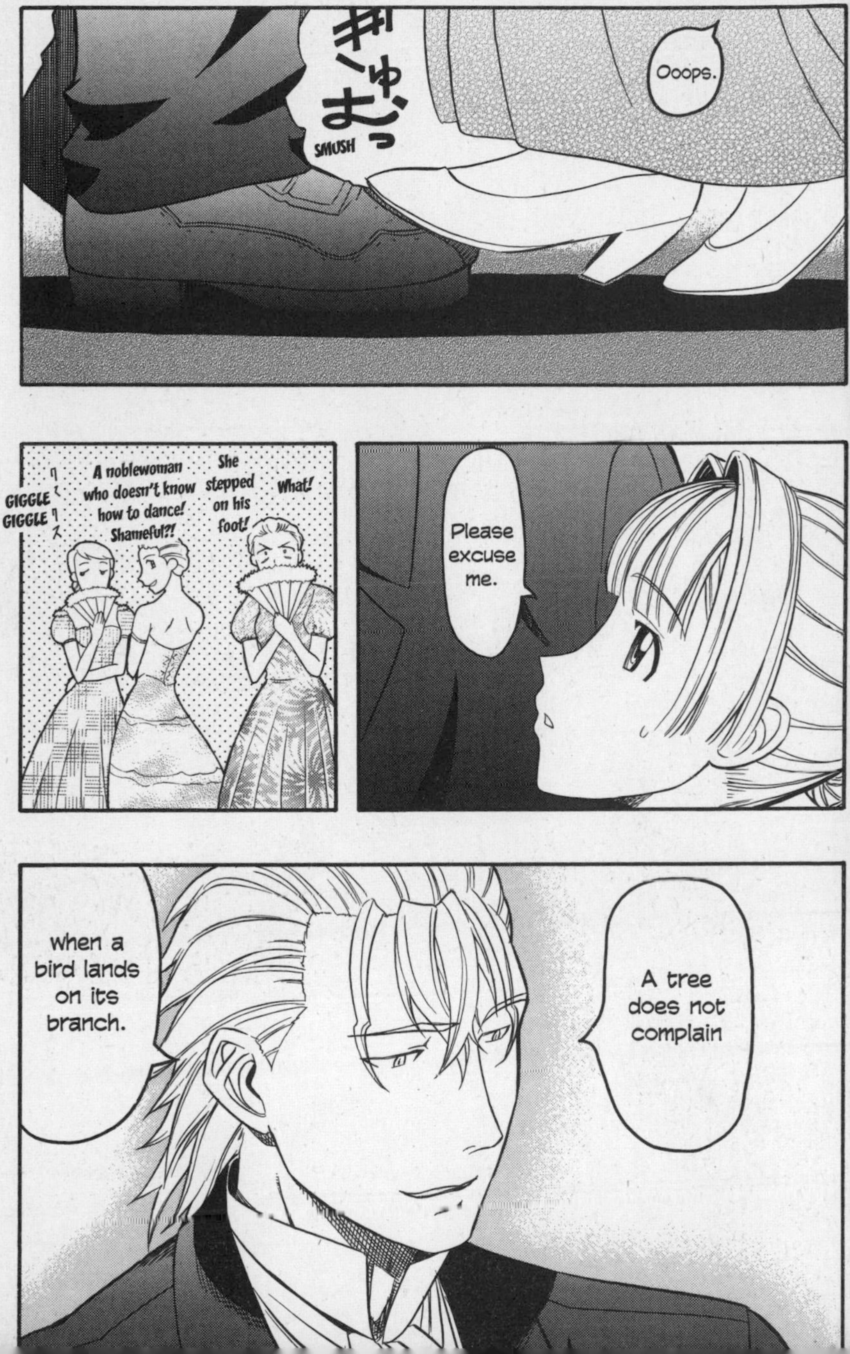
ぎゅむっ
SMUSH
Ooops.
Please excuse me.
What!
She stepped on his foot!
A noblewoman who doesn't know how to dance! Shameful?!
GIGGLE GIGGLE
A tree does not complain
when a bird lands on its branch.

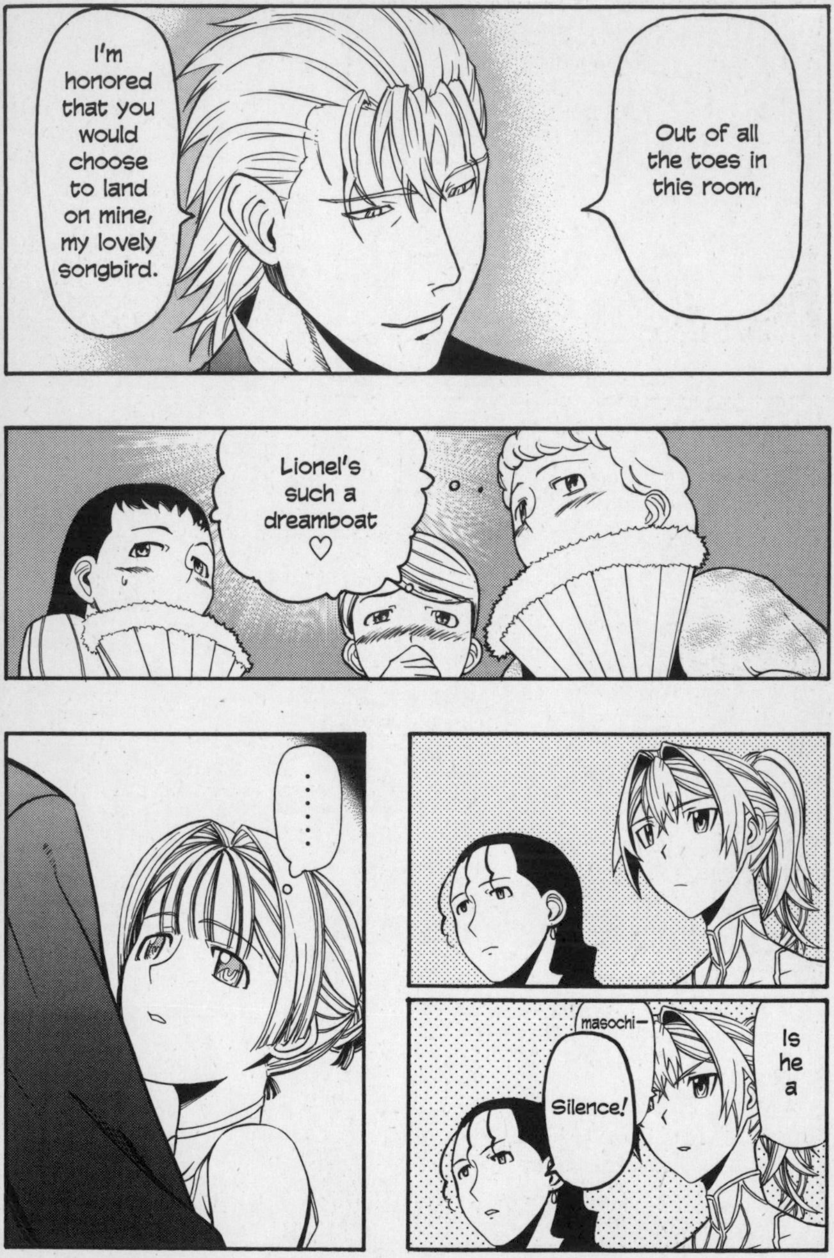
Out of all the toes in this room,
I'm honored that you would choose to land on mine, my lovely songbird.
Lionel's such a dreamboat ♡
Is he a
masochi—
Silence!
......

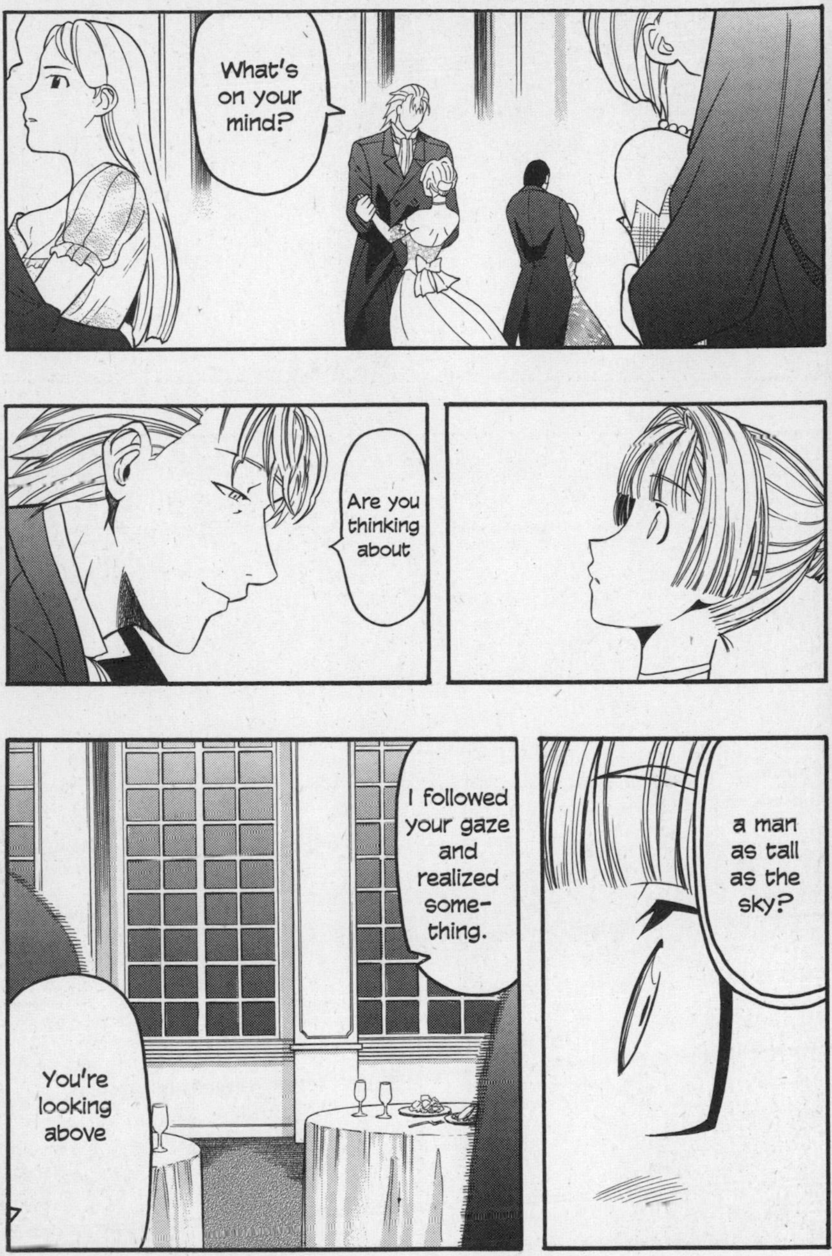
What's on your mind?
Are you thinking about
a man as tall as the sky?
I followed your gaze and realized some-thing.
You're looking above

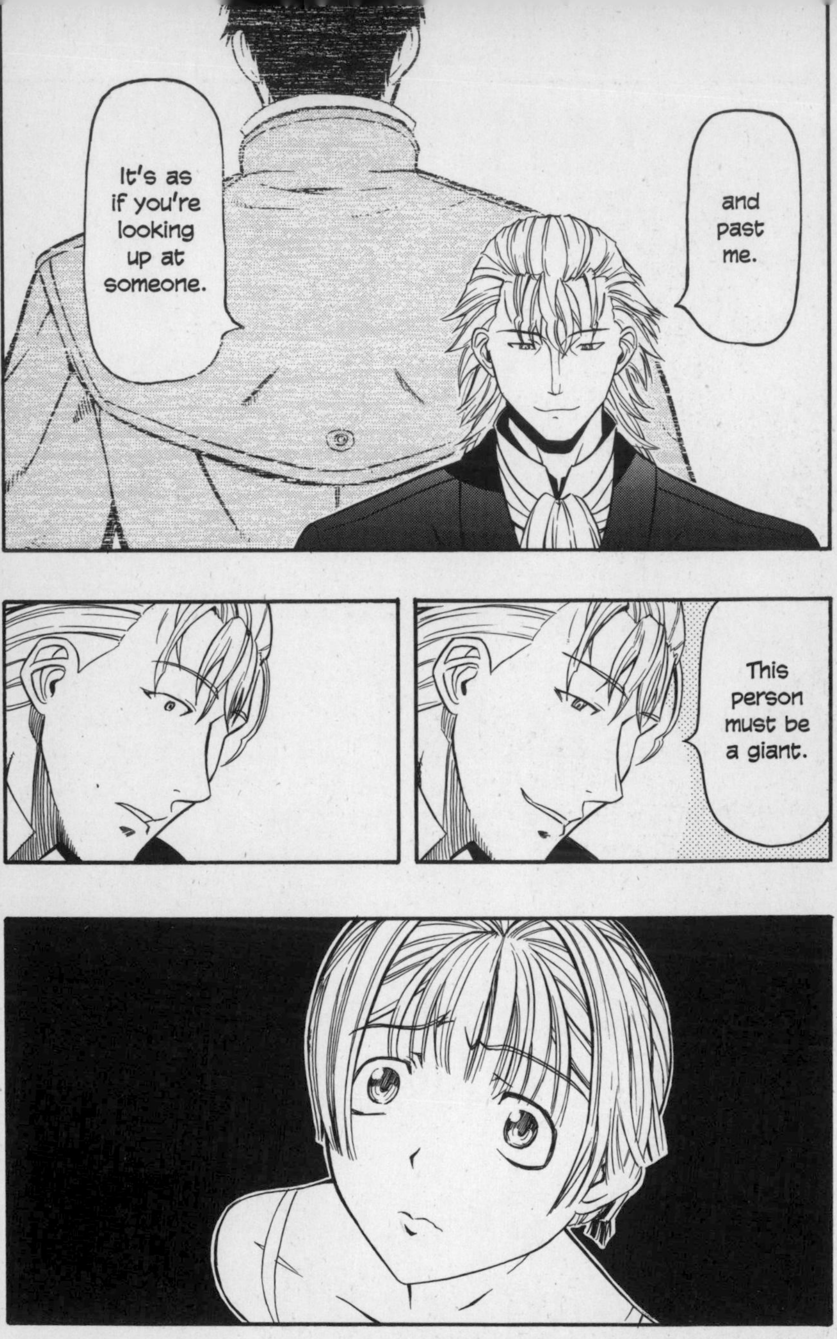
It's as if you're looking up at someone.
and past me.
This person must be a giant.

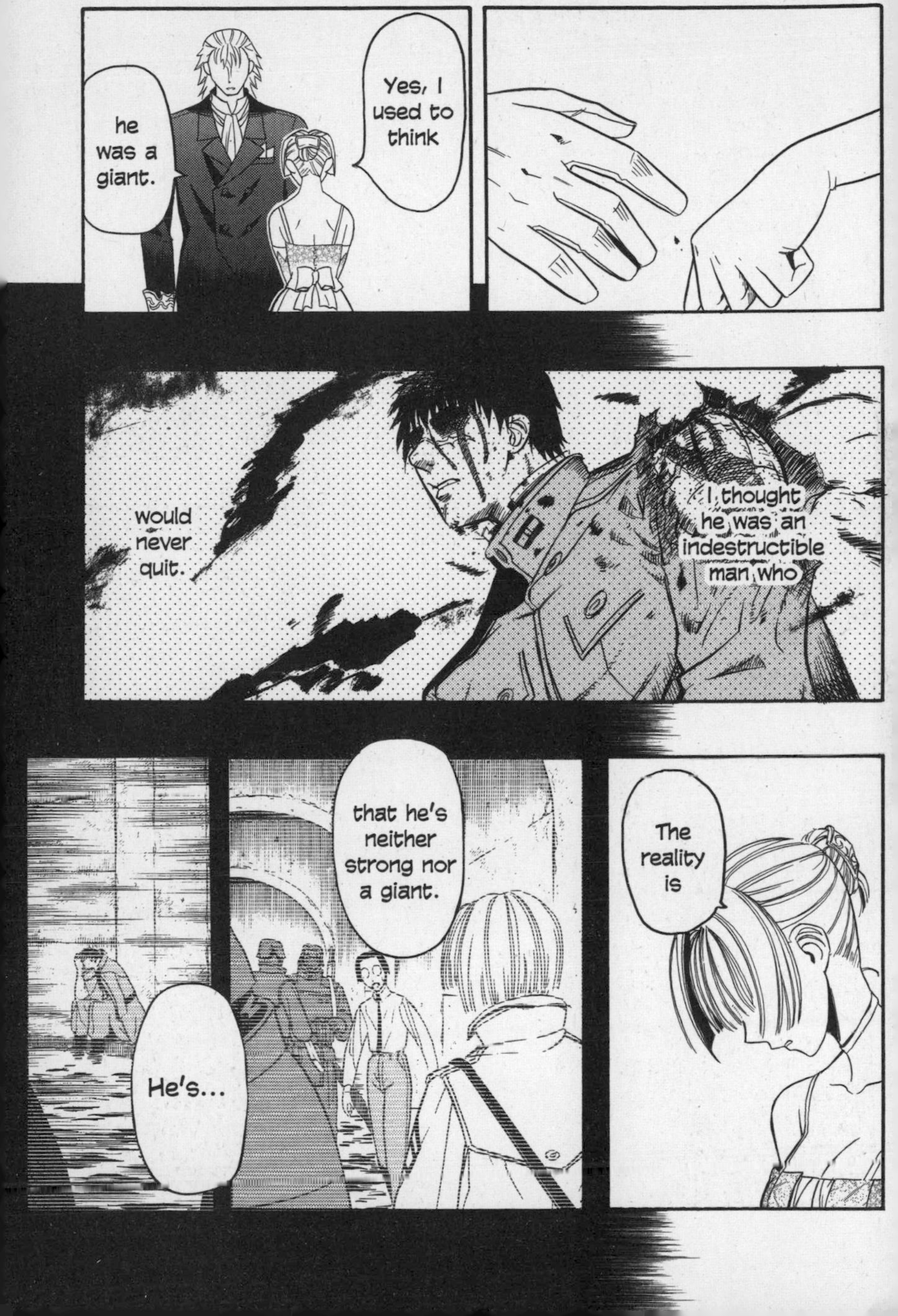
Yes, I used to think
he was a giant.
I thought he was an indestructible man who
would never quit.
The reality is
that he's neither strong nor a giant.
He's...

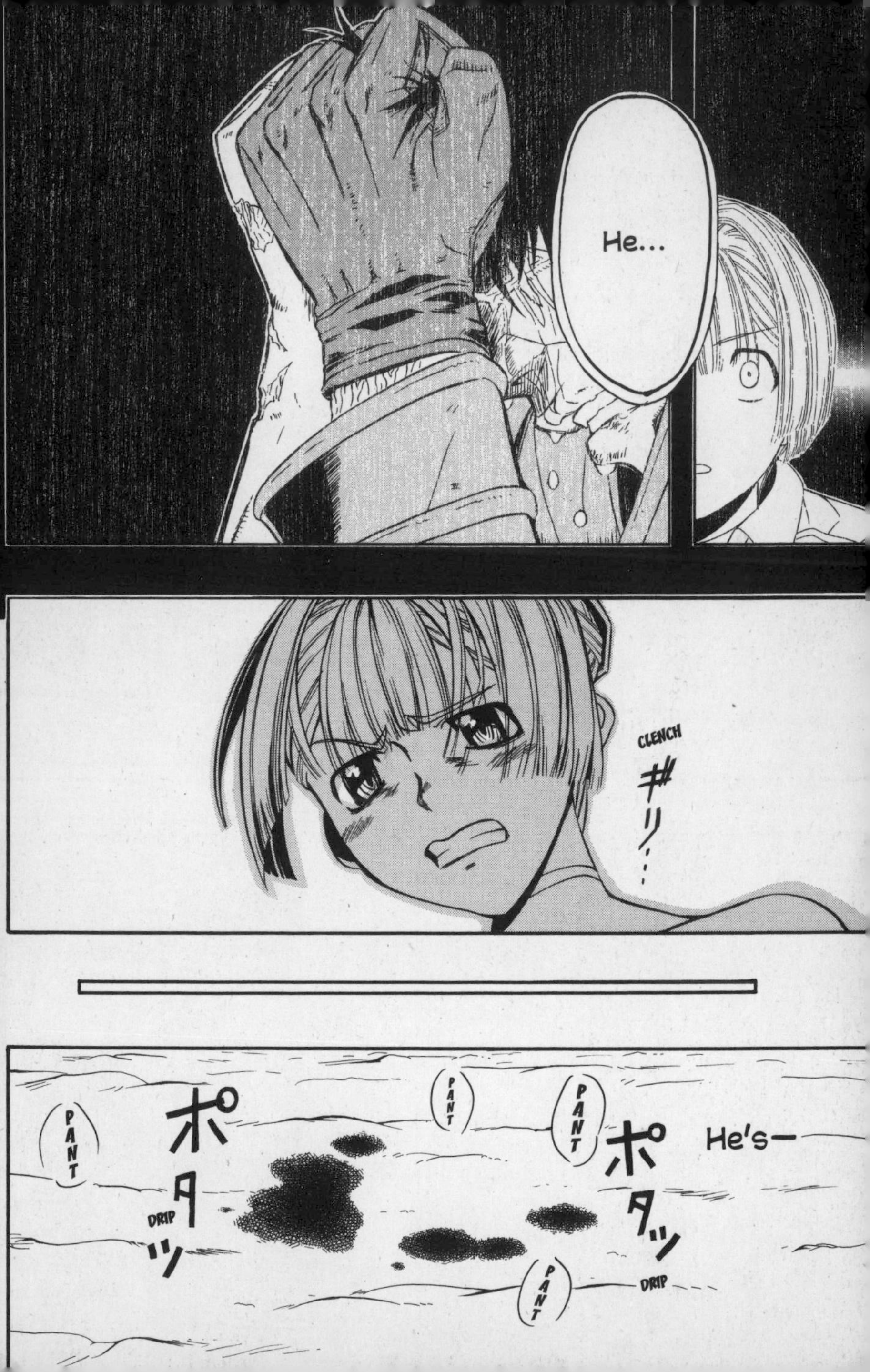
He...
CLENCH
ギリ…
He's—
PANT
ポタッ
DRIP
PANT
PANT
ポタッ
DRIP
PANT

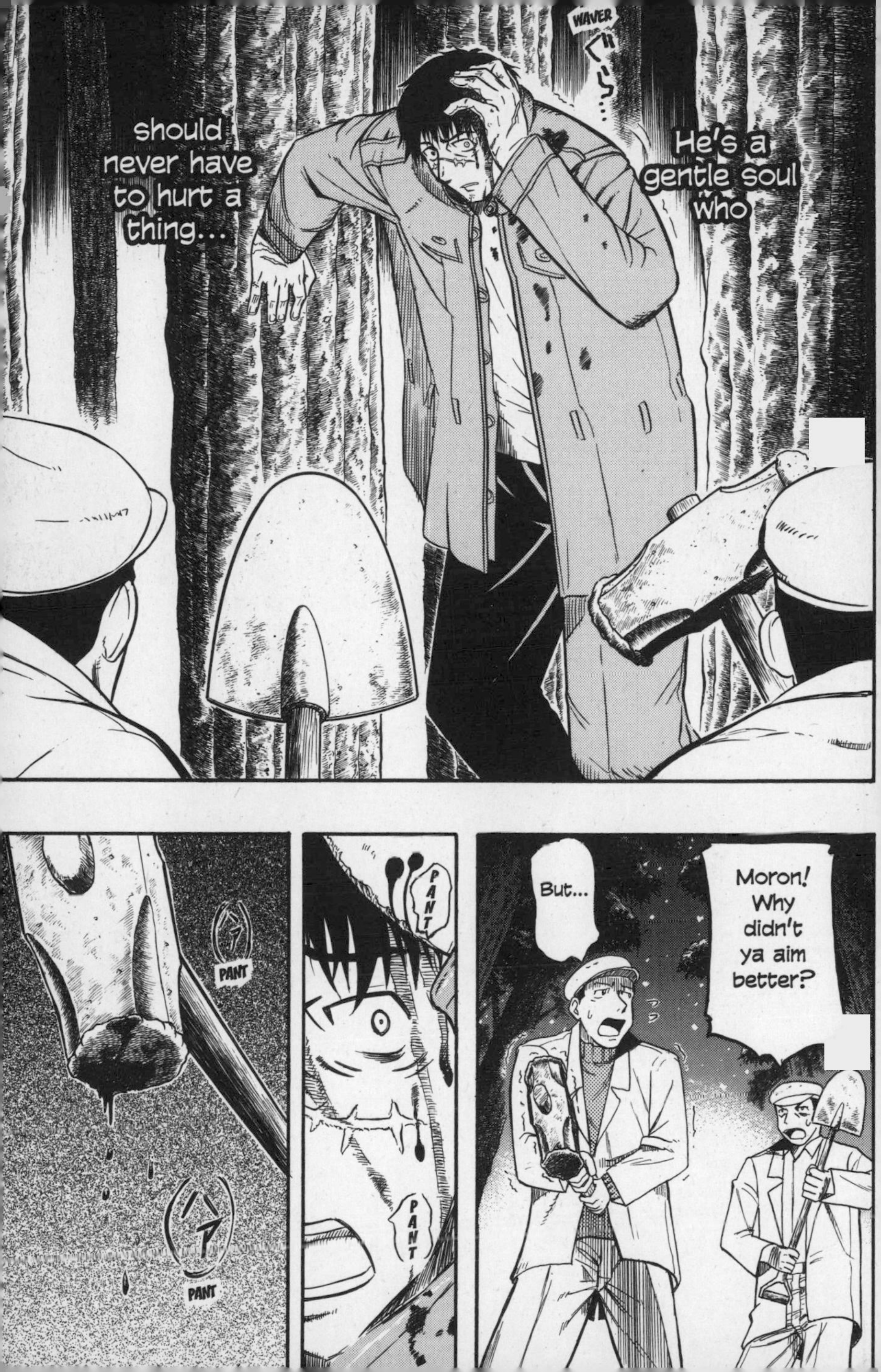
WAVER
He's a gentle soul who
should never have to hurt a thing...
Moron! Why didn't ya aim better?
But...
PANT
PANT
PANT
PANT

Don't let him get away!

DASH

GUAAAAAH

THUDD

Why...

HUFF

PUFF

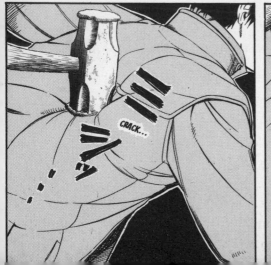

CRACK...

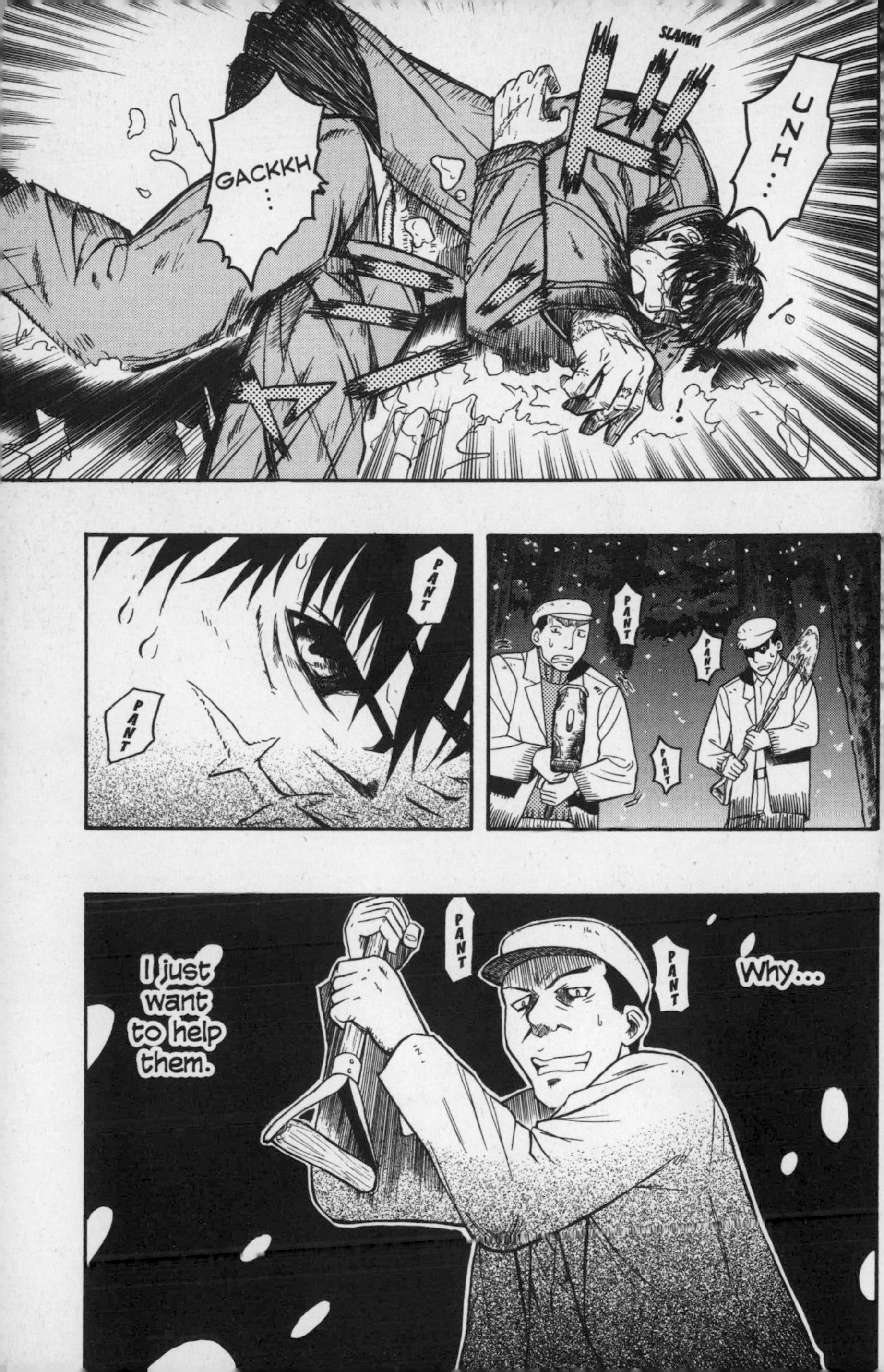
SLAMM
UNH...
!
!
GACKKH...
PANT
PANT
PANT
PANT
PANT
PANT
Why...
PANT
PANT
I just want to help them.

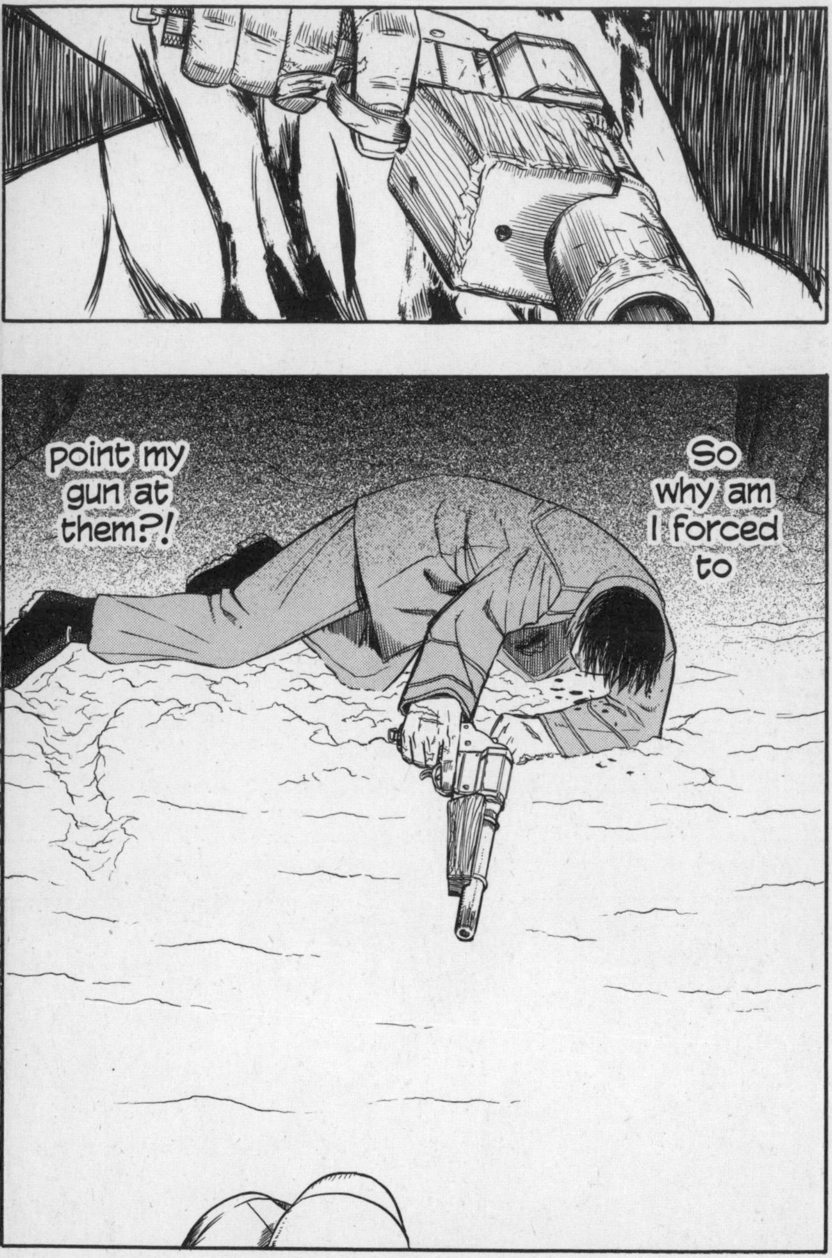
So why am I forced to
point my gun at them?!

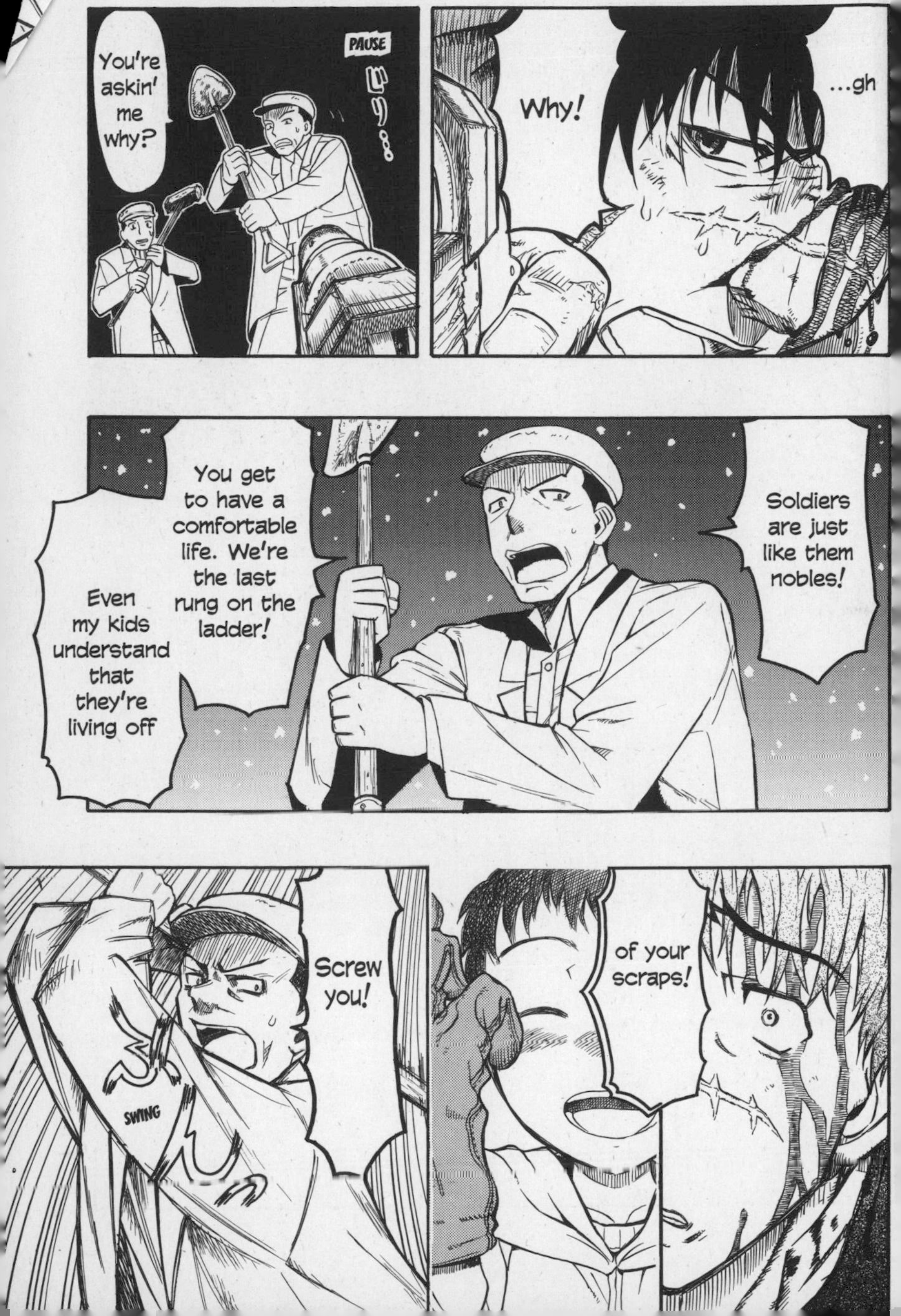
...gh
Why!
PAUSE
じり…
You're askin' me why?
Soldiers are just like them nobles!
You get to have a comfortable life. We're the last rung on the ladder!
Even my kids understand that they're living off
of your scraps!
Screw you!
SWING

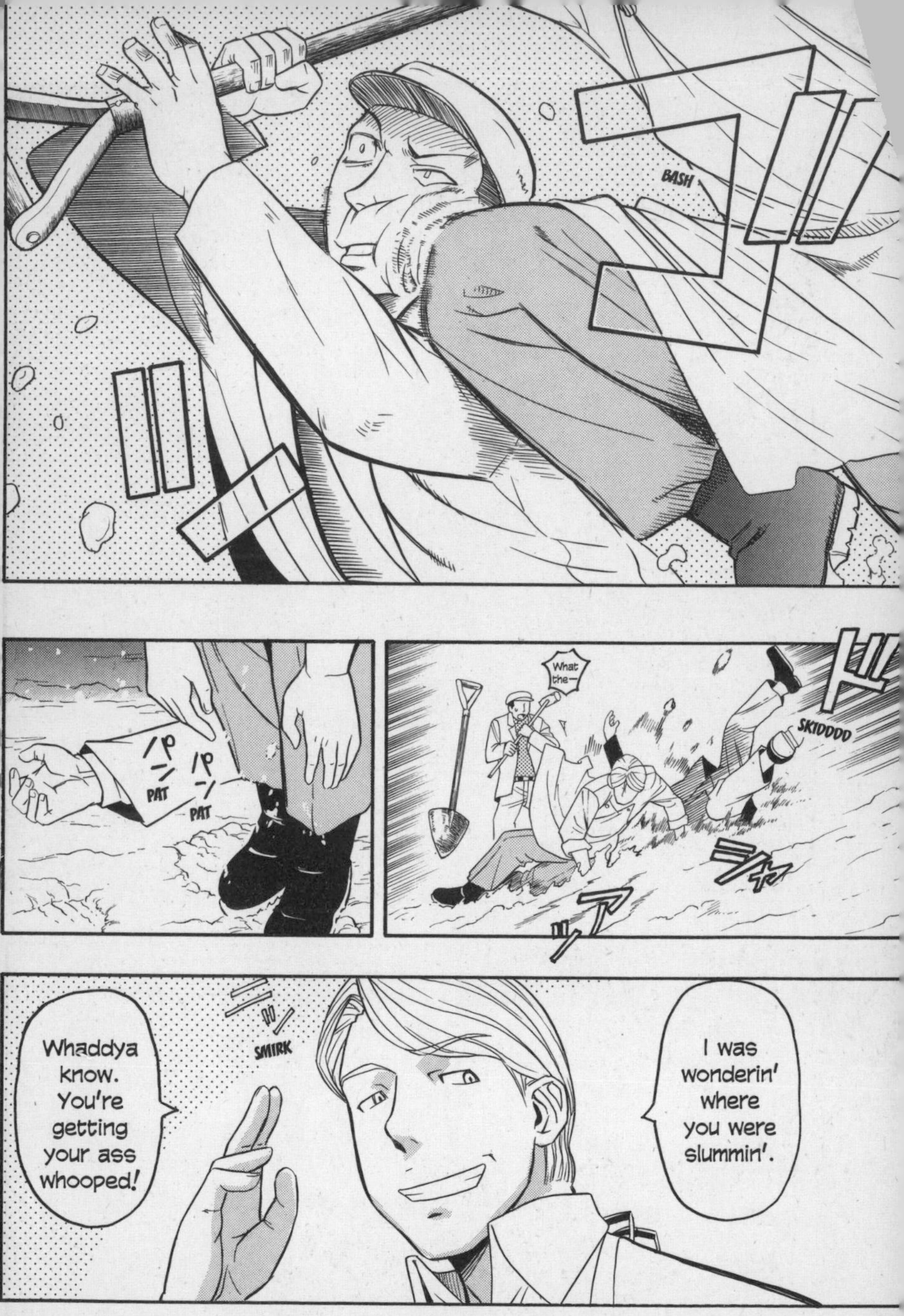
BASH
What the—
SKIDDDD
PAT
PAT
I was wonderin' where you were slummin'.
SMIRK
Whaddya know. You're getting your ass whooped!

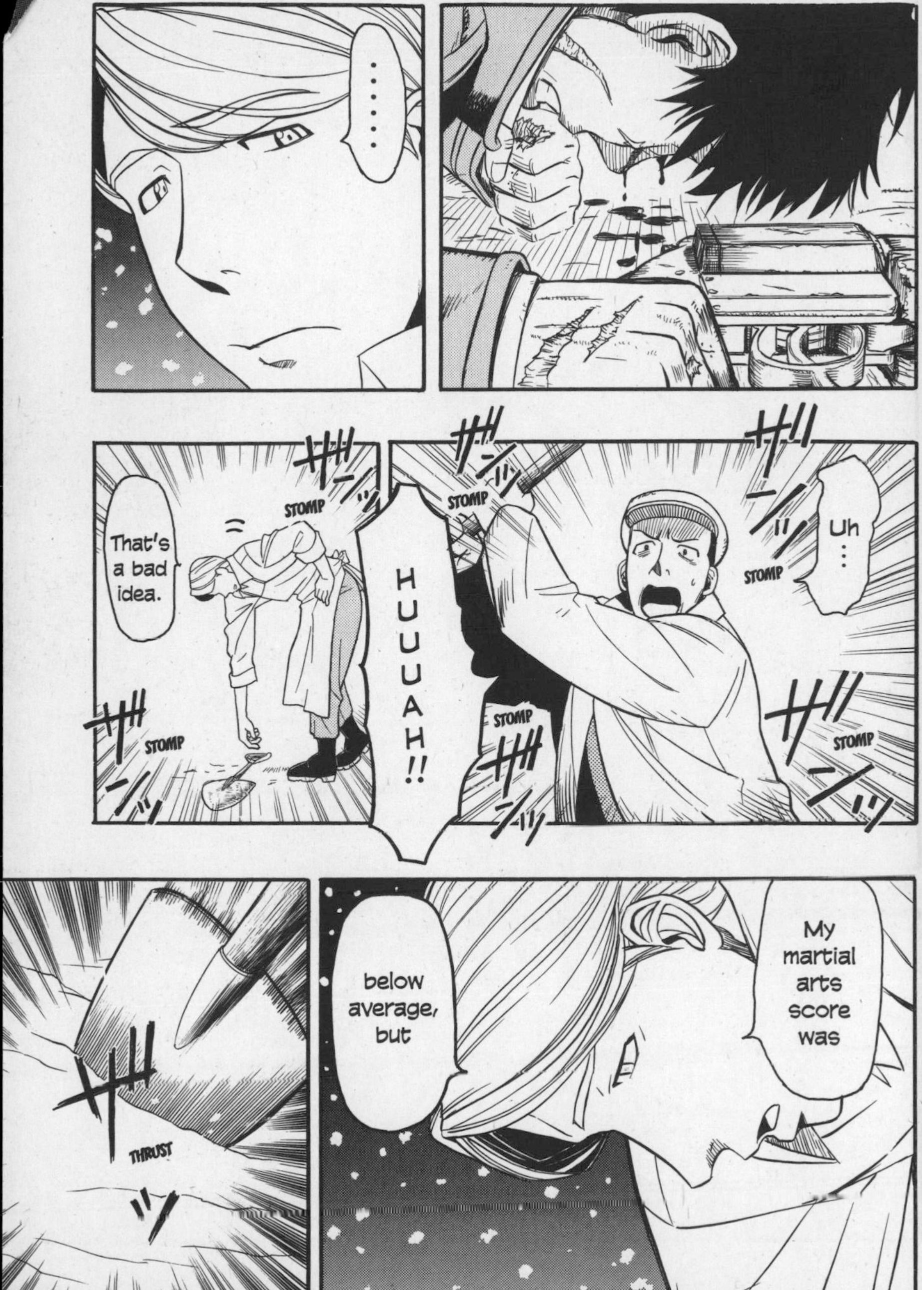
......
STOMP
Uh...
STOMP
STOMP
STOMP
HUUUAH!!
STOMP
That's a bad idea.
STOMP
My martial arts score was
below average, but
THRUST

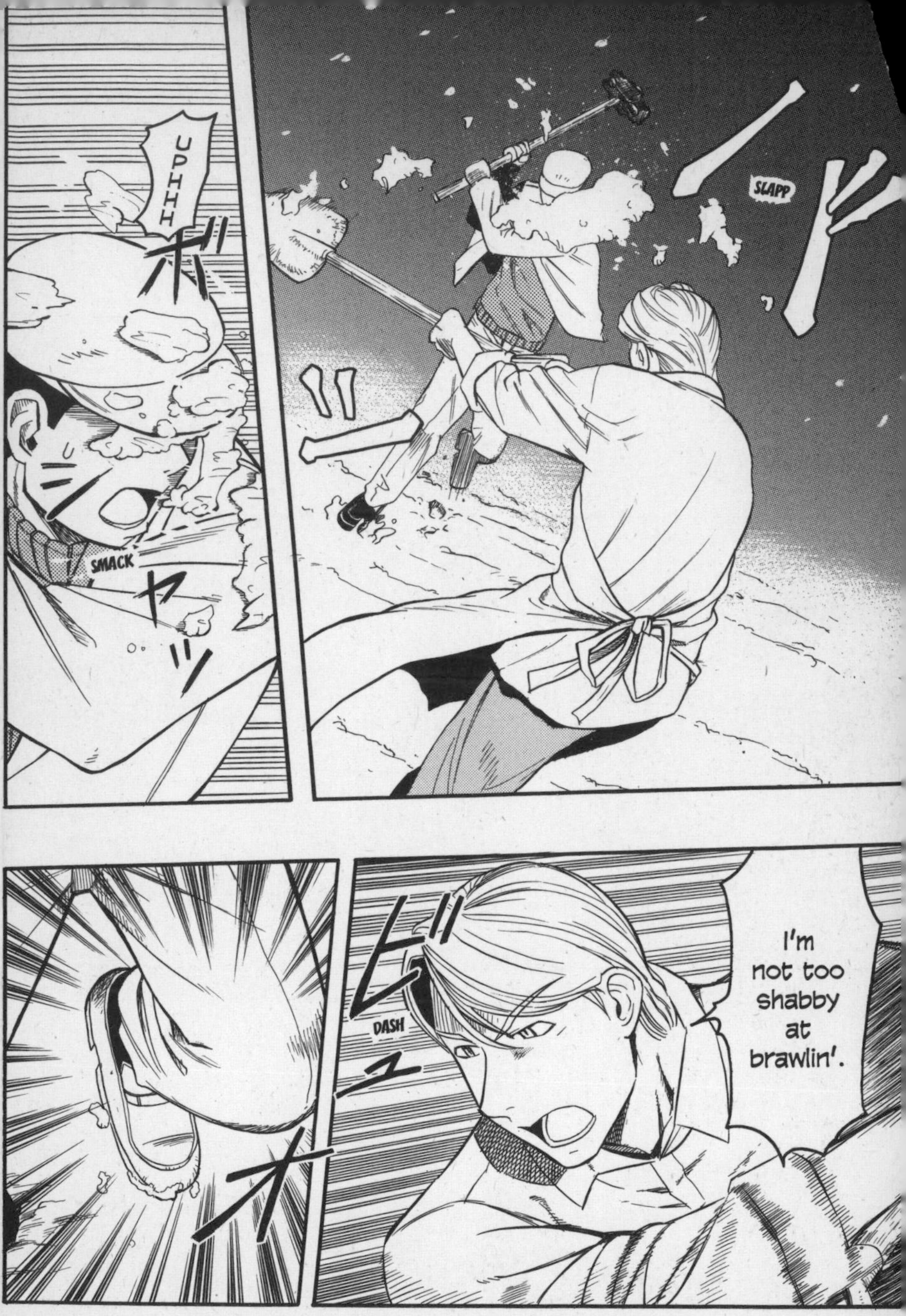
SLAPP
UPHHH
SMACK
DASH
I'm not too shabby at brawlin'.

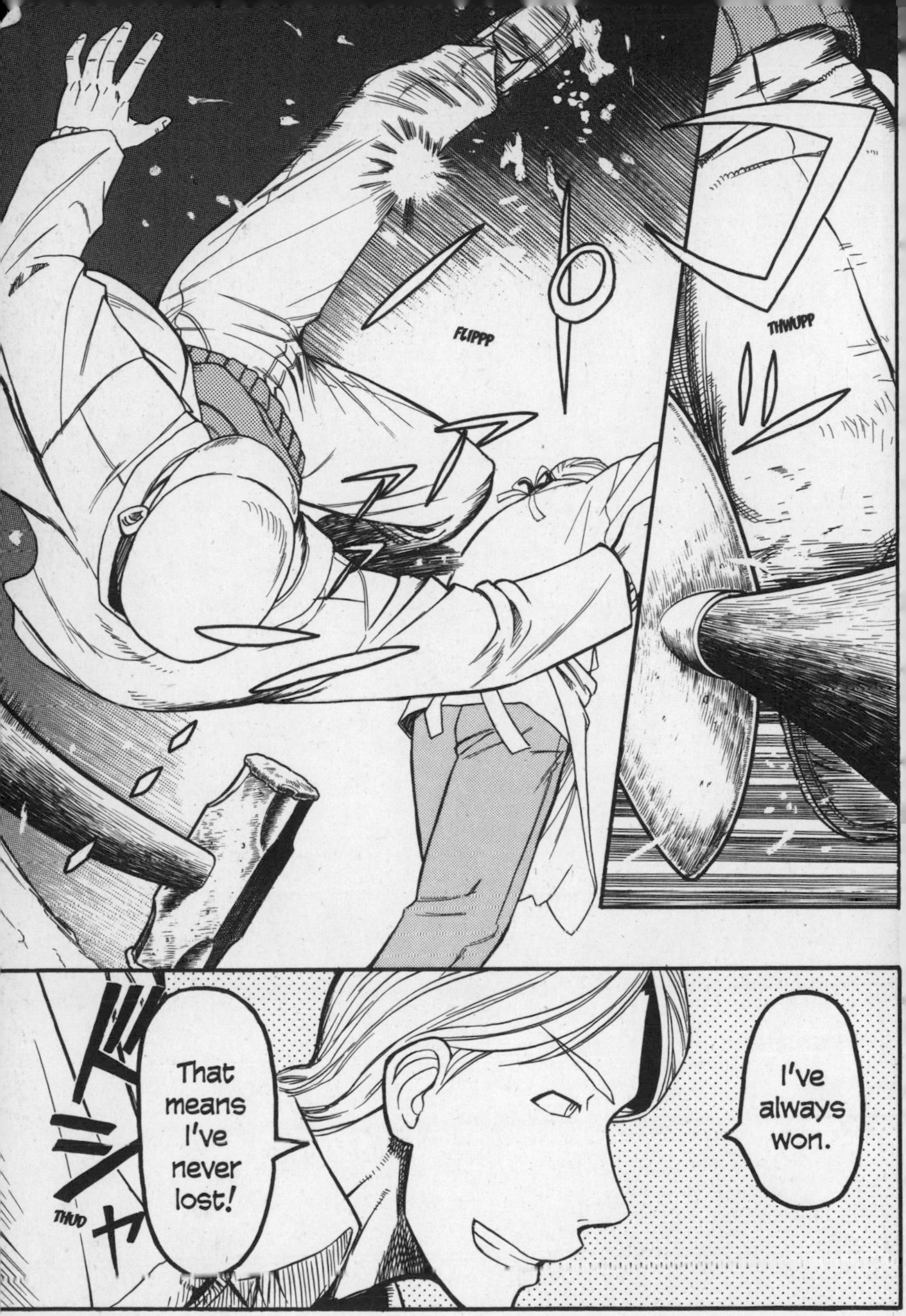
THWUPP
FLIPPP
I've always won.
That means I've never lost!
THUD

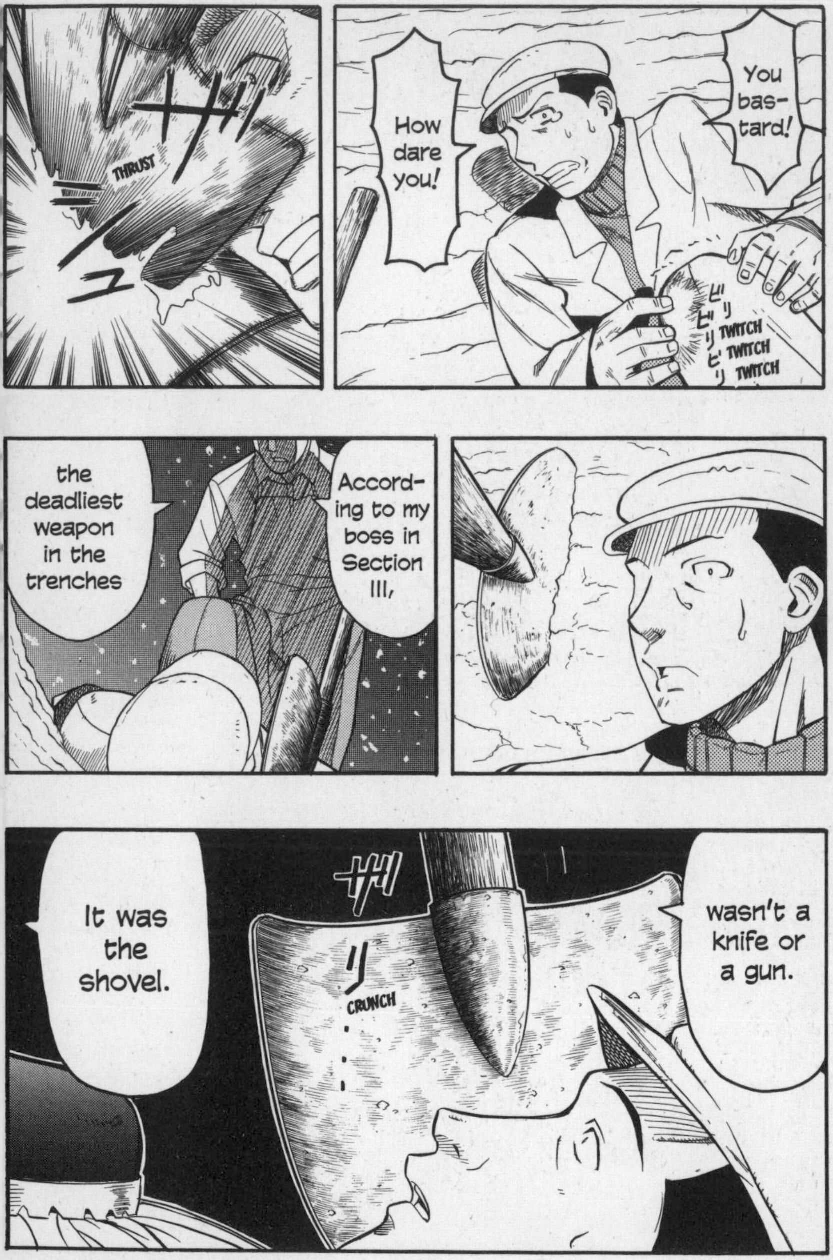
You bas-tard!
How dare you!
ビリビリビリ
TWITCH TWITCH TWITCH
THRUST
According to my boss in Section III,
the deadliest weapon in the trenches
wasn't a knife or a gun.
It was the shovel.
ザリ
CRUNCH

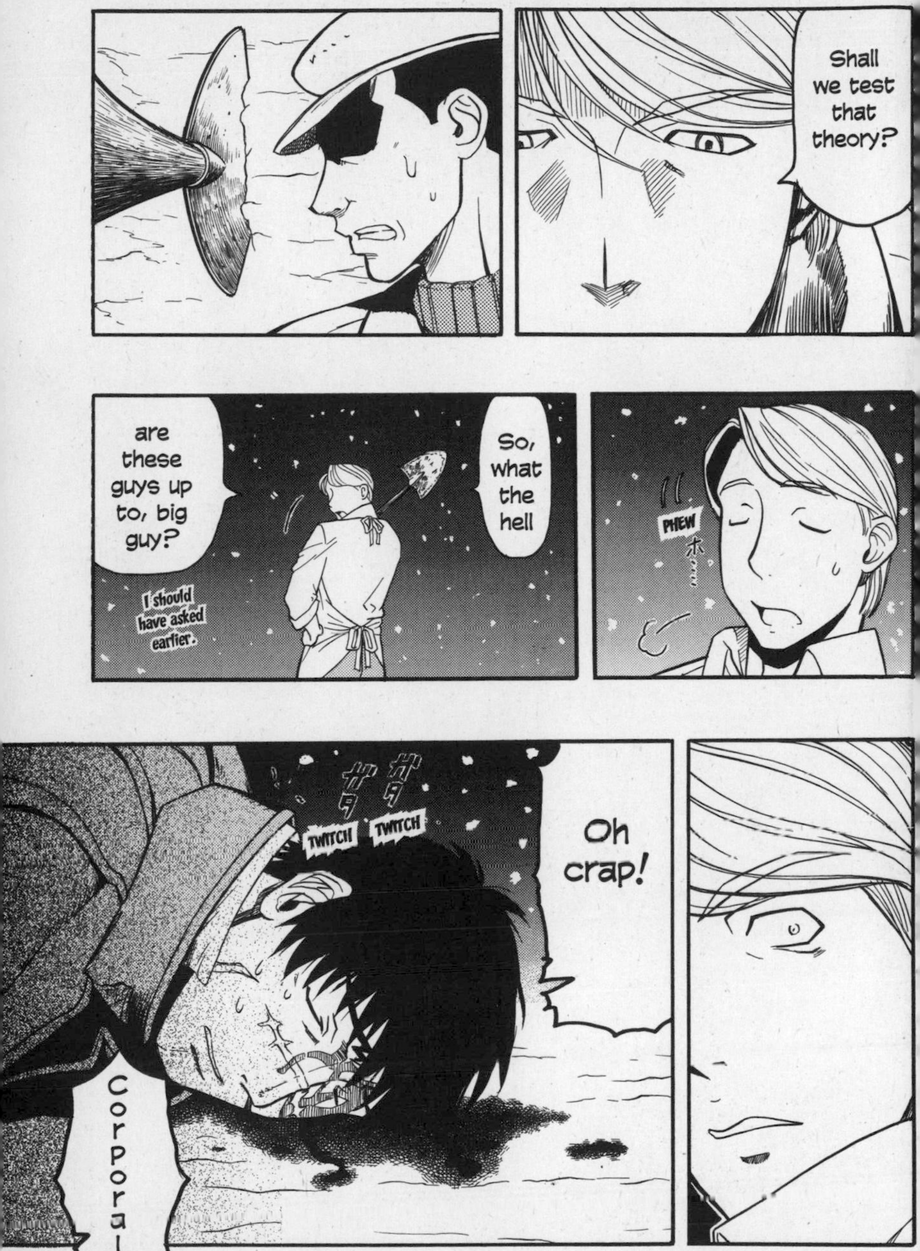

Shall we test that theory?
PHEW
So, what the hell
are these guys up to, big guy?
I should have asked earlier.
Oh crap!
TWITCH TWITCH
Corporal!

This
dream
again...

Oh...

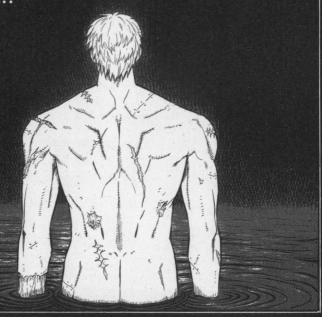

Maybe
it's not

a dream
anymore.

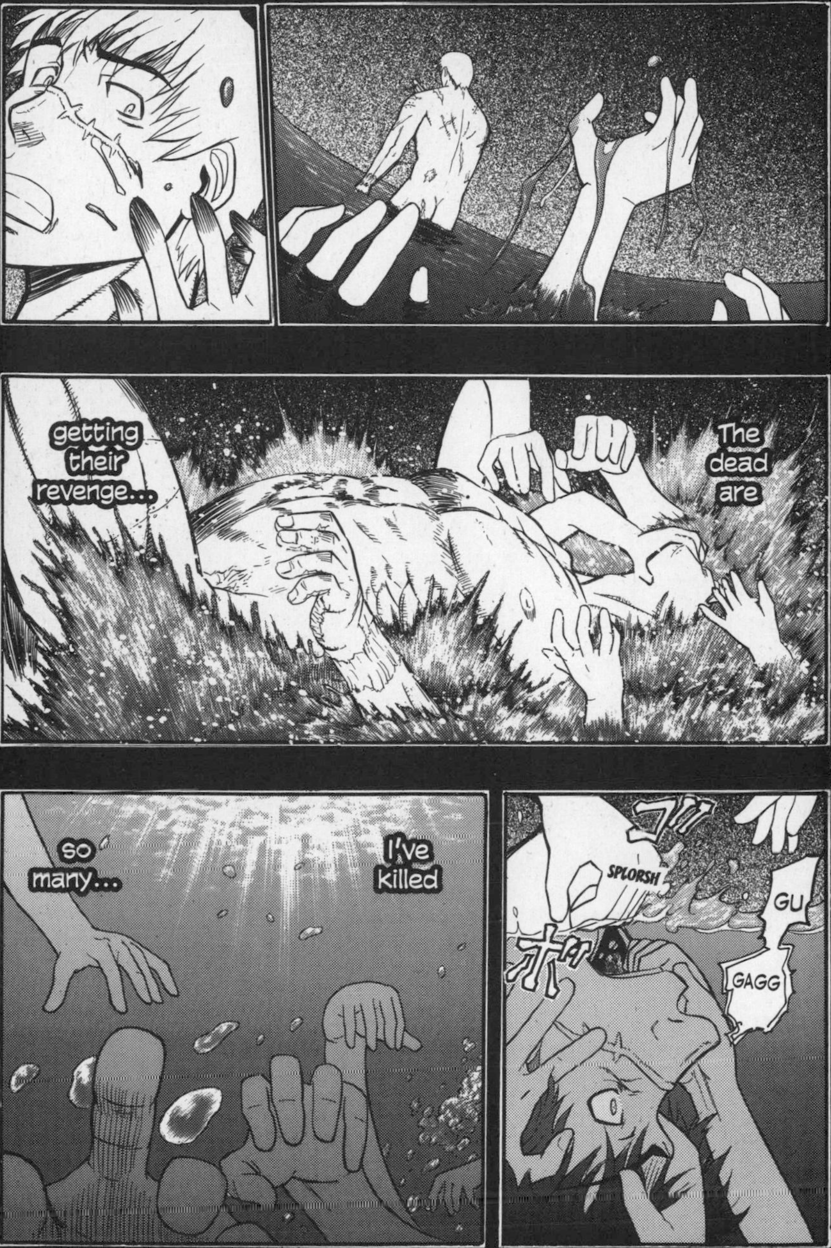
The dead are
getting their revenge...
SPLORSH
GU
GAGG
I've killed
so many...

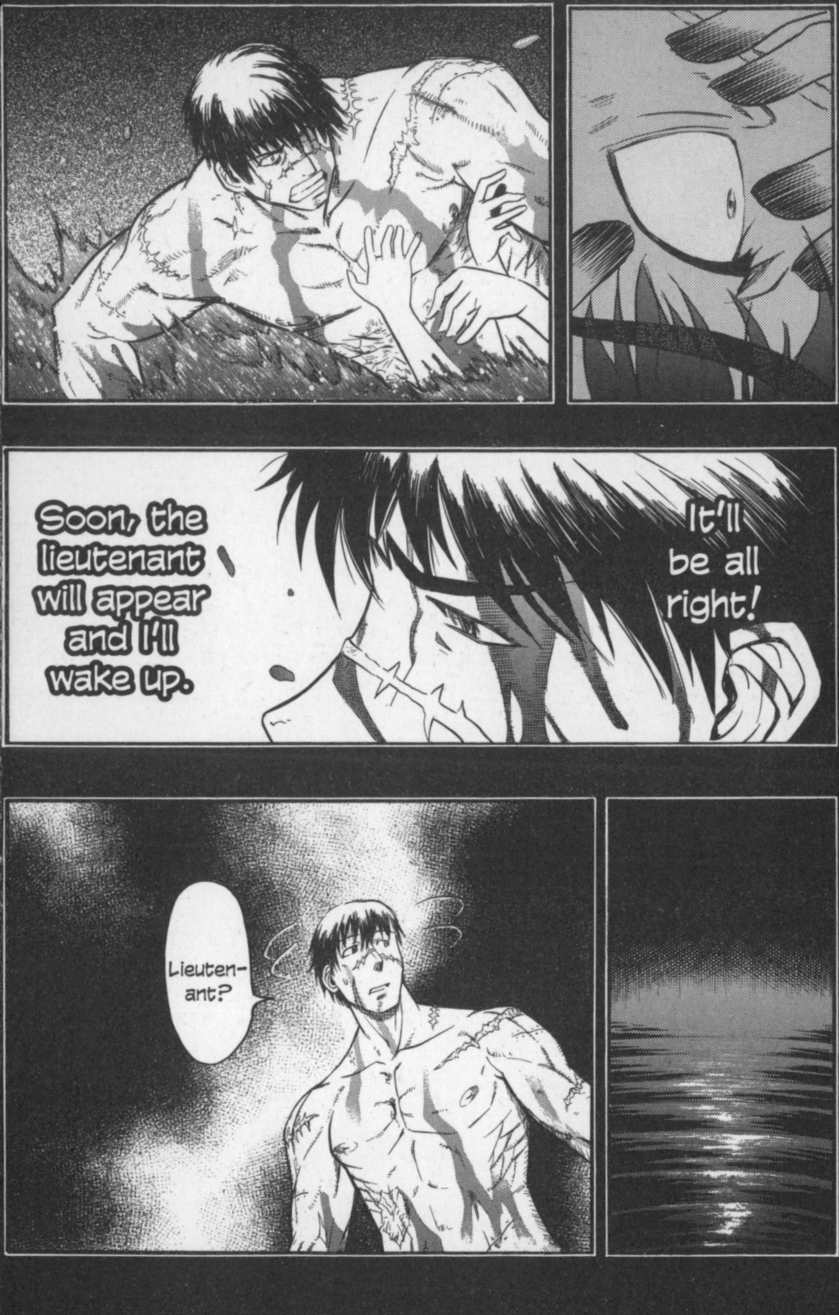
It'll be all right!
Soon, the lieutenant will appear and I'll wake up.
Lieuten-ant?

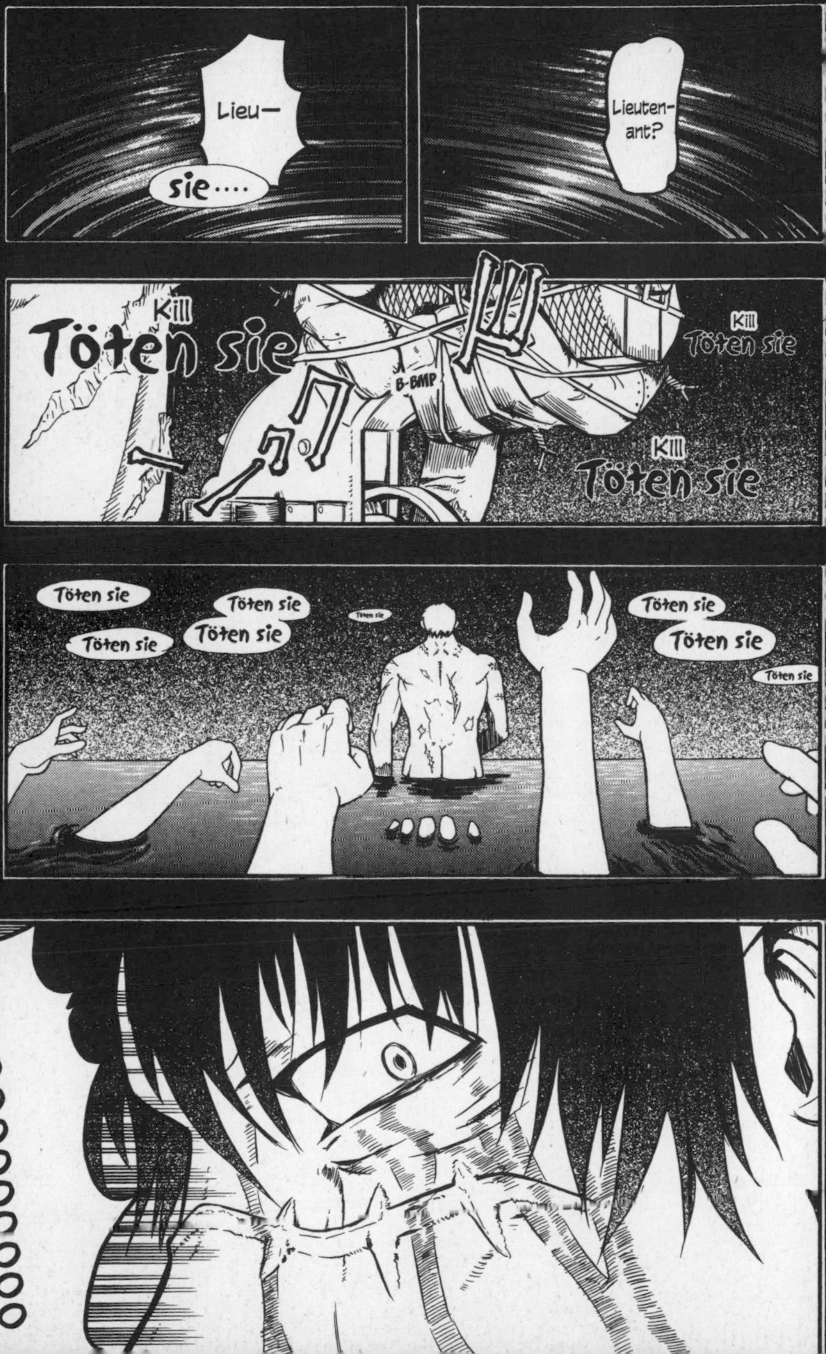
Lieuten-
ant?
Lieu—
sie....
Kill
Töten sie
Kill
Töten sie
B-BMP
Kill
Töten sie
Töten sie
Töten sie
Töten sie
Töten sie
Töten sie
Töten sie
Töten sie
Töten sie
Töten sie
NOOOOOOOOOOO

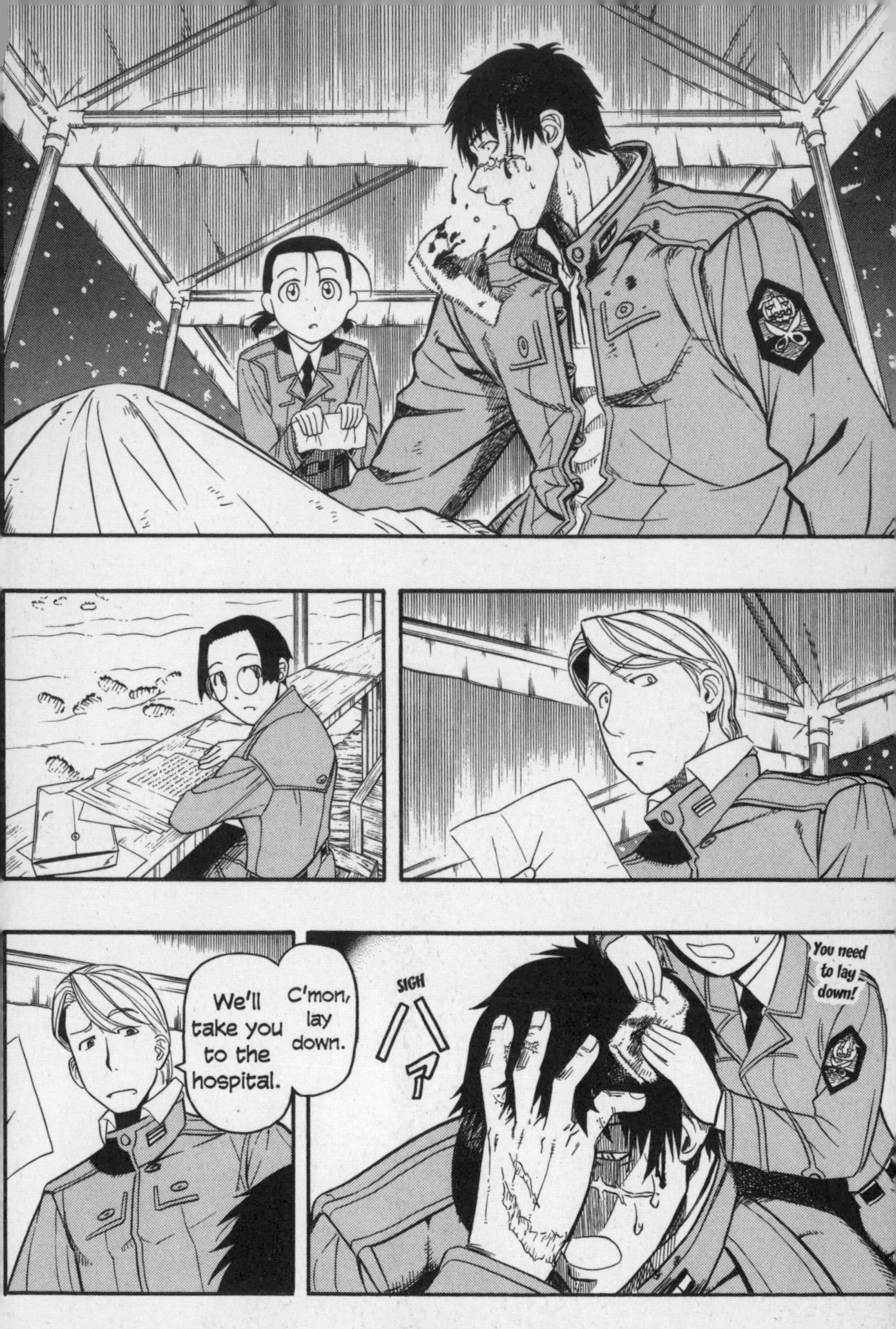
You need to lay down!
SIGH
C'mon, lay down.
We'll take you to the hospital.

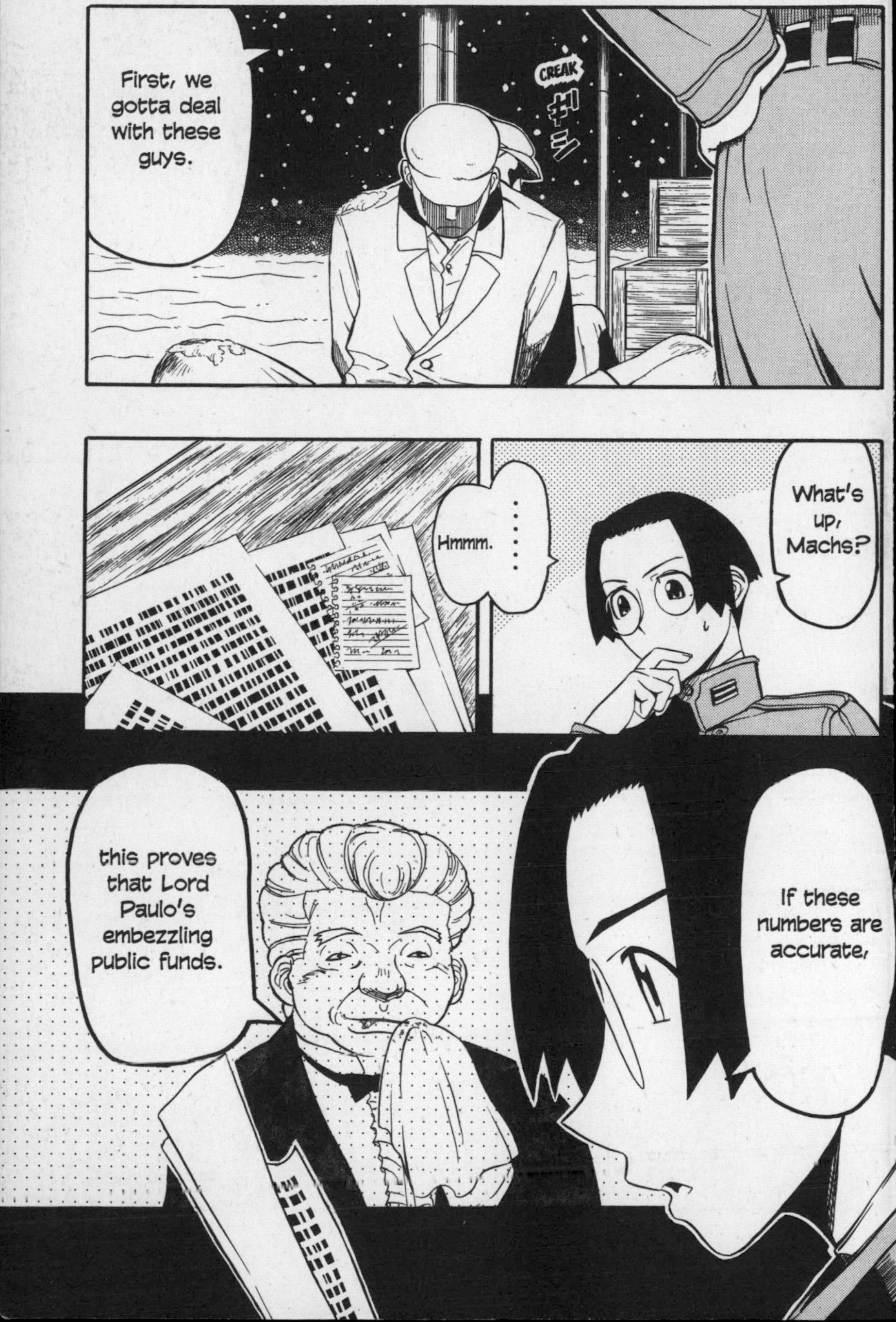
First, we gotta deal with these guys.
CREAK
What's up, Machs?
......
Hmmm.
If these numbers are accurate,
this proves that Lord Paulo's embezzling public funds.

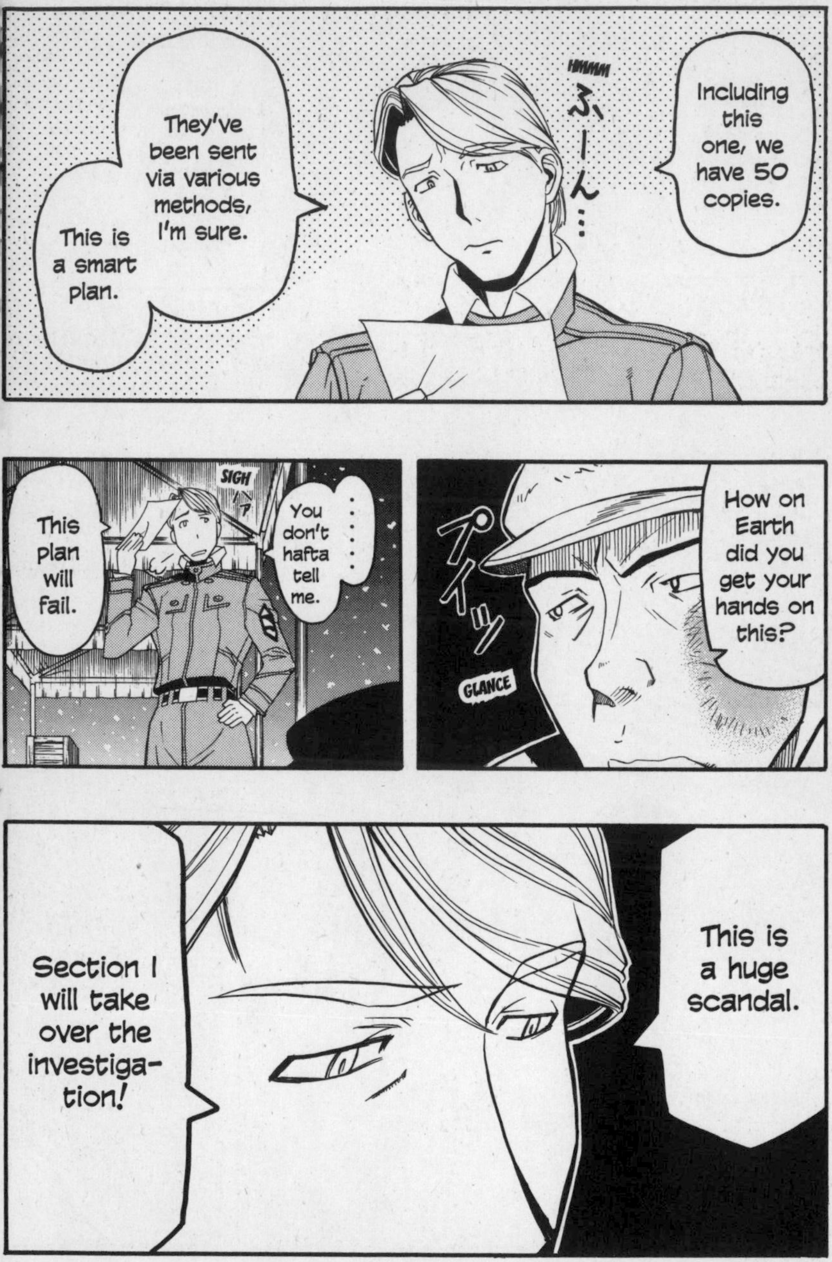
Including this one, we have 50 copies.
HMMM
ふーん…
They've been sent via various methods, I'm sure.
This is a smart plan.
How on Earth did you get your hands on this?
ピイッ
GLANCE
You don't hafta tell me.
……
SIGH
ハァ
This plan will fail.
This is a huge scandal.
Section I will take over the investiga-tion!

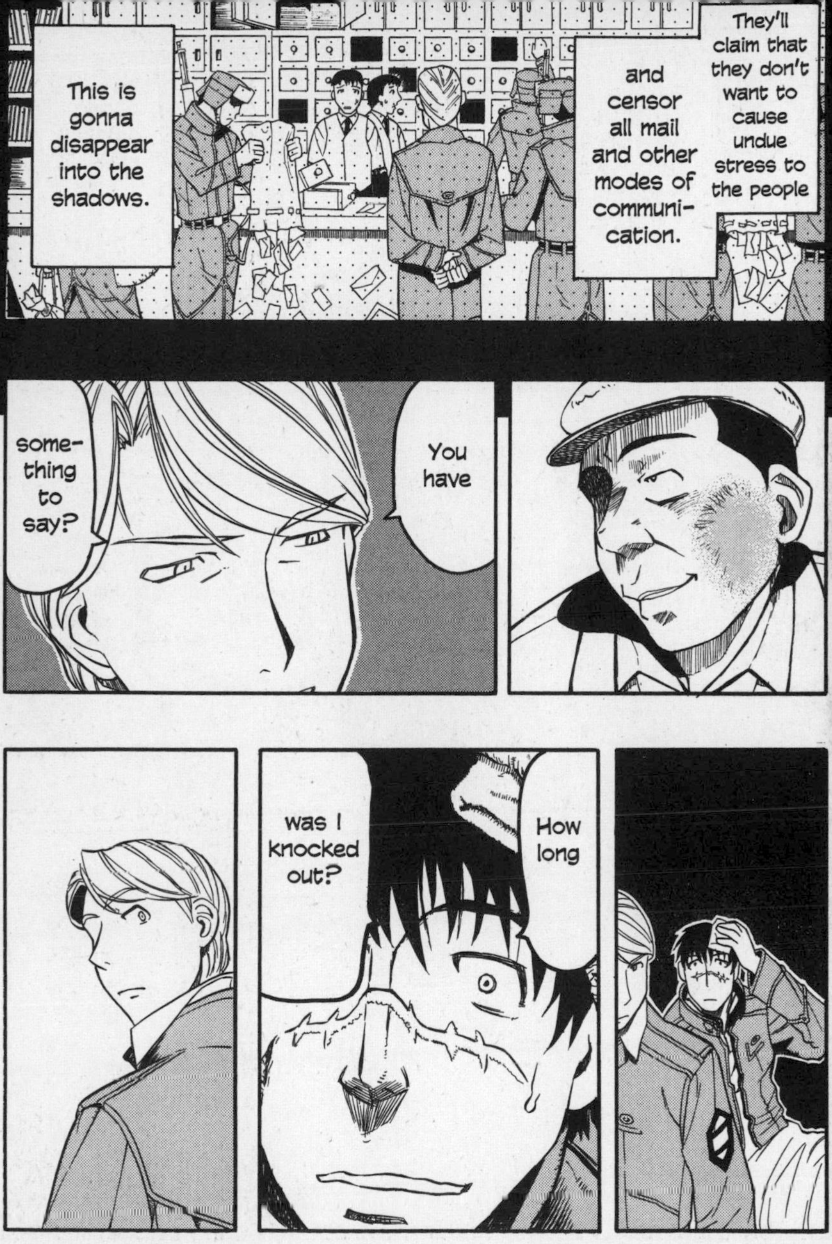
They'll claim that they don't want to cause undue stress to the people
and censor all mail and other modes of communi-cation.
This is gonna disappear into the shadows.
You have
some-thing to say?
How long
was I knocked out?

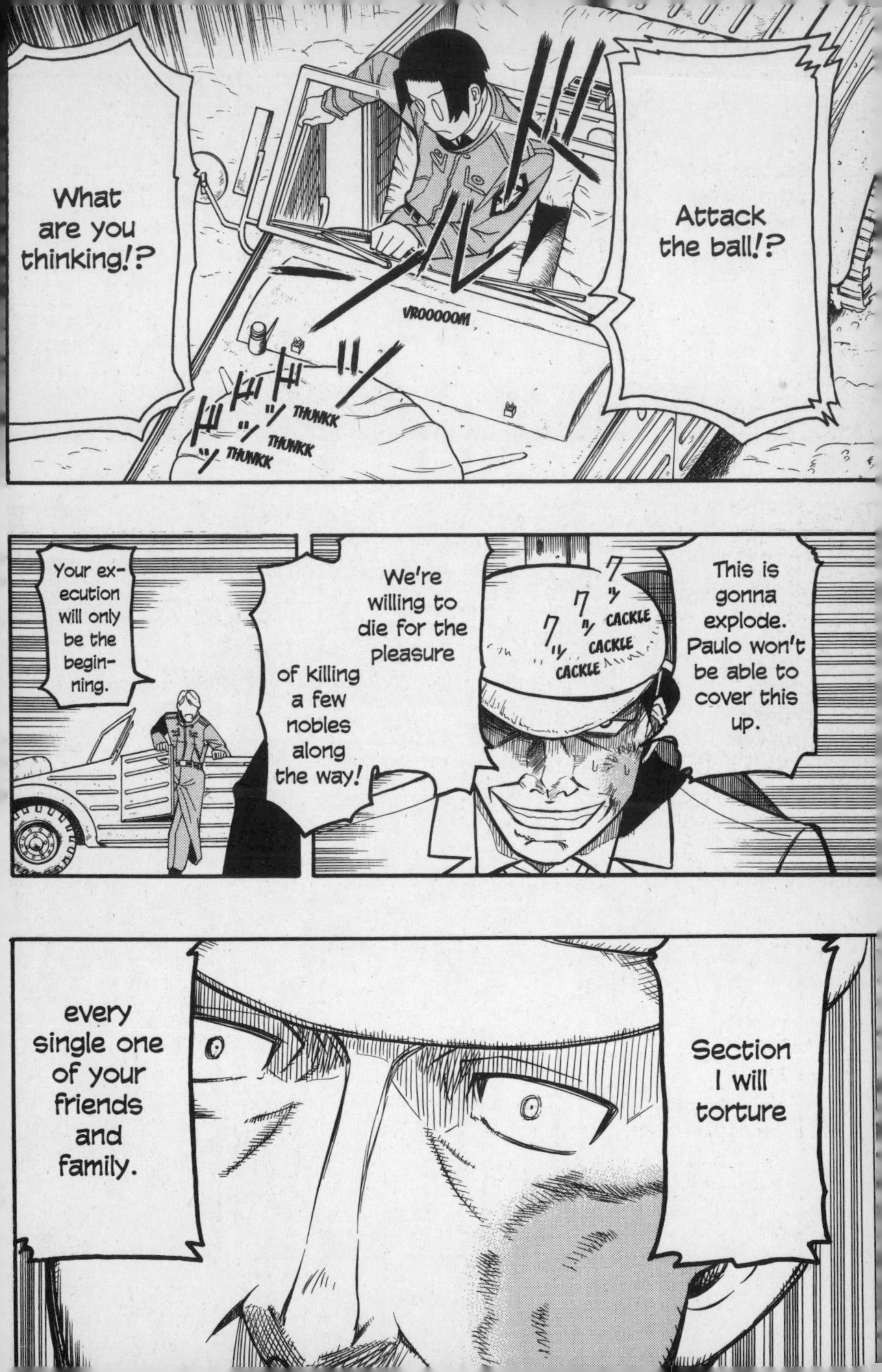
Attack the ball!?
VROOOOOM
THUNKK
THUNKK
THUNKK
What are you thinking!?
This is gonna explode. Paulo won't be able to cover this up.
CACKLE
CACKLE
CACKLE
We're willing to die for the pleasure
of killing a few nobles along the way!
Your execution will only be the beginning.
Section I will torture
every single one of your friends and family.

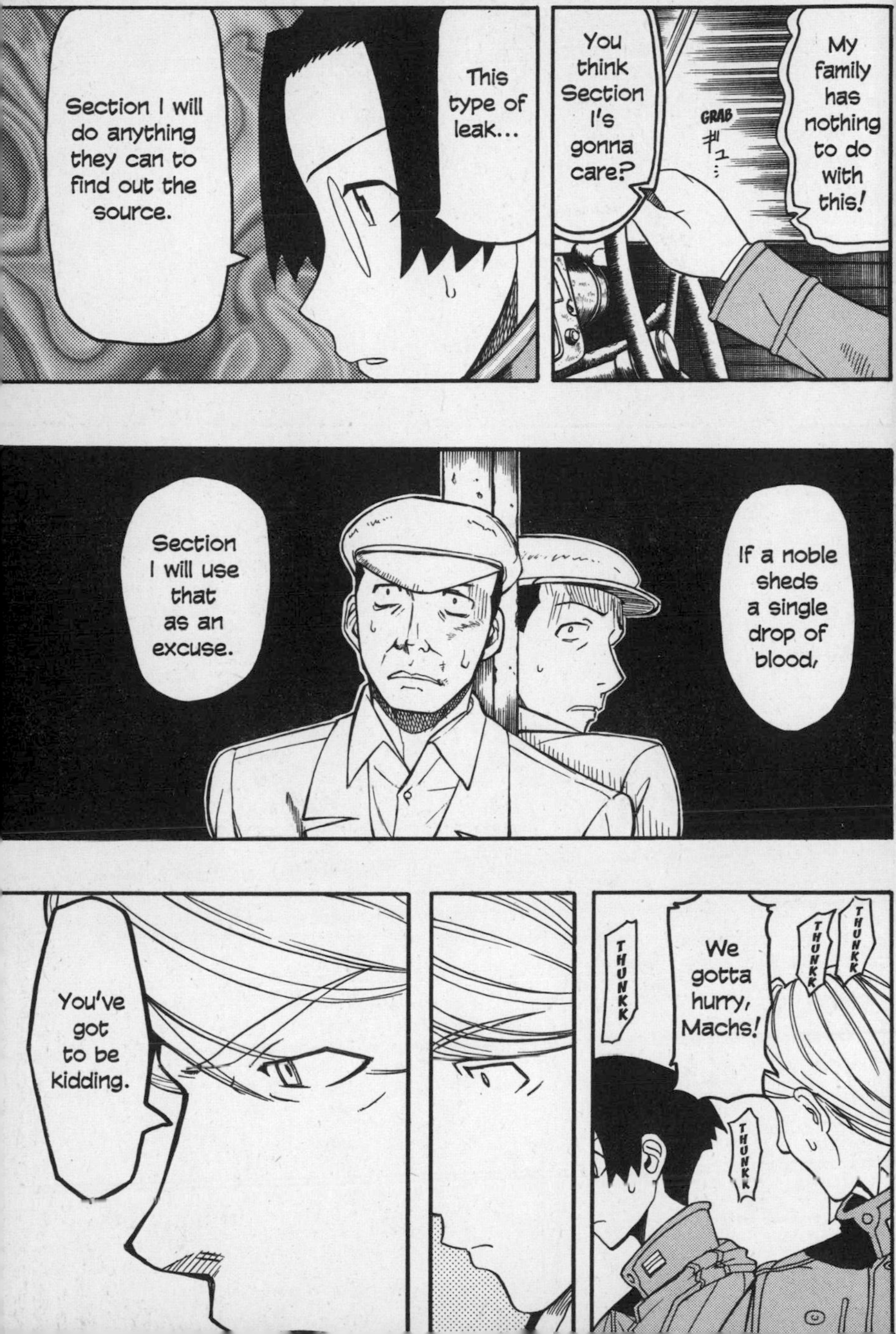
My family has nothing to do with this!
GRAB
You think Section I's gonna care?
This type of leak...
Section I will do anything they can to find out the source.
If a noble sheds a single drop of blood,
Section I will use that as an excuse.
THUNKK
THUNKK
We gotta hurry, Machs!
THUNKK
THUNKK
You've got to be kidding.

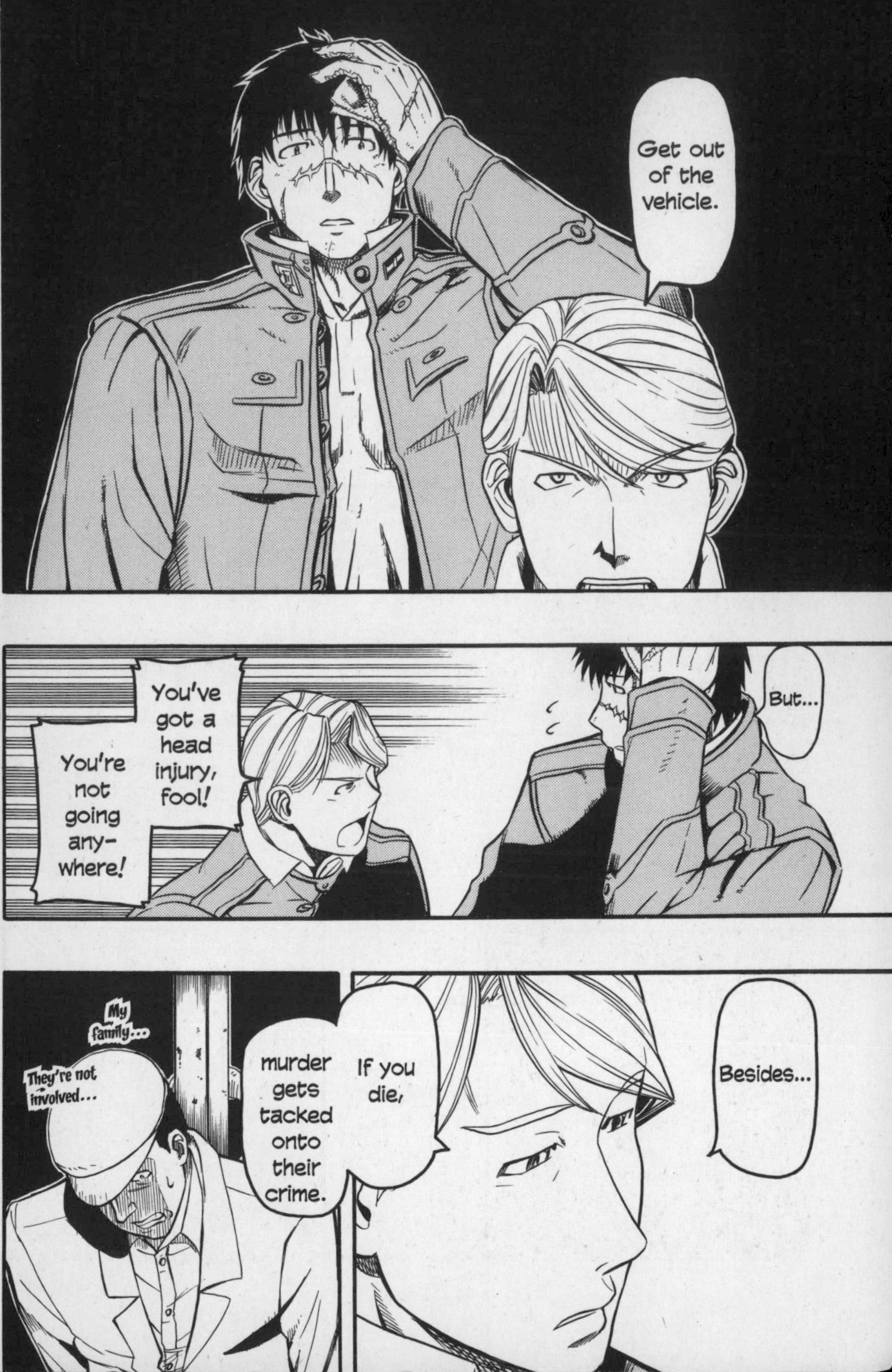
Get out of the vehicle.
But...
You've got a head injury, fool!
You're not going anywhere!
Besides...
If you die,
murder gets tacked onto their crime.
My family...
They're not involved...

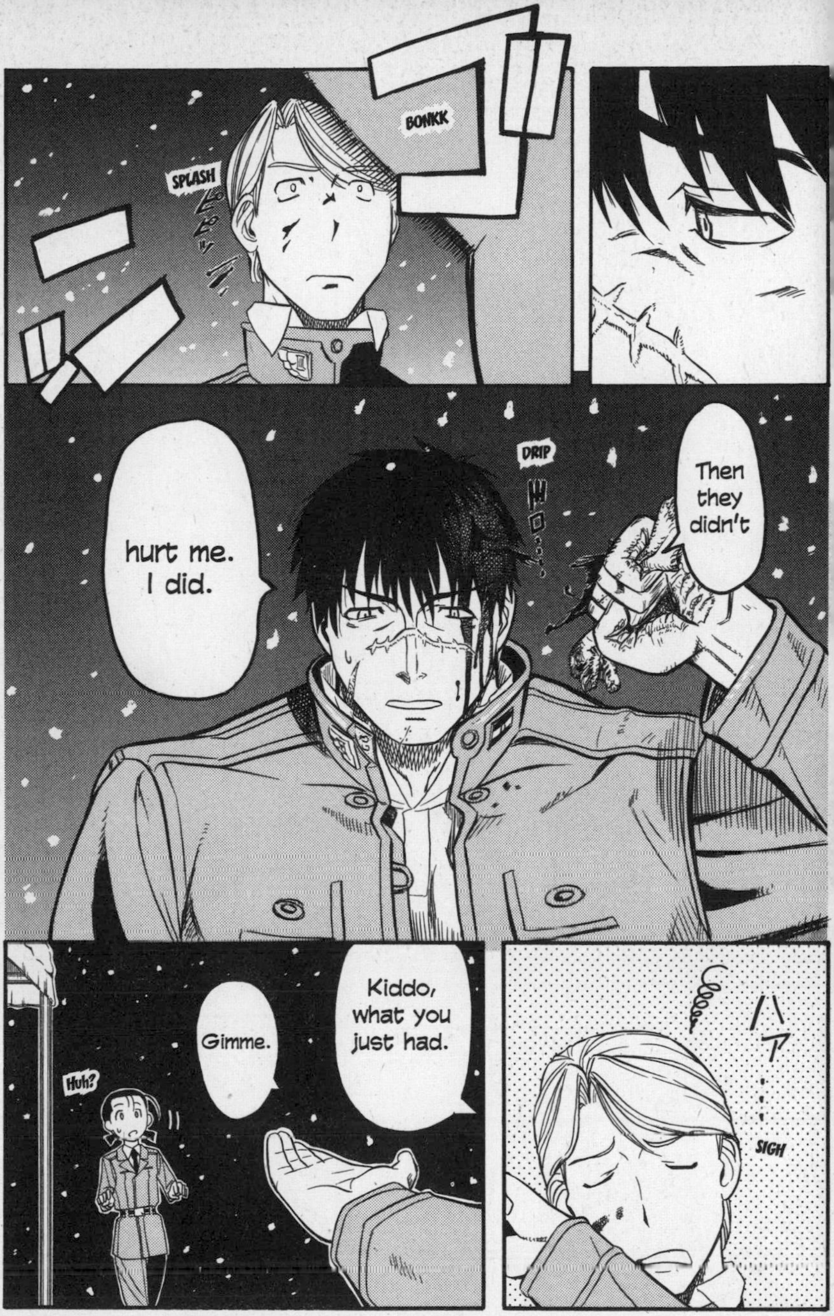
BONKK
SPLASH
Then they didn't
DRIP
hurt me. I did.
ハア…
SIGH
Kiddo, what you just had.
Gimme.
Huh?

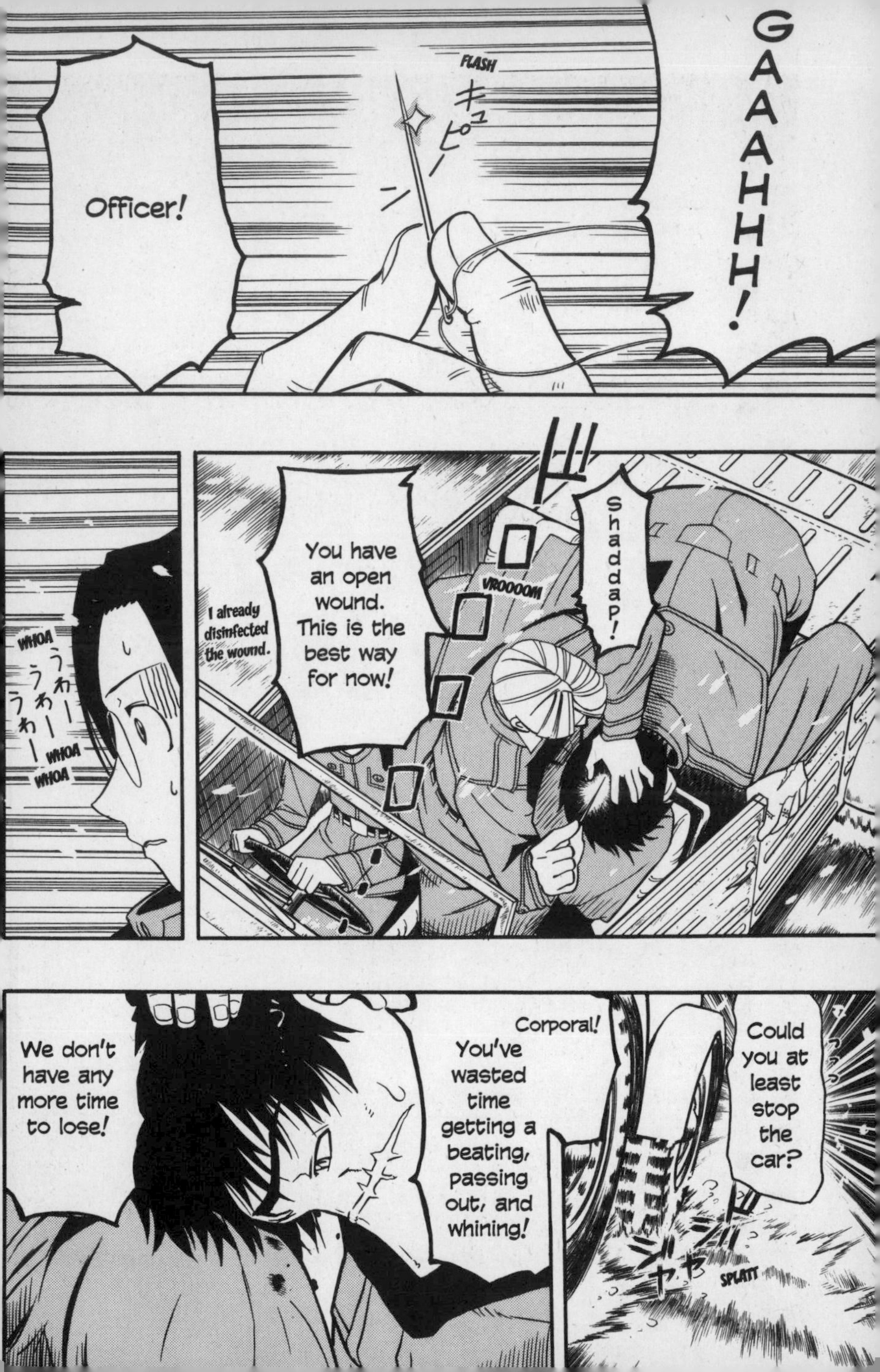
GAAAHHH!
FLASH
Officer!
Shaddap!
VROOOOM
You have an open wound. This is the best way for now!
I already disinfected the wound.
WHOA
うわーうわーうわー
WHOA
WHOA
Could you at least stop the car?
SPLATT
Corporal!
You've wasted time getting a beating, passing out, and whining!
We don't have any more time to lose!

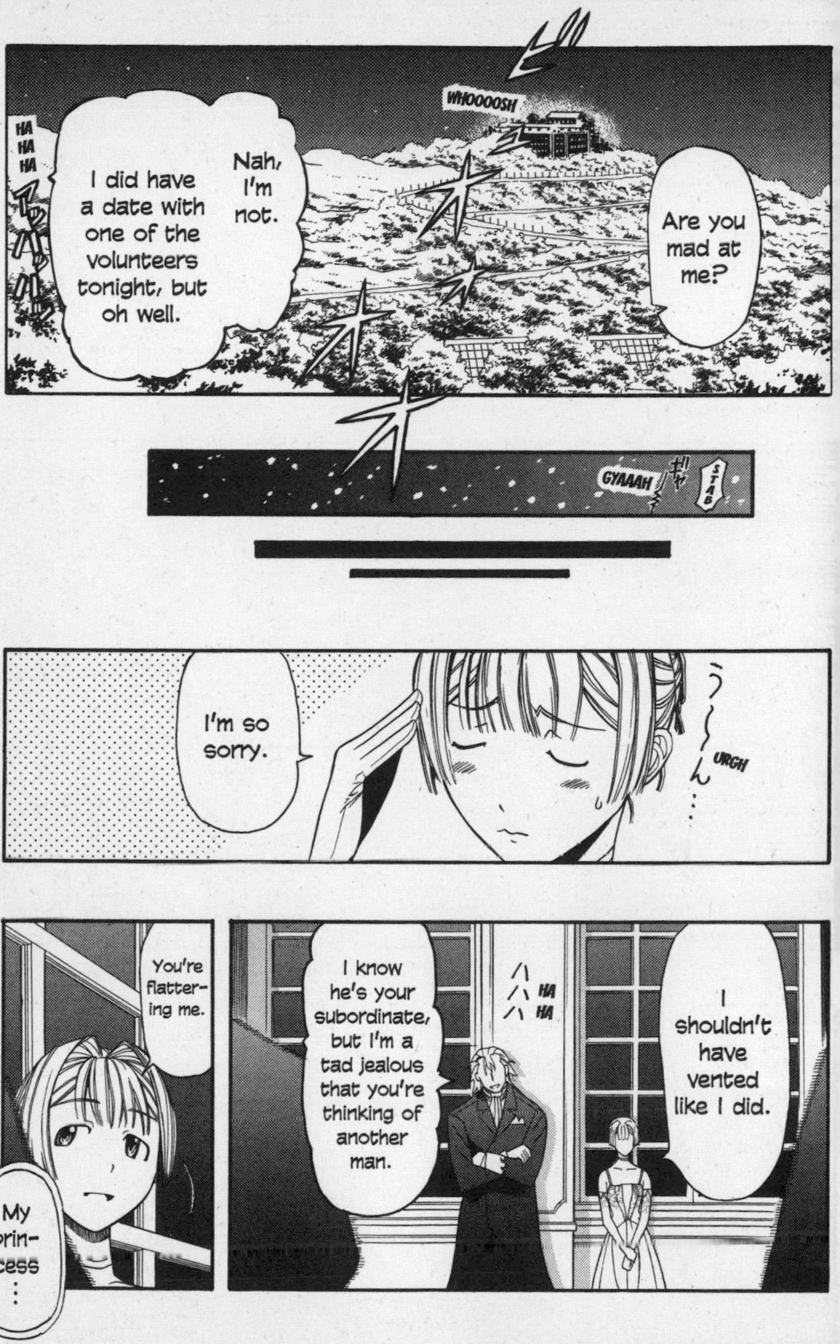
WHOOOOSH
Are you mad at me?
Nah, I'm not.
I did have a date with one of the volunteers tonight, but oh well.
HA HA HA
STAB
GYAAAH
URGH
I'm so sorry.
I shouldn't have vented like I did.
HA HA
I know he's your subordinate, but I'm a tad jealous that you're thinking of another man.
You're flattering me.
My prin-cess…

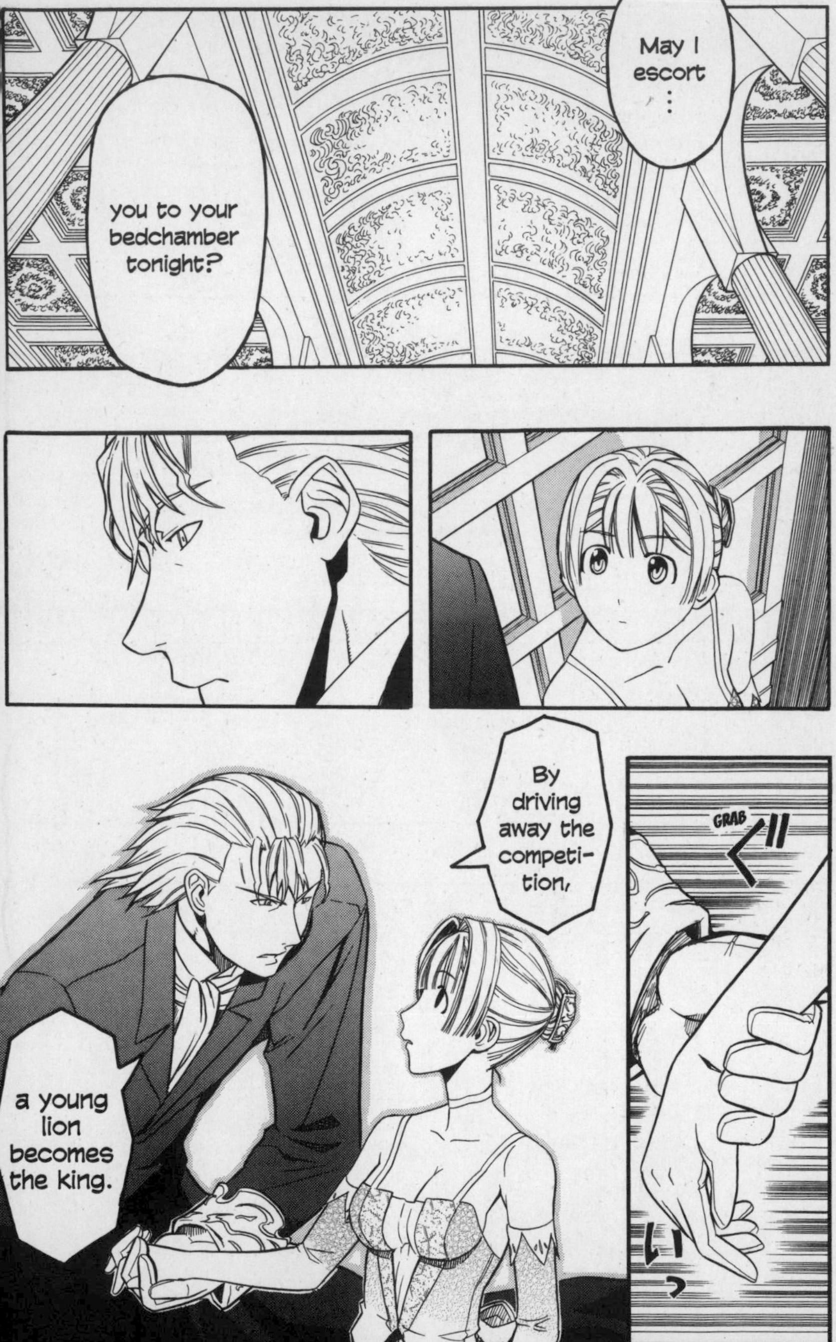
May I escort ...
you to your bedchamber tonight?
GRAB
By driving away the competition,
a young lion becomes the king.

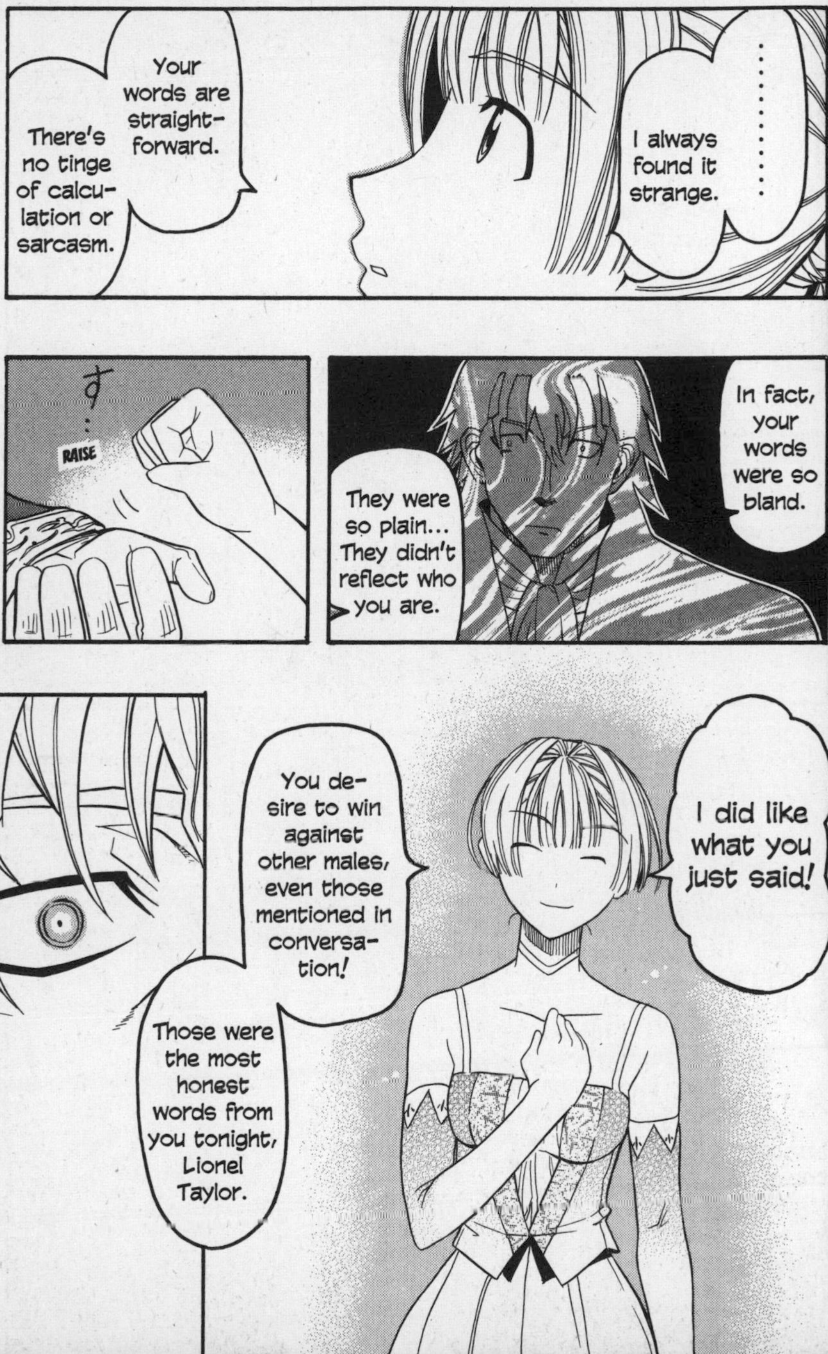

......
I always found it strange.
Your words are straight-forward.
There's no tinge of calcu-lation or sarcasm.
In fact, your words were so bland.
They were so plain... They didn't reflect who you are.
す...
RAISE
I did like what you just said!
You de-sire to win against other males, even those mentioned in conversa-tion!
Those were the most honest words from you tonight, Lionel Taylor.

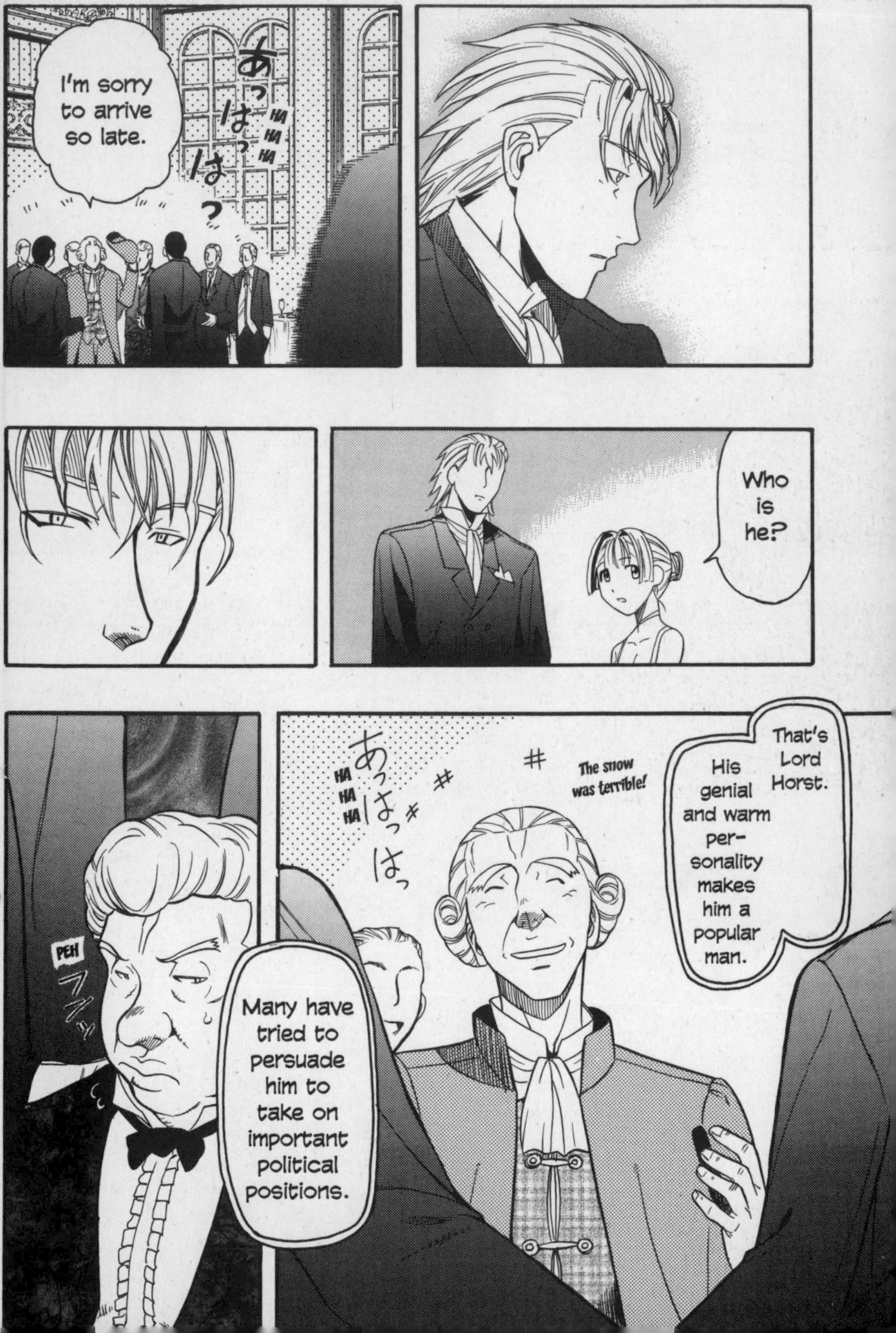
I'm sorry to arrive so late.
あっはっはっ
HA HA HA
Who is he?
That's Lord Horst.
His genial and warm personality makes him a popular man.
The snow was terrible!
あっはっはっ
HA HA HA
Many have tried to persuade him to take on important political positions.
PEH

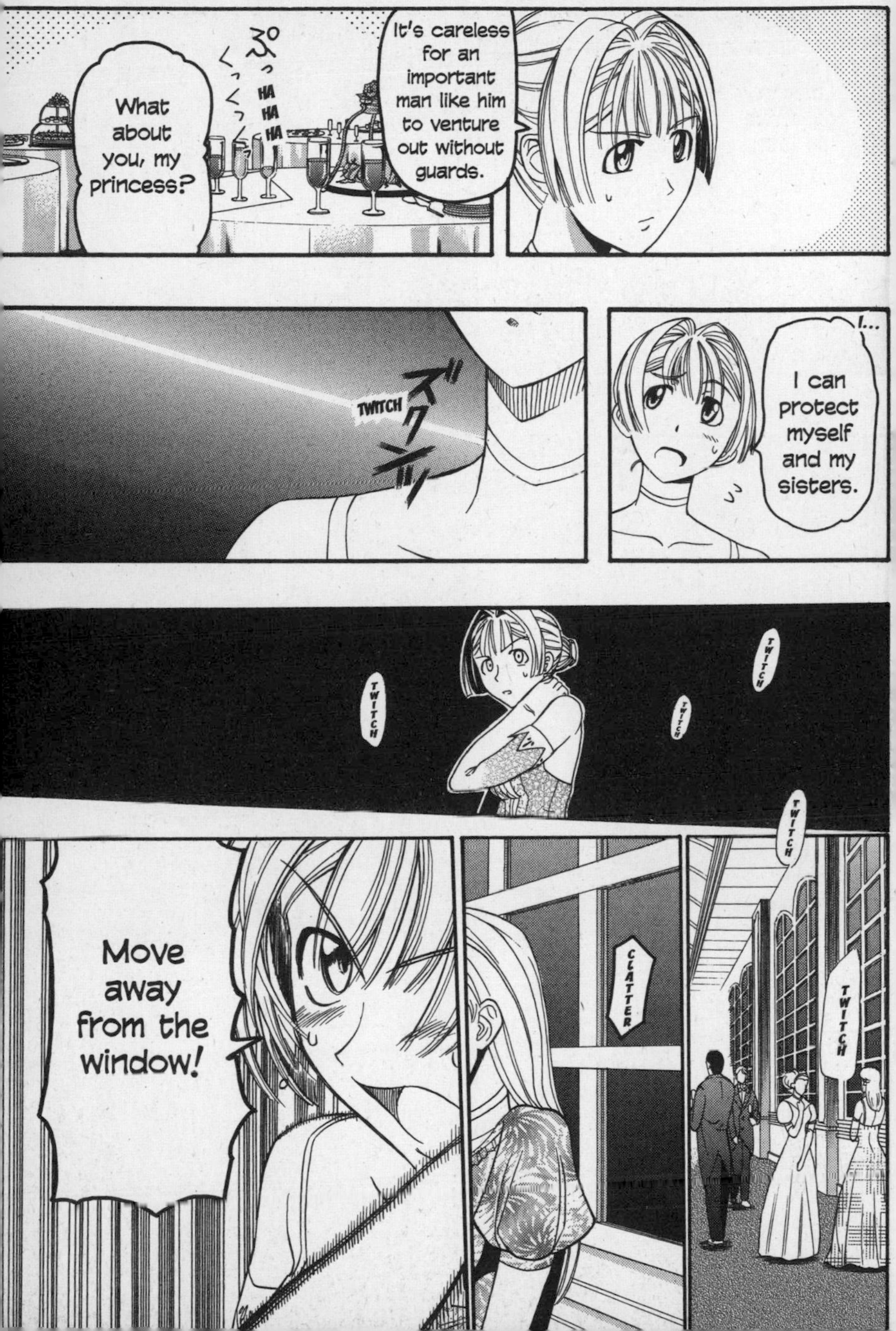

It's careless for an important man like him to venture out without guards.
ぷっ
HA HA HA
What about you, my princess?
I...
I can protect myself and my sisters.
TWITCH
TWITCH
TWITCH
TWITCH
TWITCH
TWITCH
CLATTER
Move away from the window!

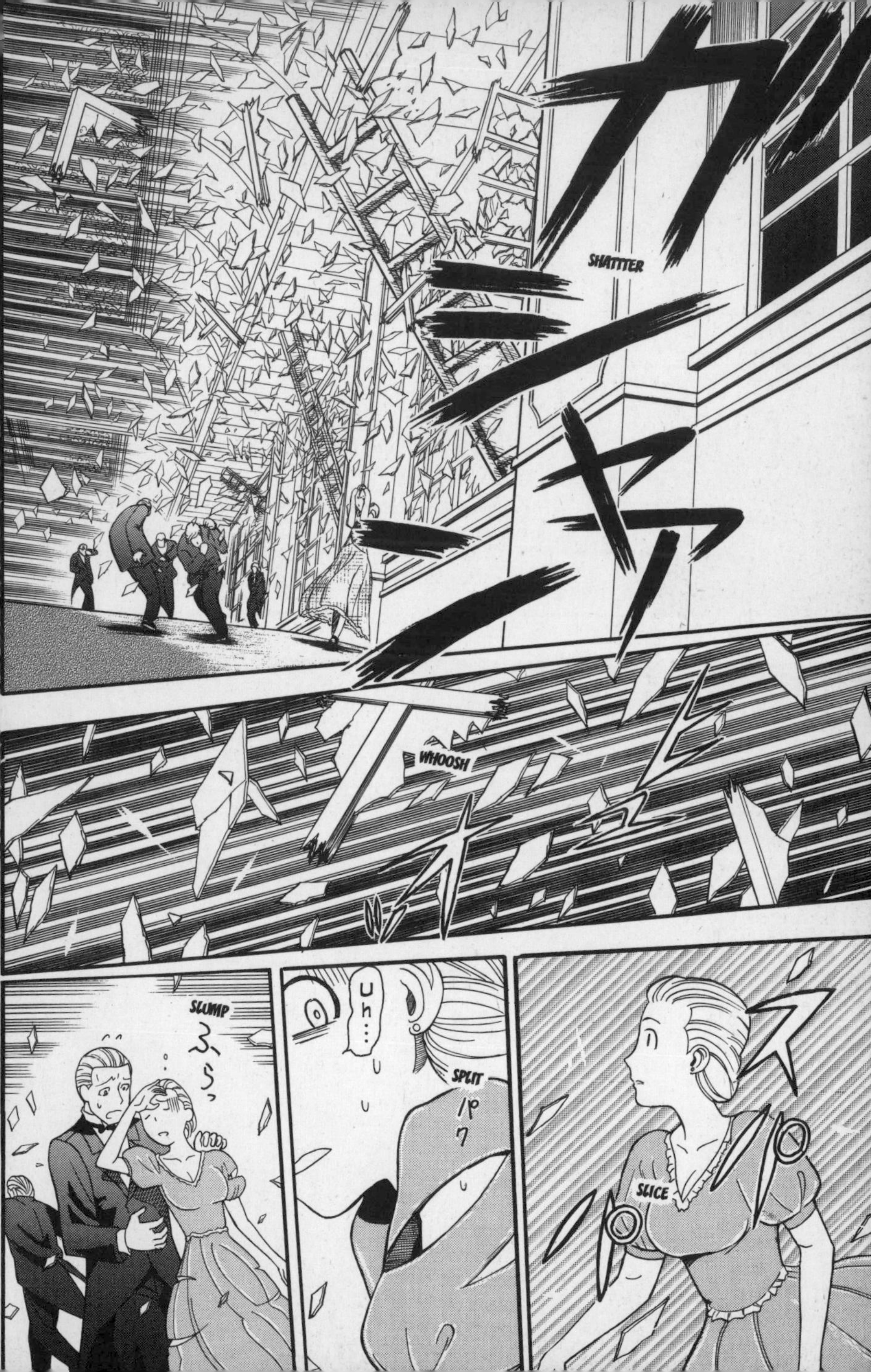
SHATTER
WHOOSH
SLICE
Uh…
SPLIT
パク
SLUMP
ふらっ

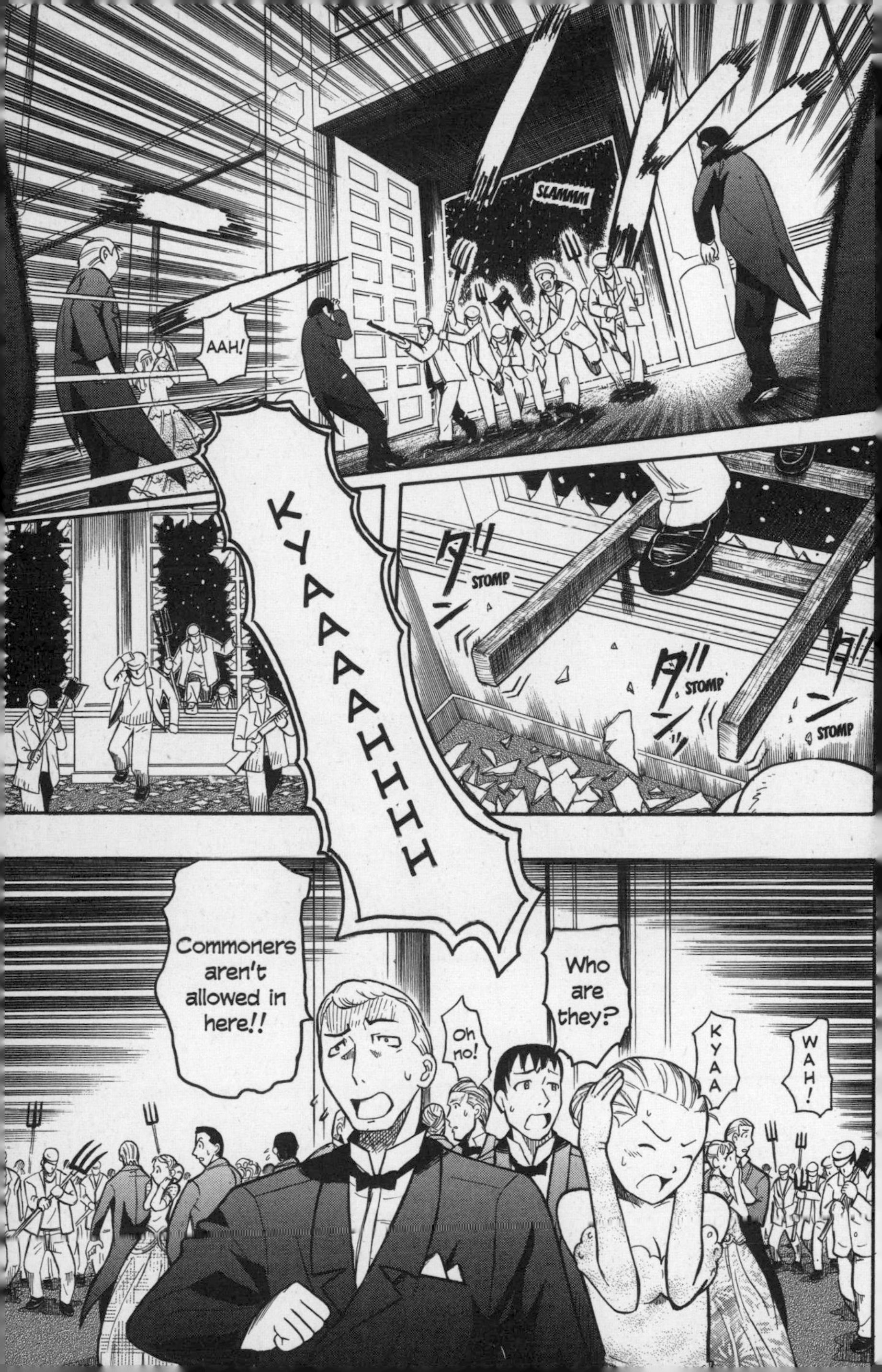
SLAMMM
AAH!
KYAAAAHHHH
STOMP
STOMP
STOMP
WAH!
KYAA
Who are they?
Oh no!
Commoners aren't allowed in here!!

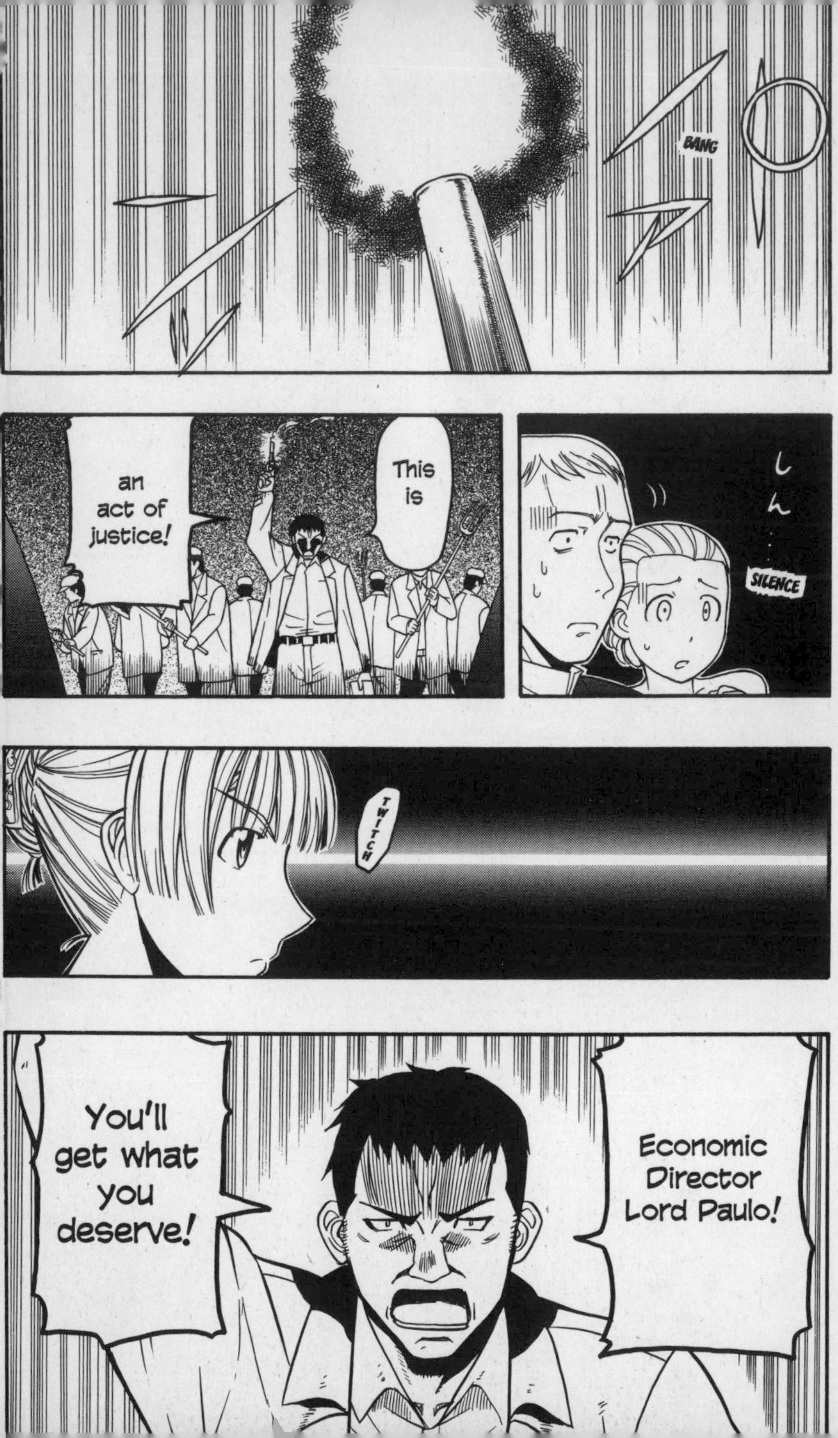
BANG
しん
SILENCE
This is
an act of justice!
TWITCH
Economic Director Lord Paulo!
You'll get what you deserve!

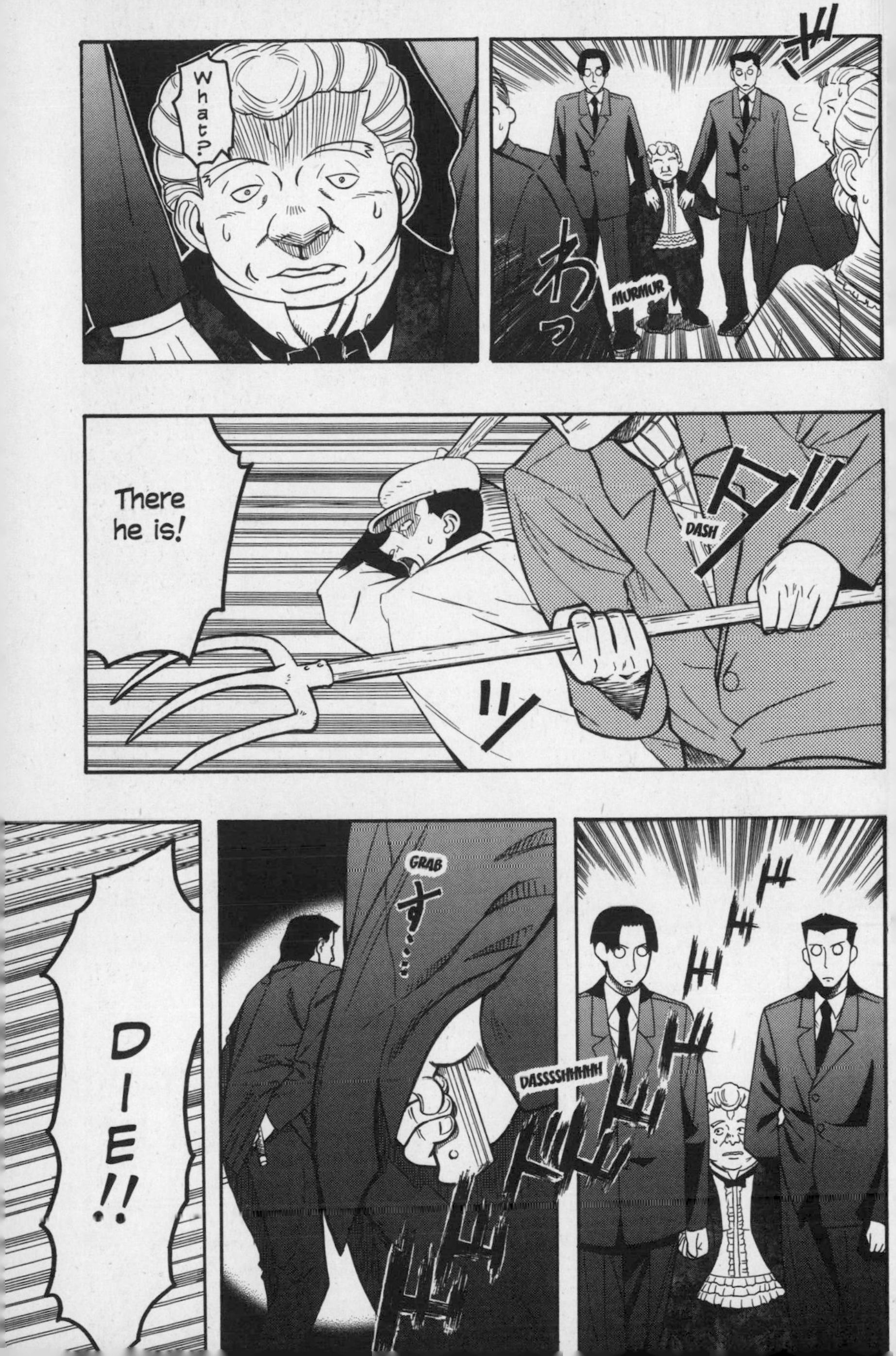
MURMUR
What?
There he is!
DASH
DASSSSHHHHH
GRAB
DIE!!

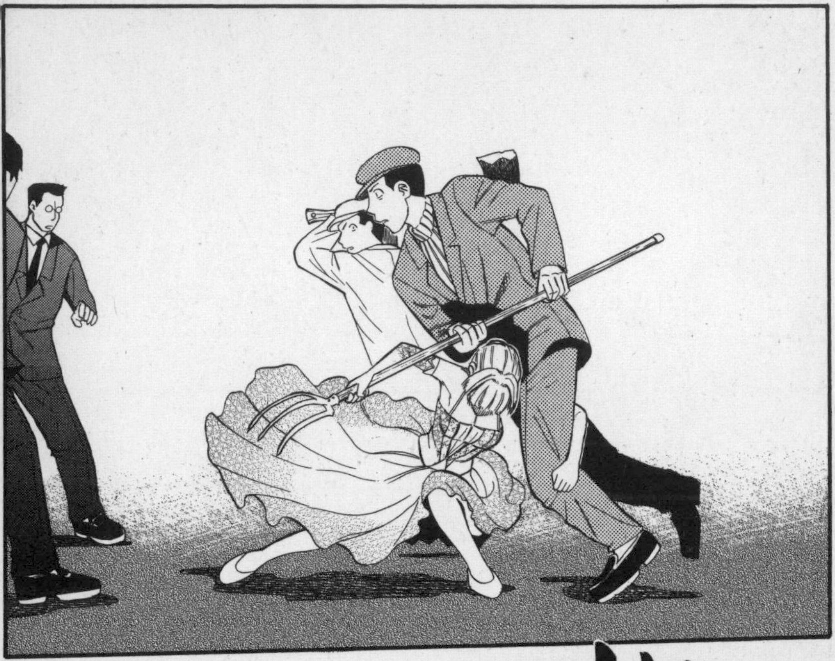

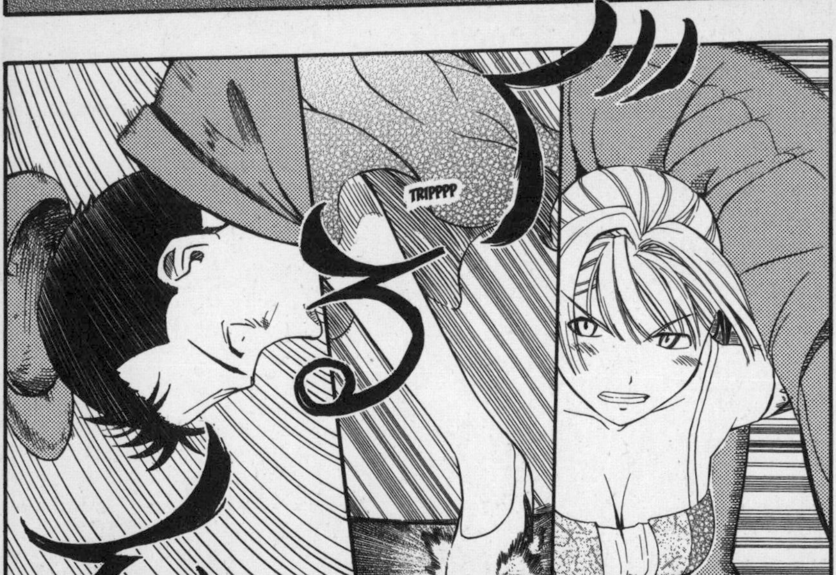
TRIPPPP

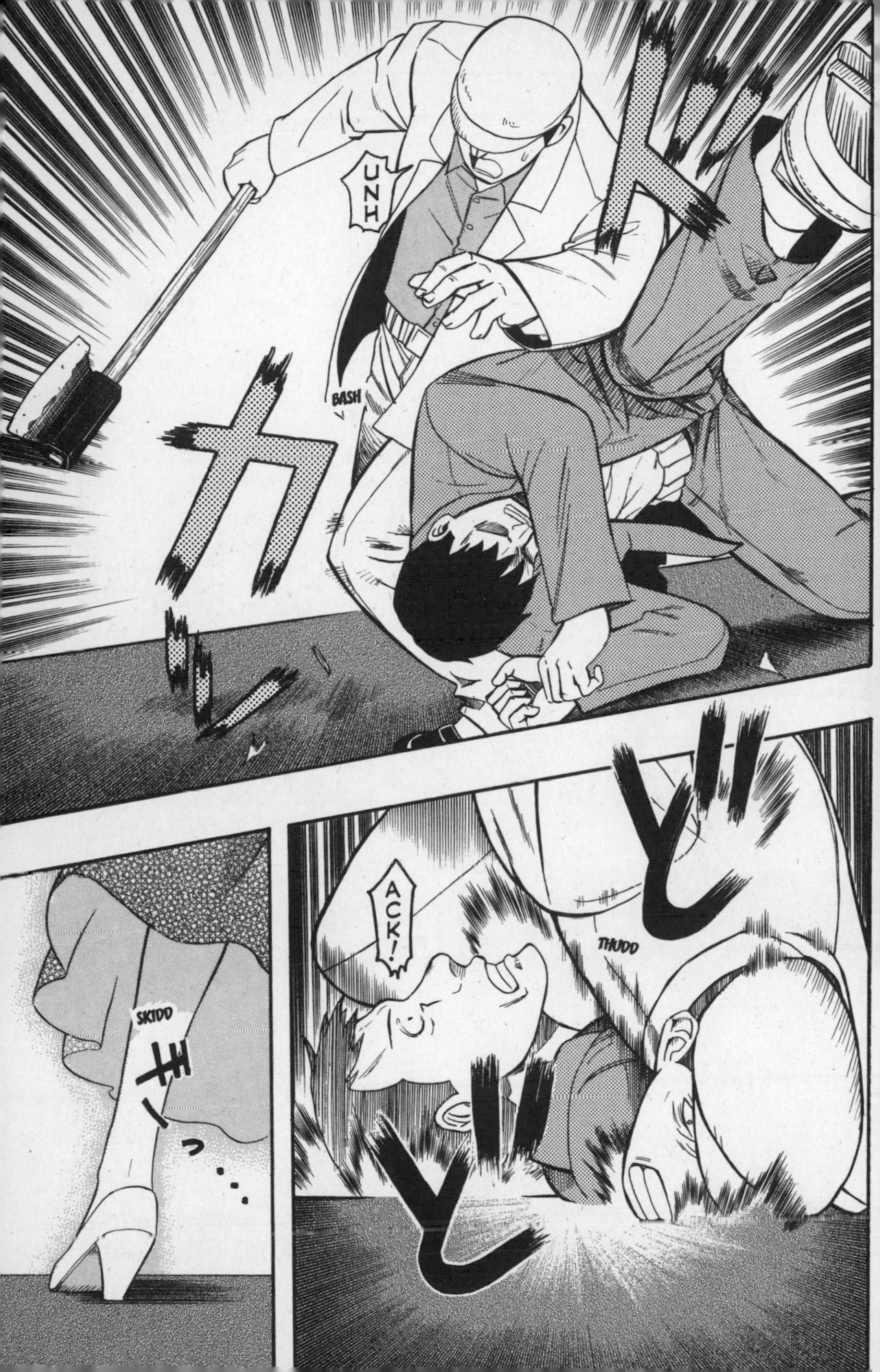

UNH
ドカッ
BASH
ACK!
THUDD
SKIDD

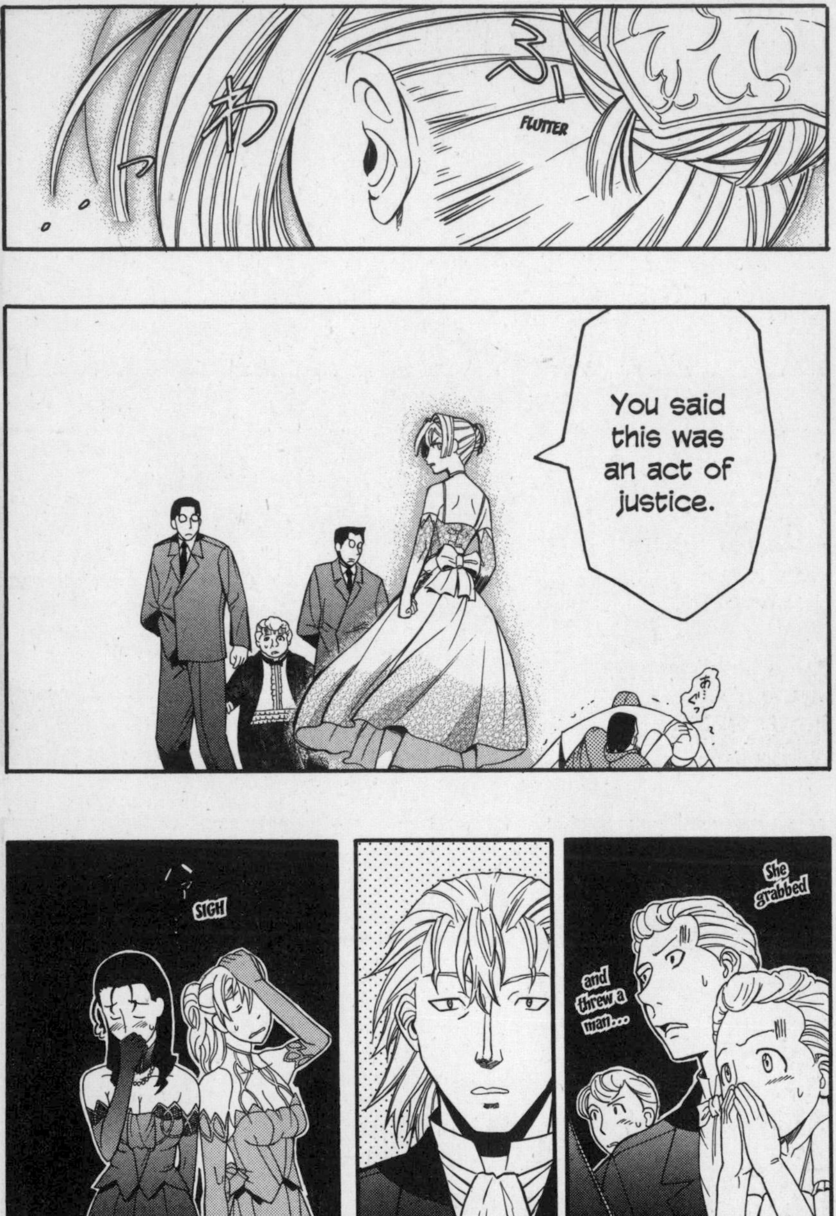
FLUTTER
You said this was an act of justice.
She grabbed
and threw a man...
SIGH

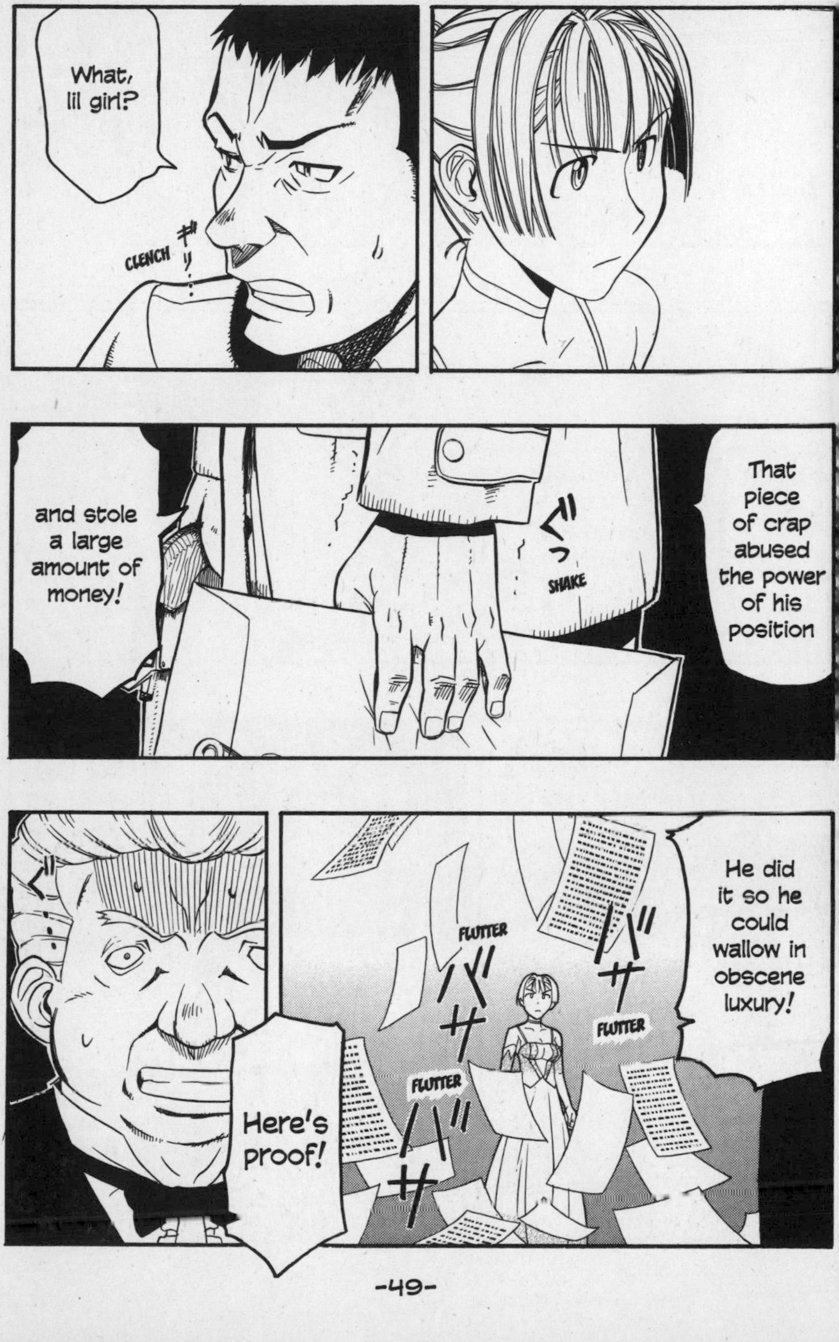
What, lil girl?
CLENCH
That piece of crap abused the power of his position
SHAKE
and stole a large amount of money!
He did it so he could wallow in obscene luxury!
FLUTTER
FLUTTER
FLUTTER
Here's proof!

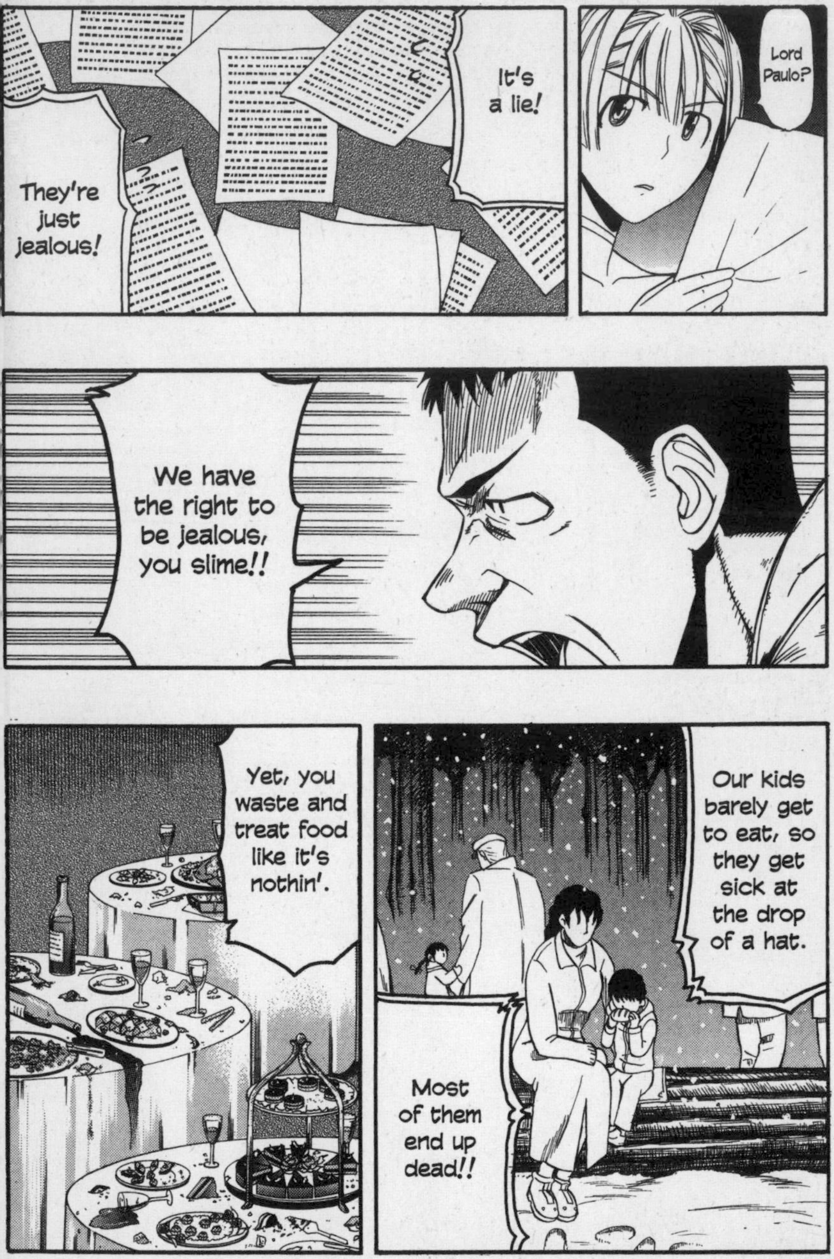
Lord Paulo?
It's a lie!
They're just jealous!
We have the right to be jealous, you slime!!
Our kids barely get to eat, so they get sick at the drop of a hat.
Most of them end up dead!!
Yet, you waste and treat food like it's nothin'.

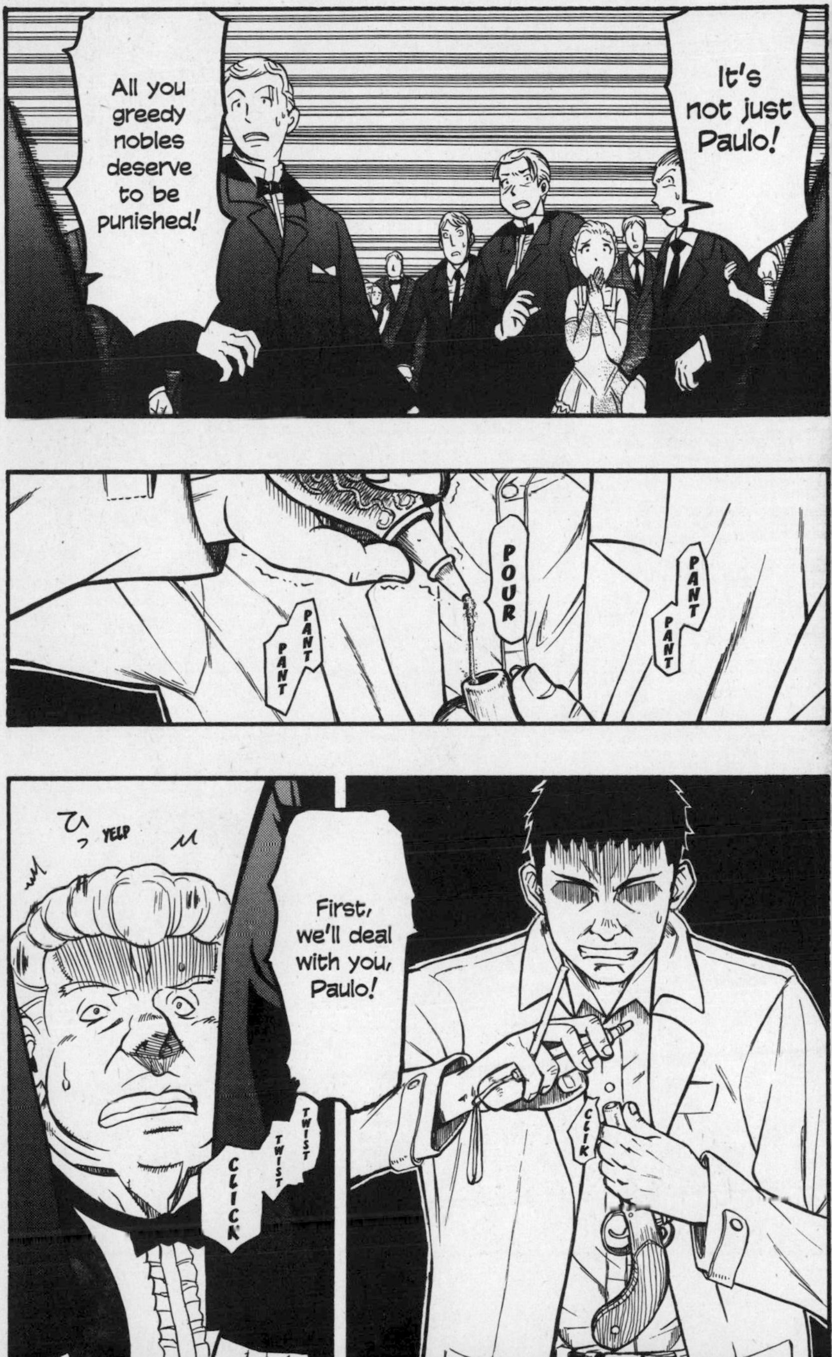

It's not just Paulo!
All you greedy nobles deserve to be punished!
PANT PANT
POUR
PANT PANT
CLIK
First, we'll deal with you, Paulo!
YELP
TWIST TWIST
CLICK

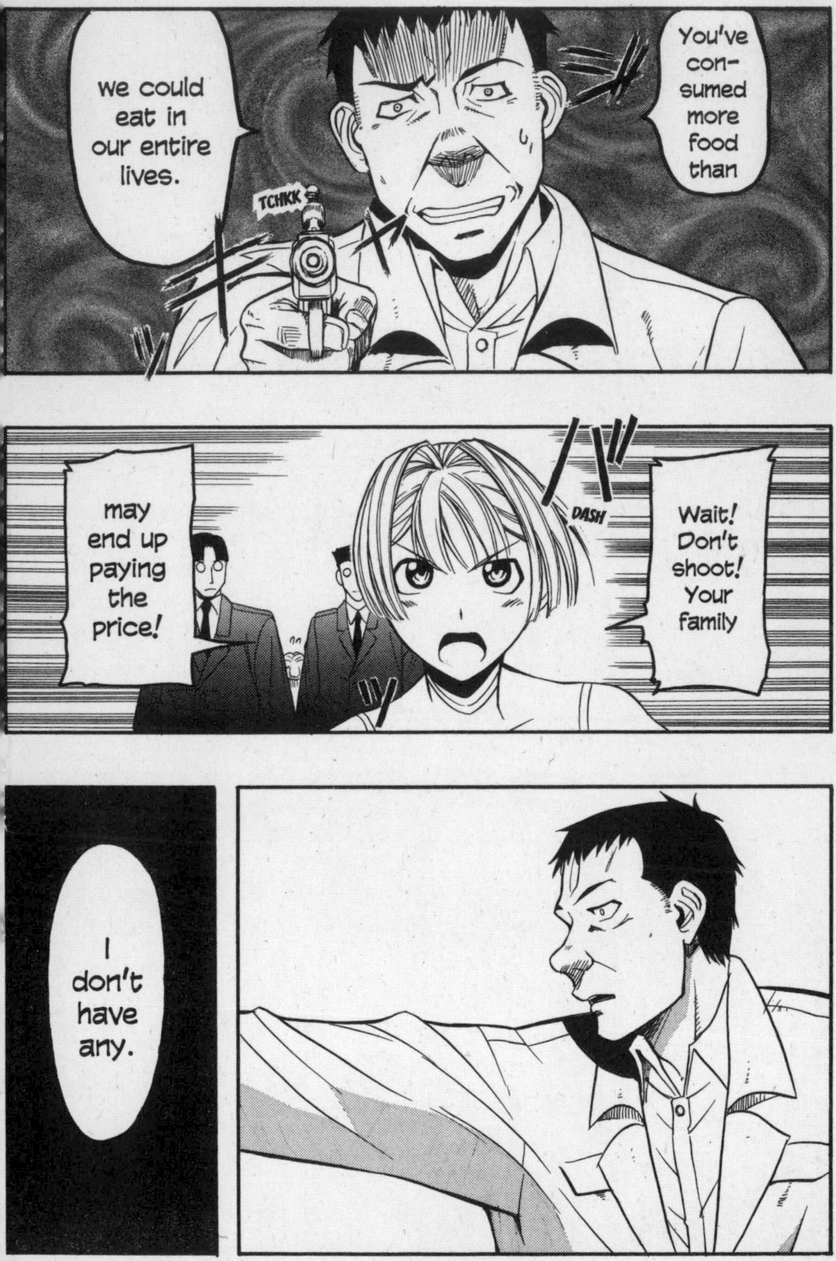
You've con- sumed more food than
we could eat in our entire lives.
TCHKK
DASH
Wait! Don't shoot! Your family
may end up paying the price!
I don't have any.

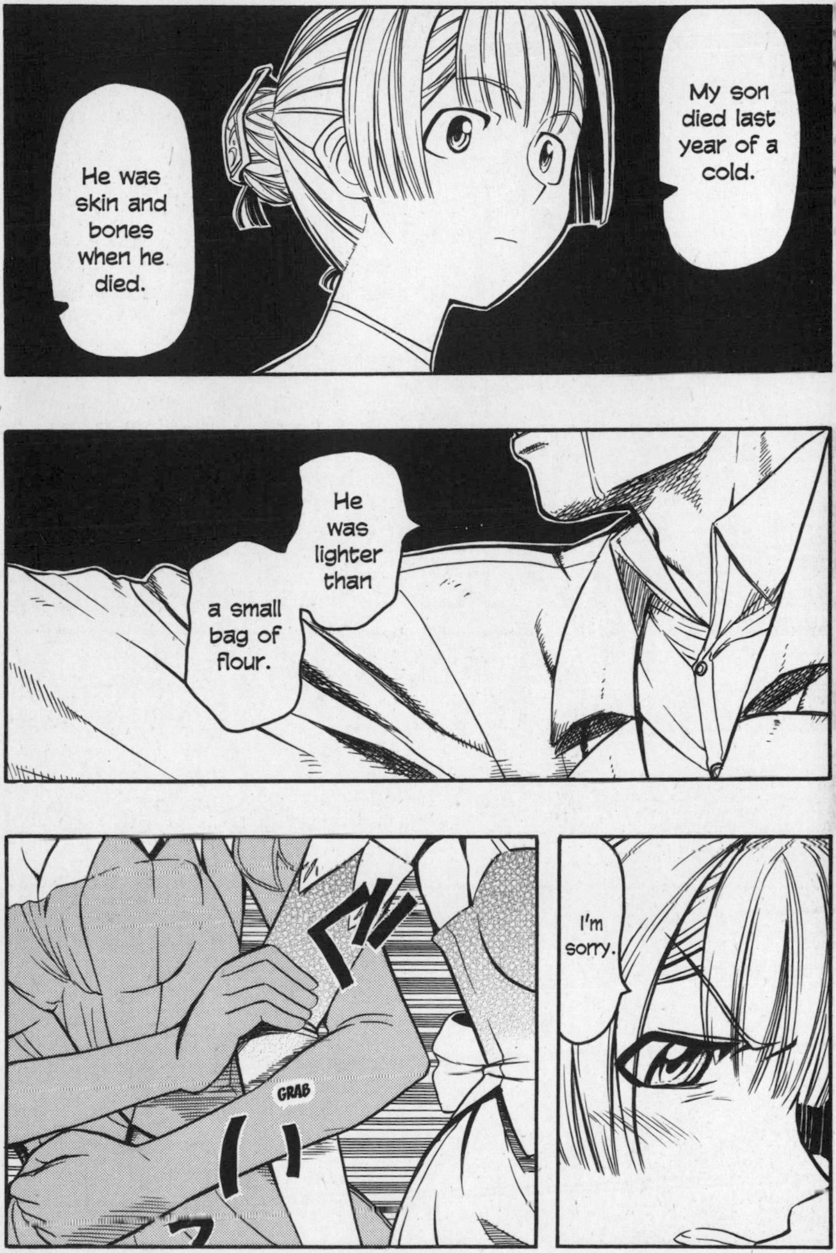
My son died last year of a cold.
He was skin and bones when he died.
He was lighter than
a small bag of flour.
I'm sorry.
GRAB

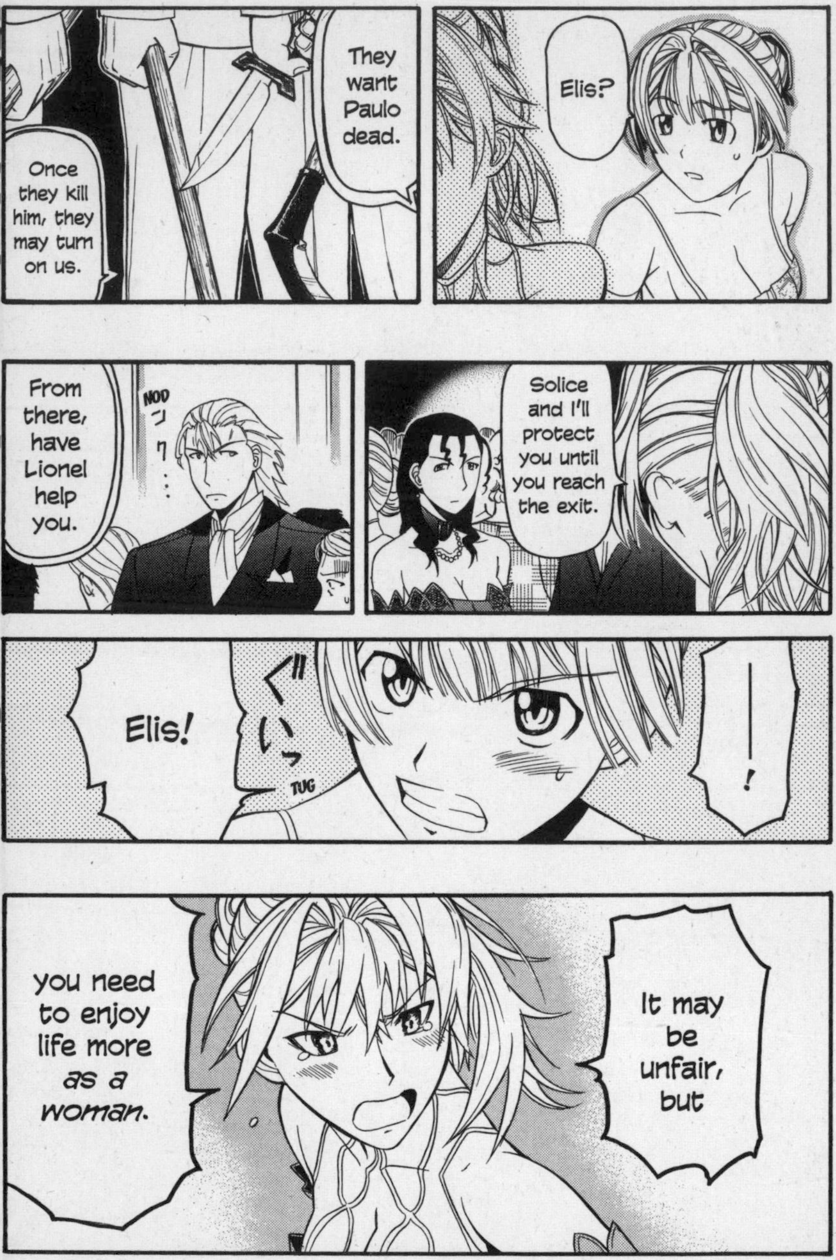
Elis?
They want Paulo dead.
Once they kill him, they may turn on us.
Solice and I'll protect you until you reach the exit.
From there, have Lionel help you.
NOD
—!
TUG
Elis!
It may be unfair, but
you need to enjoy life more *as a woman*.

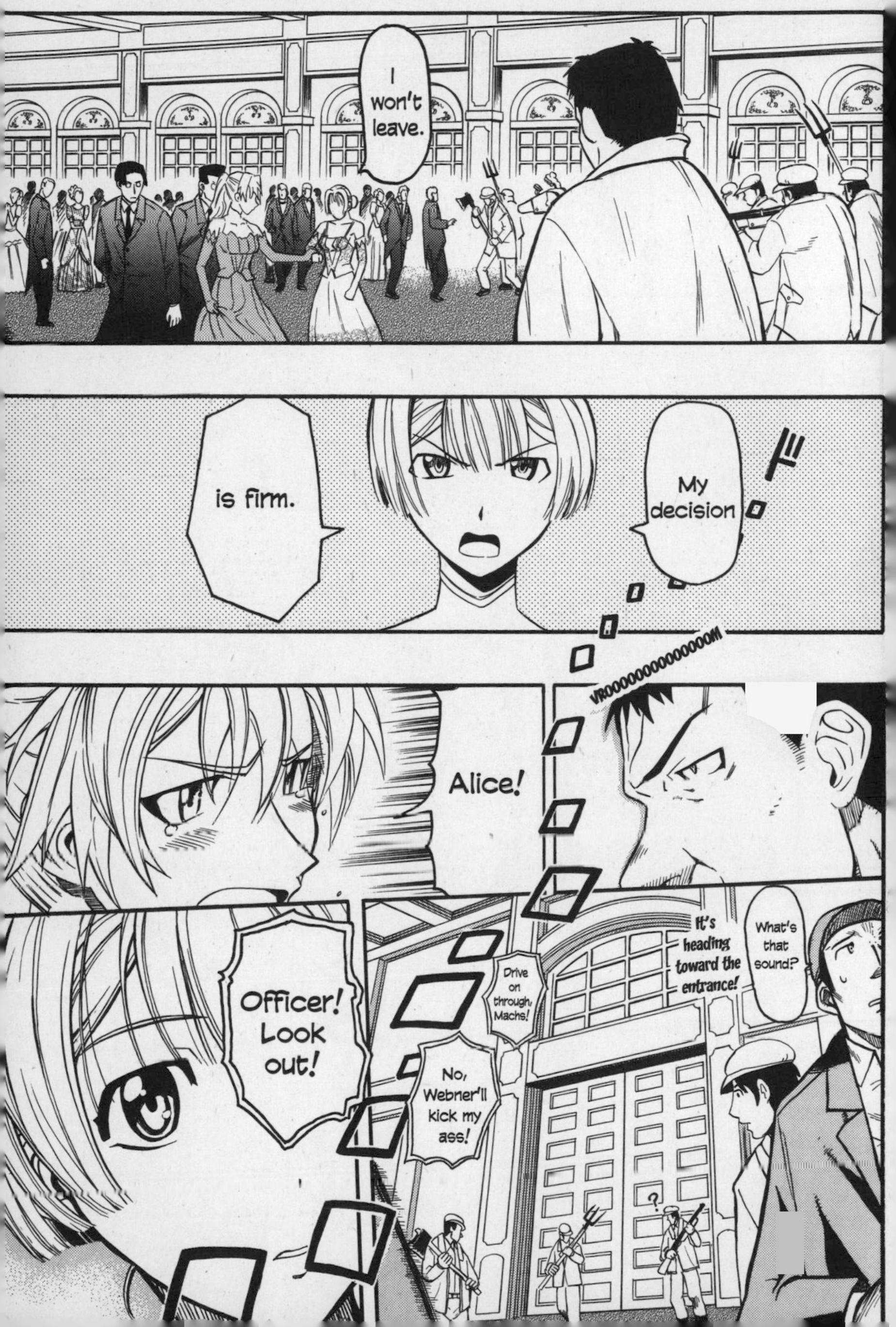
I won't leave.
My decision
is firm.
VROOOOOOOOOOOOOOOM
Alice!
What's that sound?
It's heading toward the entrance!
Drive on through, Machs!
No, Webner'll kick my ass!
Officer! Look out!

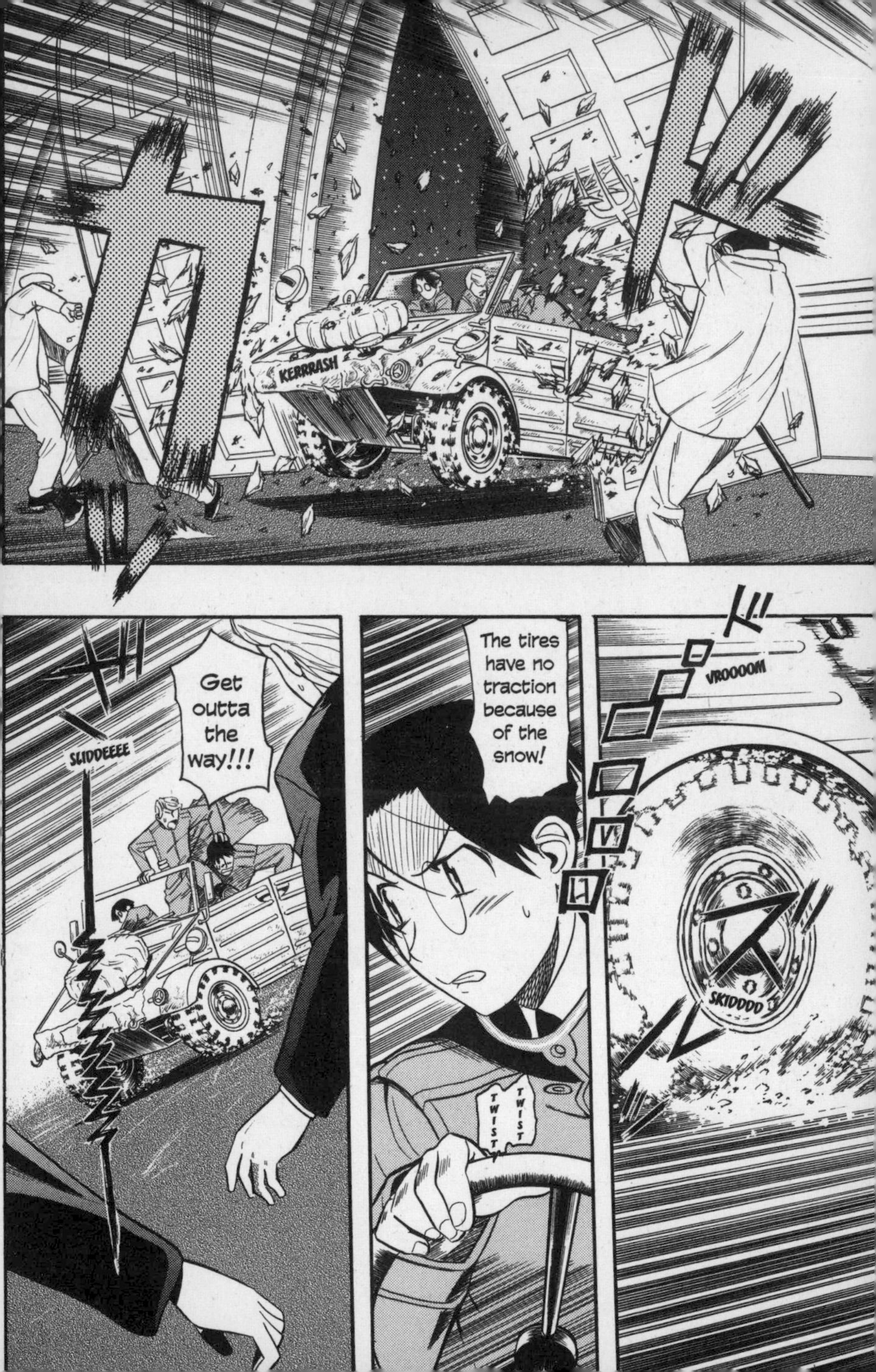
KERRRASH
VROOOOM
SKIDDDD
The tires have no traction because of the snow!
TWIST TWIST
Get outta the way!!!
SLIDDEEEE

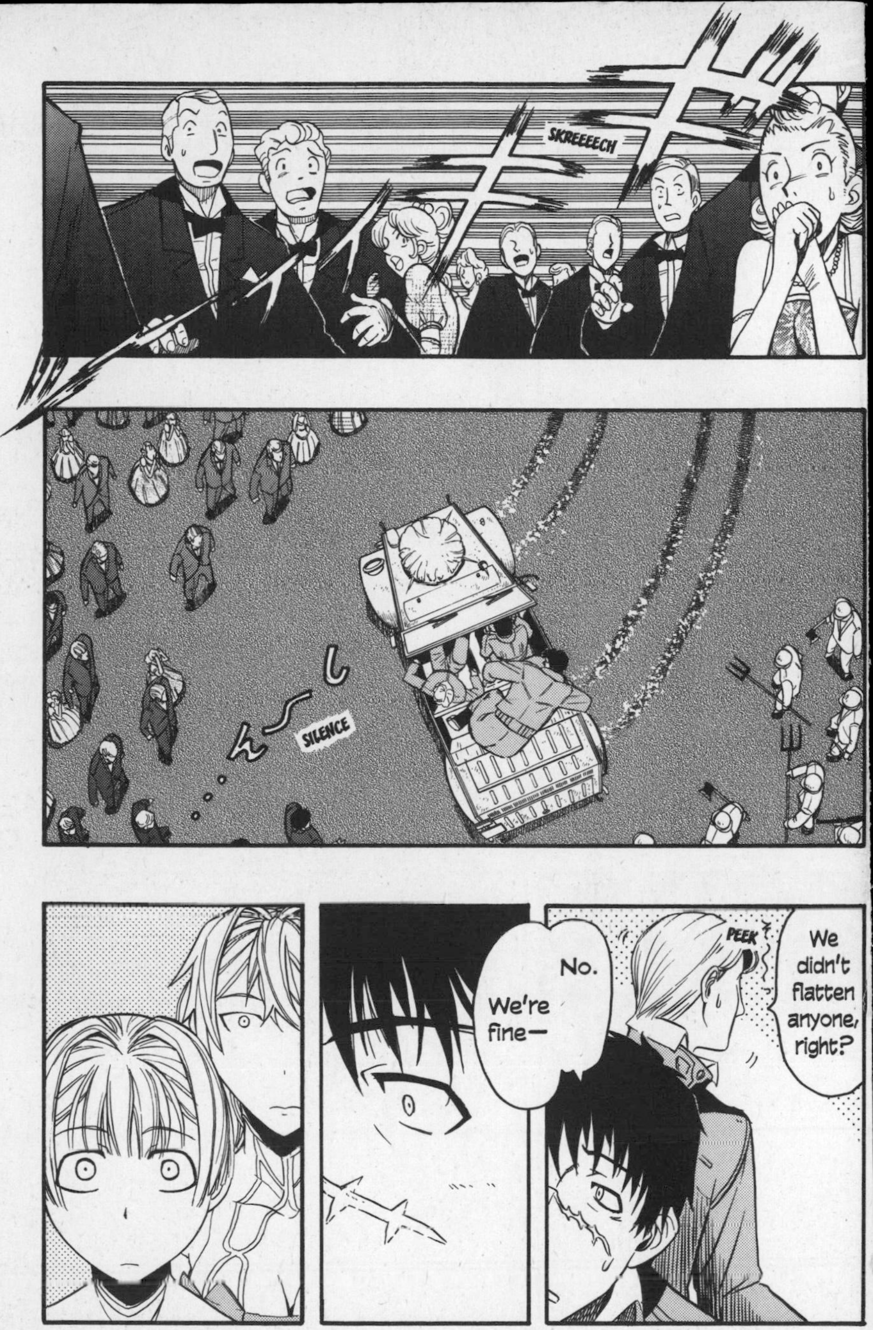
SKREEEECH
SILENCE
PEEK
We didn't flatten anyone, right?
No.
We're fine—

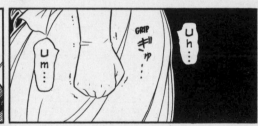

Um...

GRIP
キリッ...

Uh...

You look
amazing.

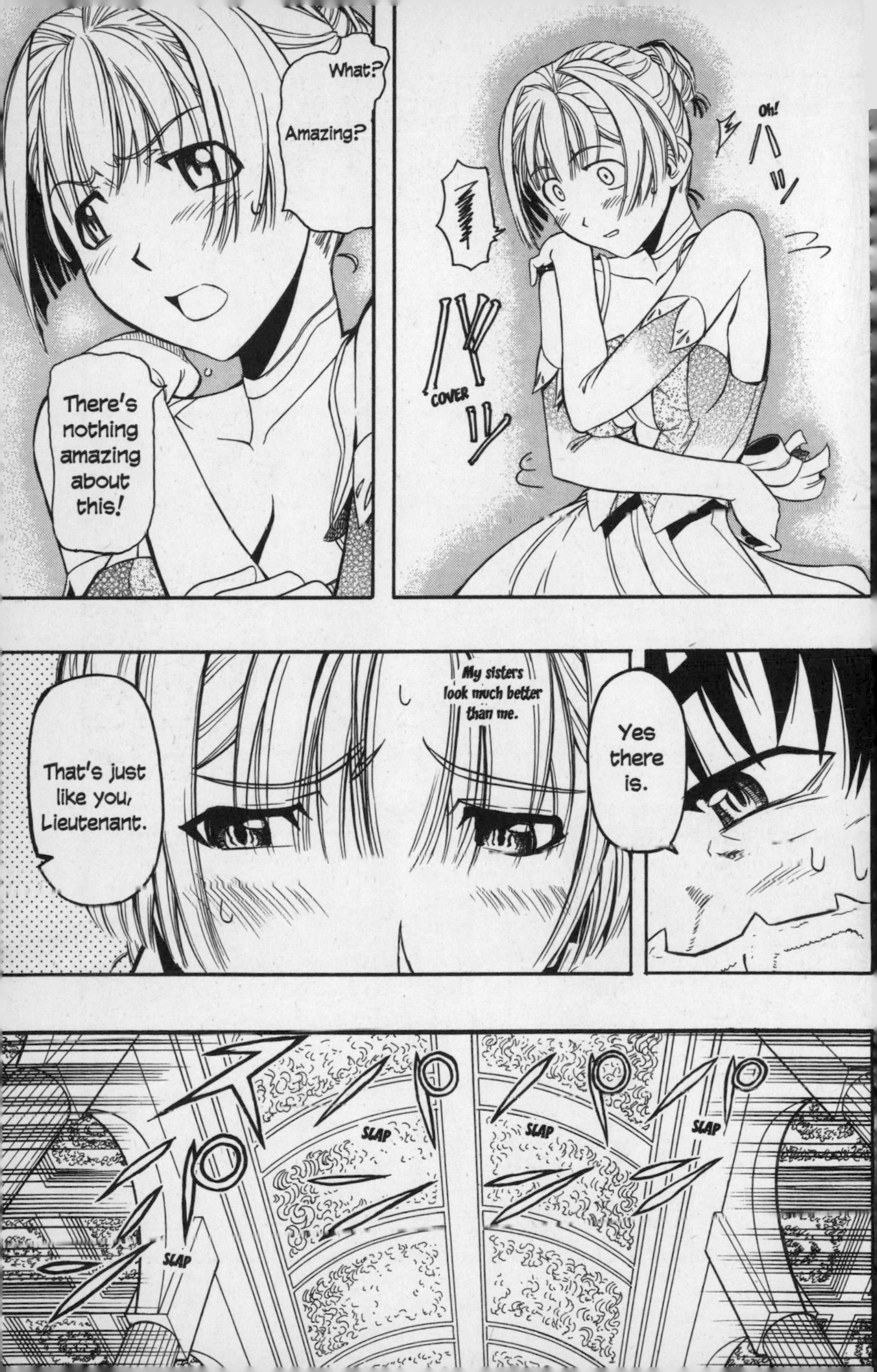

Oh!
COVER
What?
Amazing?
There's nothing amazing about this!
Yes there is.
My sisters look much better than me.
That's just like you, Lieutenant.
SLAP
SLAP
SLAP
SLAP

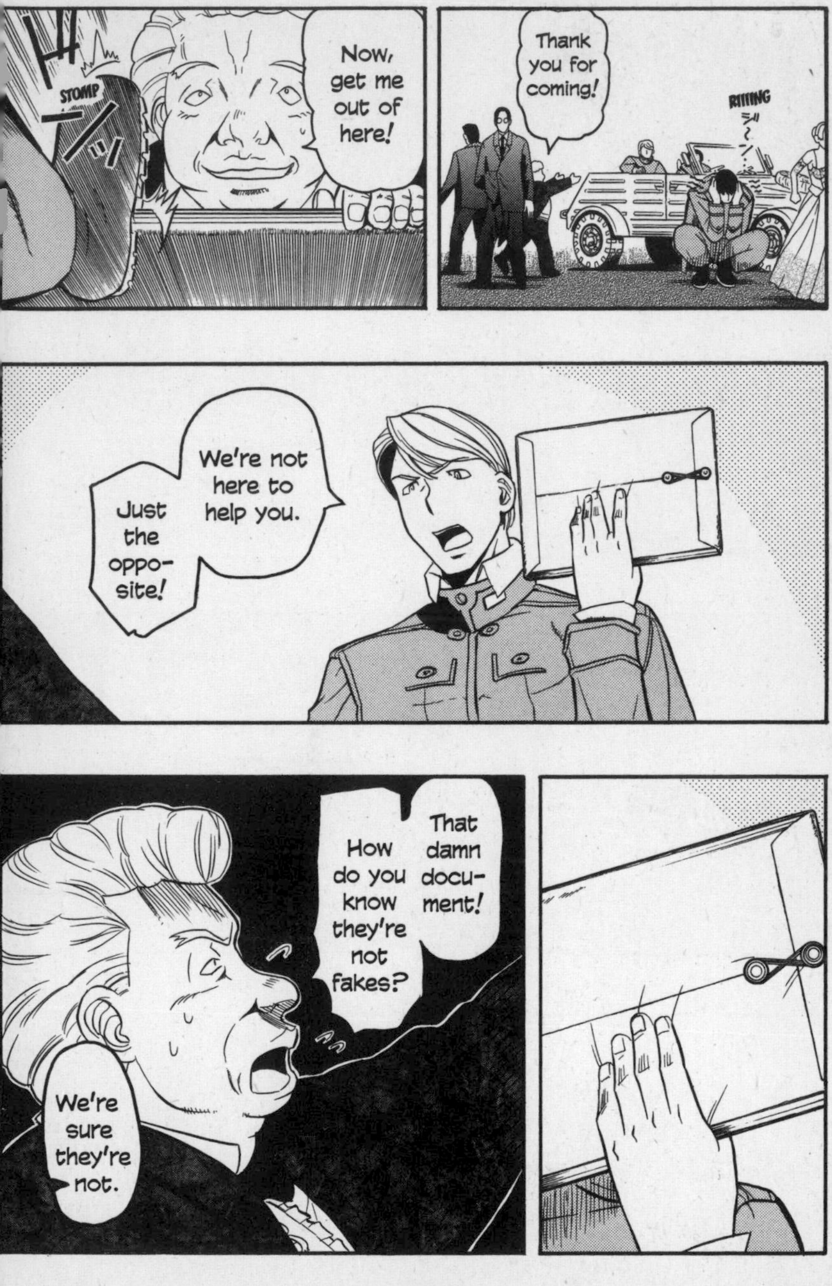
Thank you for coming!
RIIIING
Now, get me out of here!
STOMP
We're not here to help you.
Just the opposite!
That damn document!
How do you know they're not fakes?
We're sure they're not.

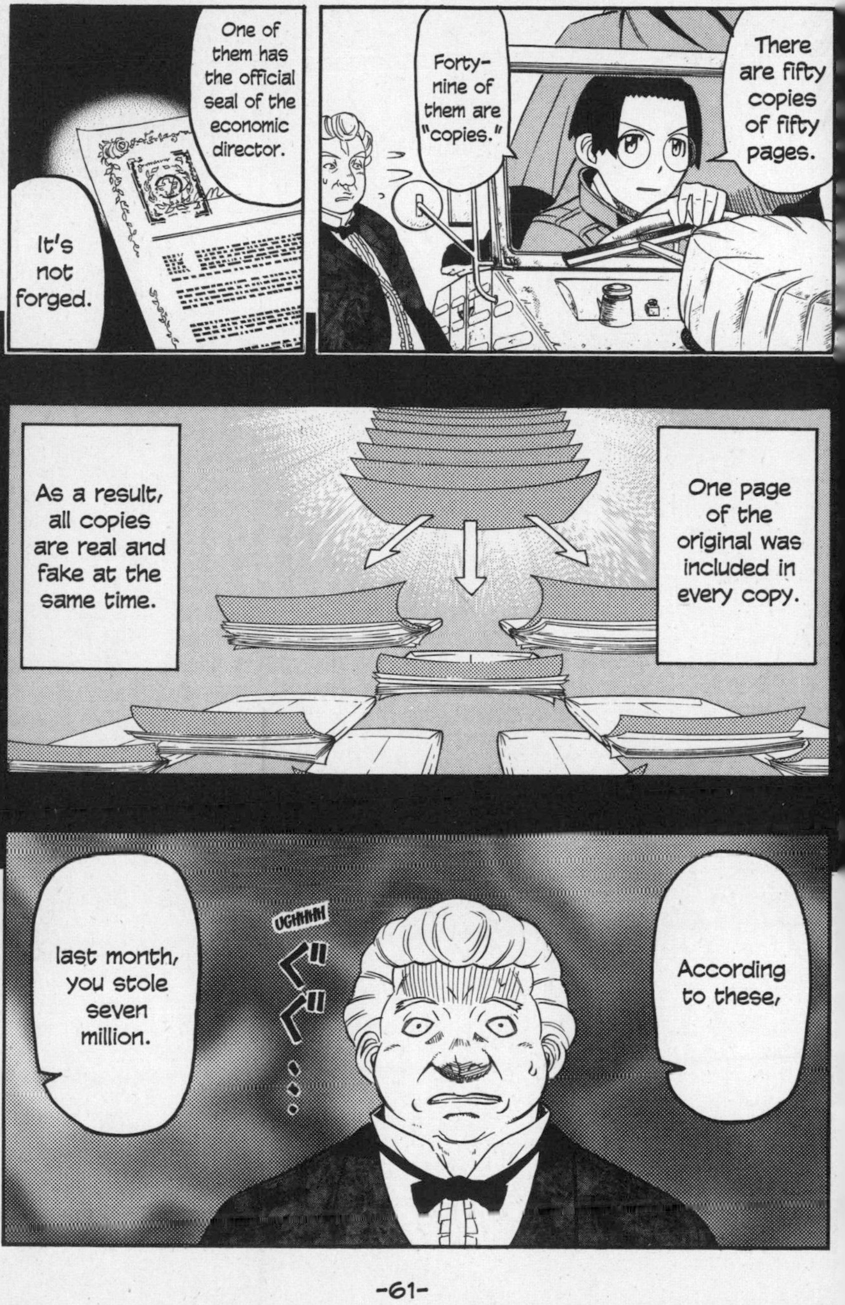
There are fifty copies of fifty pages.
Forty-nine of them are "copies."
One of them has the official seal of the economic director.
It's not forged.
One page of the original was included in every copy.
As a result, all copies are real and fake at the same time.
According to these,
UGHHHH
last month, you stole seven million.

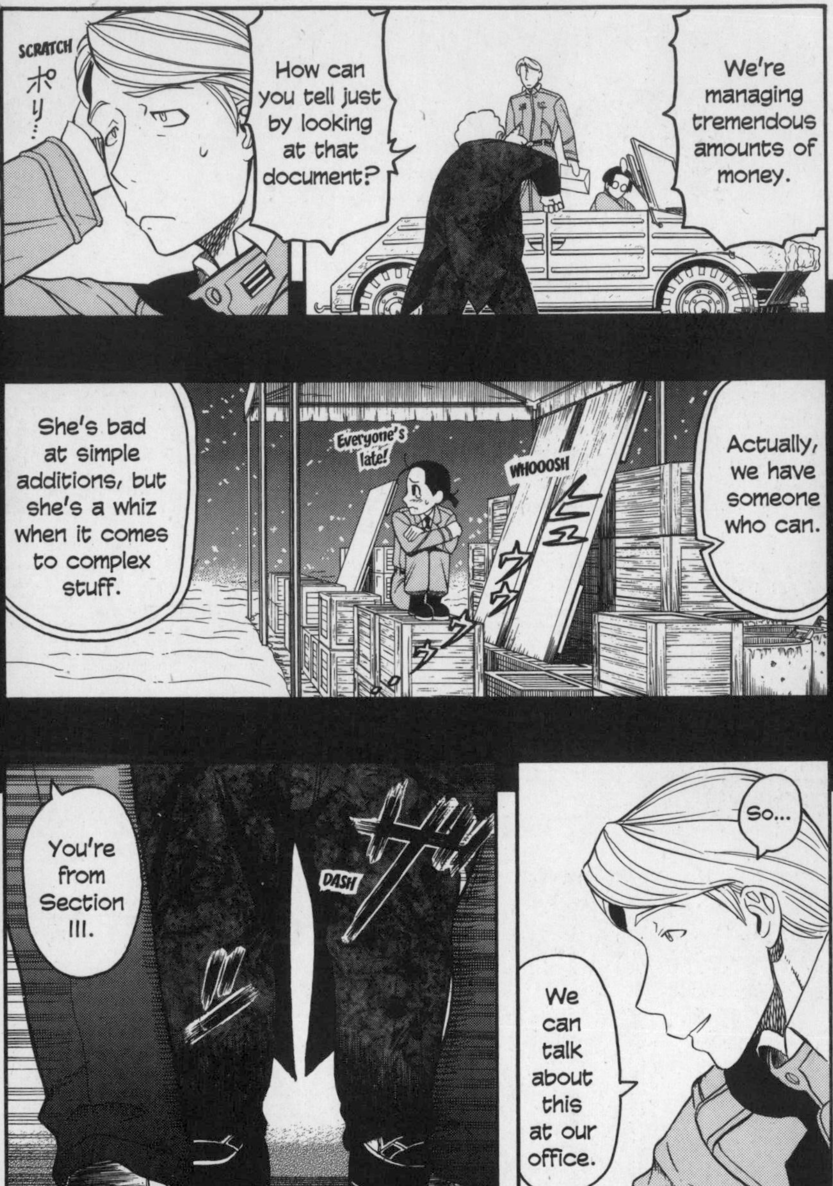
We're managing tremendous amounts of money.
How can you tell just by looking at that document?
SCRATCH
ポリ…
Actually, we have someone who can.
Everyone's late!
WHOOOSH
She's bad at simple additions, but she's a whiz when it comes to complex stuff.
So...
We can talk about this at our office.
DASH
You're from Section III.

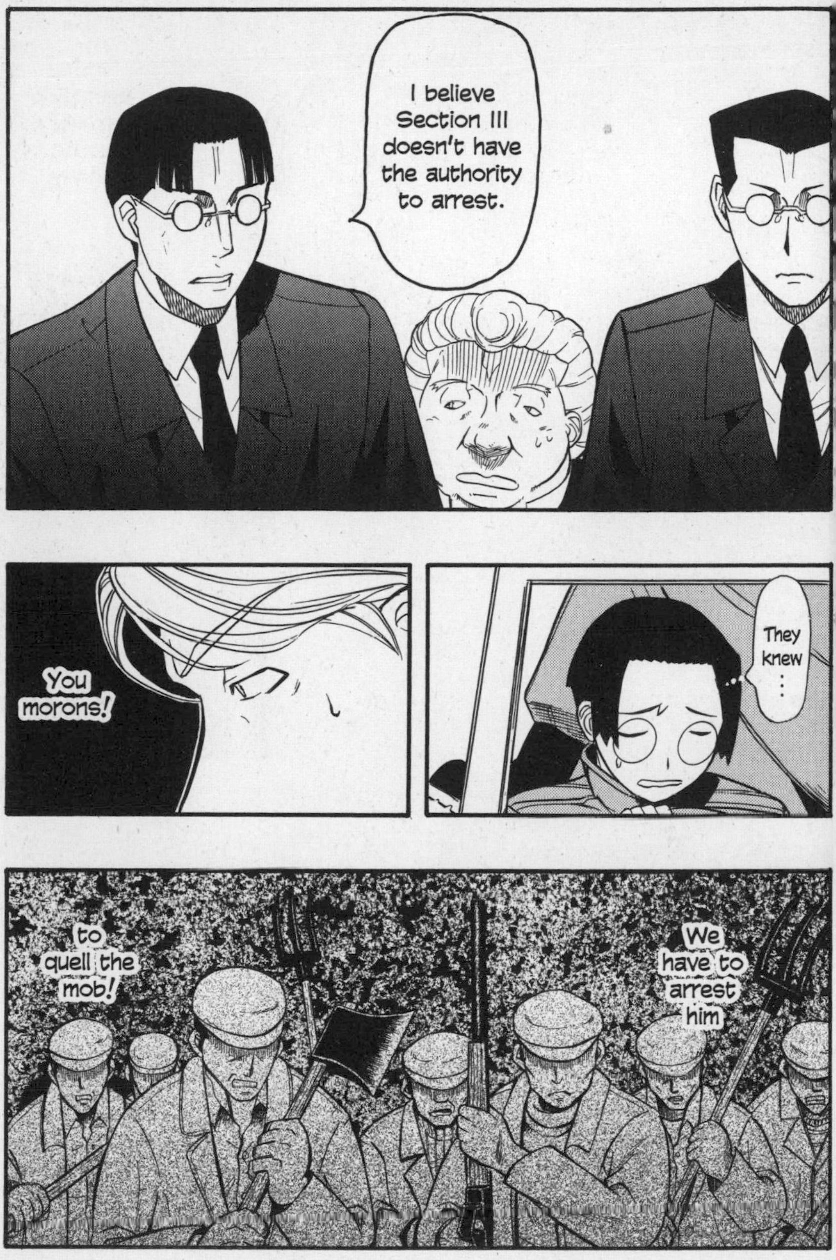
I believe Section III doesn't have the authority to arrest.
They knew . . .
You morons!
We have to arrest him
to quell the mob!

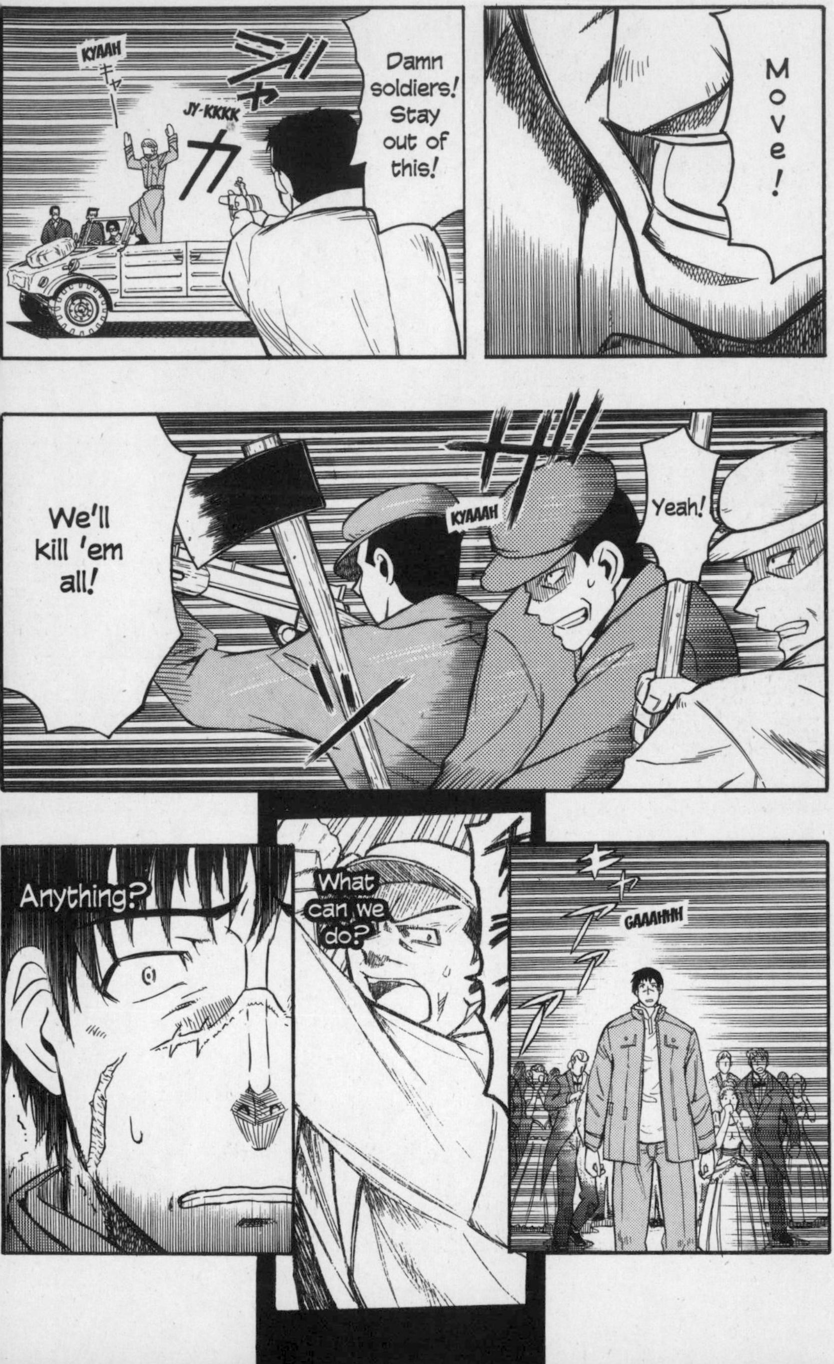
Move!
Damn soldiers! Stay out of this!
KYAAH
キャー
JY-KKKK
Yeah!
KYAAAH
We'll kill 'em all!
GAAAHHH
What can we do?
Anything?

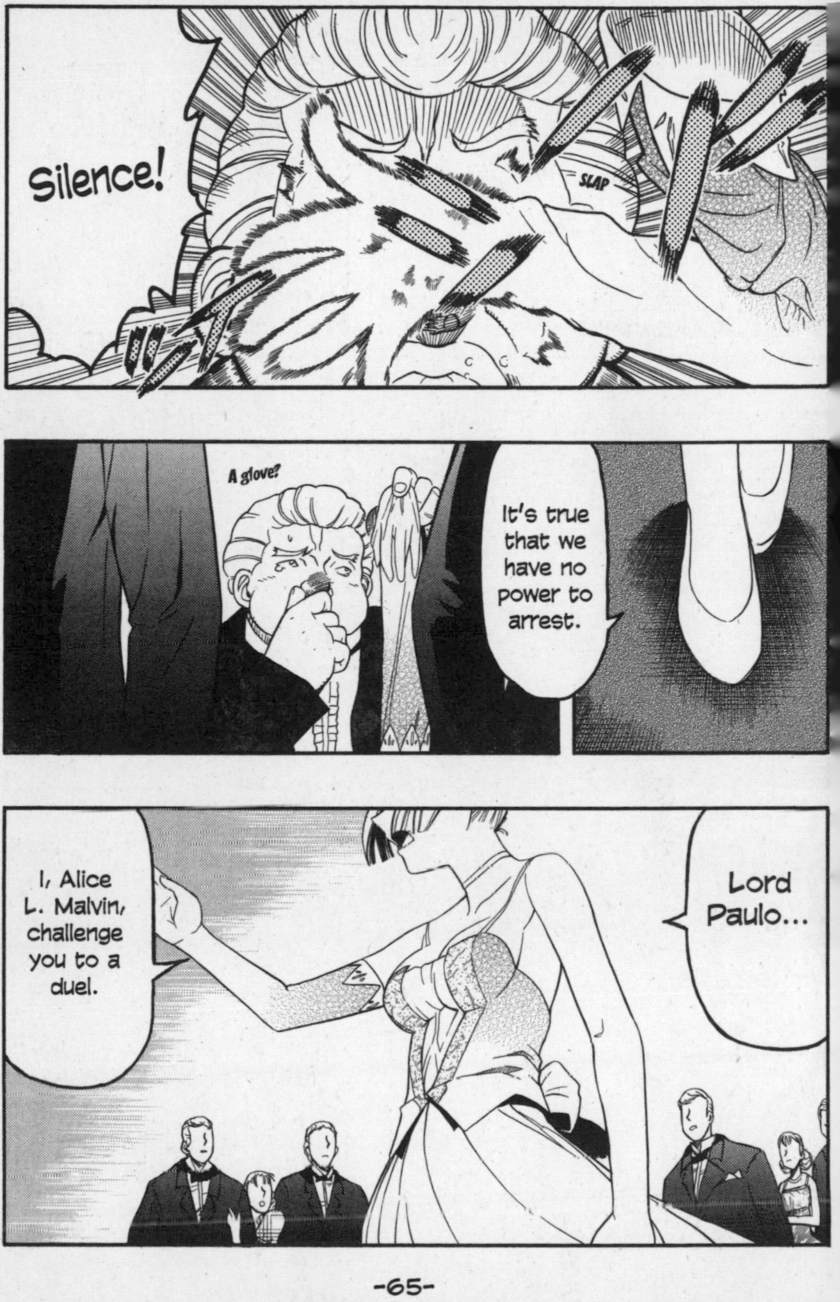
SLAP
Silence!
It's true that we have no power to arrest.
A glove?
Lord Paulo...
I, Alice L. Malvin, challenge you to a duel.

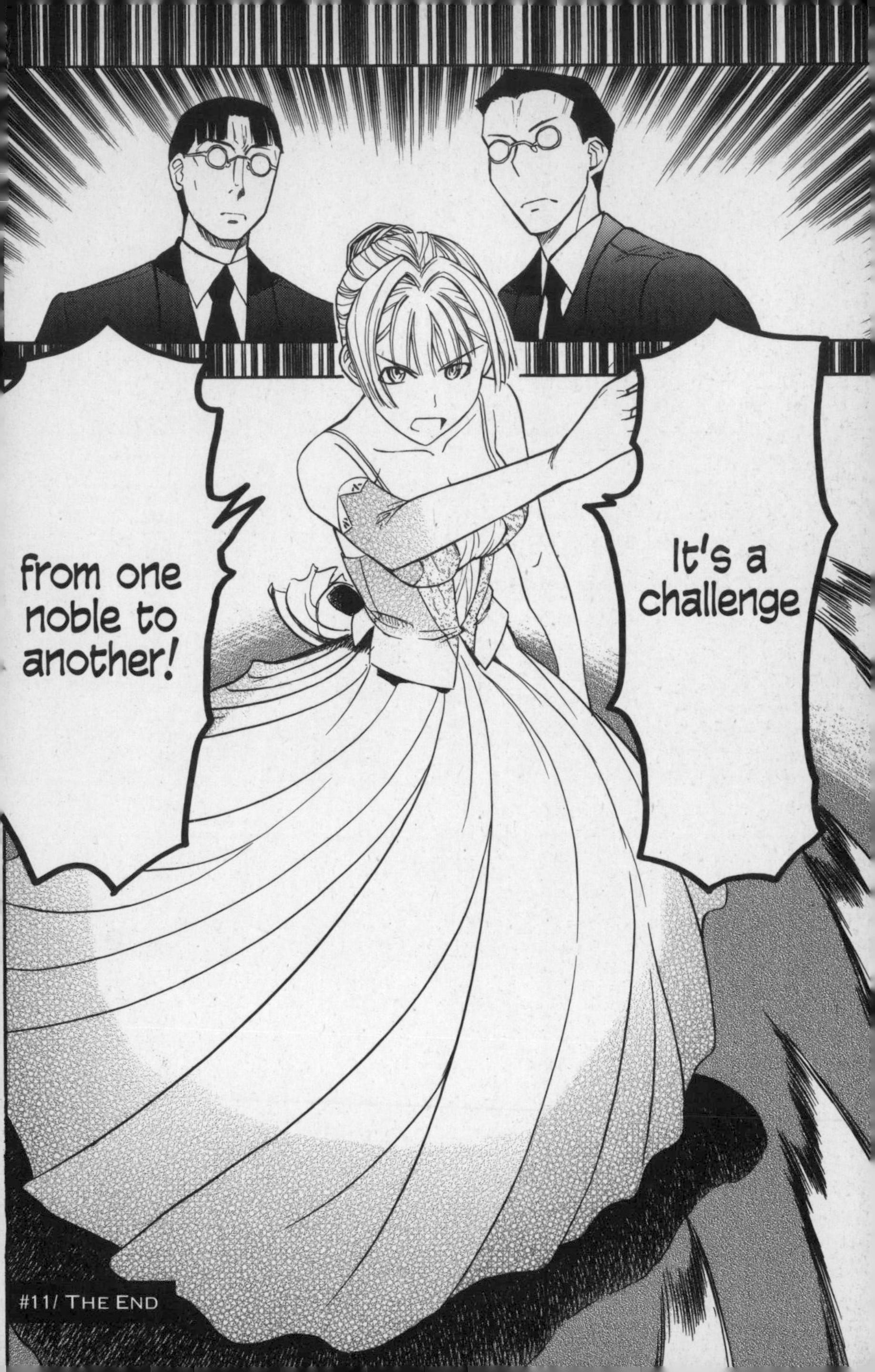
It's a challenge
from one noble to another!
#11/ The End

PumpkinScissors

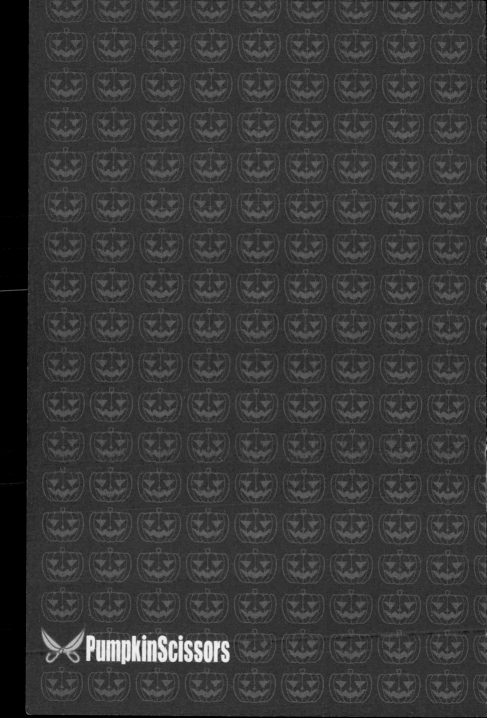

PumpkinScissors

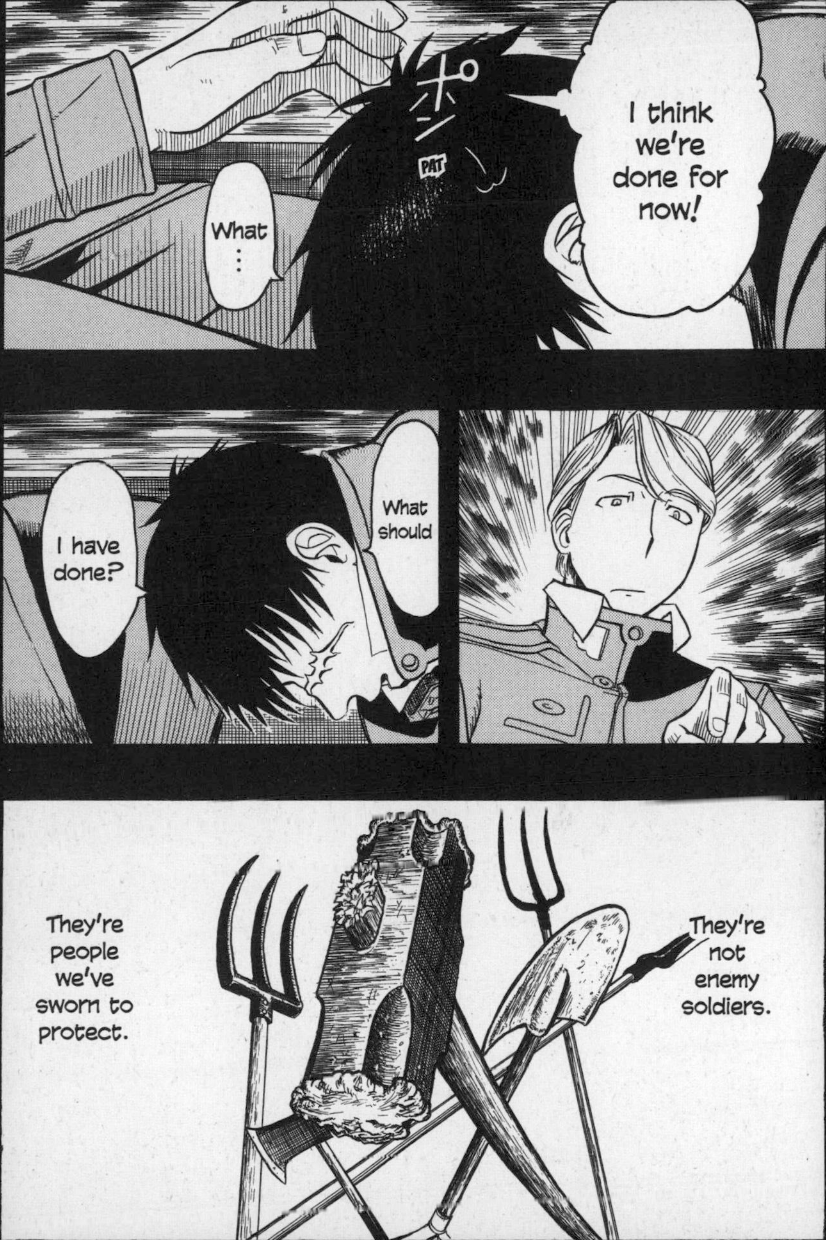
I think we're done for now!
PAT
What ...
What should
I have done?
They're not enemy soldiers.
They're people we've sworn to protect.

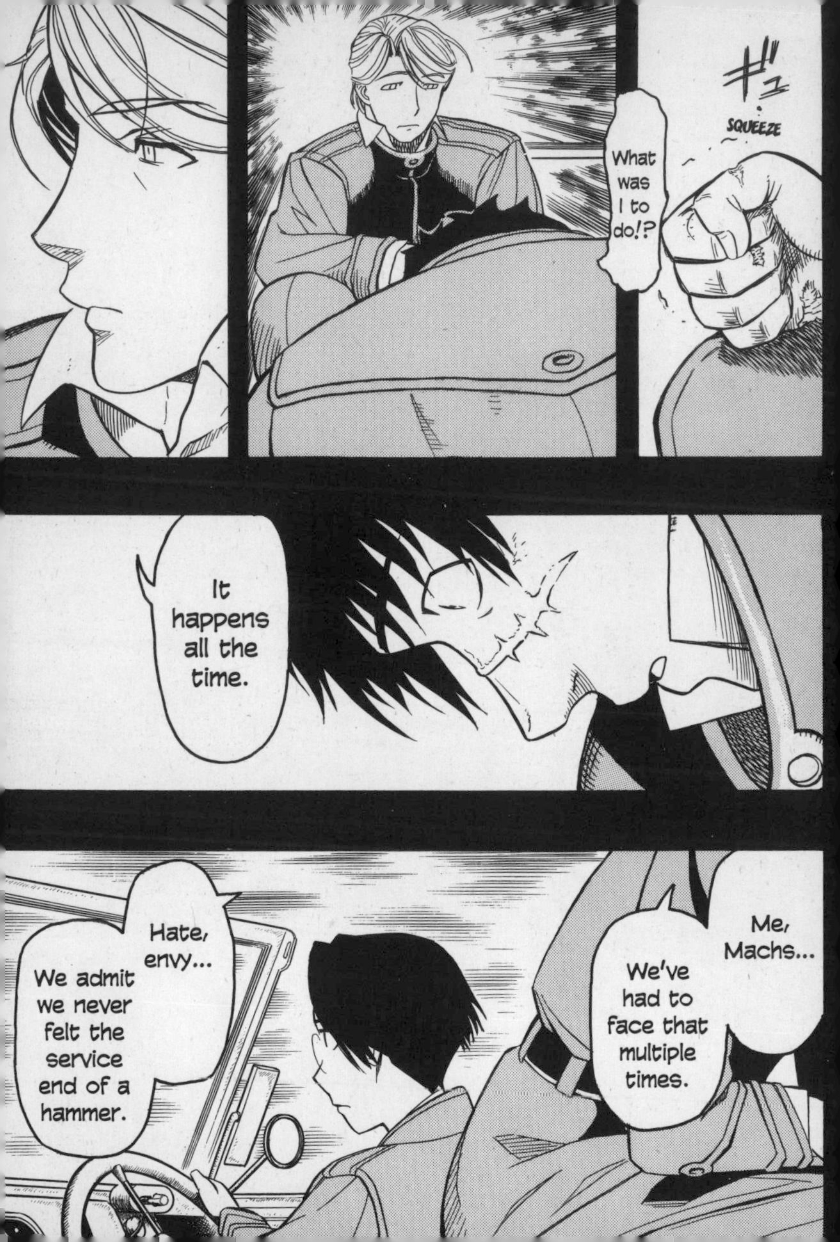

ギュ
SQUEEZE
What was I to do!?
It happens all the time.
Me, Machs...
We've had to face that multiple times.
Hate, envy...
We admit we never felt the service end of a hammer.

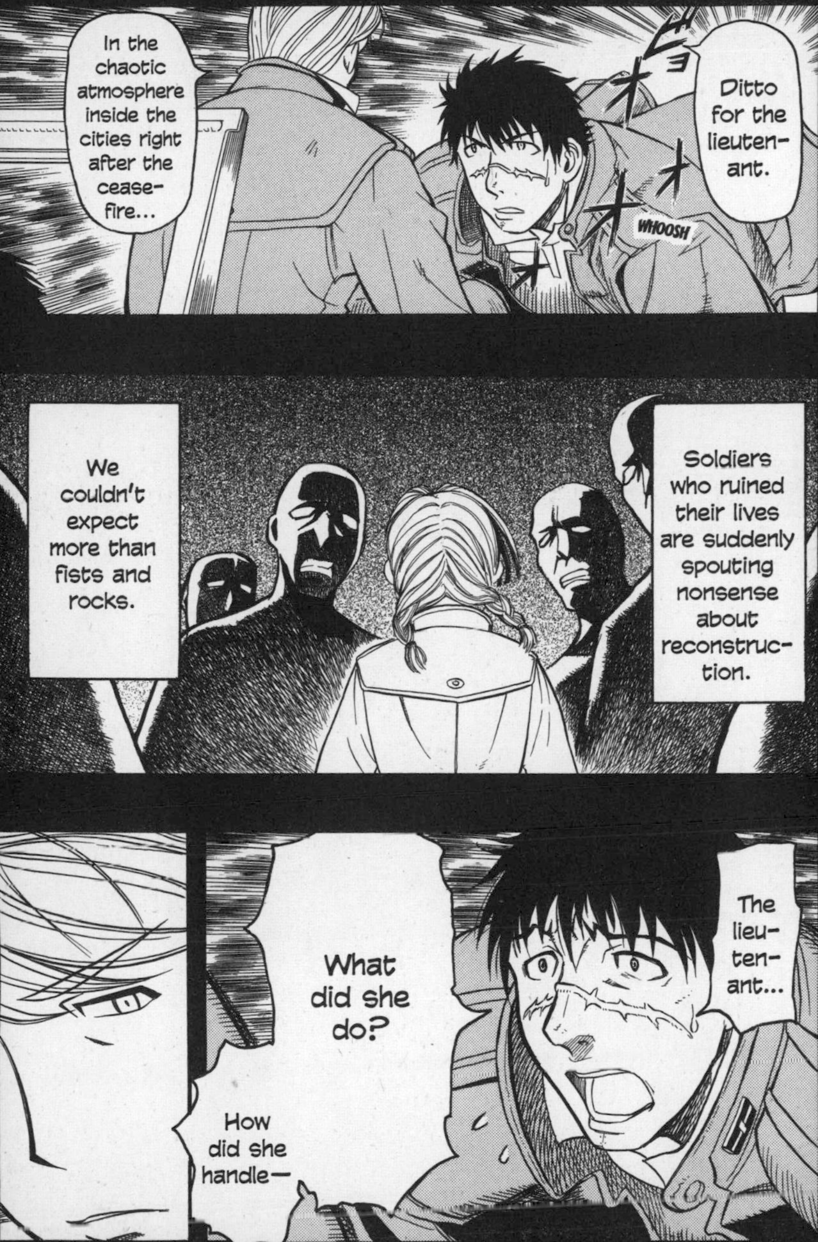
Ditto for the lieutenant.
WHOOSH
In the chaotic atmosphere inside the cities right after the cease-fire...
Soldiers who ruined their lives are suddenly spouting nonsense about reconstruction.
We couldn't expect more than fists and rocks.
The lieutenant...
What did she do?
How did she handle—

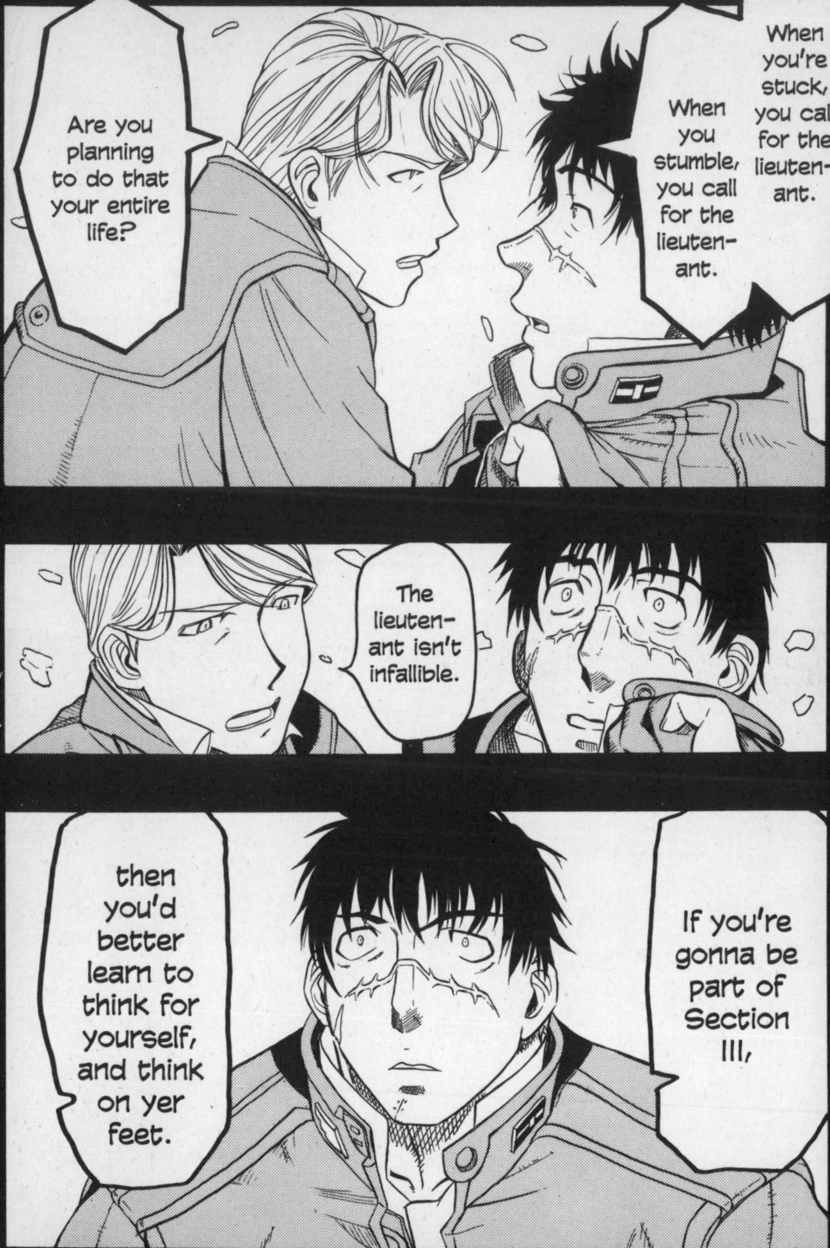
When you're stuck, you call for the lieutenant.
When you stumble, you call for the lieutenant.
Are you planning to do that your entire life?
The lieutenant isn't infallible.
If you're gonna be part of Section III,
then you'd better learn to think for yourself, and think on yer feet.

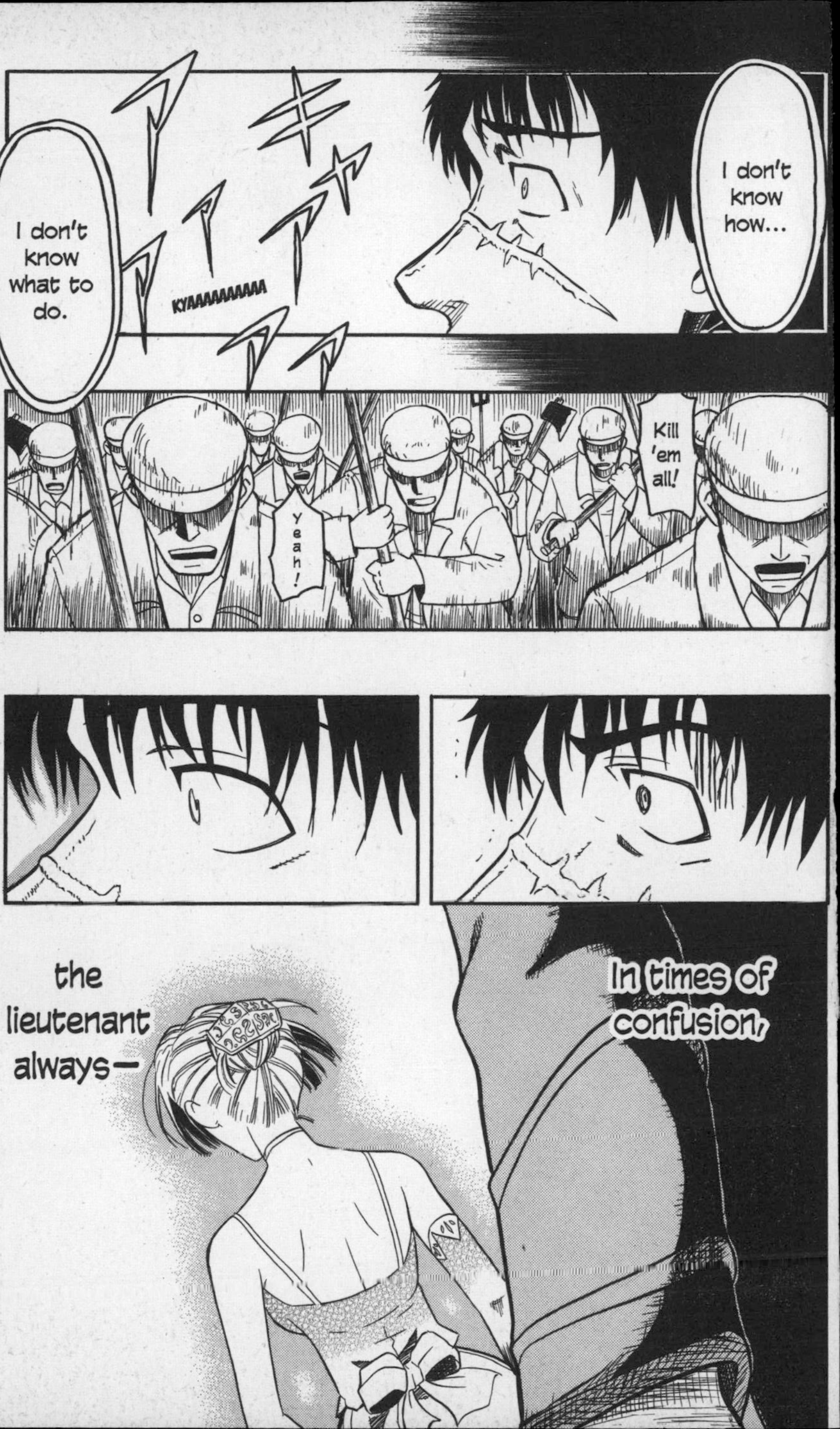
I don't know how...
I don't know what to do.
KYAAAAAAAAAA
Kill 'em all!
Yeah!
In times of confusion,
the lieutenant always—

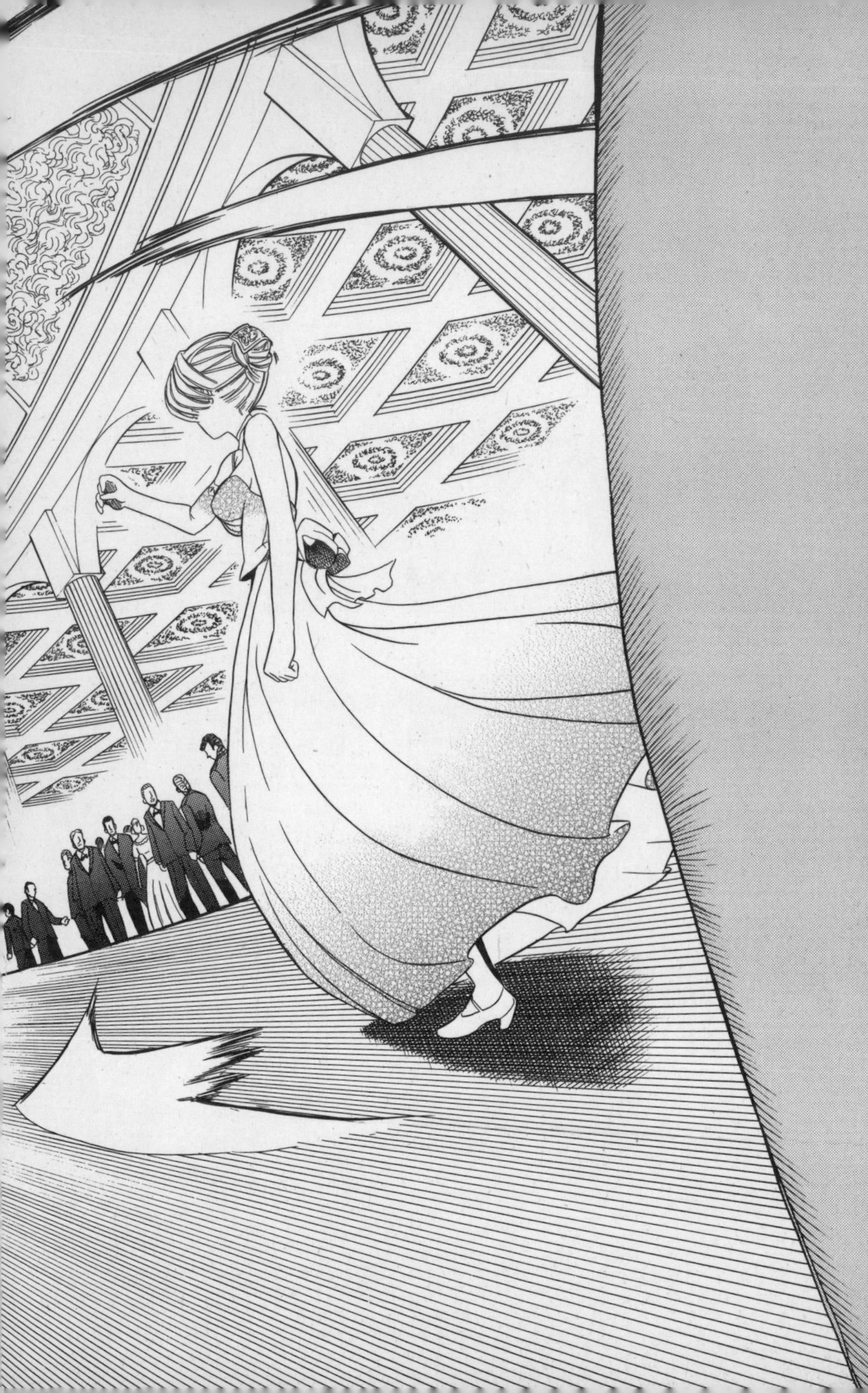

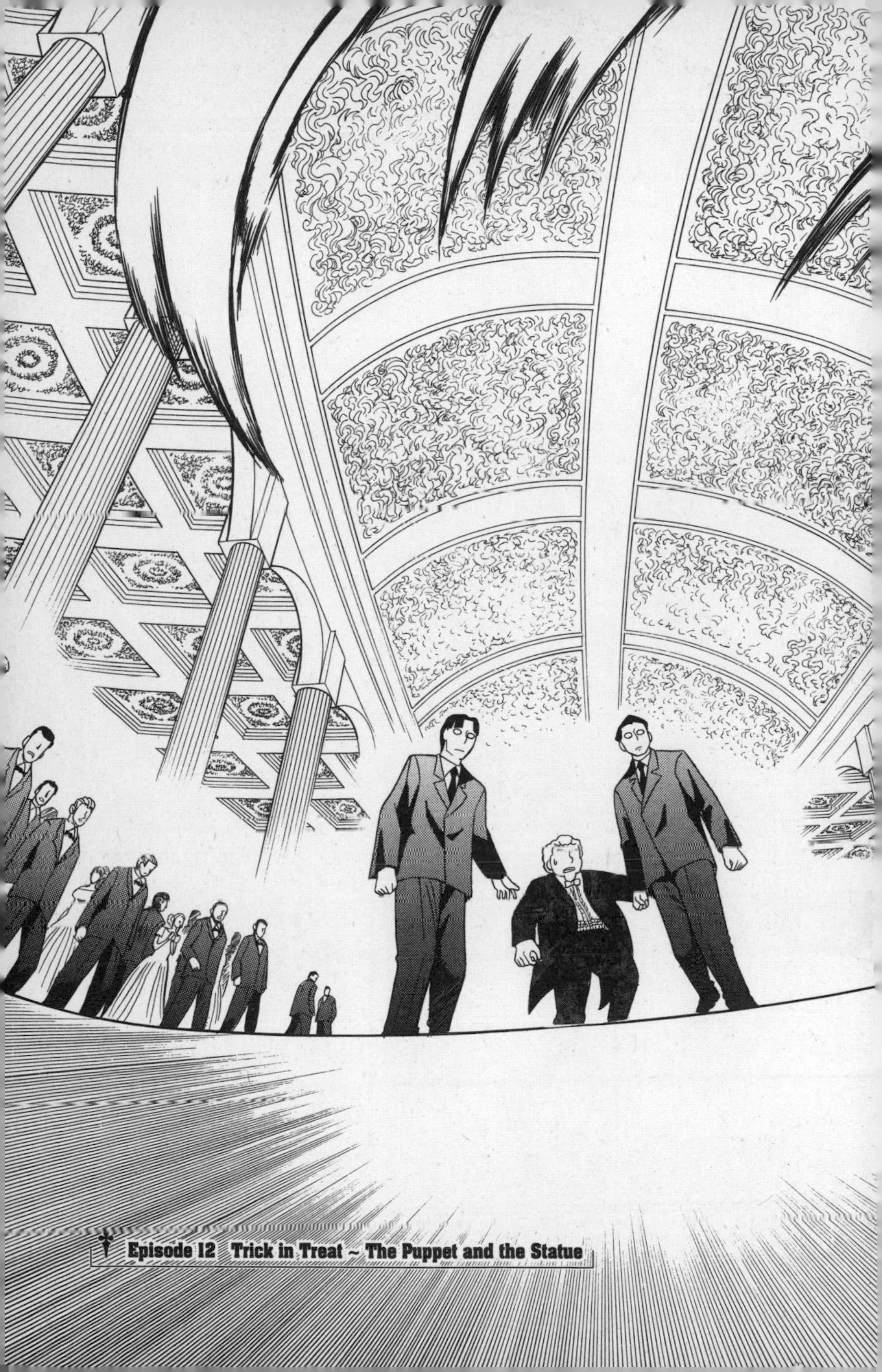
Episode 12 Trick in Treat ~ The Puppet and the Statue

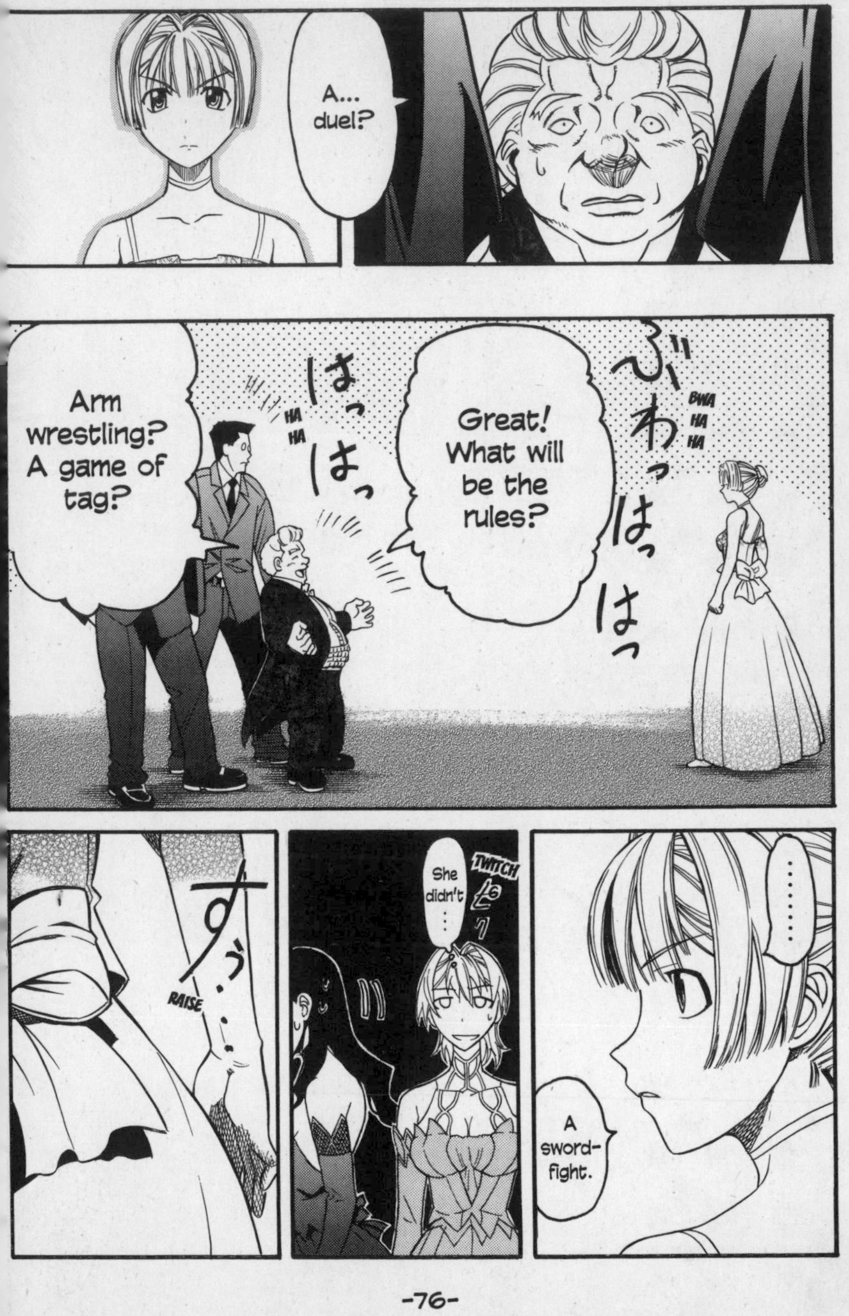
A... duel?
ぶわっはっはっ
BWA HA HA
Great! What will be the rules?
はっはっ
HA HA
Arm wrestling? A game of tag?
......
A sword-fight.
TWITCH
She didn't ...
RAISE

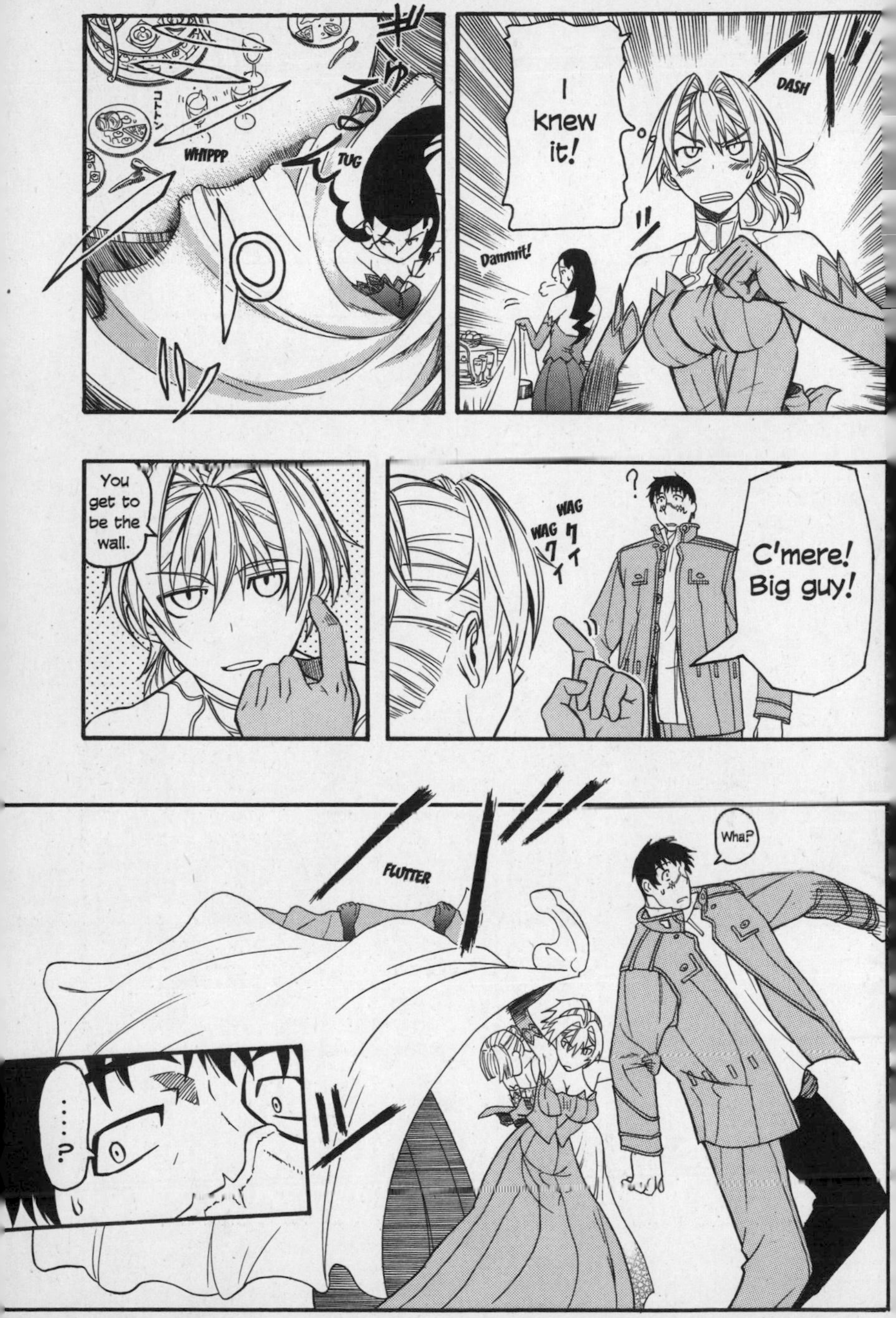
DASH
I knew it!
Dammit!
WHIPPP
TUG
C'mere! Big guy!
WAG
WAG
?
You get to be the wall.
Wha?
FLUTTER
?.....

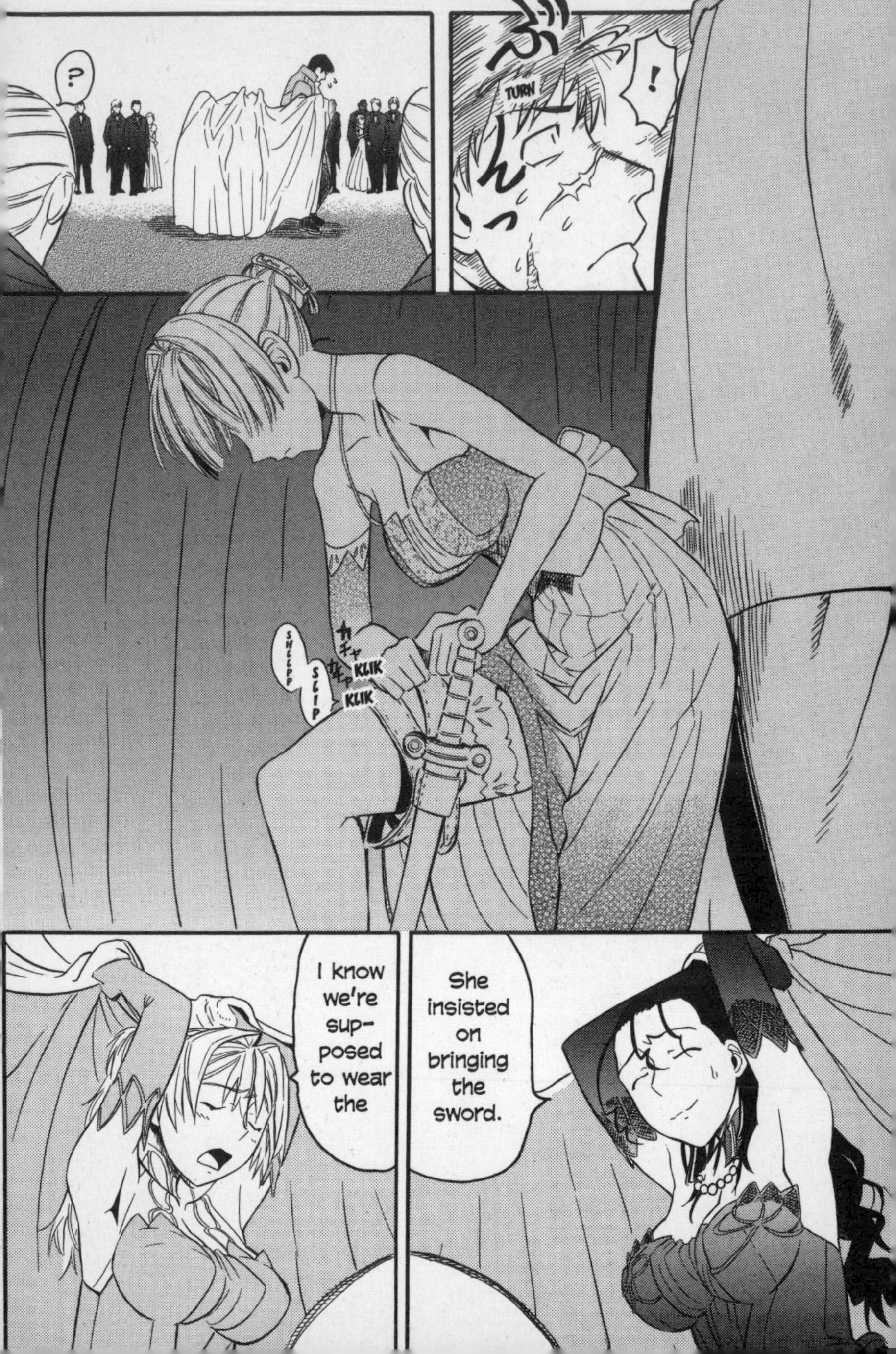
TURN
!
?
SHLLPP
SLIP
KLIK
KLIK
She insisted on bringing the sword.
I know we're sup-posed to wear the

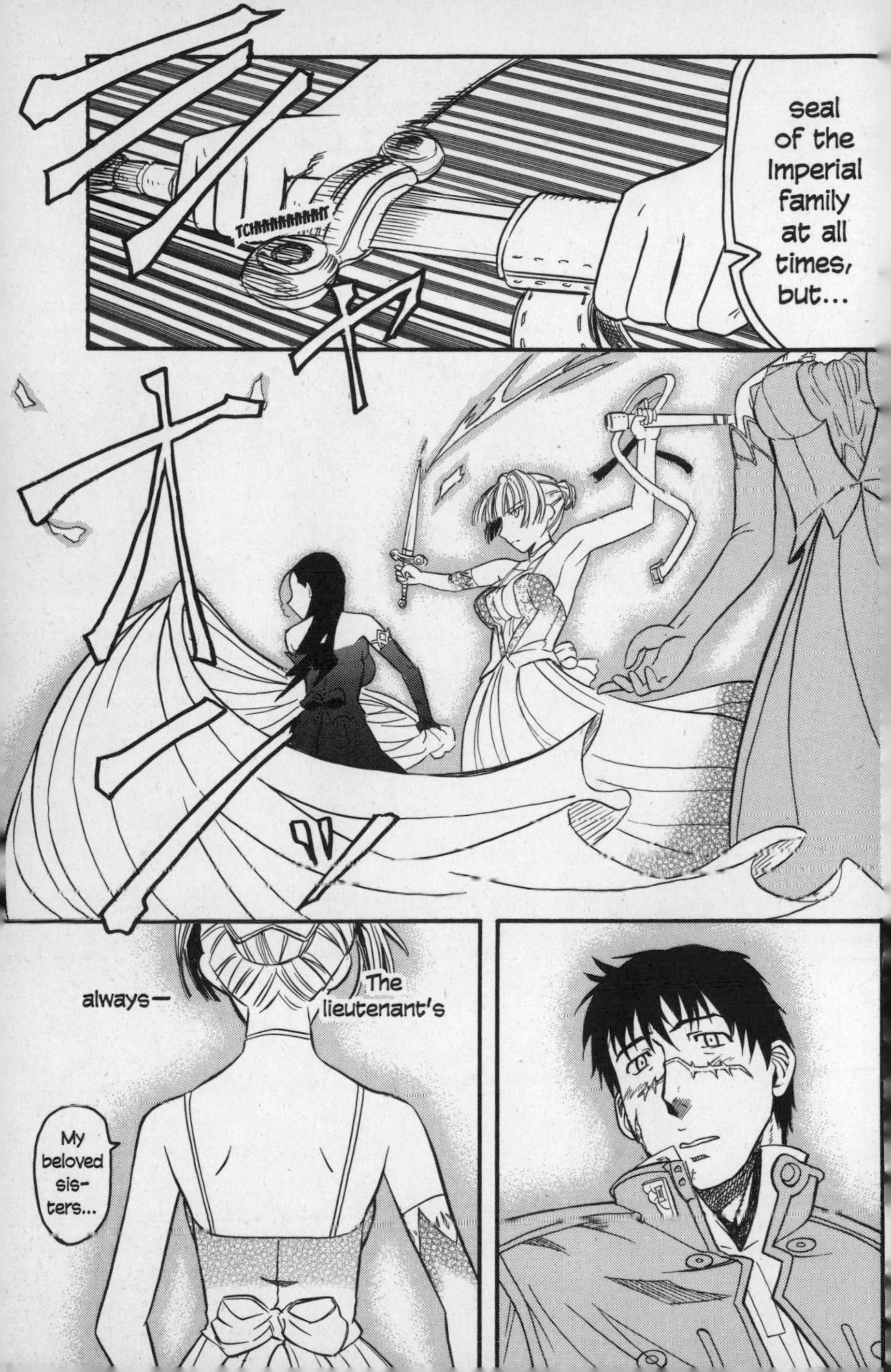
seal of the Imperial family at all times, but...
TCHHHHHHHHHT
The lieutenant's
always—
My beloved sis-ters...

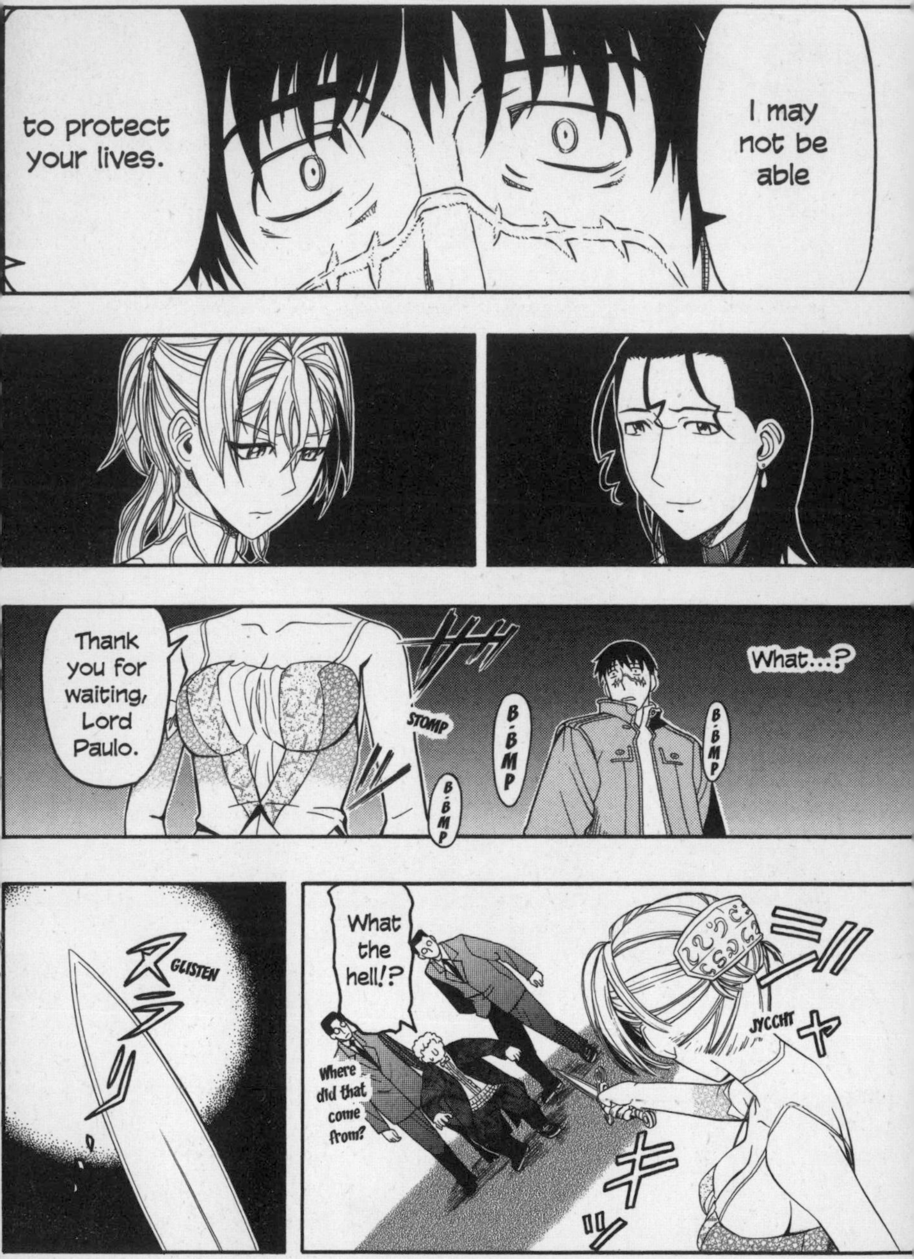

I may not be able
to protect your lives.
What...?
B-BMP
B-BMP
STOMP
B-BMP
Thank you for waiting, Lord Paulo.
JYCCHT
What the hell!?
Where did that come from?
GLISTEN

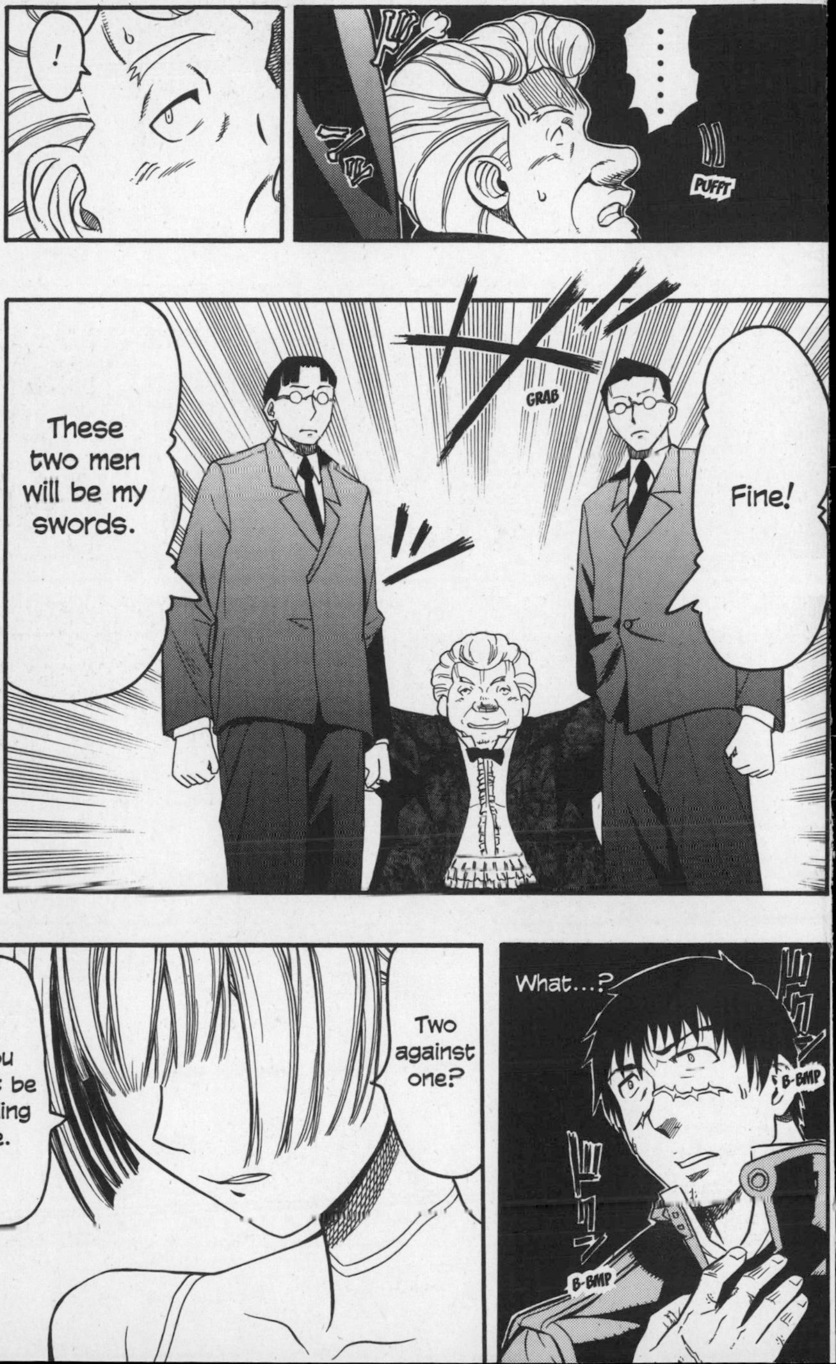

......
PUFFT
!
Fine!
GRAB
These two men will be my swords.
What...?
B-BMP
B-BMP
Two against one?
You must be kidding me.

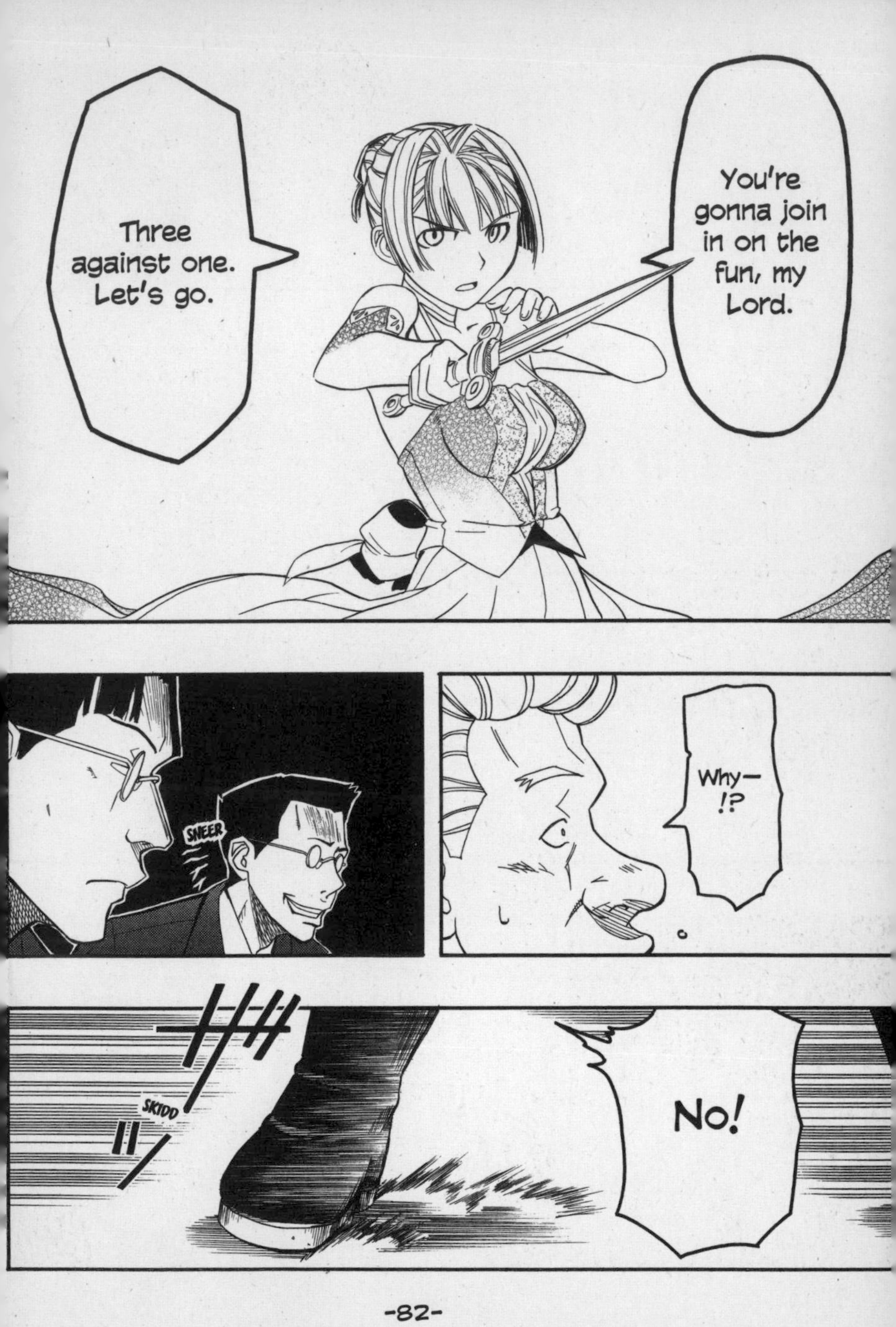
You're gonna join in on the fun, my Lord.
Three against one. Let's go.
Why— !?
SNEER
No!
SKIDD

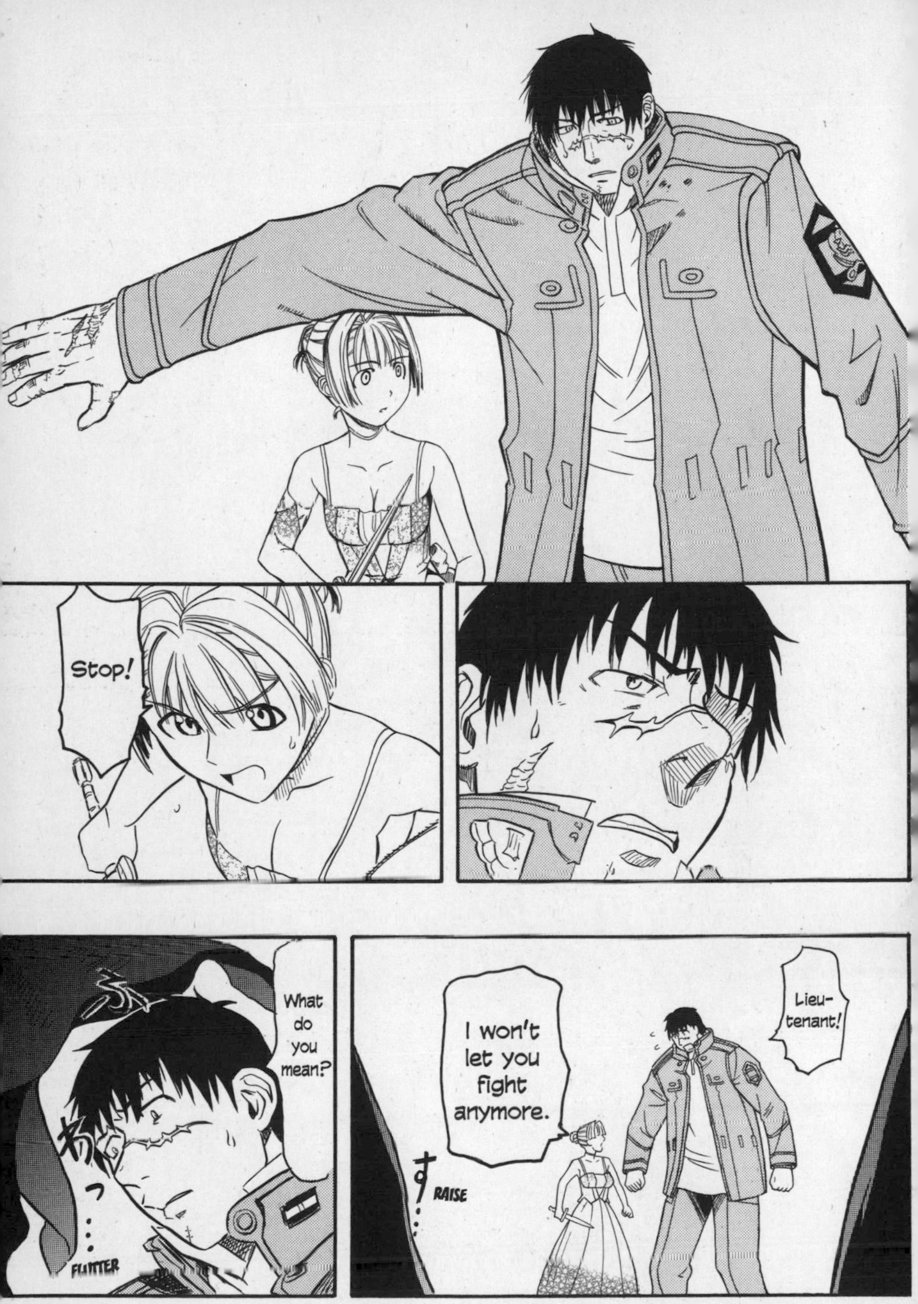
Stop!
Lieu-tenant!
I won't let you fight anymore.
RAISE
What do you mean?
FLUTTER

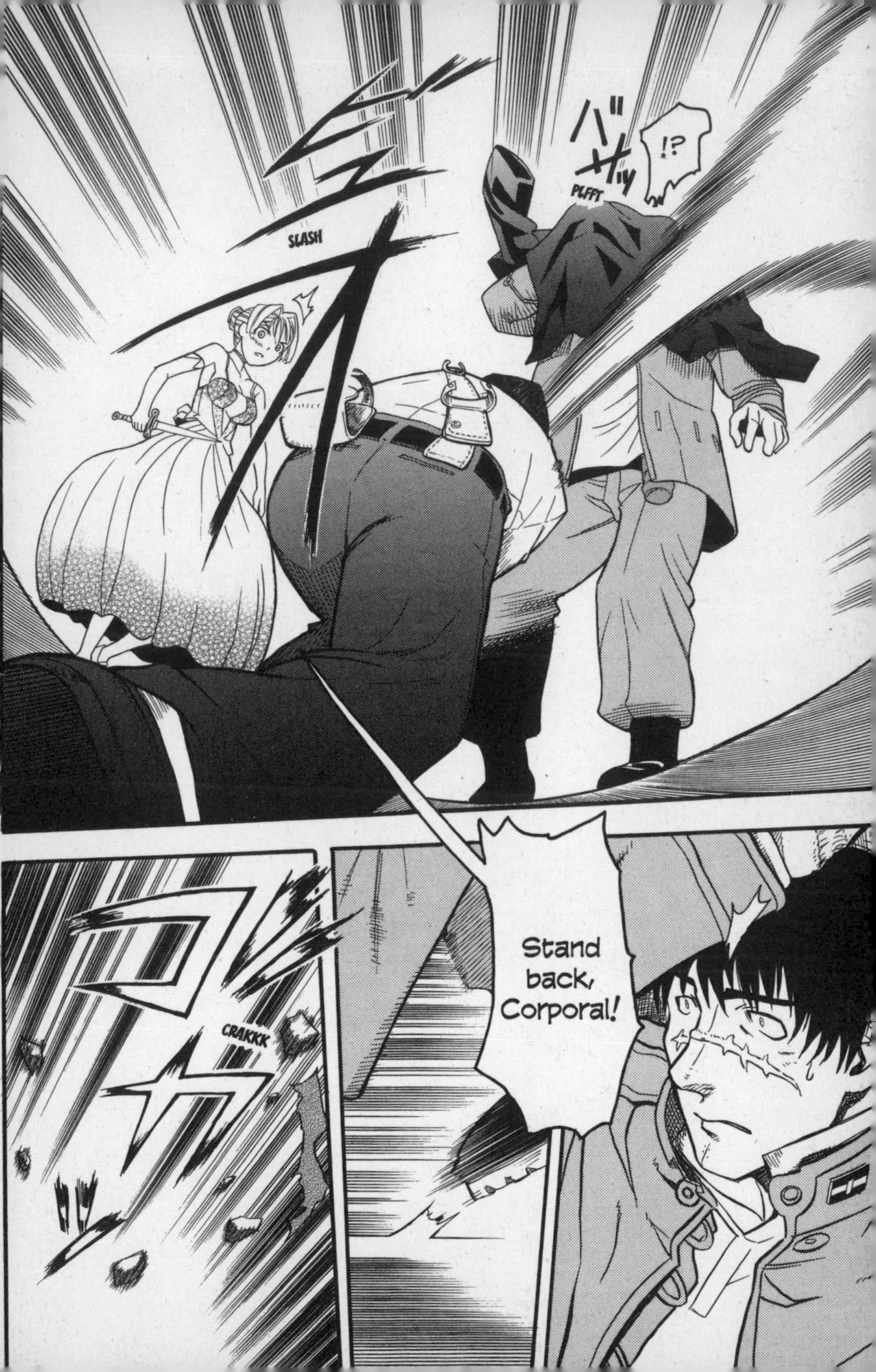
!?
PLFFT
SLASH
Stand back, Corporal!
CRAKKK

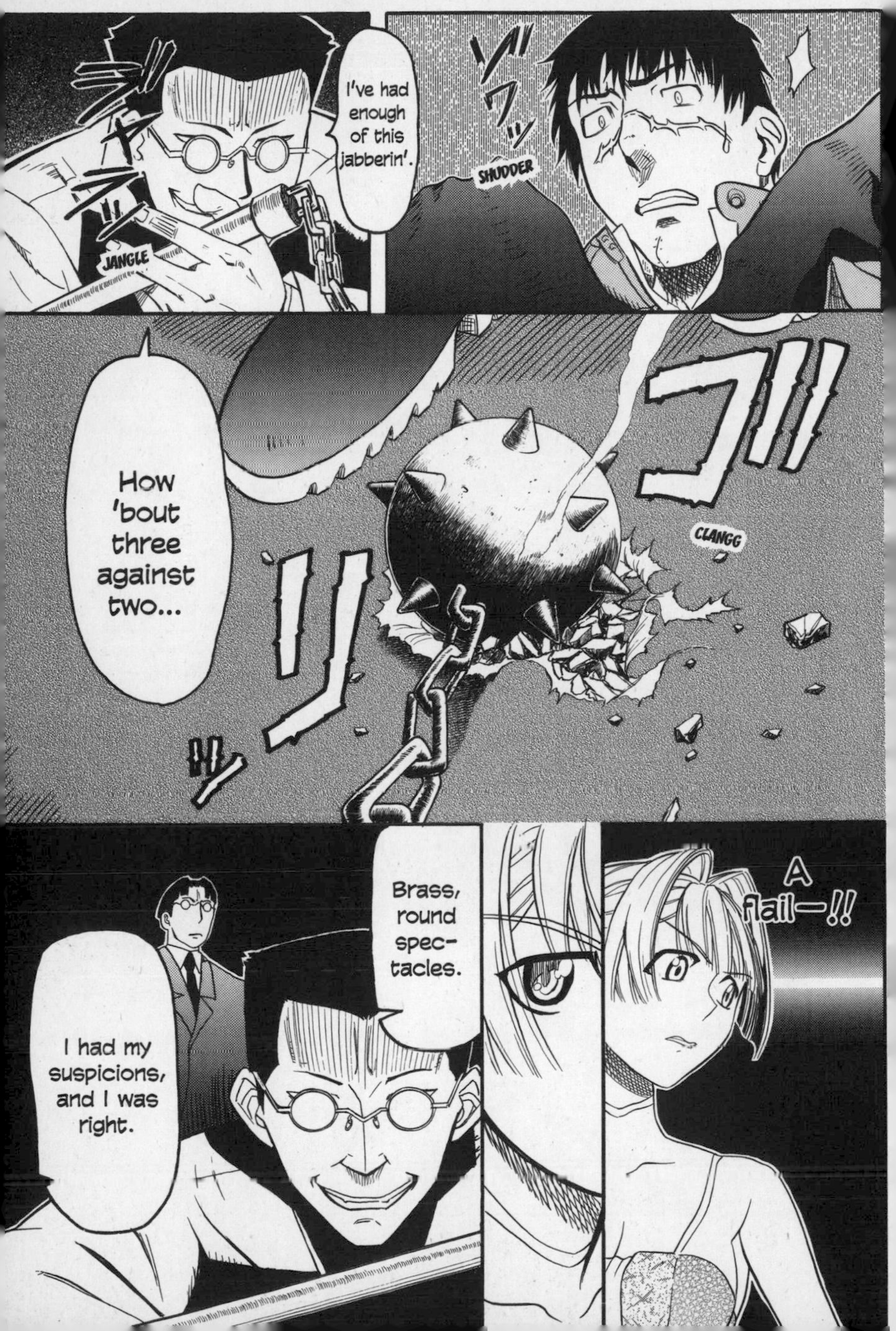
SHUDDER
I've had enough of this jabberin'.
JANGLE
How 'bout three against two...
CLANGG
A flail—!!
Brass, round spec-tacles.
I had my suspicions, and I was right.

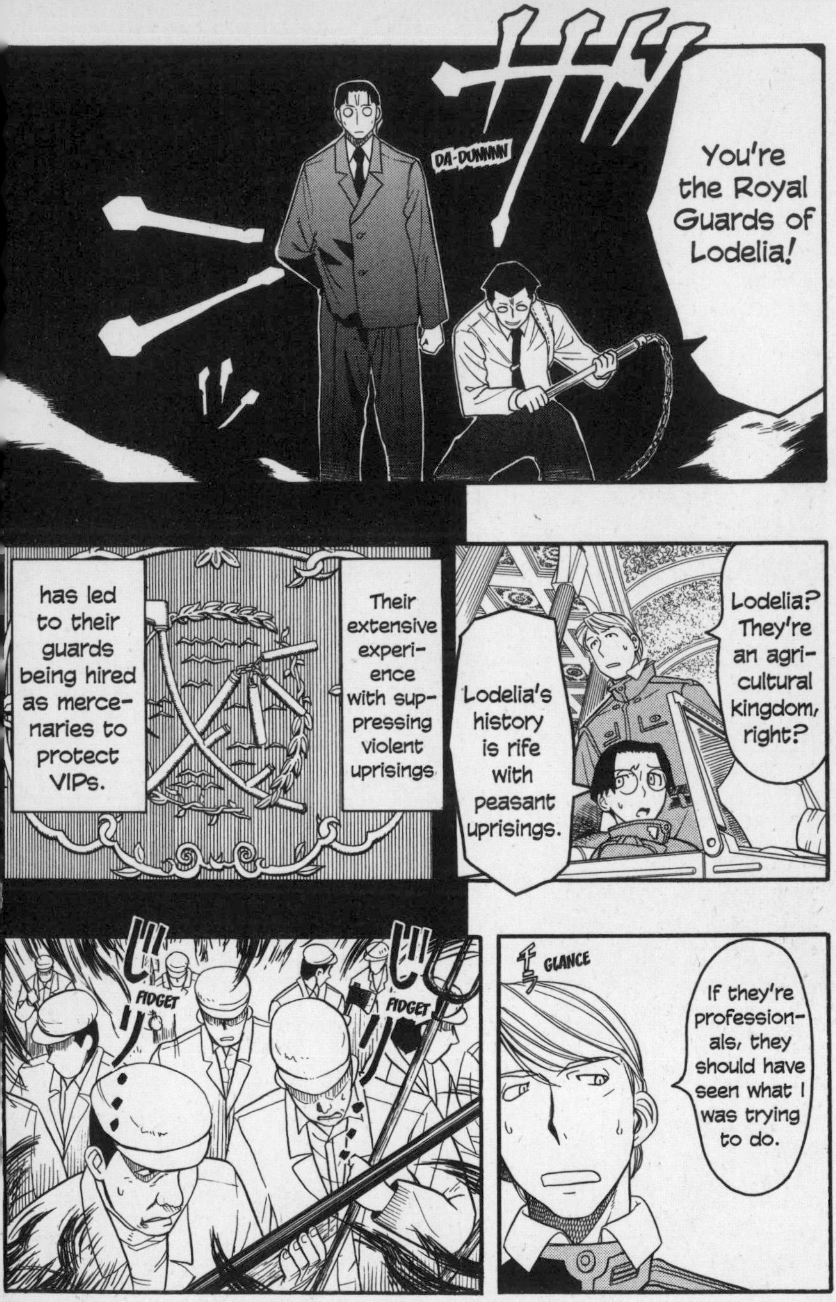

You're the Royal Guards of Lodelia!
DA-DUNNNN
Lodelia? They're an agricultural kingdom, right?
Lodelia's history is rife with peasant uprisings.
Their extensive experience with suppressing violent uprisings
has led to their guards being hired as mercenaries to protect VIPs.
GLANCE
If they're professionals, they should have seen what I was trying to do.
FIDGET
FIDGET

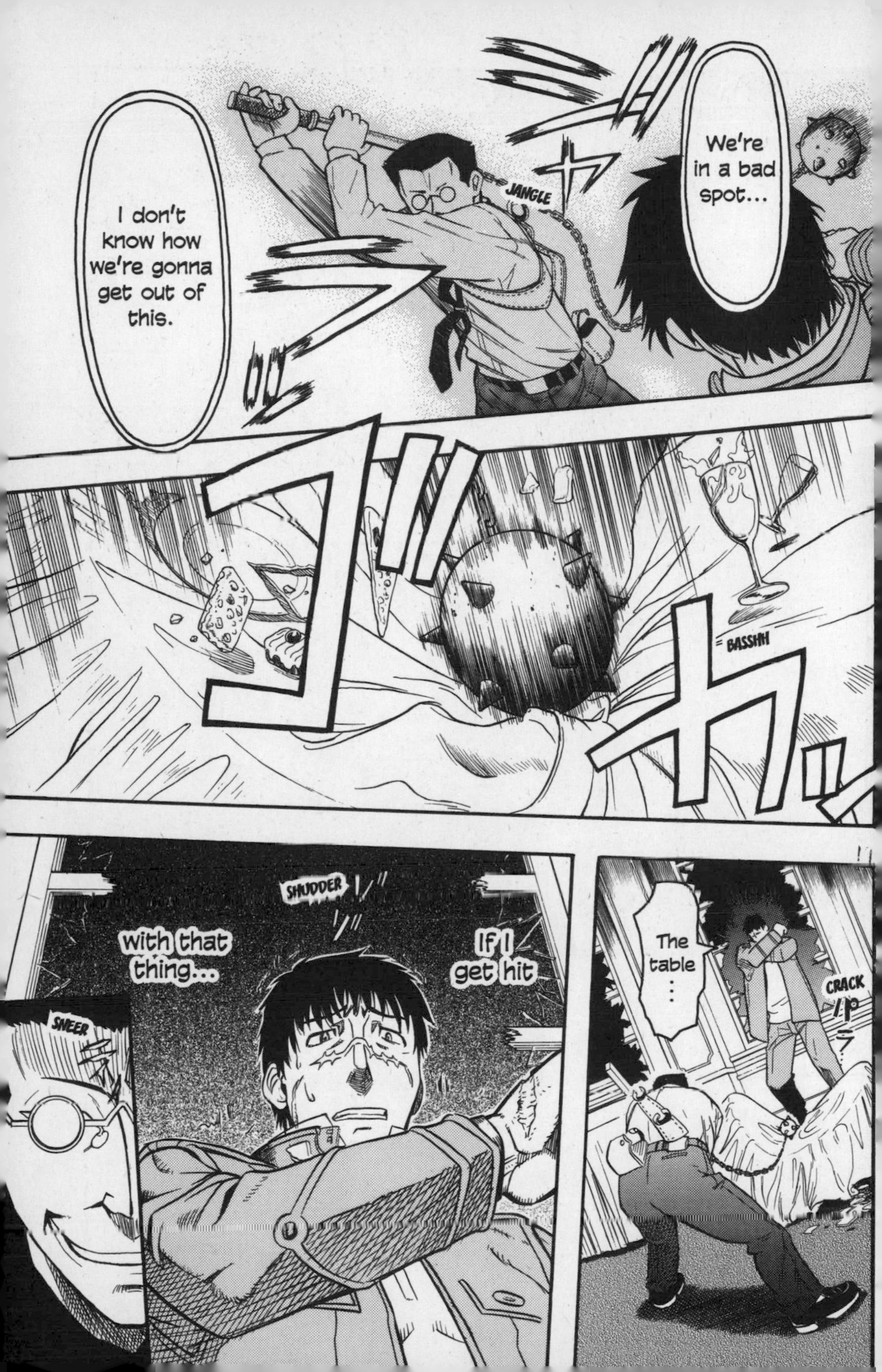
JANGLE
We're in a bad spot...
I don't know how we're gonna get out of this.
BASSHH
The table...
CRACK
SHUDDER
If I get hit
with that thing...
SNEER

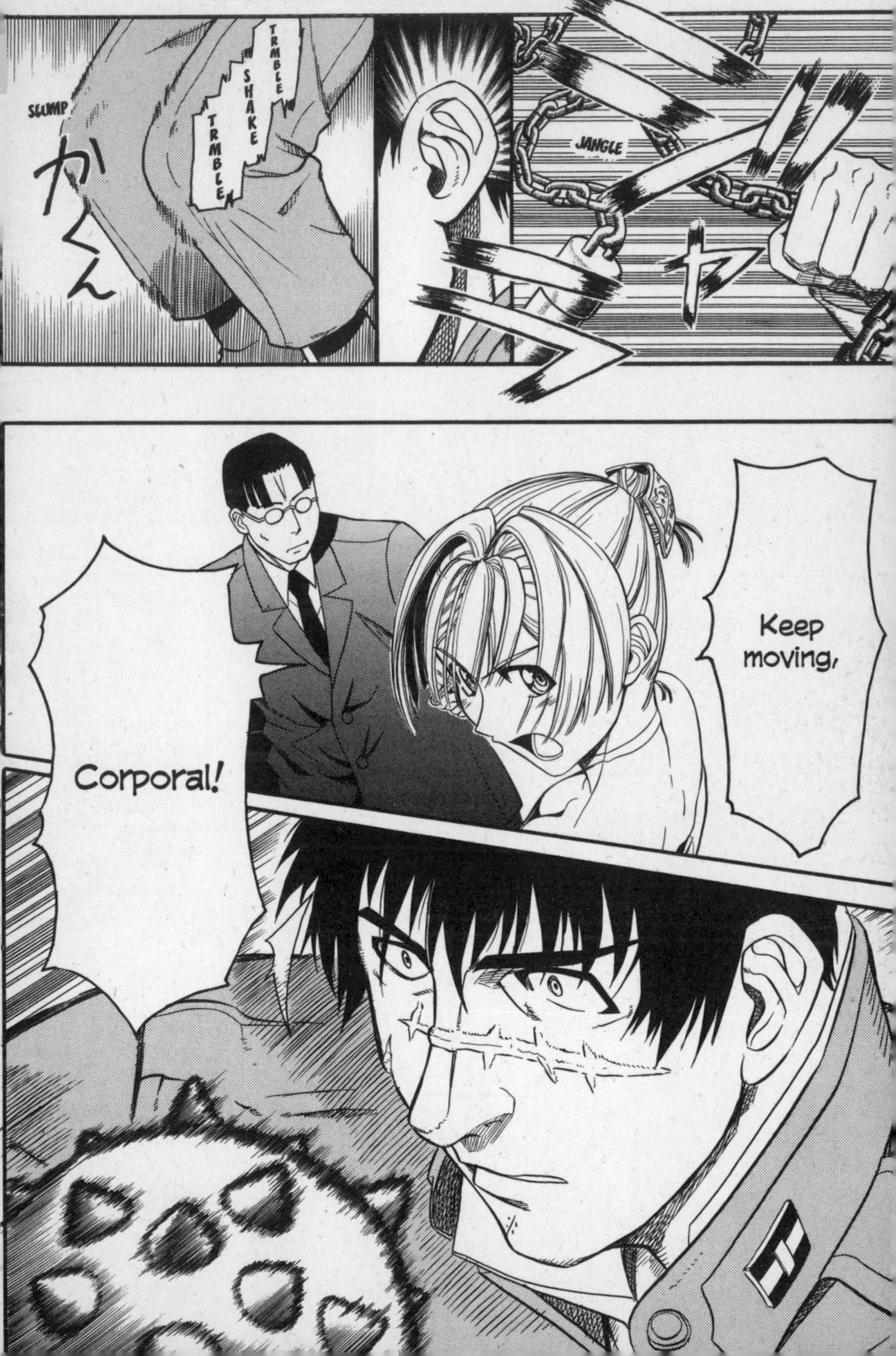
JANGLE
TRMBLE
SHAKE
TRMBLE
SLUMP
かくん
Keep moving,
Corporal!

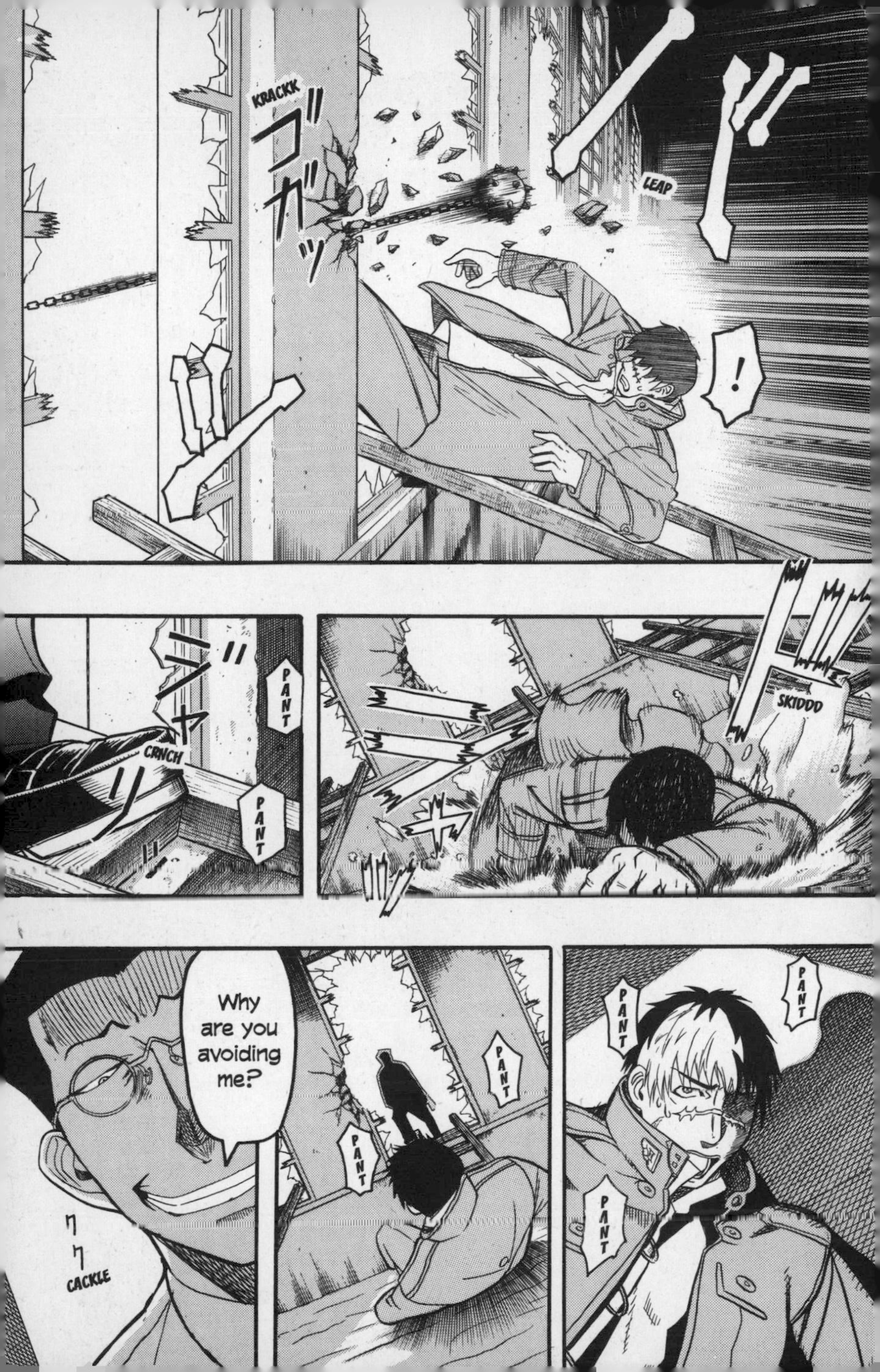
LEAP
!
KRACKK
SKIDDD
PANT PANT
CRNCH
PANT PANT
PANT
PANT
PANT
PANT
PANT
Why are you avoiding me?
CACKLE

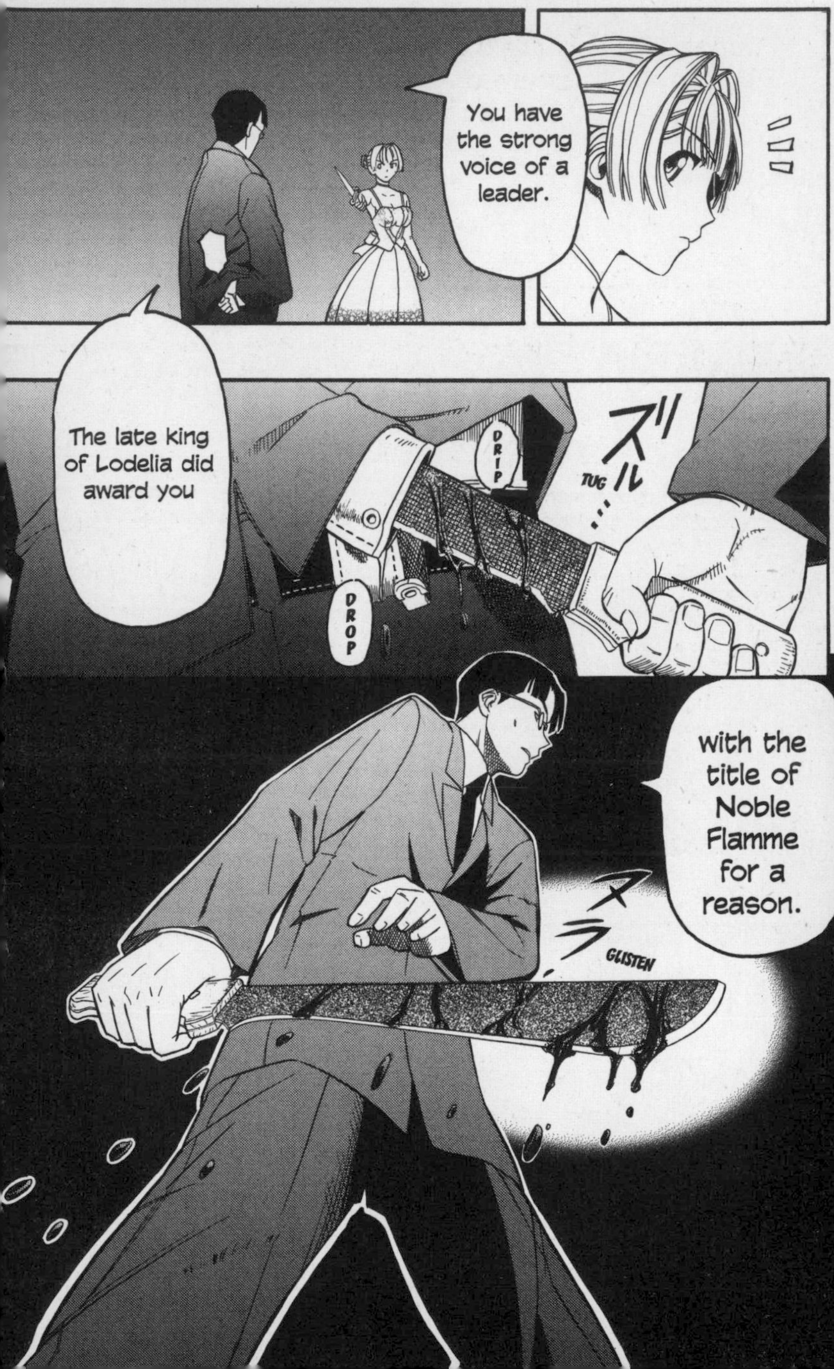
You have the strong voice of a leader.
The late king of Lodelia did award you
ズル
TUG
DRIP
DROP
with the title of Noble Flamme for a reason.
ヌラ
GLISTEN

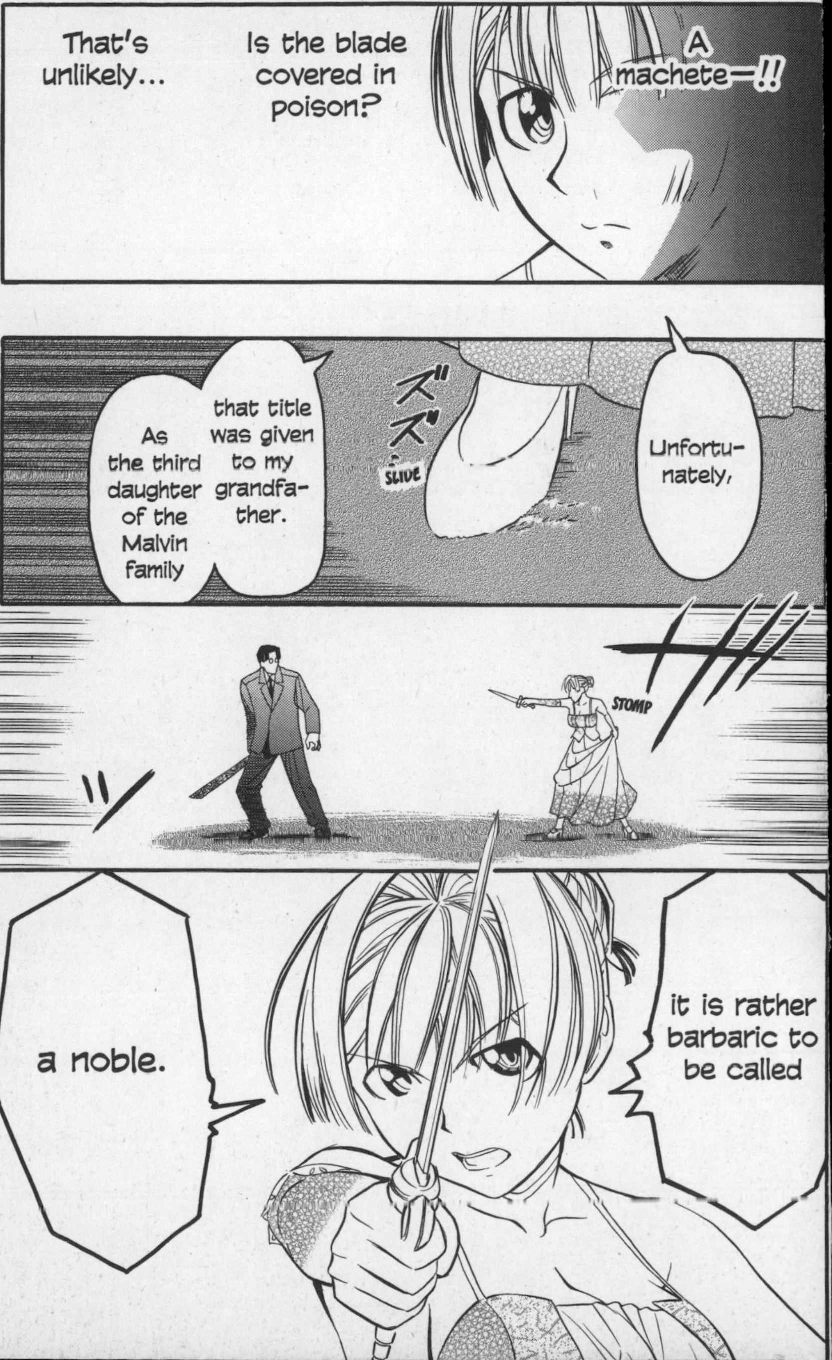
A machete—!!
Is the blade covered in poison?
That's unlikely...
Unfortunately,
ズズ
SLIDE
that title was given to my grandfather.
As the third daughter of the Malvin family
STOMP
it is rather barbaric to be called
a noble.

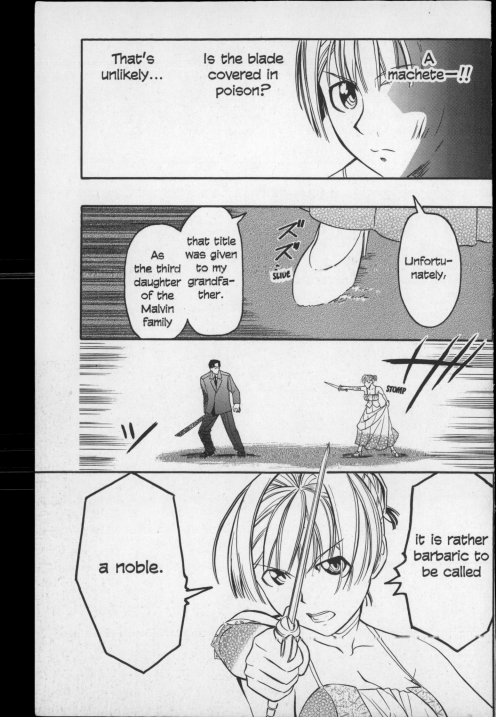

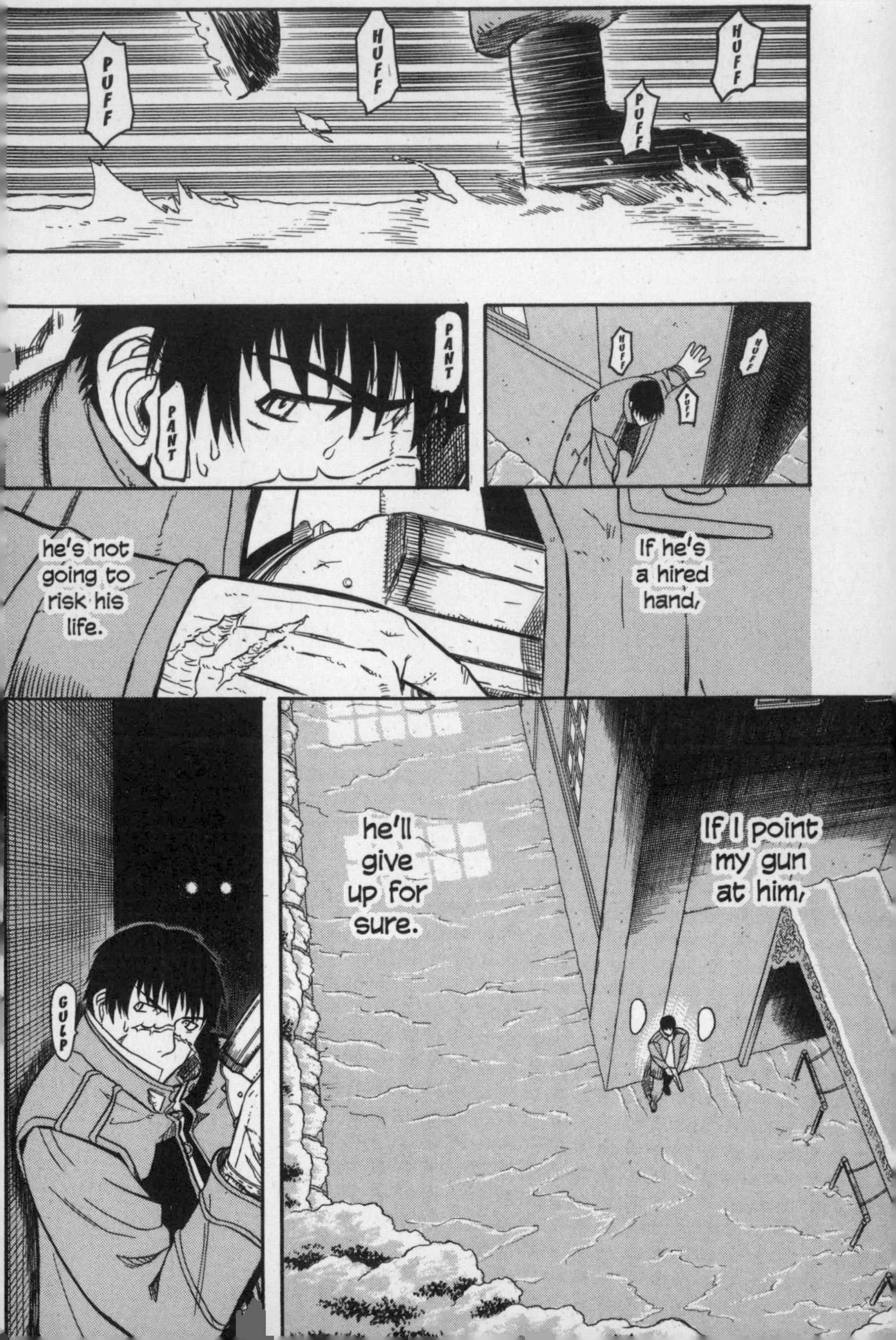
HUFF
PUFF
HUFF
PUFF
HUFF
PUFF
HUFF
PANT
PANT
If he's a hired hand,
he's not going to risk his life.
If I point my gun at him,
he'll give up for sure.
GULP

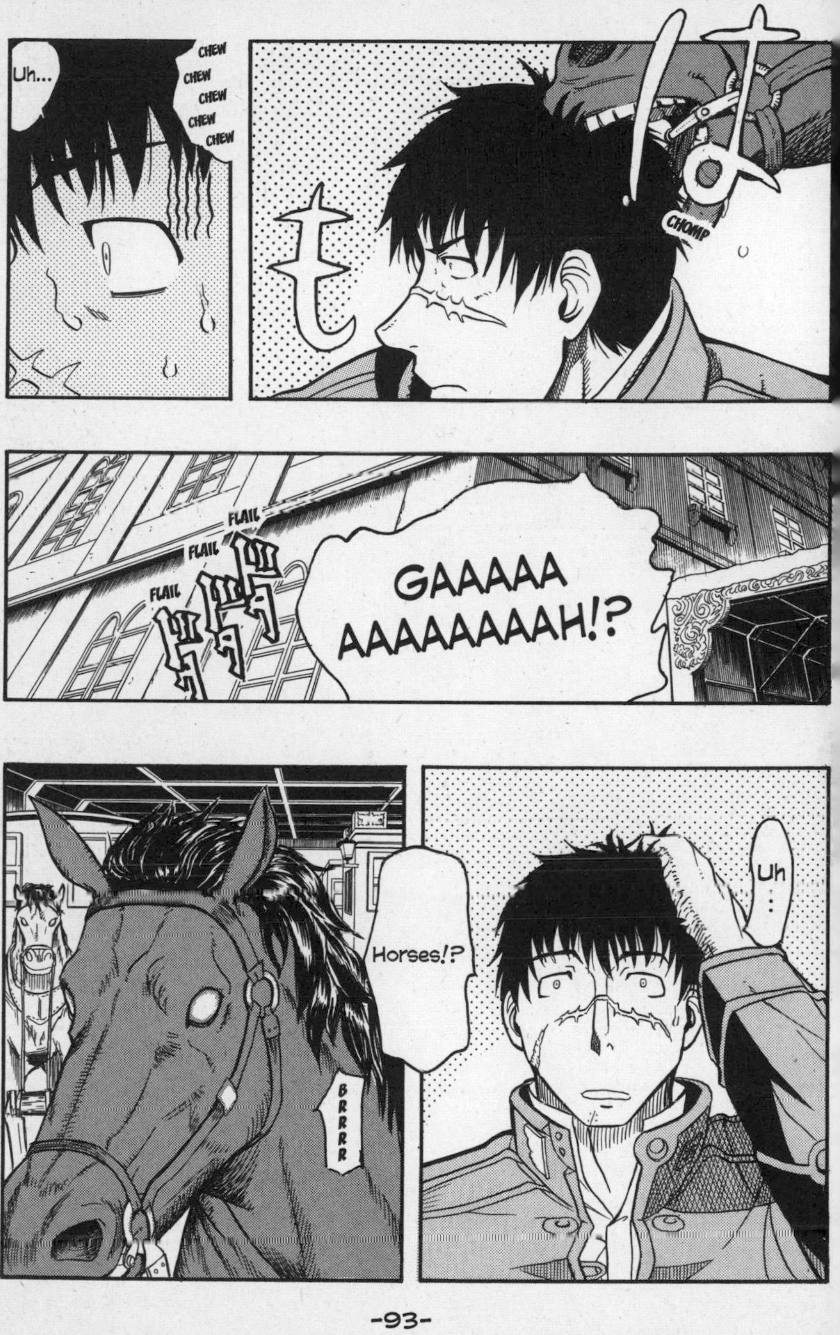
CHOMP
Uh...
CHEW
CHEW
CHEW
CHEW
CHEW
GAAAAA AAAAAAAAH!?
FLAIL
FLAIL
FLAIL
Uh ...
Horses!?
BRRRR

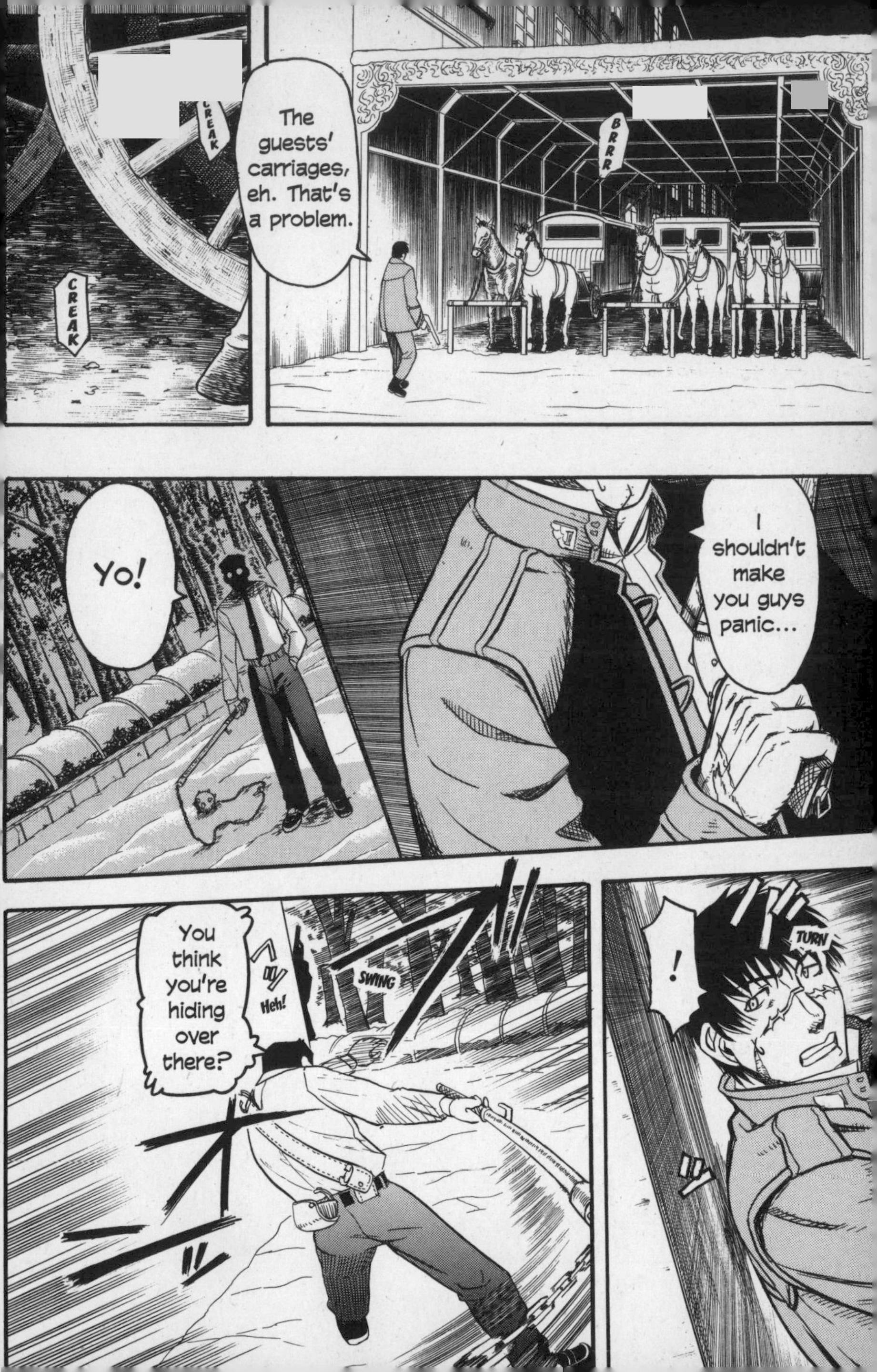
BRRR
The guests' carriages, eh. That's a problem.
CREAK
CREAK
I shouldn't make you guys panic...
Yo!
TURN
!
You think you're hiding over there?
Heh!
SWING

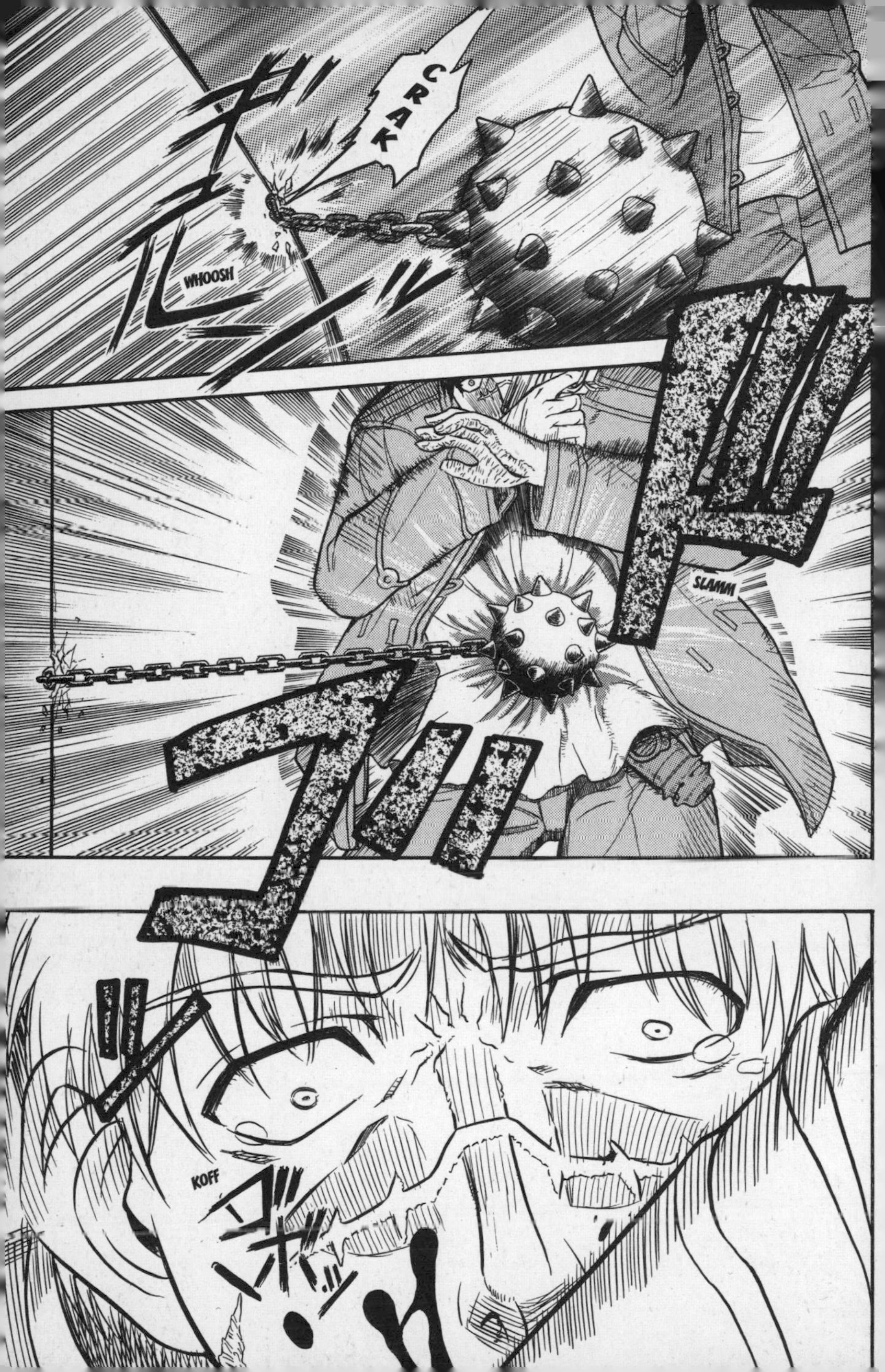
CRAK
WHOOSH
SLAMM
KOFF

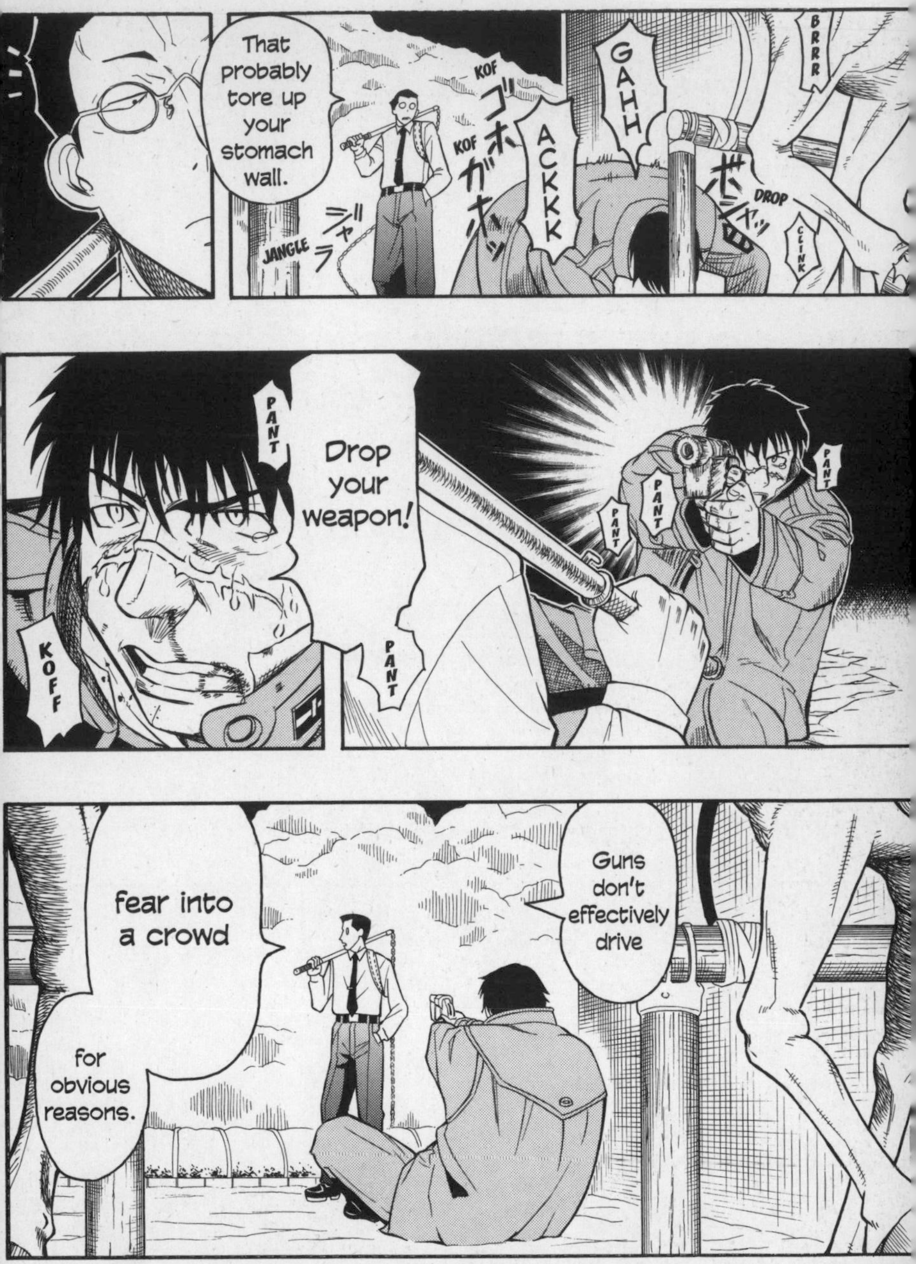
BRRR
GAHH
ACKKK
DROP
ボシャッ
CLINK
KOF
ゴホ
KOF
ガホッ
That probably tore up your stomach wall.
JANGLE
ジャラ
!!!
PANT
PANT
PANT
Drop your weapon!
PANT
PANT
KOFF
Guns don't effectively drive
fear into a crowd
for obvious reasons.

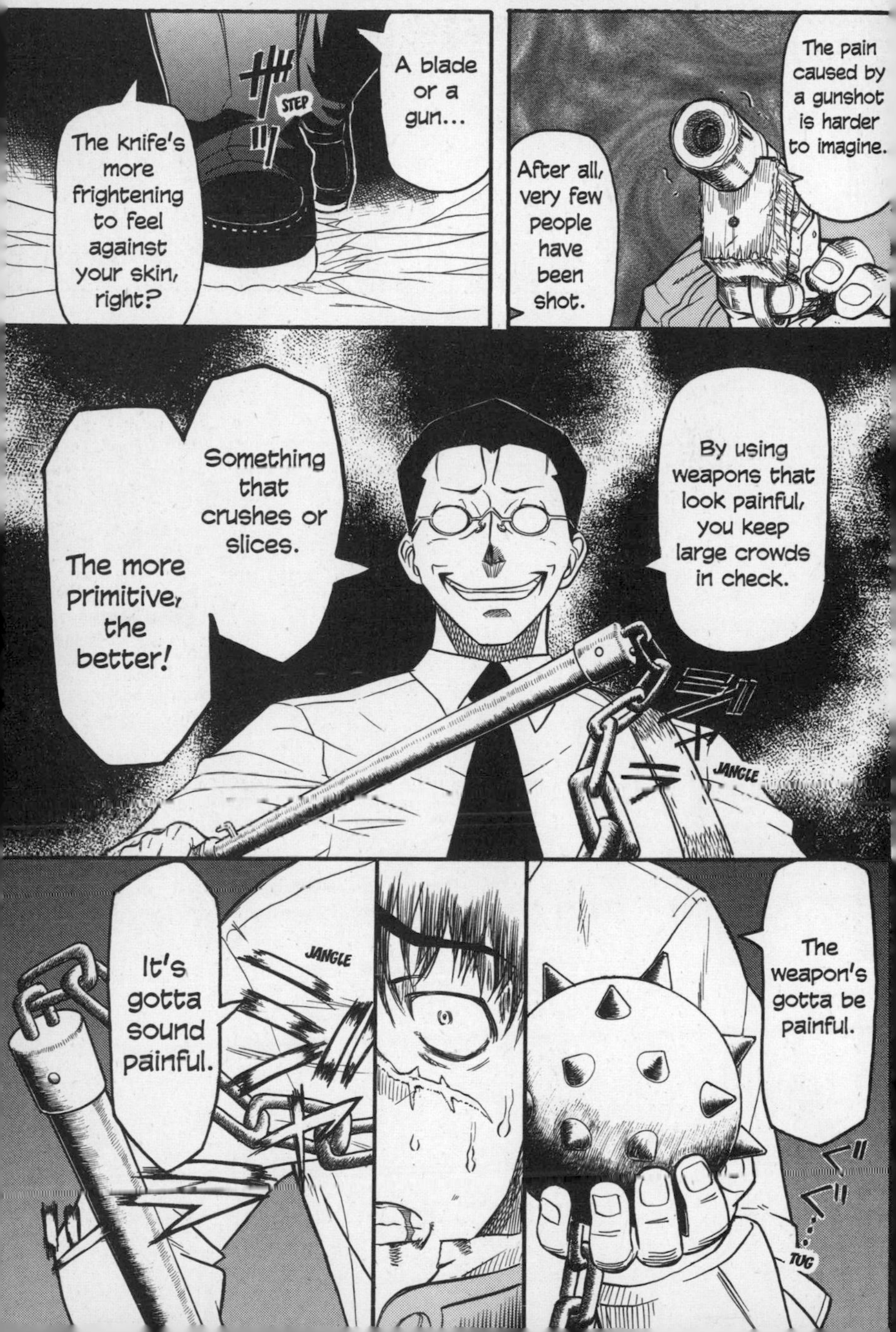
The pain caused by a gunshot is harder to imagine.
After all, very few people have been shot.
A blade or a gun...
STEP
The knife's more frightening to feel against your skin, right?
By using weapons that look painful, you keep large crowds in check.
JANGLE
Something that crushes or slices.
The more primitive, the better!
The weapon's gotta be painful.
TUG
JANGLE
It's gotta sound painful.

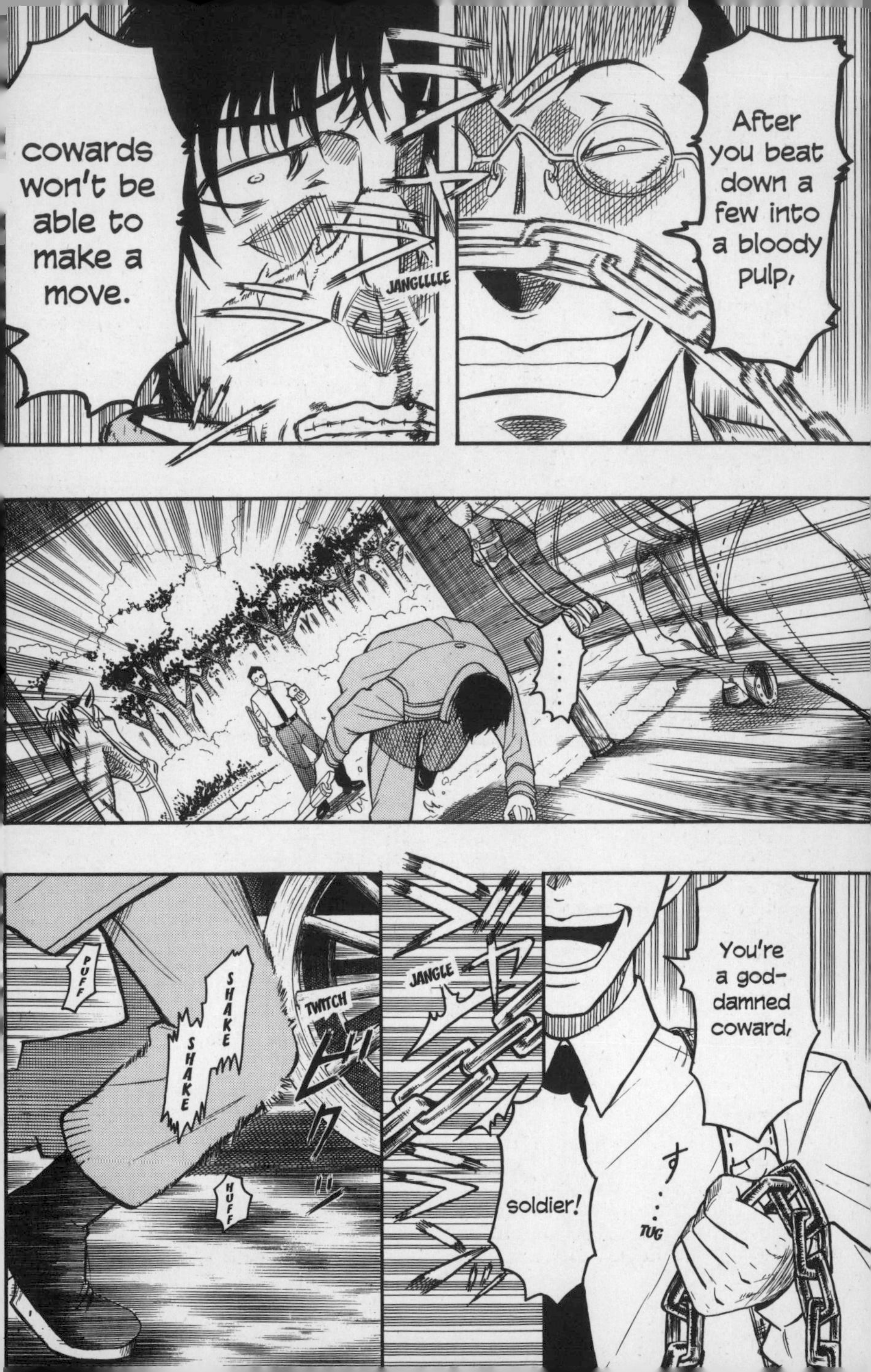
After you beat down a few into a bloody pulp,
JANGLLLLE
cowards won't be able to make a move.
......
You're a god-damned coward,
soldier!
TUG
JANGLE
TWITCH
PUFF
SHAKE
SHAKE
HUFF

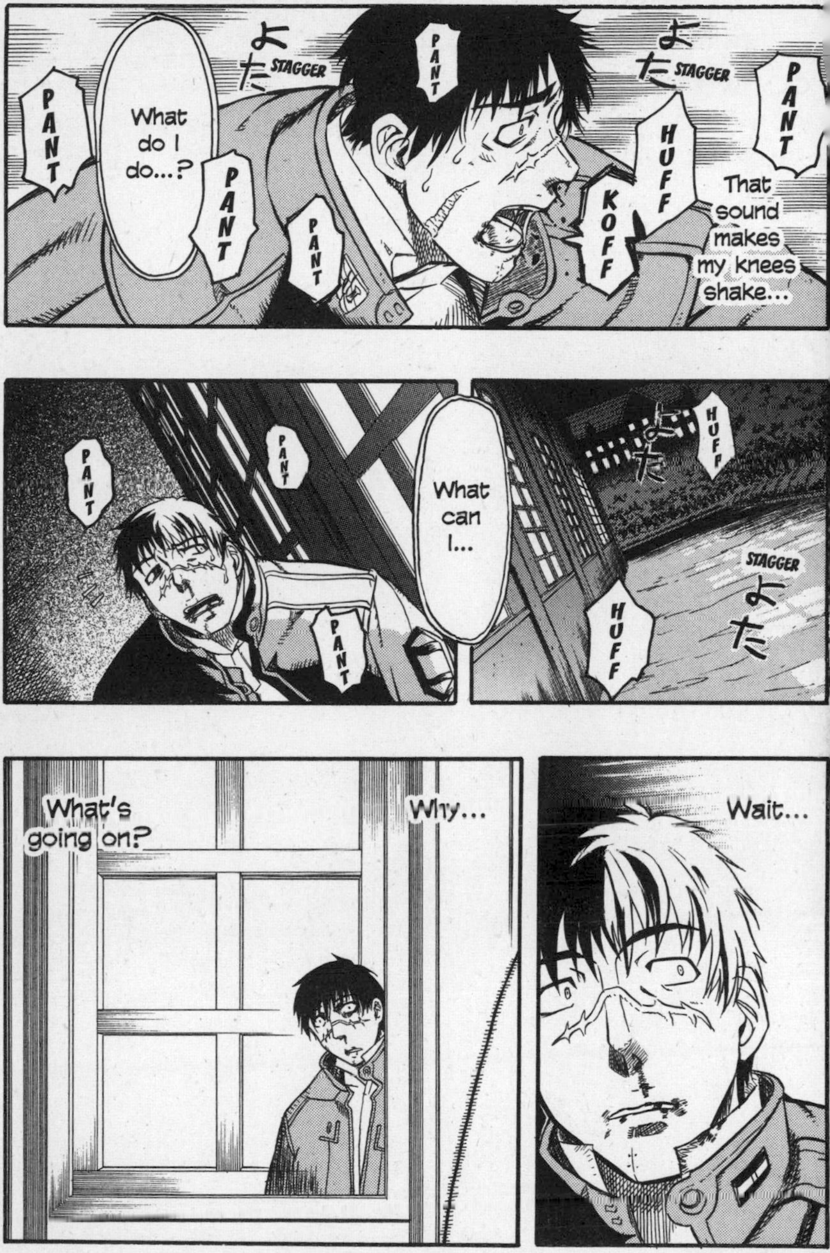
PANT
That sound makes my knees shake...
よた STAGGER
HUFF
KOFF
PANT
PANT
PANT
What do I do...?
よた STAGGER
PANT
HUFF
よた
STAGGER よた
HUFF
What can I...
PANT
PANT
PANT
Wait...
Why...
What's going on?

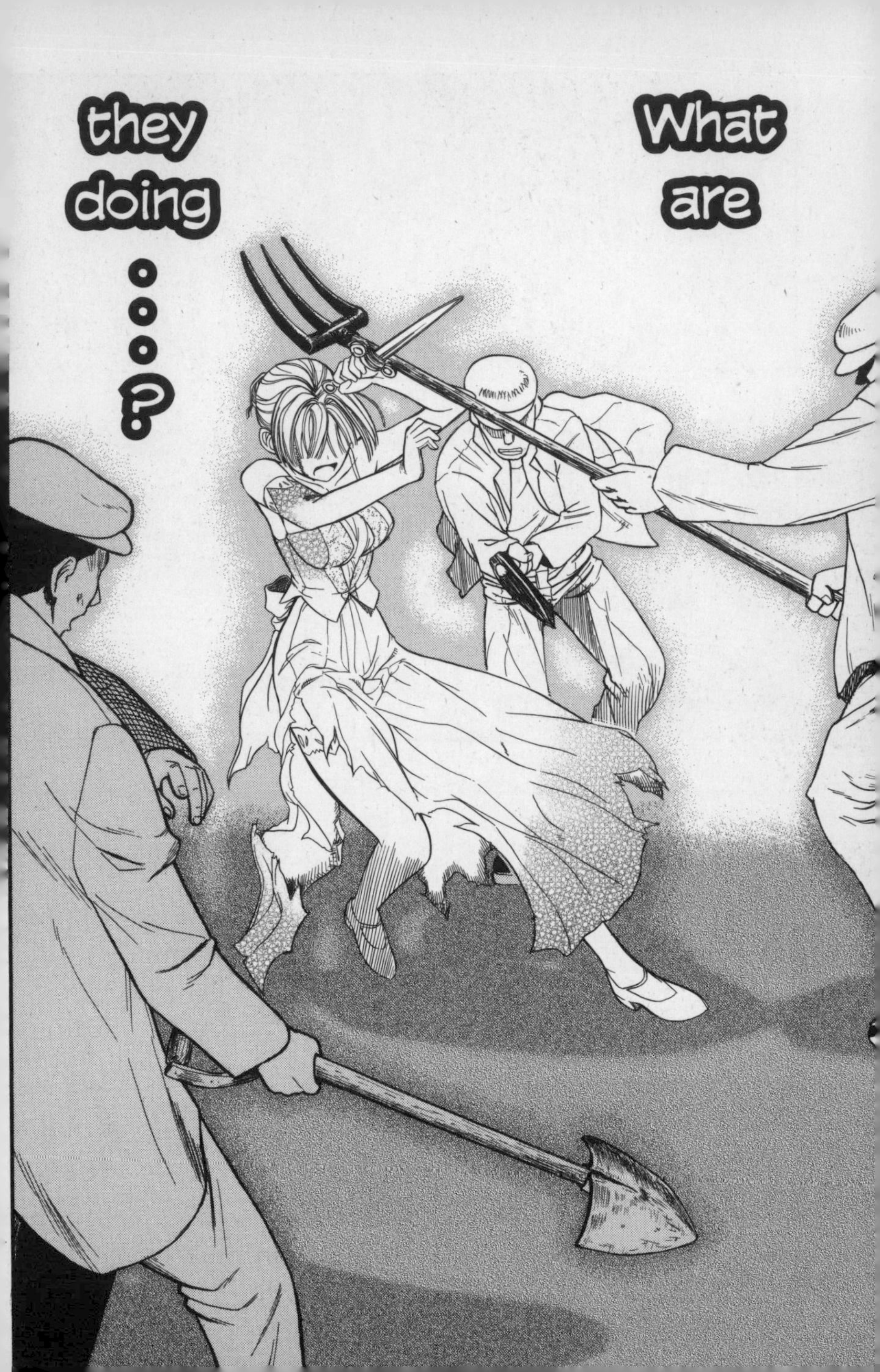
What are
they doing ....?

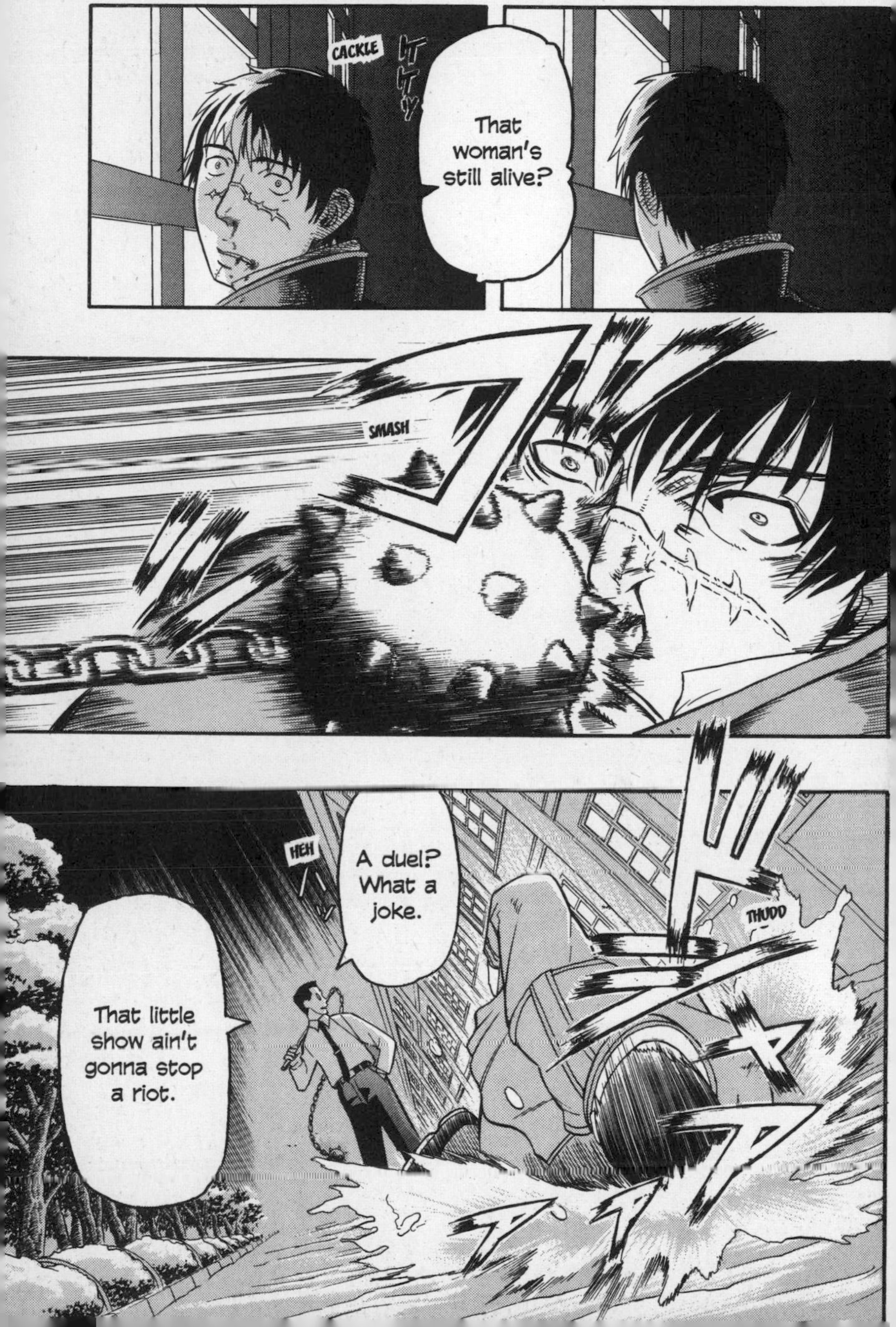
That woman's still alive?
CACKLE
SMASH
THUDD
A duel? What a joke.
HEH
That little show ain't gonna stop a riot.

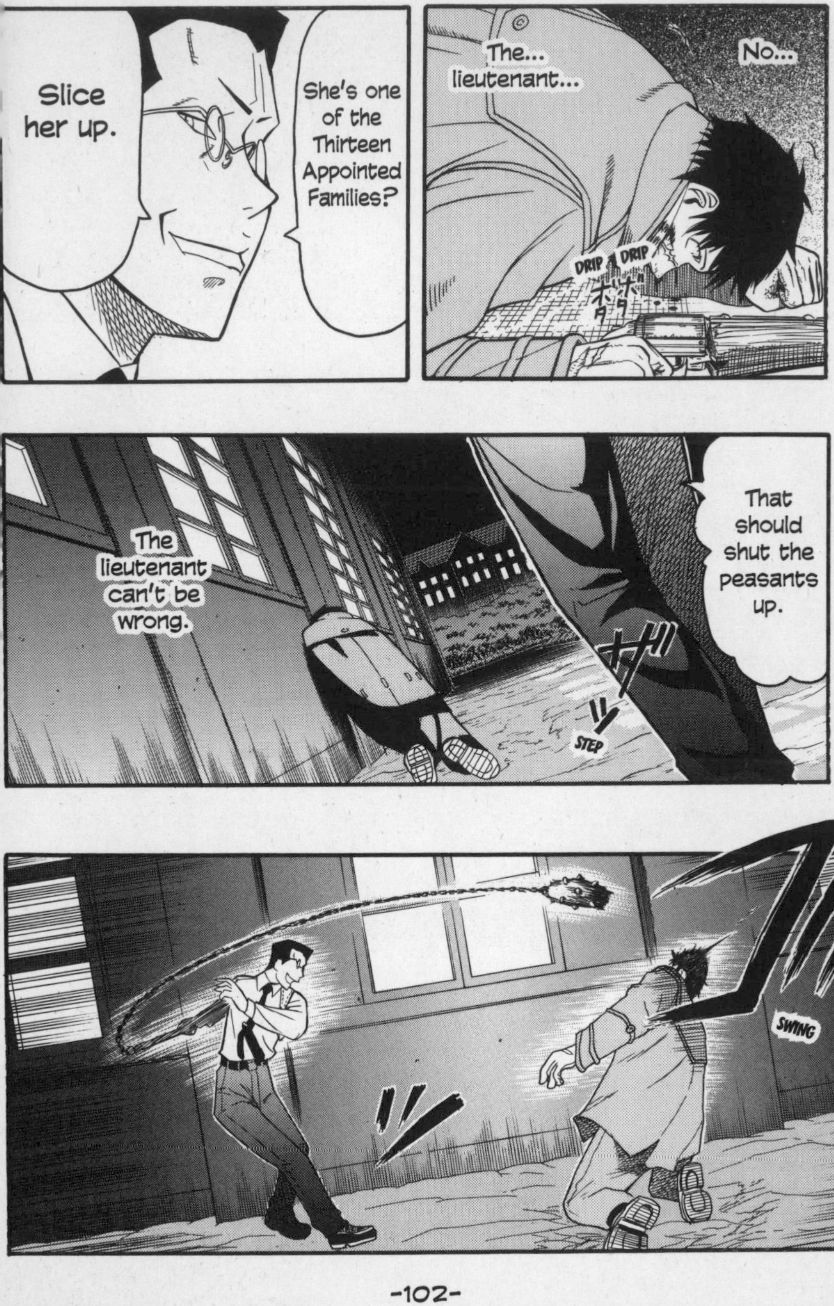
No...
The... lieutenant...
DRIP DRIP
She's one of the Thirteen Appointed Families?
Slice her up.
That should shut the peasants up.
STEP
The lieutenant can't be wrong.
SWING

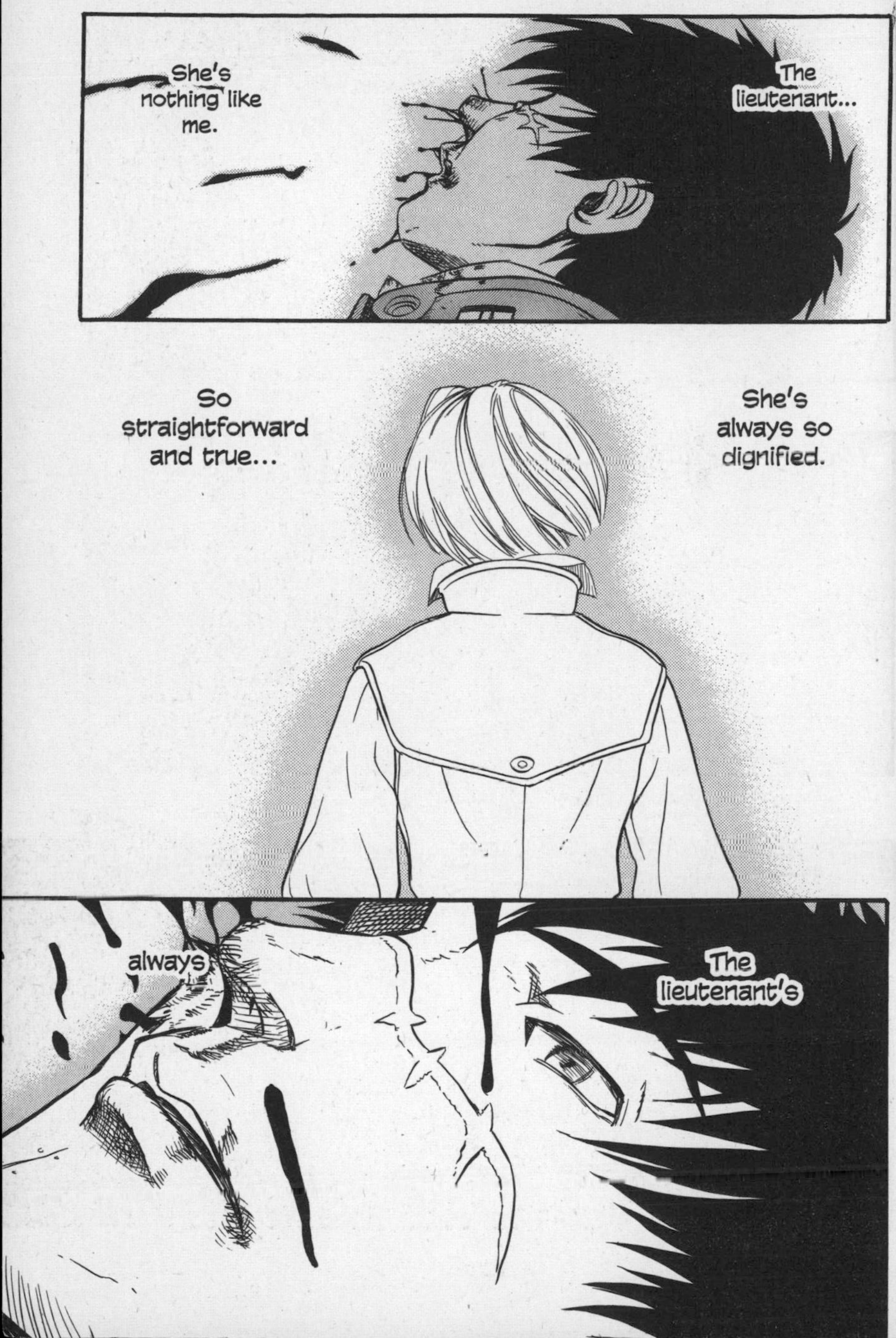
The lieutenant...
She's nothing like me.
She's always so dignified.
So straightforward and true...
The lieutenant's
always

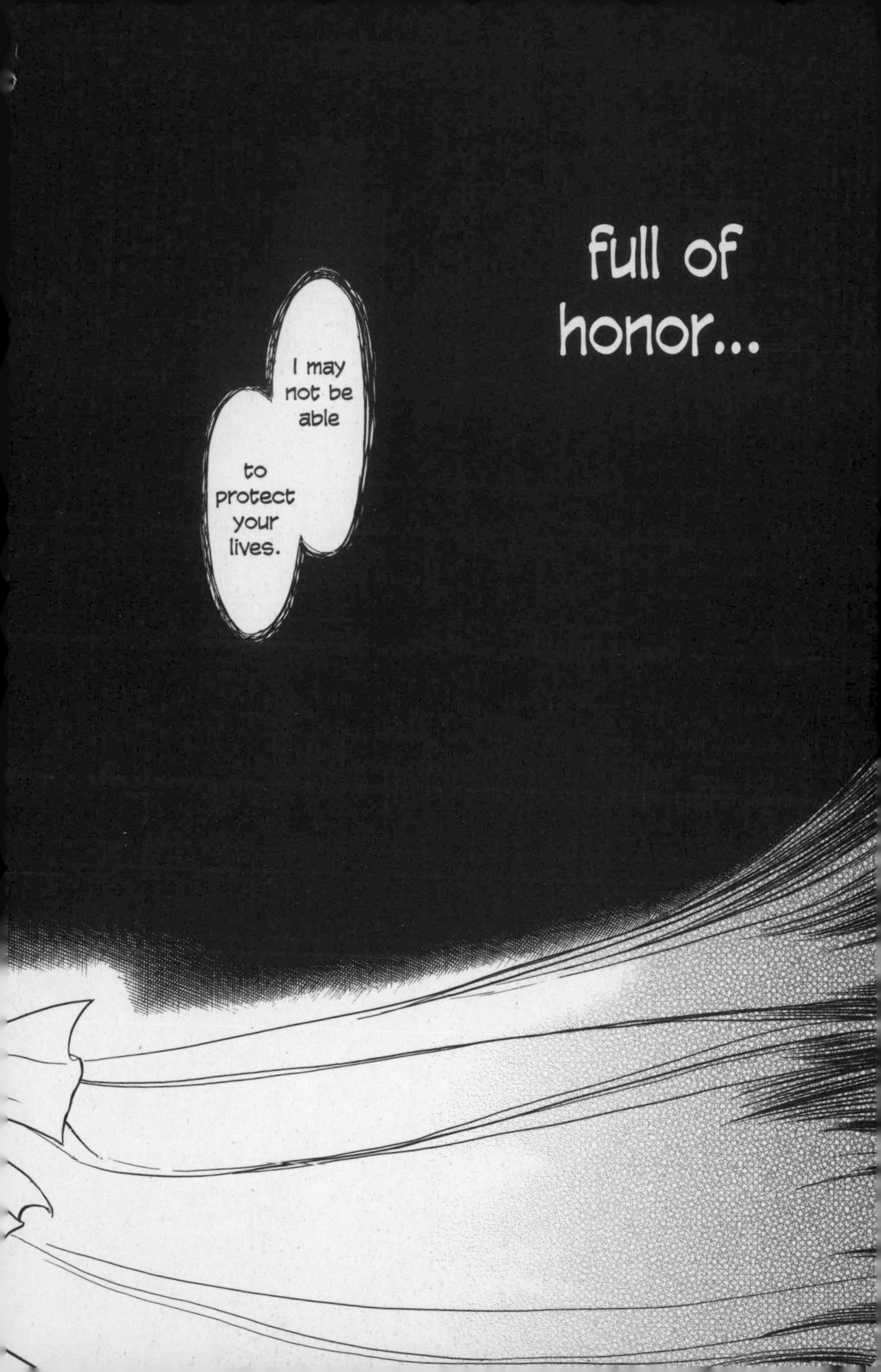
full of honor...
I may not be able to protect your lives.

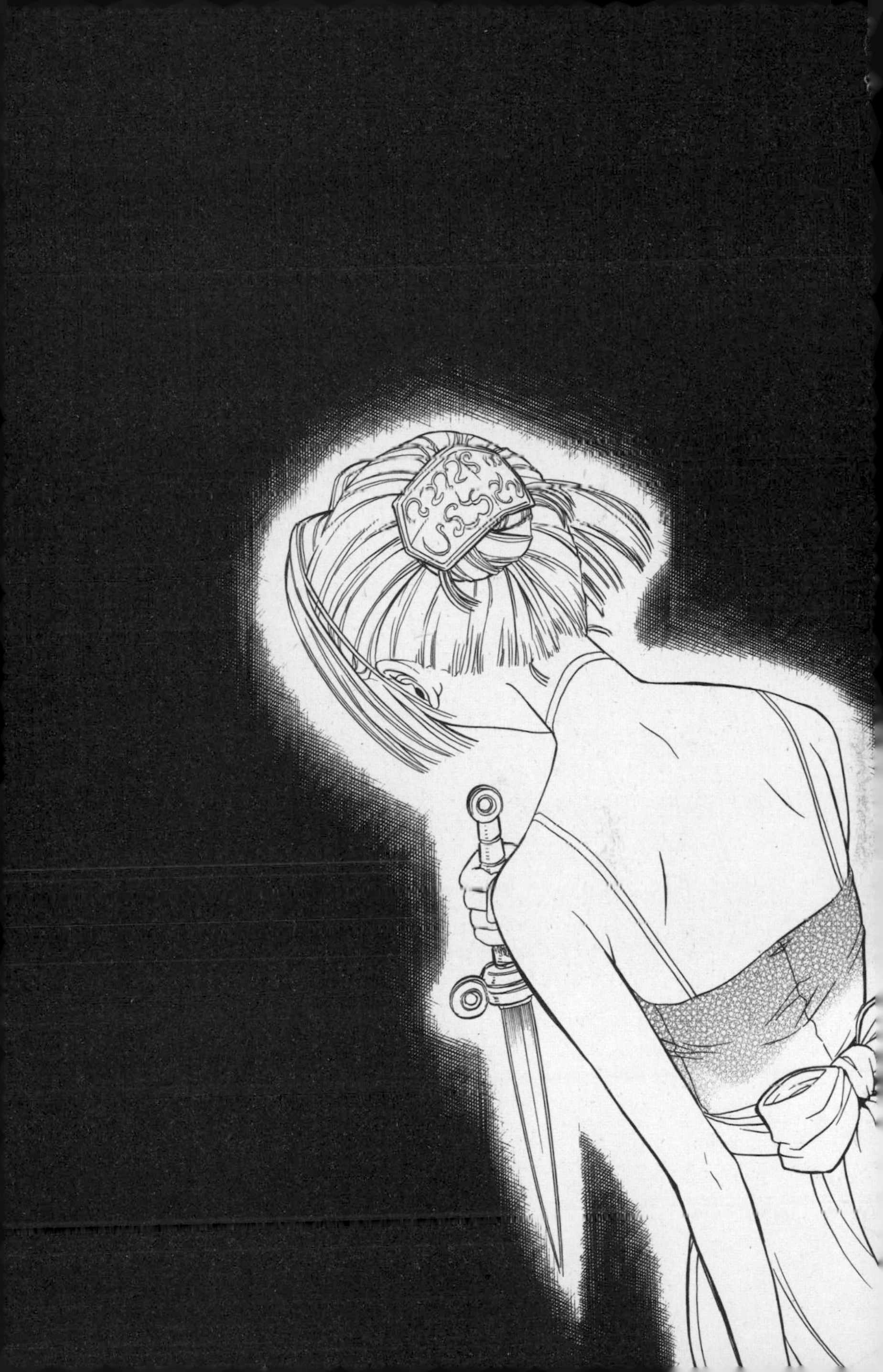

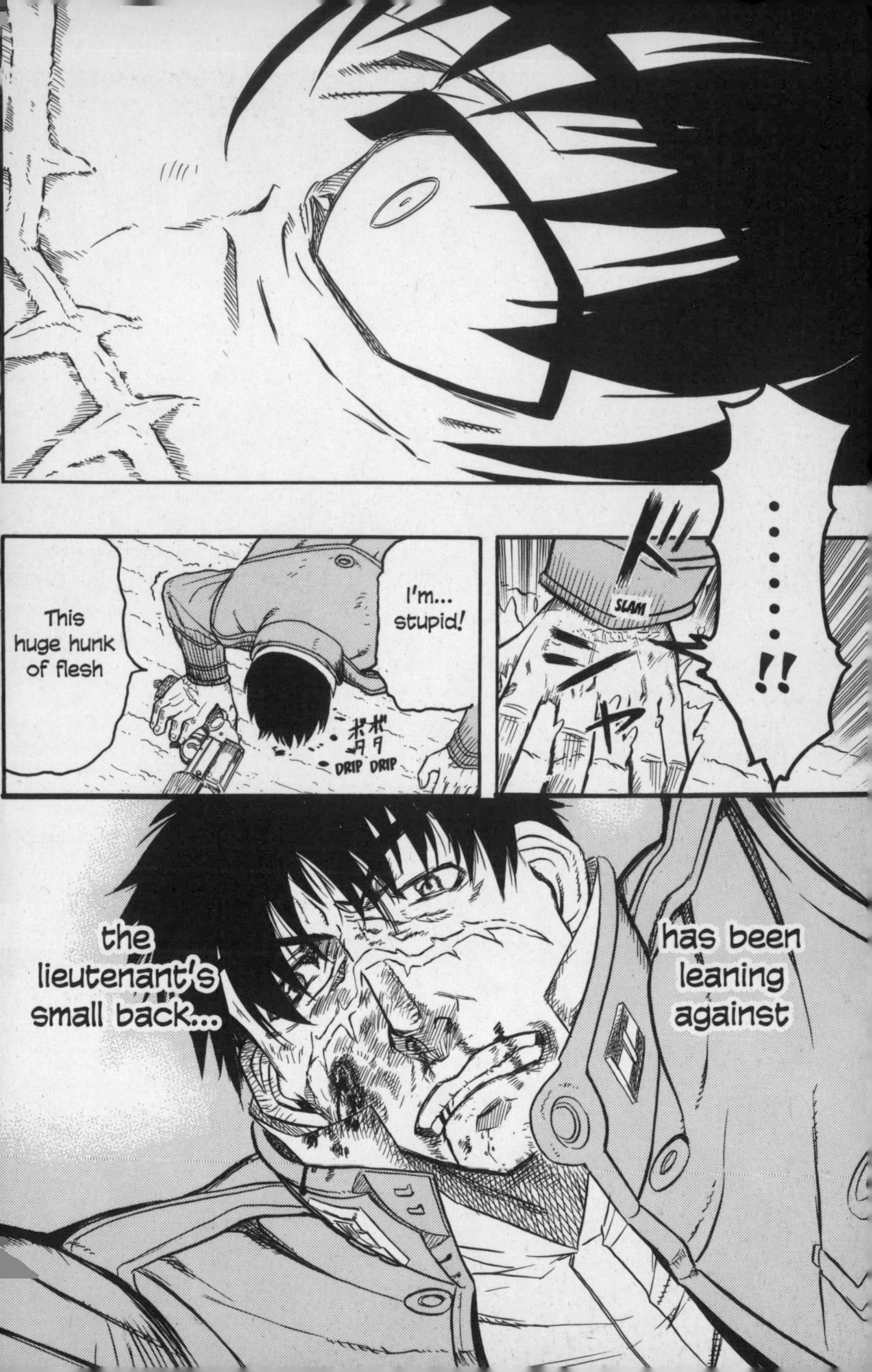

......!!
SLAM
I'm... stupid!
This huge hunk of flesh
DRIP DRIP
has been leaning against
the lieutenant's small back...

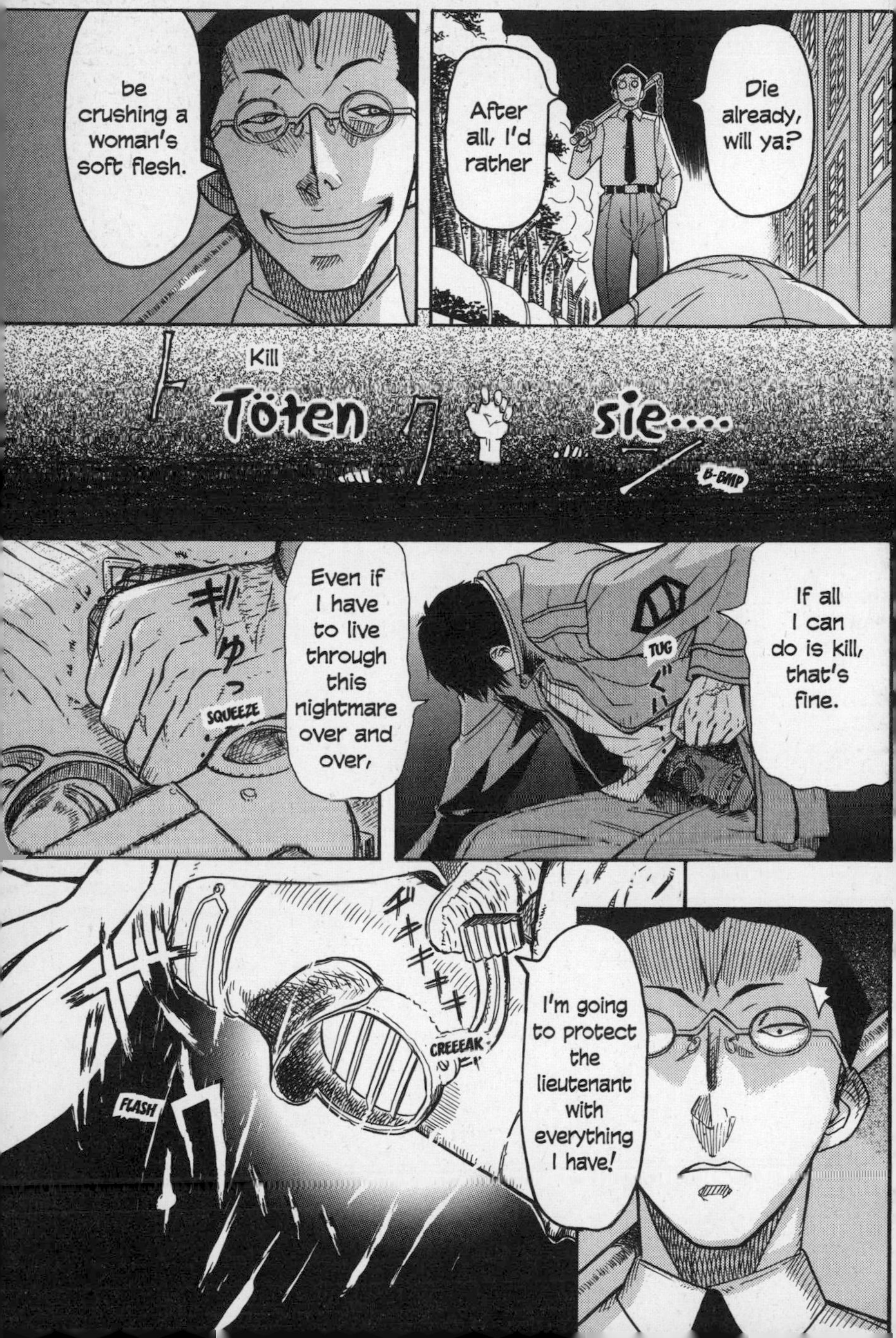
Die already, will ya?
After all, I'd rather
be crushing a woman's soft flesh.
Kill
Töten
sie....
B-BMP
If all I can do is kill, that's fine.
TUG
Even if I have to live through this nightmare over and over,
SQUEEZE
I'm going to protect the lieutenant with everything I have!
CREEEAK
FLASH

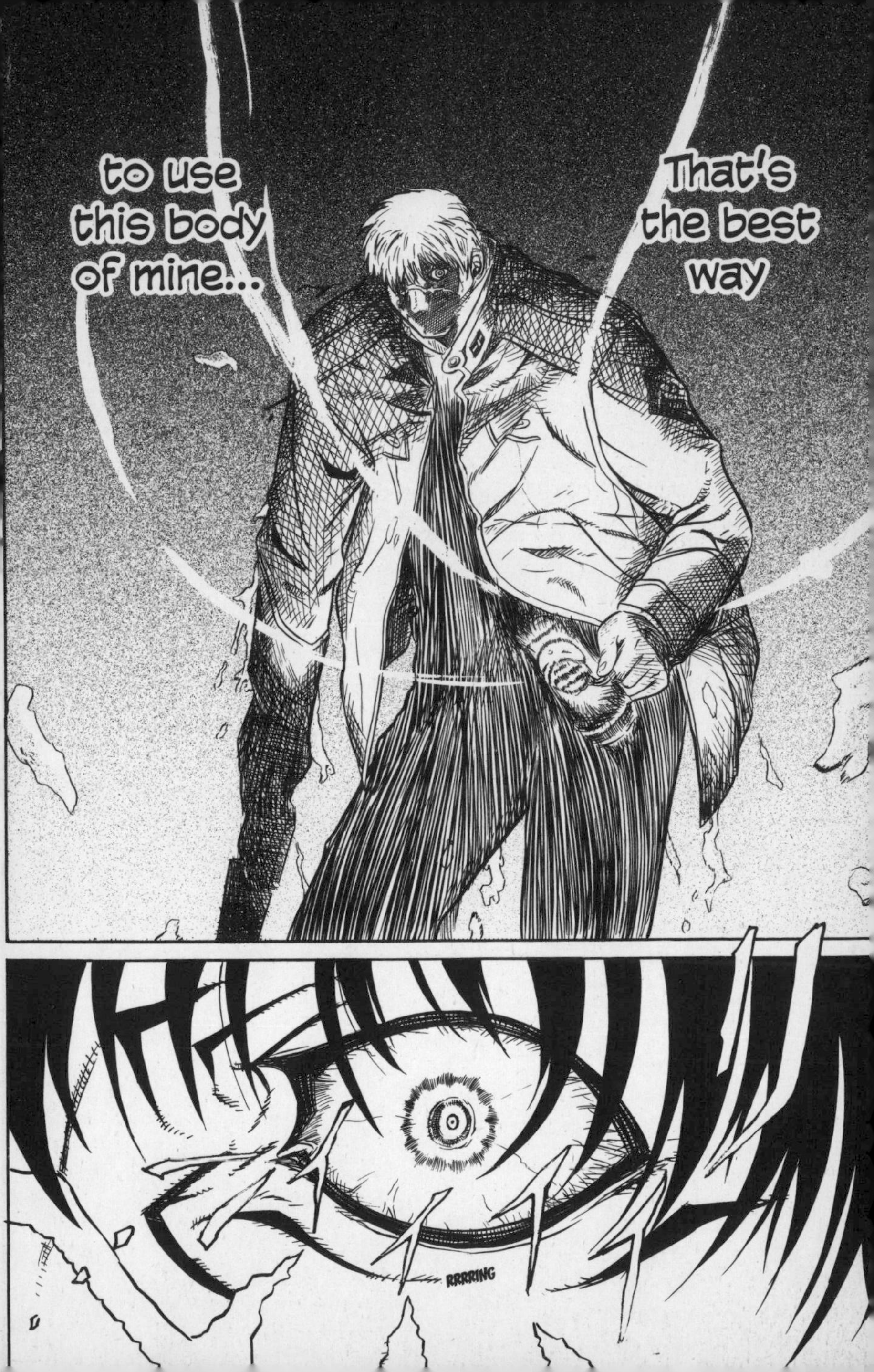
That's the best way
to use this body of mine...
RRRRING

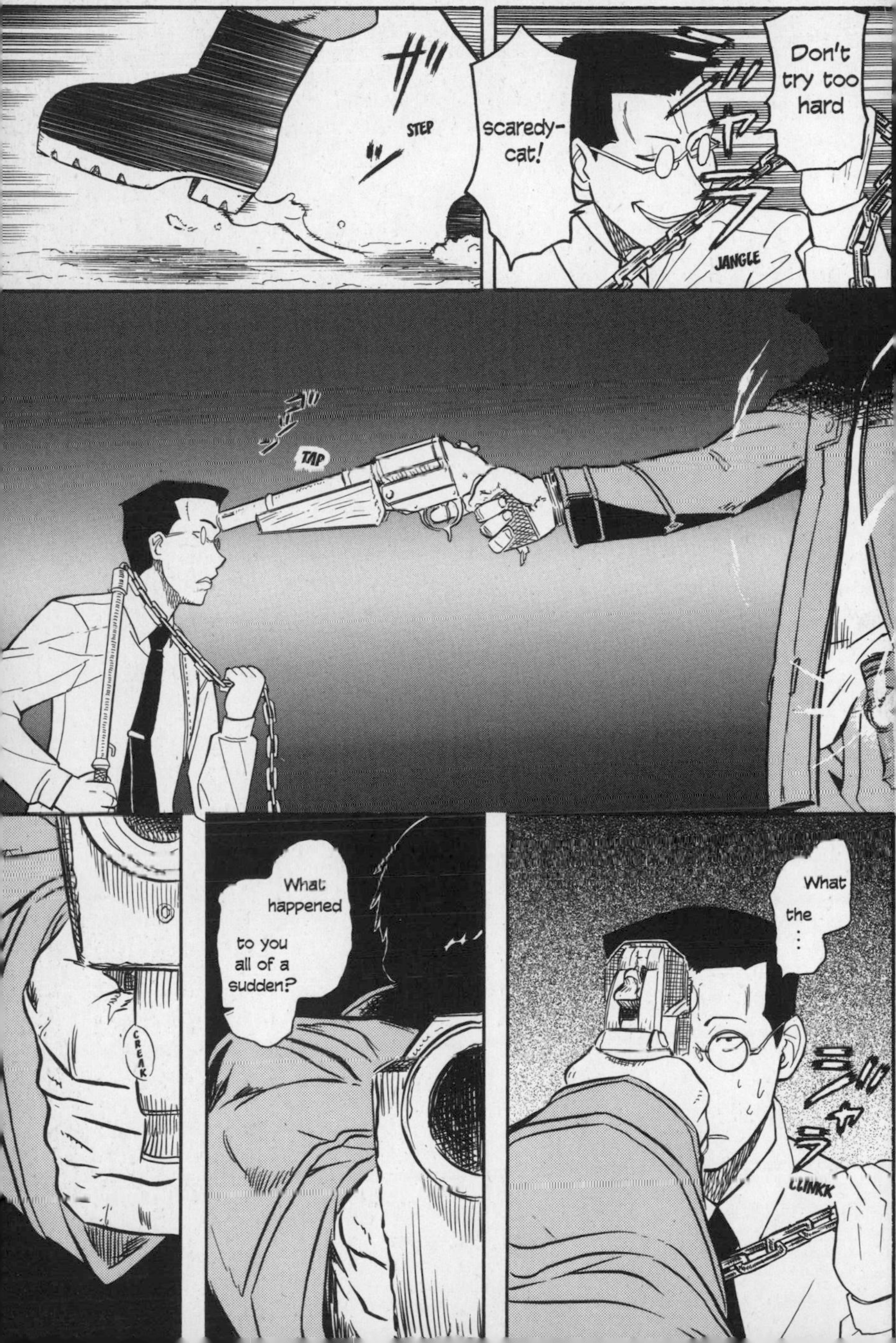
Don't try too hard
scaredy-cat!
JANGLE
STEP
TAP
What the . . .
CLINKK
What happened to you all of a sudden?
CREAK

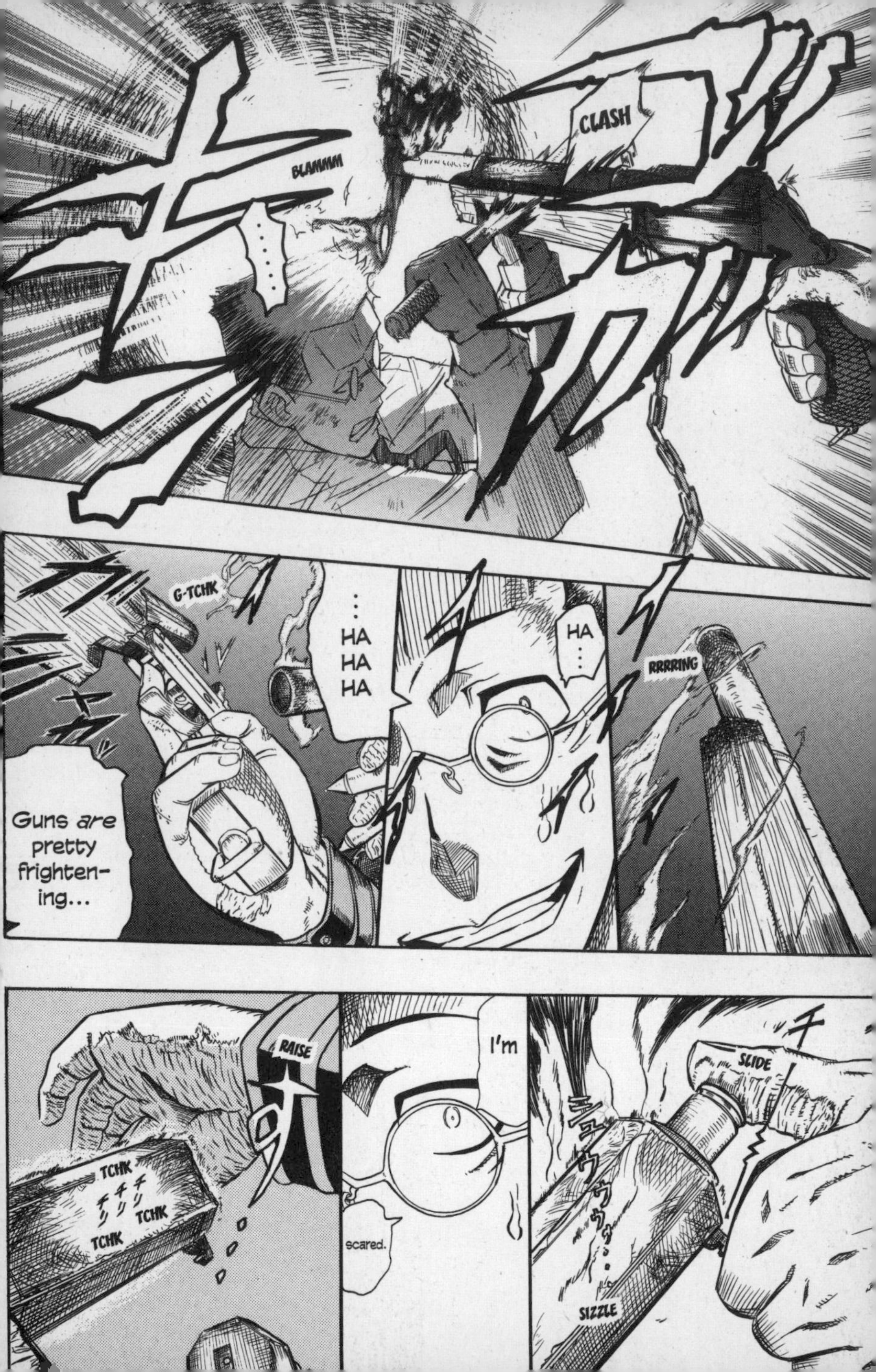
CLASH
BLAMMM
......
RRRRING
HA...
...HA HA HA
G-TCHK
Guns are pretty frighten-ing...
SLIDE
SIZZLE
I'm
scared.
RAISE
TCHK
TCHK
TCHK

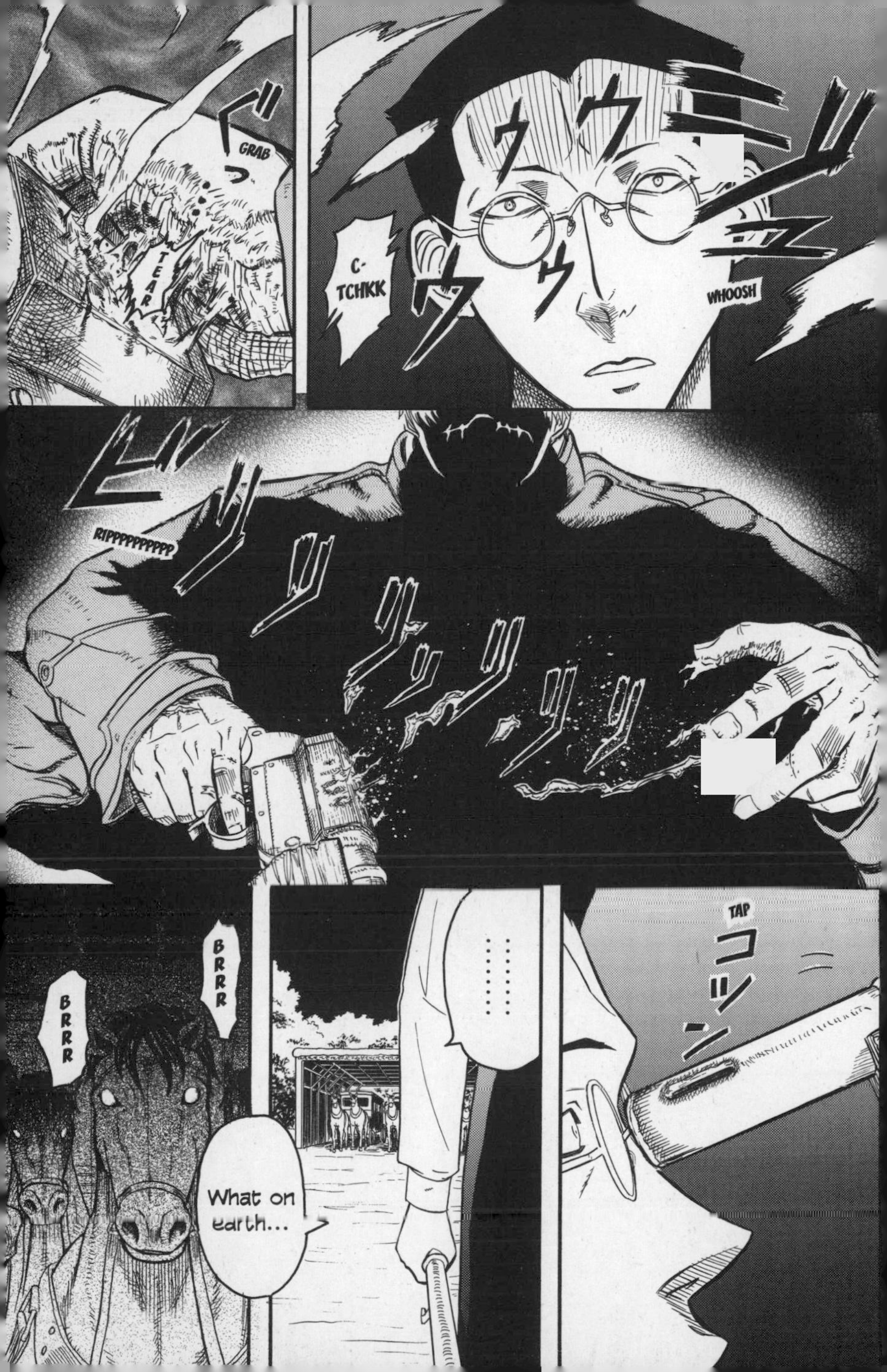
WHOOSH
C-TCHKK
GRAB
TEAR
RIPPPPPPPPPP
TAP
BRRR
BRRR
What on earth...

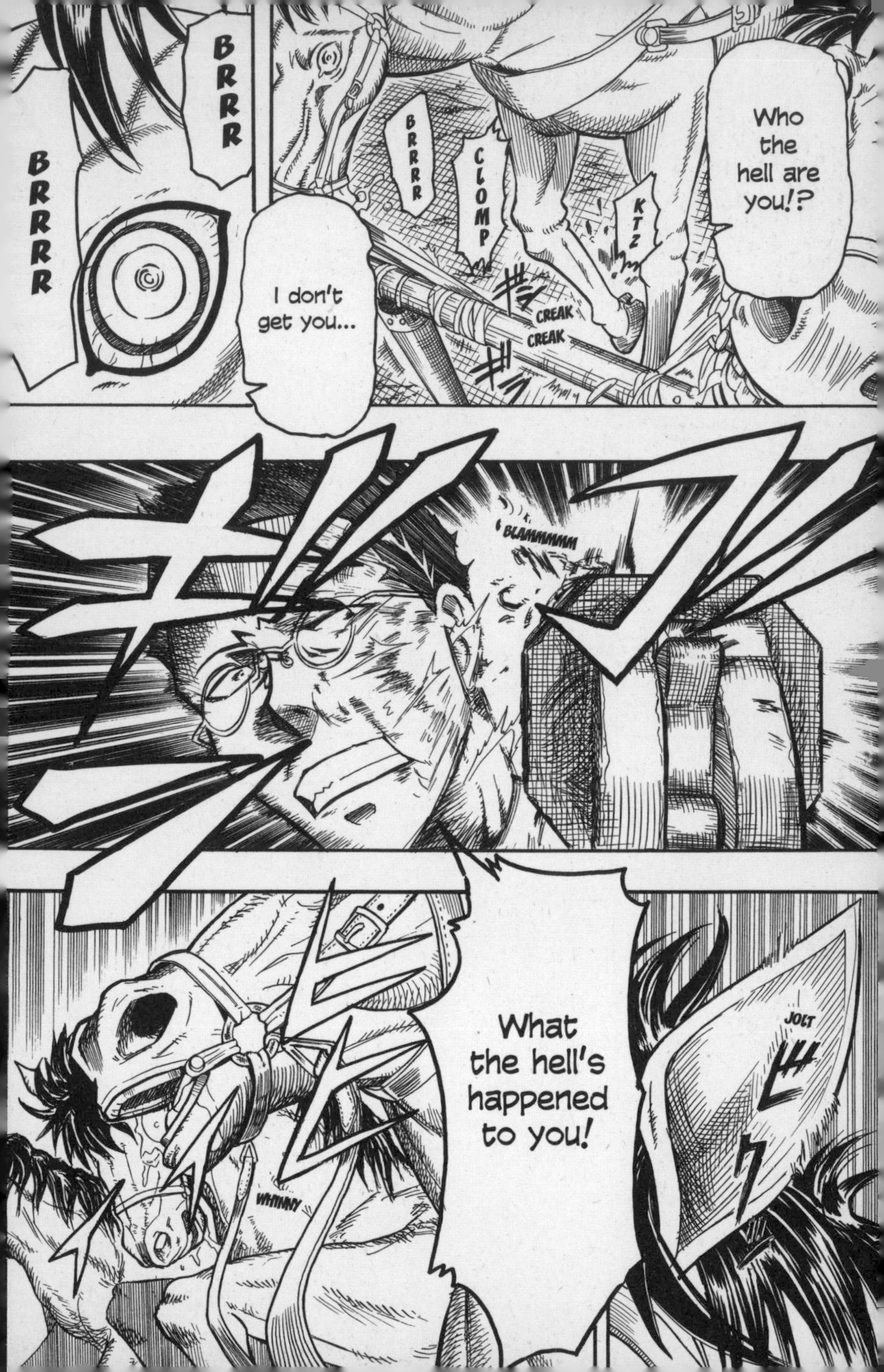
Who the hell are you!?
KTZ
CLOMP
BRRRR
CREAK
CREAK
I don't get you...
BRRR
BRRRR
BLAMMMMM
JOLT
What the hell's happened to you!
WHINNY

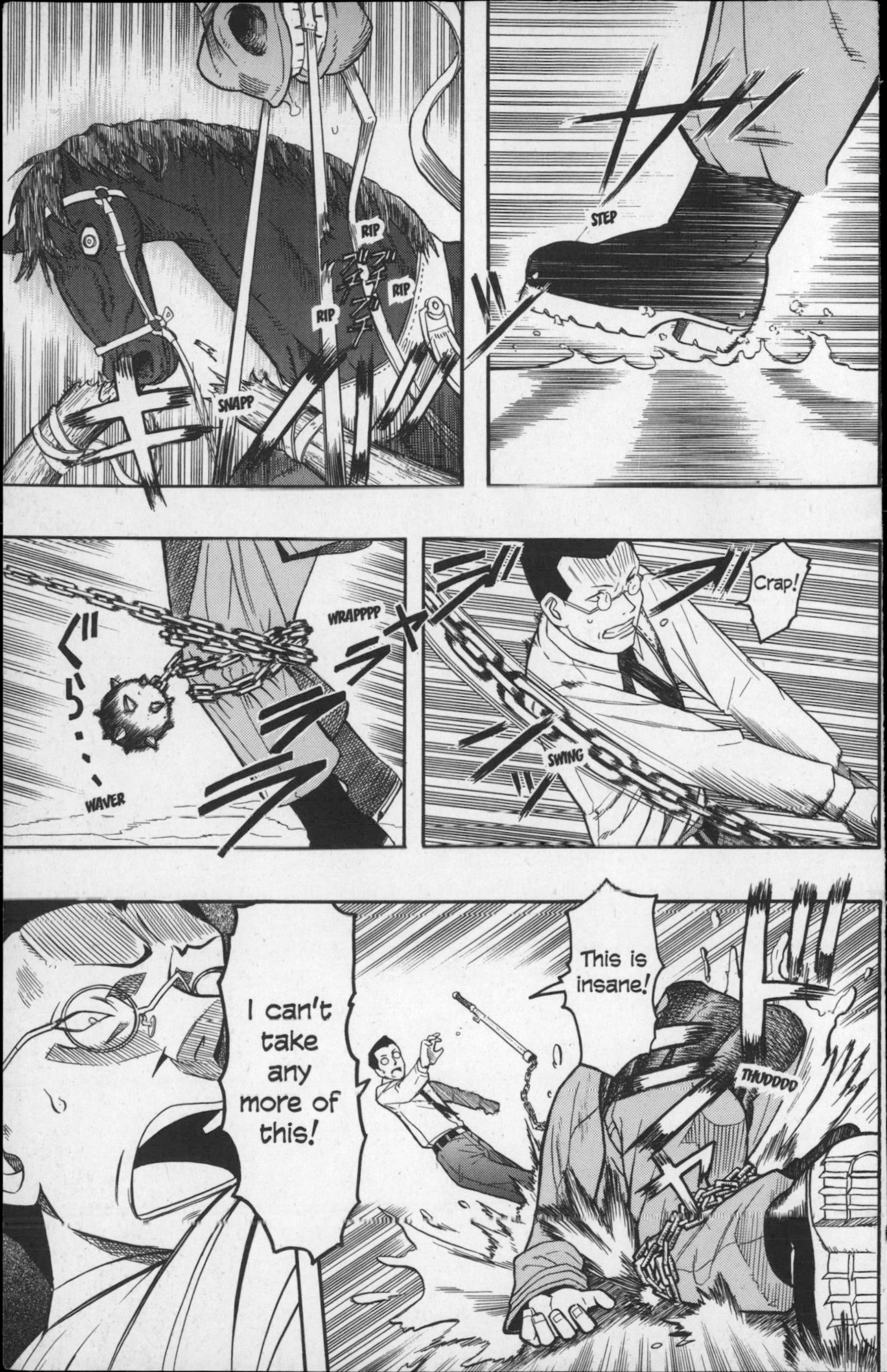
STEP
RIP
RIP
RIP
SNAPP
Crap!
SWING
WRAPPPP
WAVER
This is insane!
THUDDDD
I can't take any more of this!

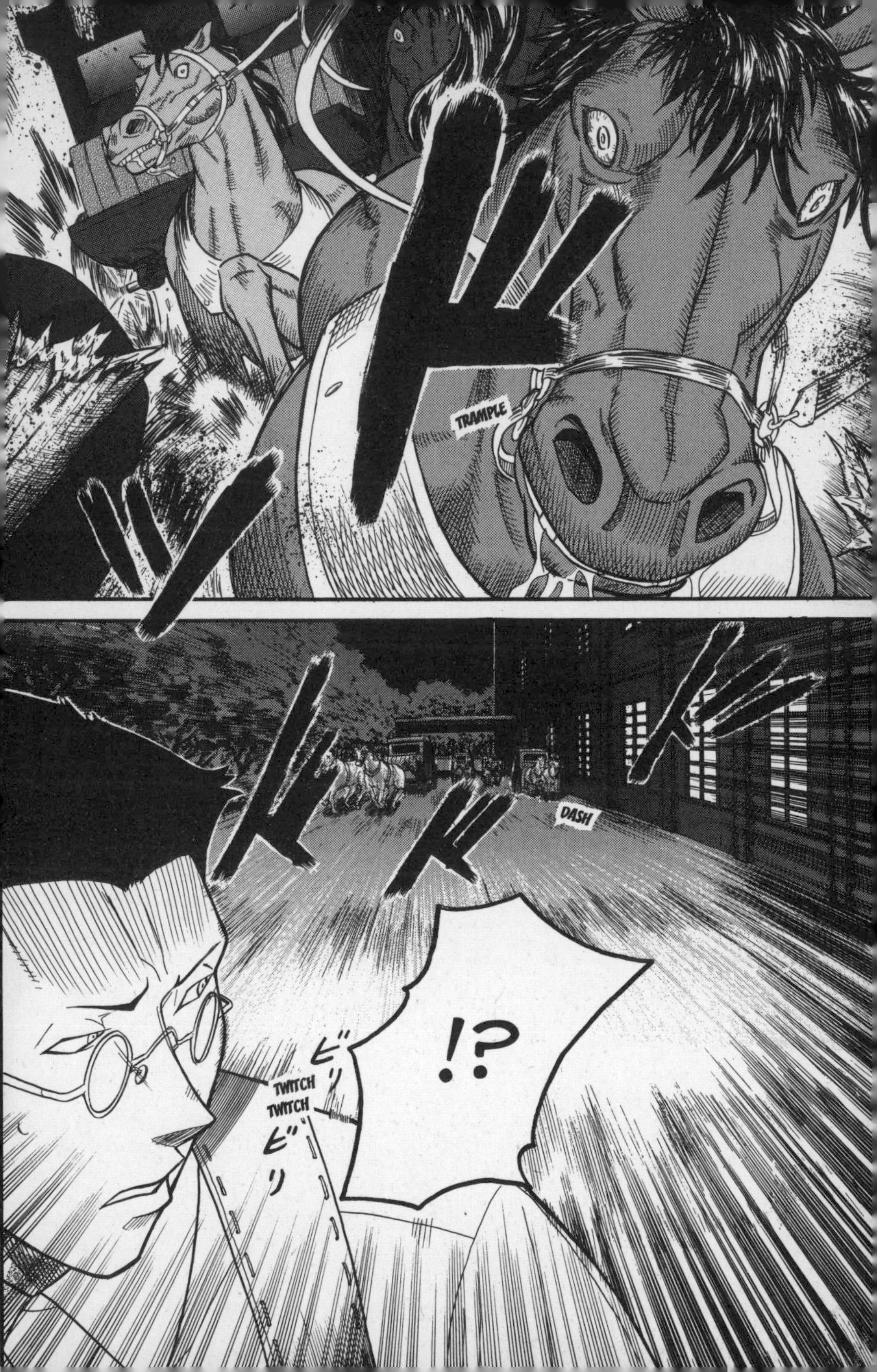
TRAMPLE
DASH
!?
TWITCH
TWITCH
ビリ
ビリ

DASH
The gun-shots
Damn!
!!
DASH
GRABB
SLUMP
......
Hey...
DASH
DASH
Stop being
DASH
DASH
DASH
DASH
GRIP
DASH
crazy!
DASH
DASH
DASH

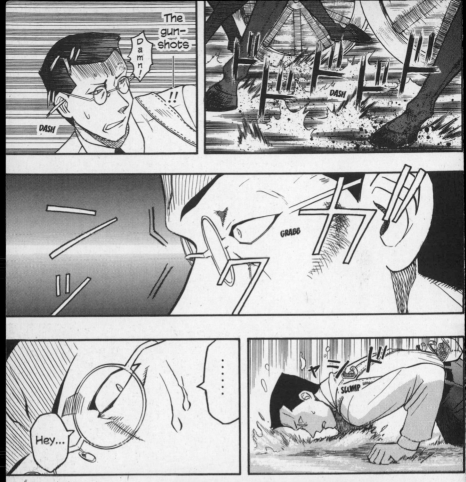

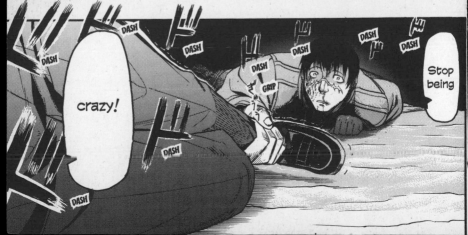

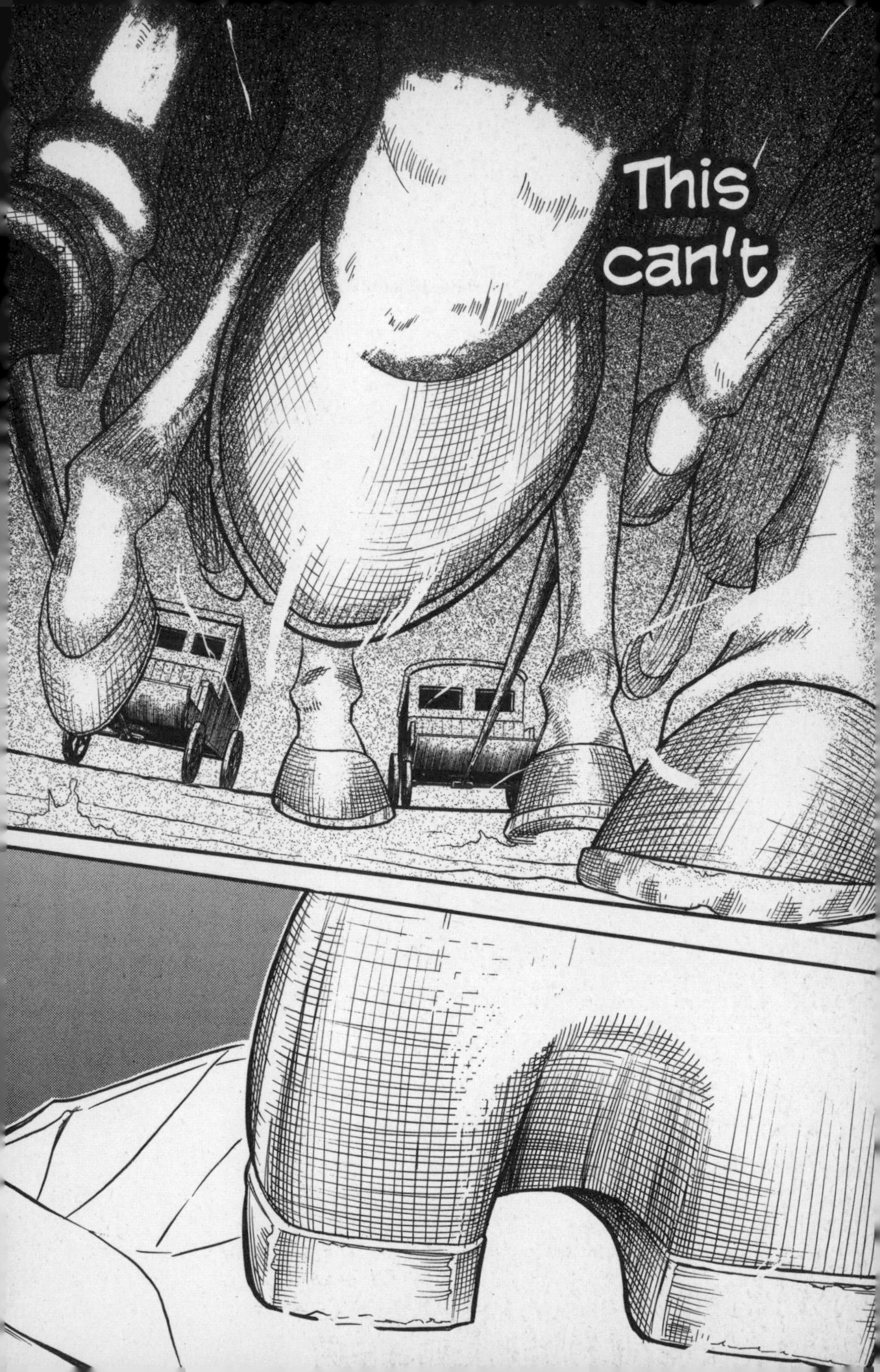
This can't

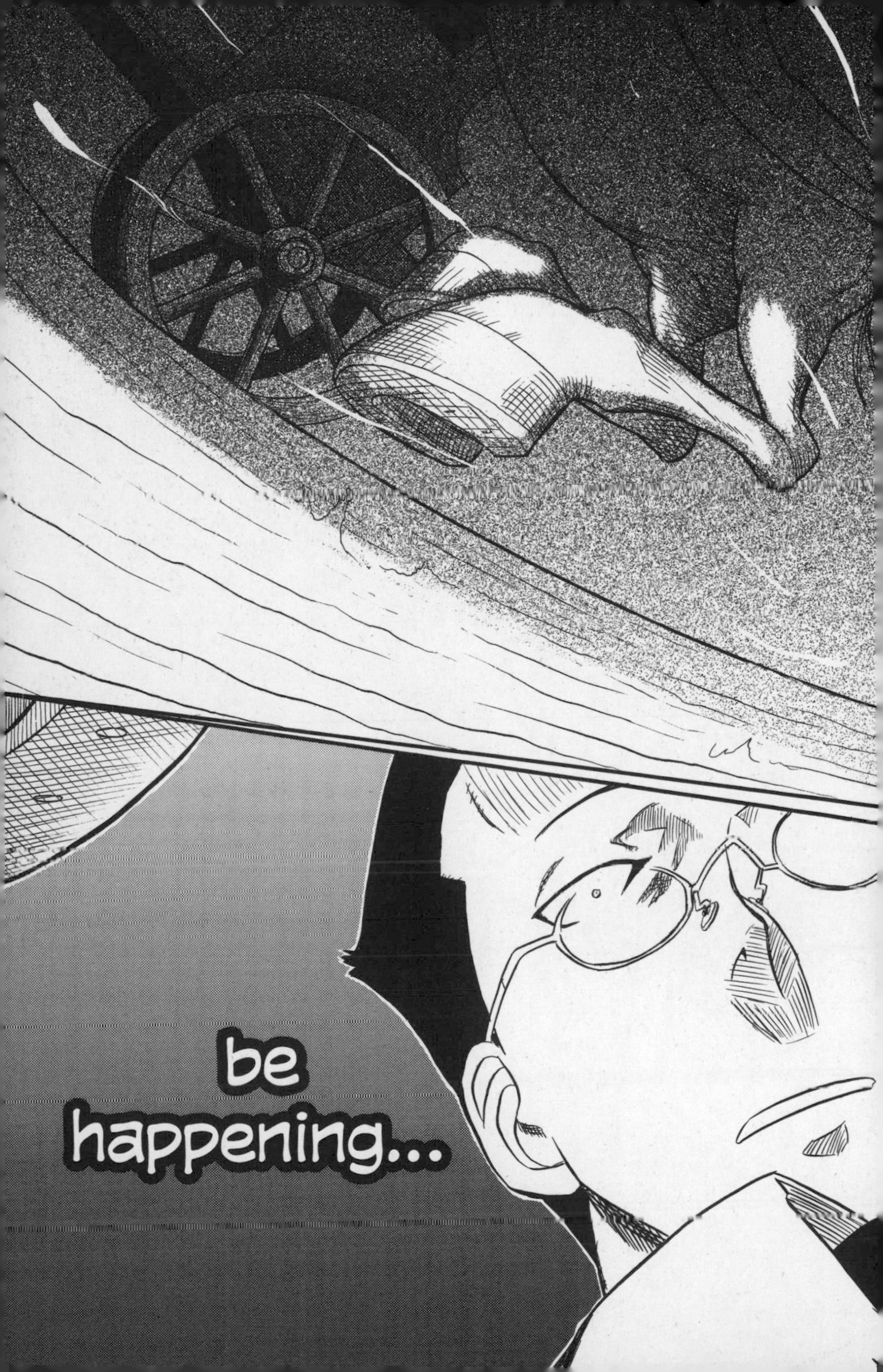
be
happening...

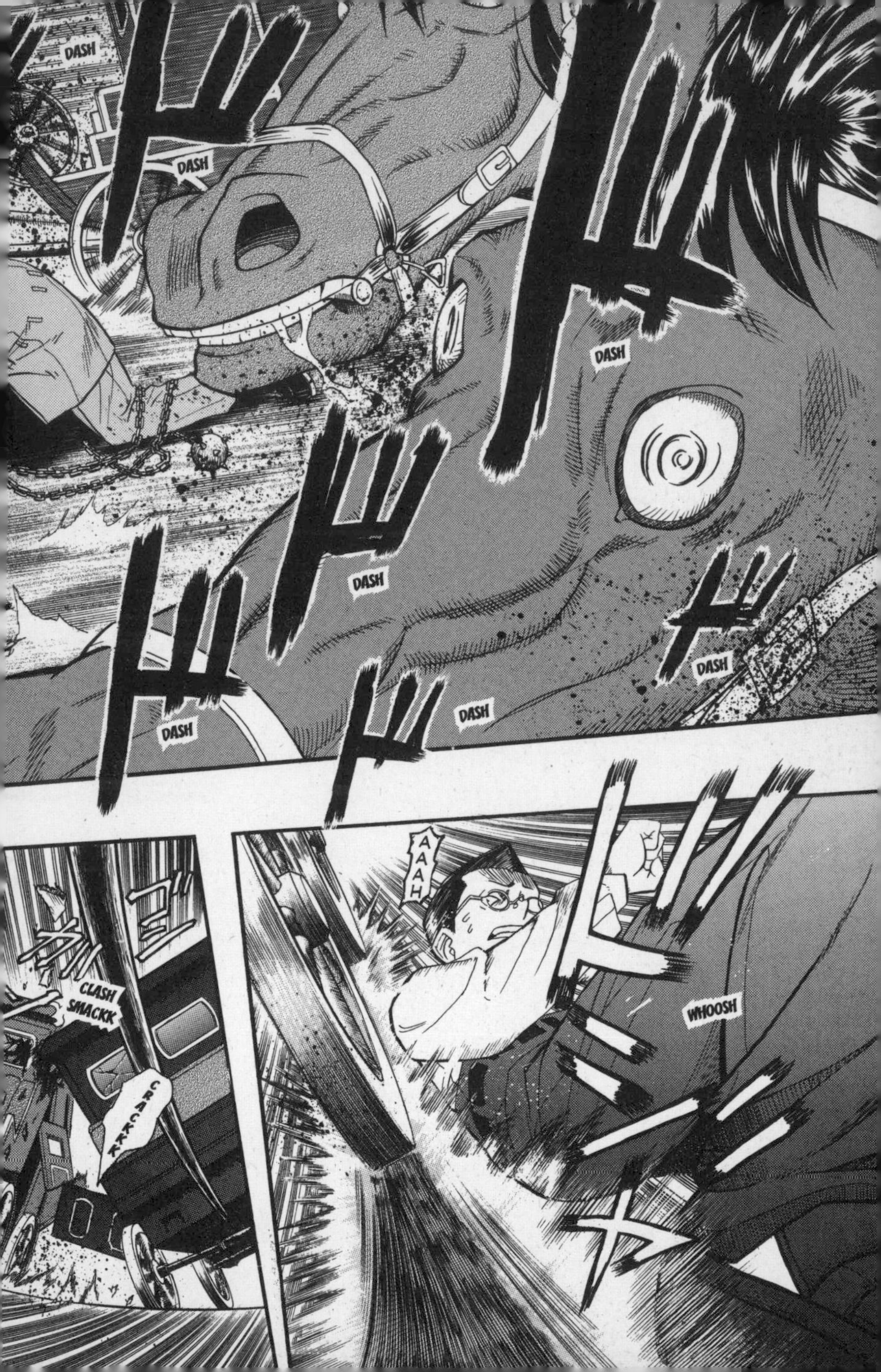
DASH
DASH
DASH
DASH
DASH
DASH
DASH
AAAH
WHOOSH
CLASH
SMACKK
CRACKKK

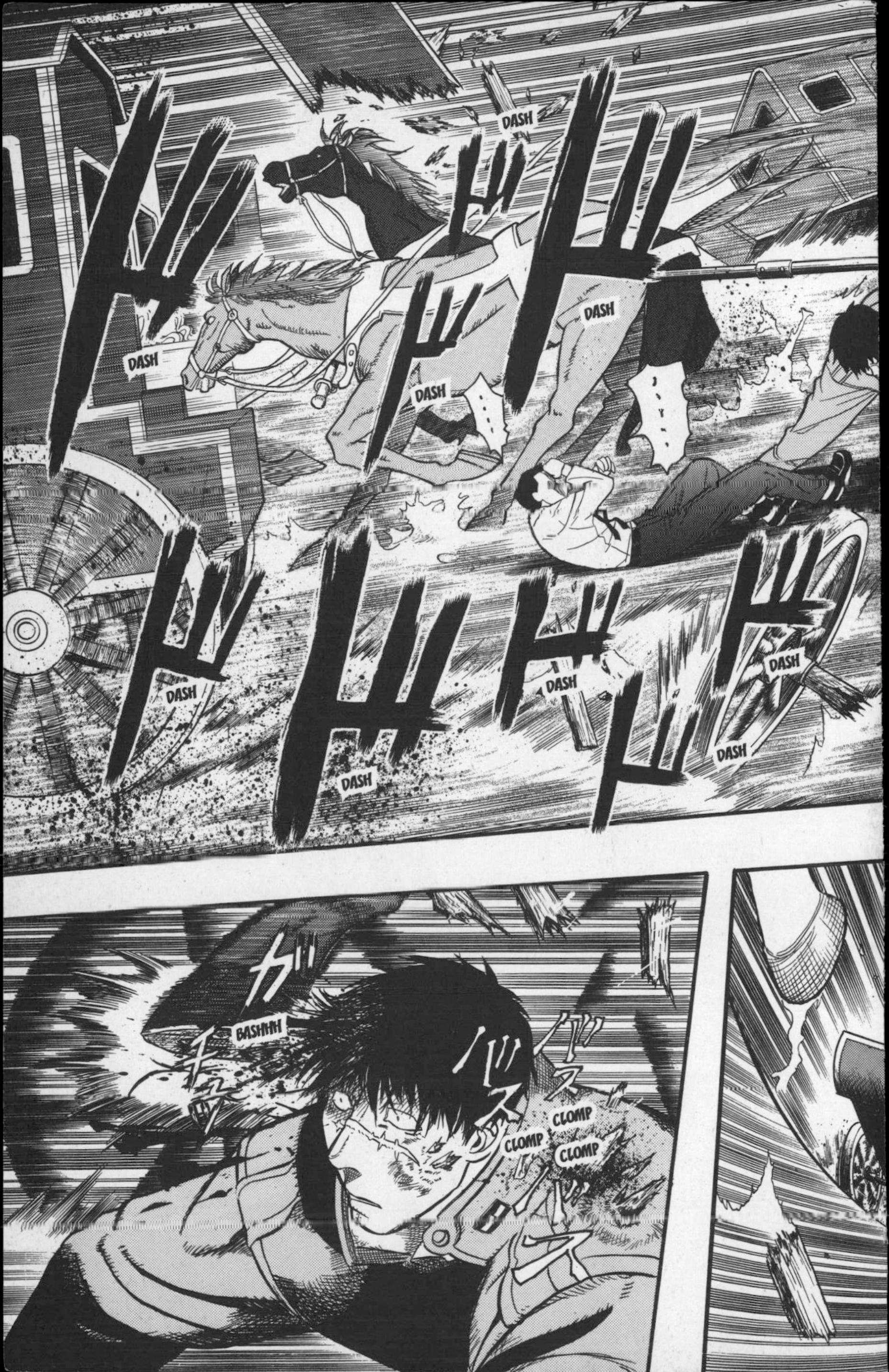
DASH
DASH
DASH
DASH
DASH
DASH
DASH
DASH
DASH
BASHHH
CLOMP
CLOMP
CLOMP
CLOMP

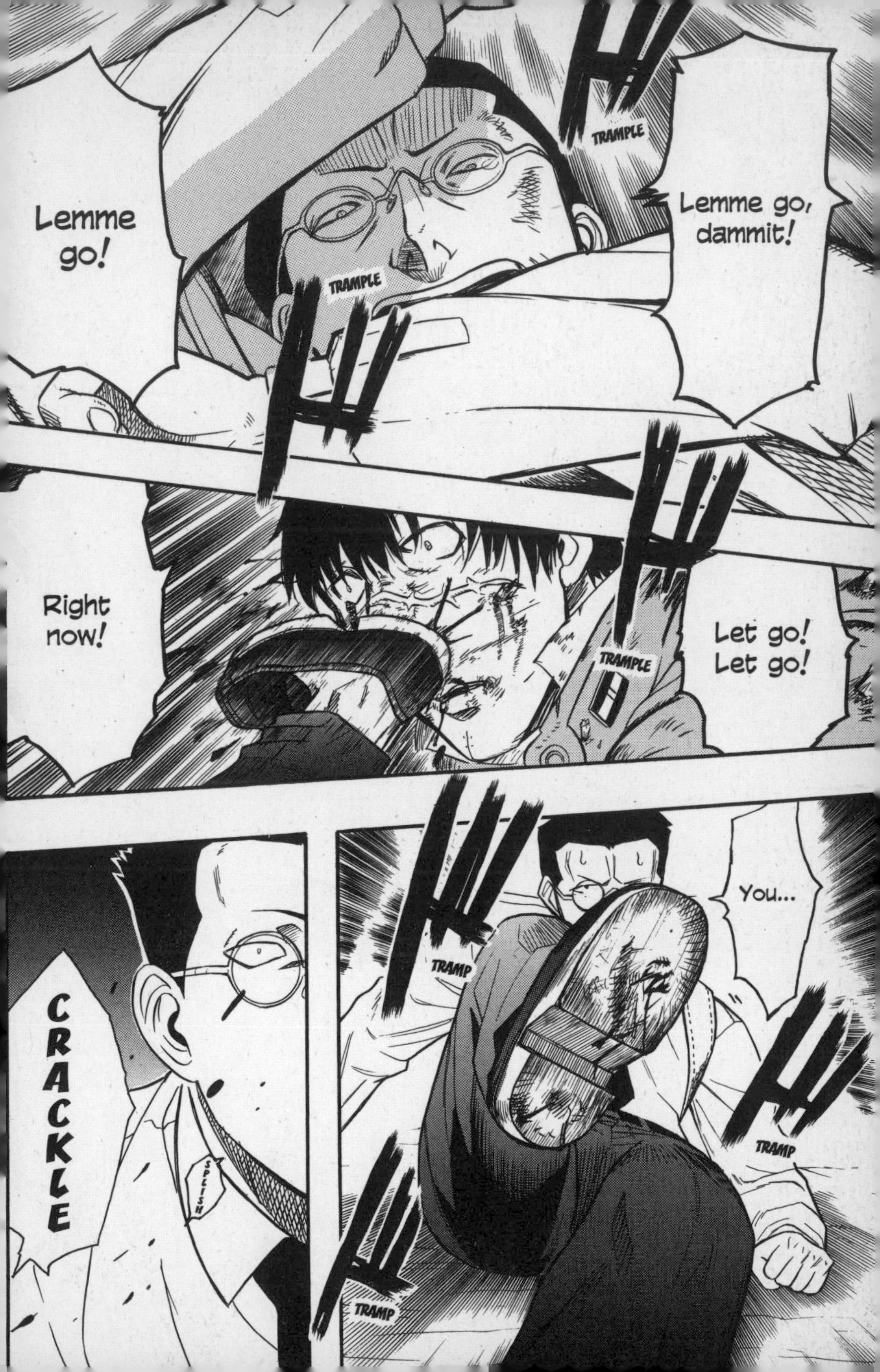
TRAMPLE
Lemme go, dammit!
Lemme go!
TRAMPLE
Let go! Let go!
TRAMPLE
Right now!
You...
TRAMP
TRAMP
TRAMP
CRACKLE
SPLISH

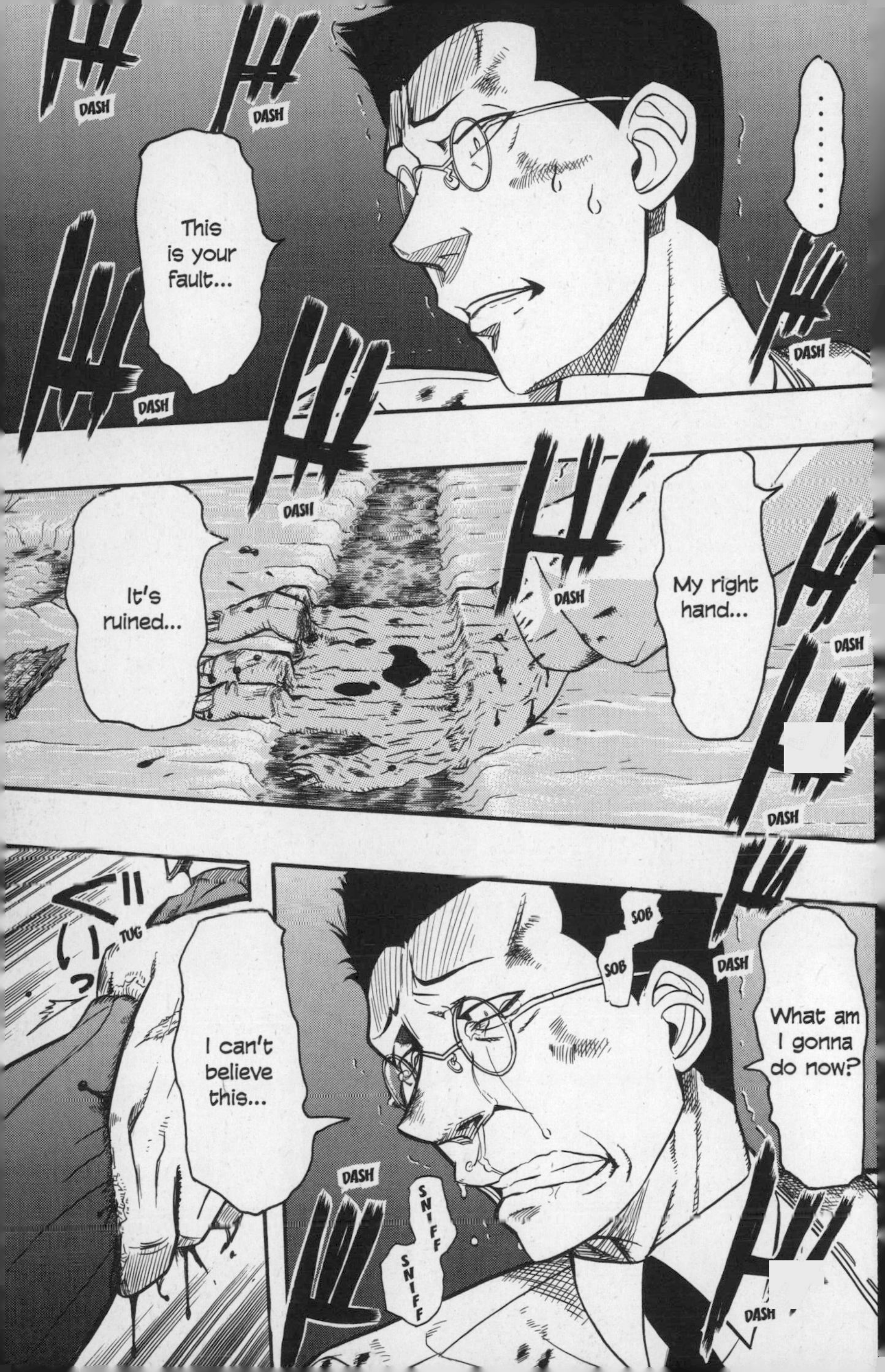
......
DASH
DASH
DASH
This is your fault...
DASH
My right hand...
DASH
DASH
DASH
It's ruined...
DASH
DASH
What am I gonna do now?
SOB
SOB
DASH
SNIFF
SNIFF
I can't believe this...
TUG

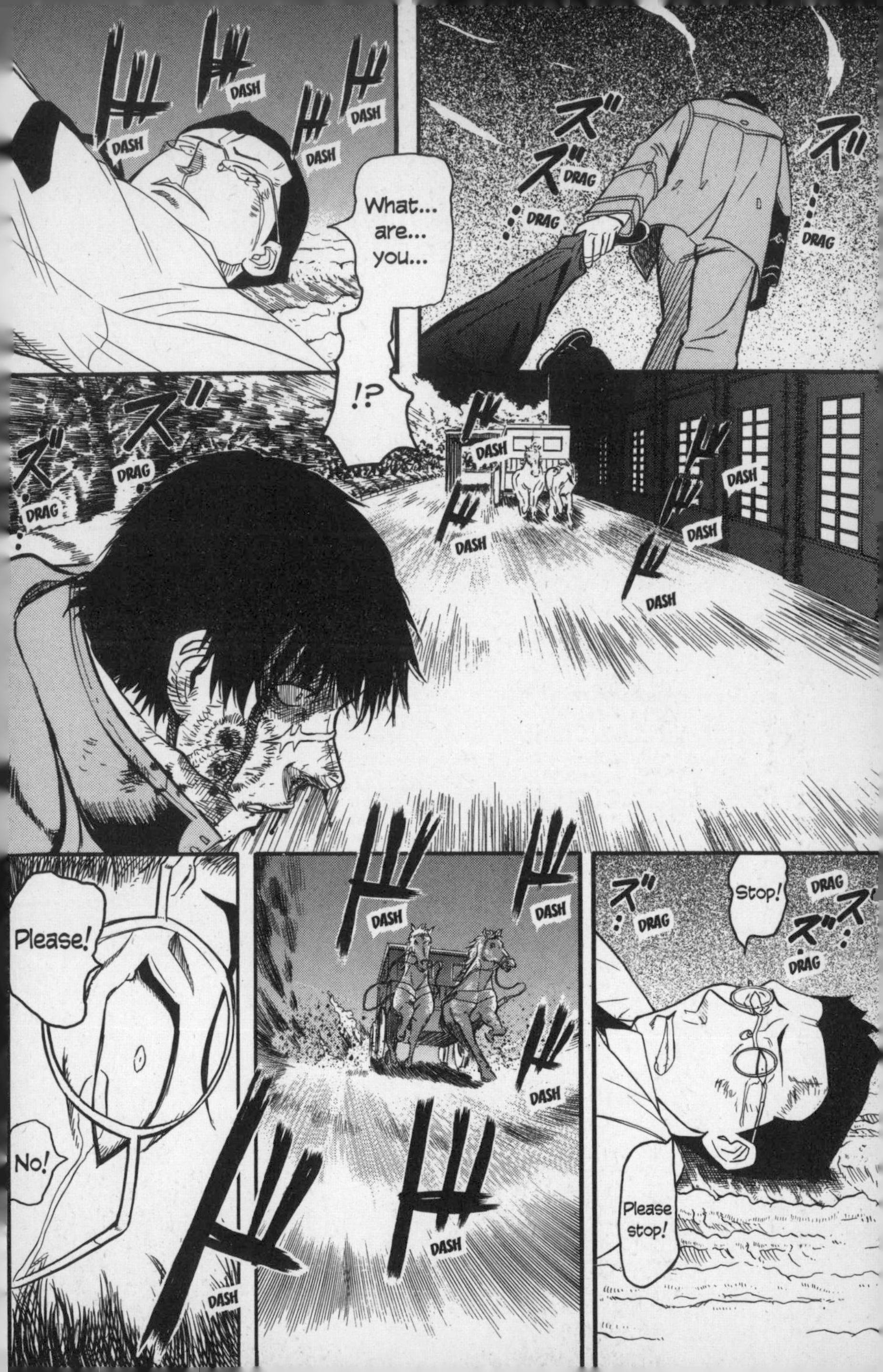
DRAG
DRAG
DRAG
DASH
DASH
DASH
DASH
What... are... you...
!?
DASH
DASH
DASH
DASH
DASH
DRAG
DRAG
DRAG
Stop!
DRAG
DRAG
Please stop!
DASH
DASH
DASH
DASH
Please!
No!
DASH

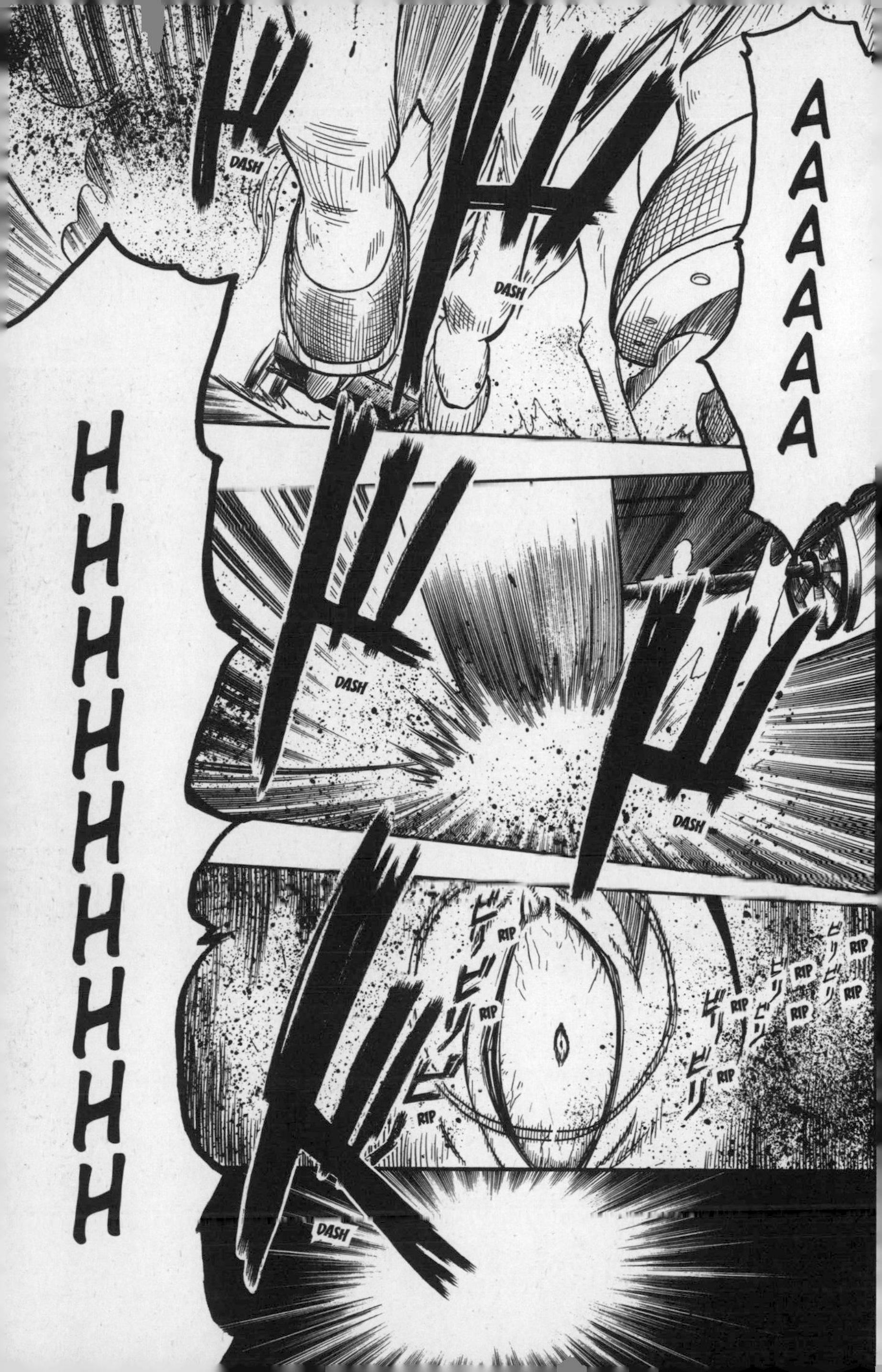
AAAAAAA
DASH
DASH
DASH
DASH
RIP
RIP
RIP
RIP
RIP
RIP
RIP
RIP
RIP
RIP
DASH
HHHHHHH

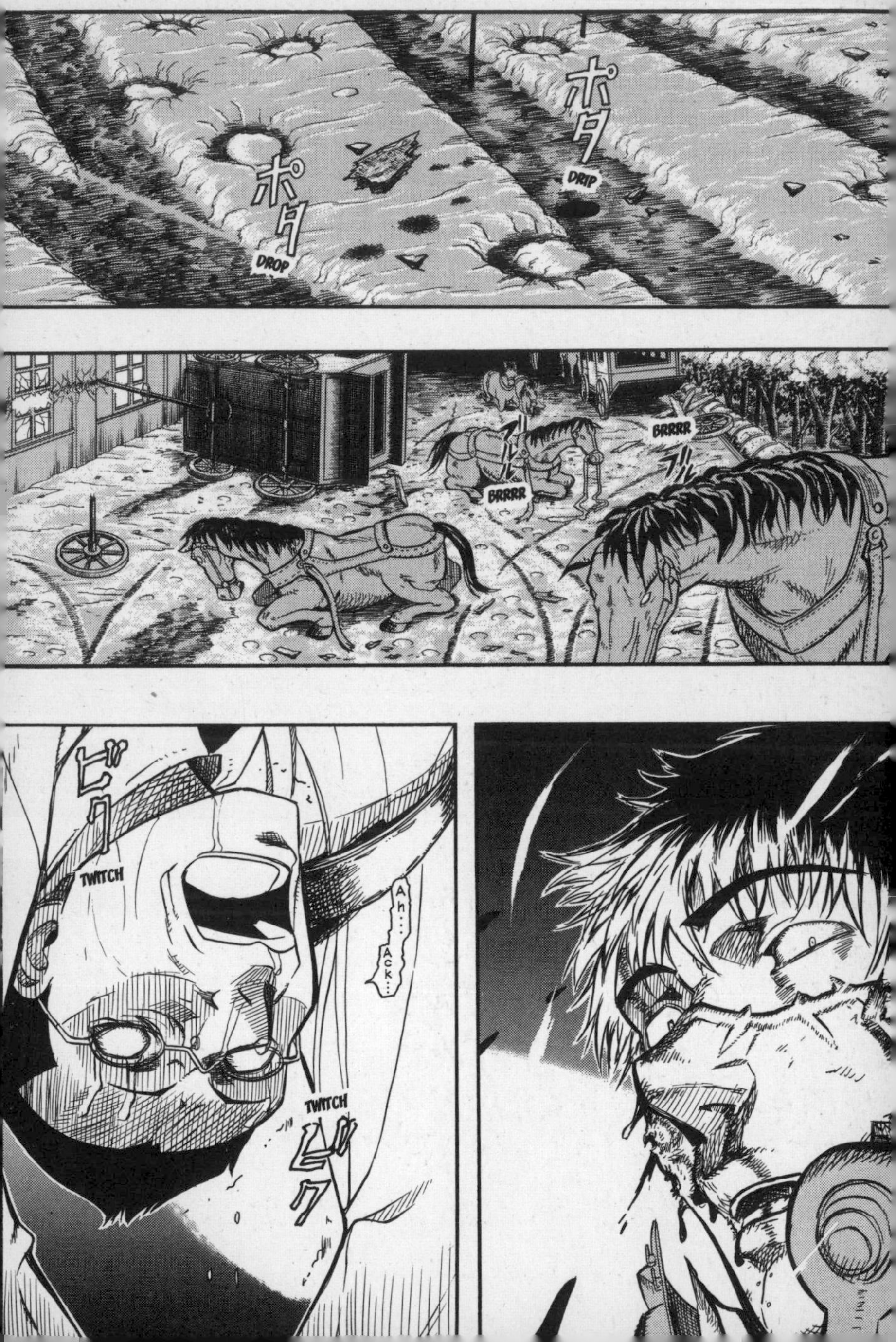

ポタ
DRIP
ポタ
DROP
BRRRR
BRRRR
ビク
TWITCH
Ah... Ack...
TWITCH
ビク

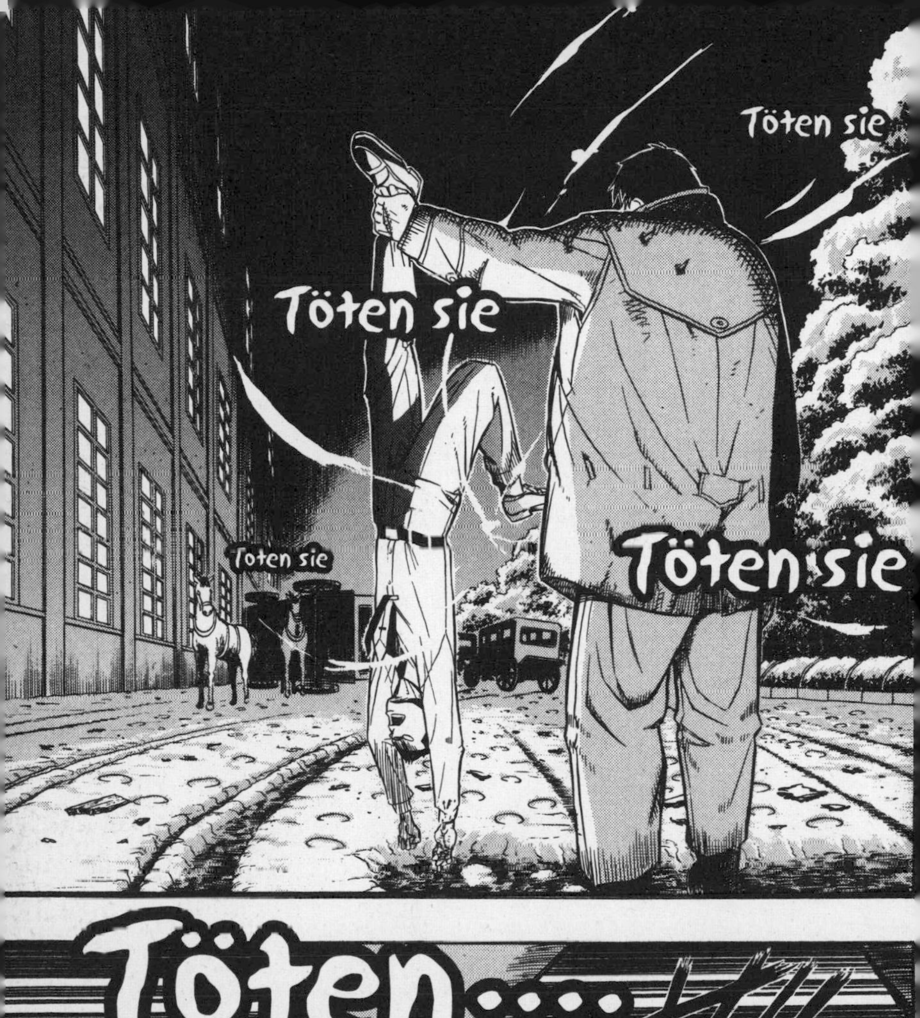
Töten sie
Töten sie
Töten sie
Töten sie

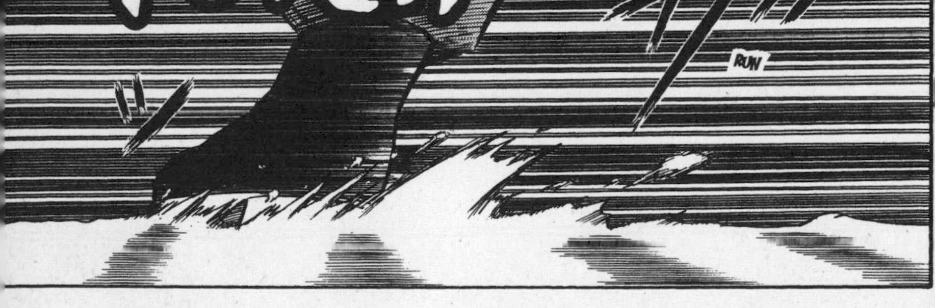
Töten....
RUN

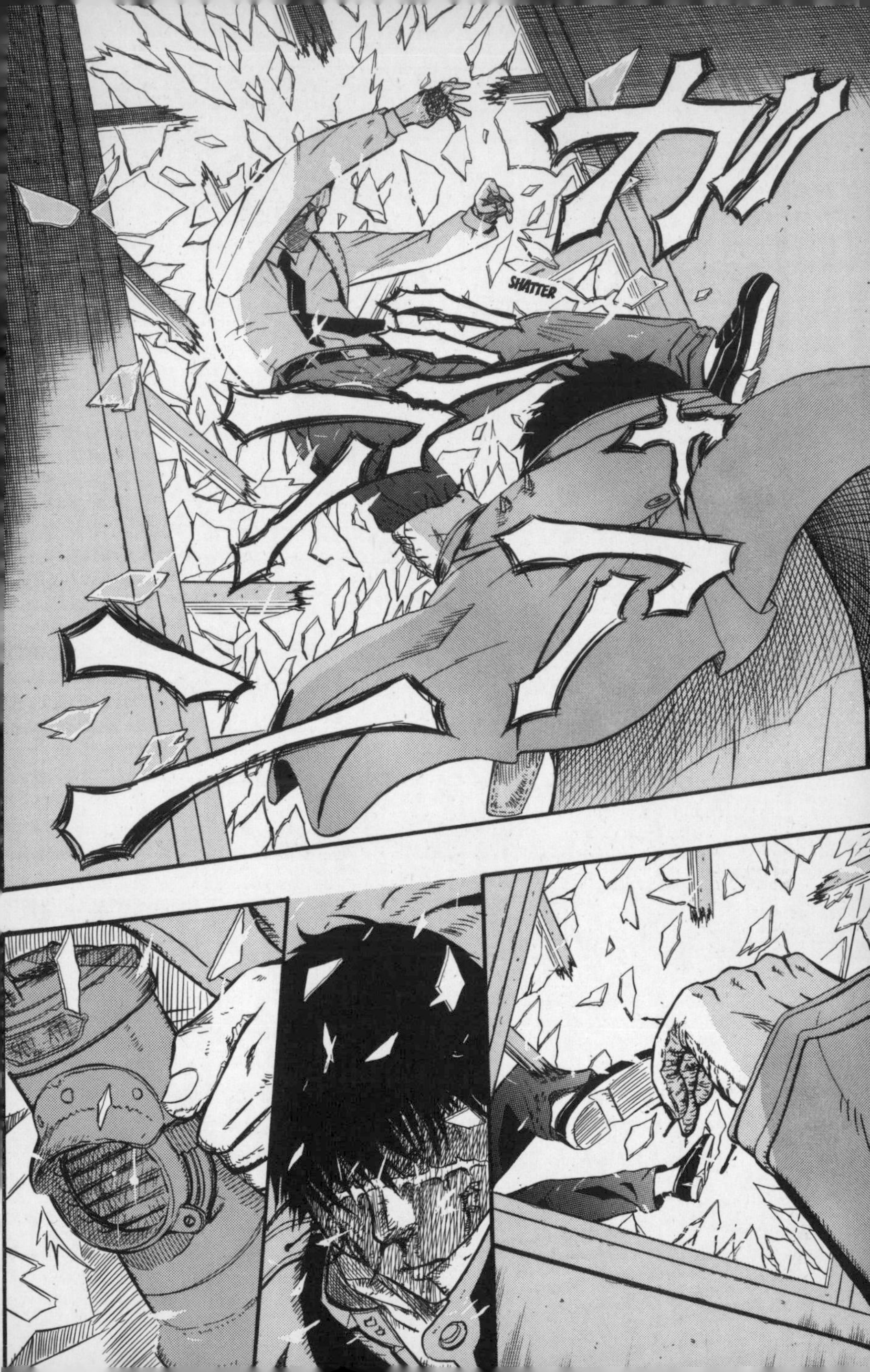
SHATTER

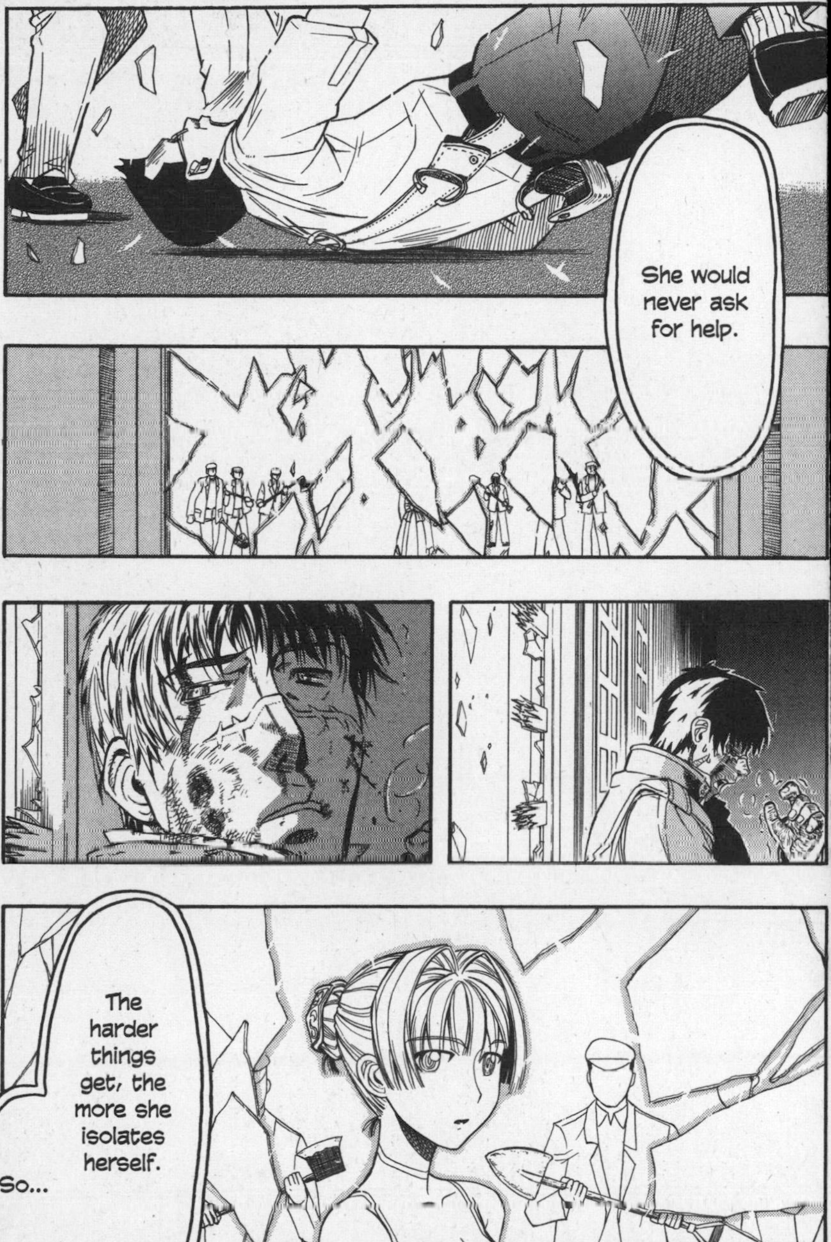
She would never ask for help.
The harder things get, the more she isolates herself.
So...

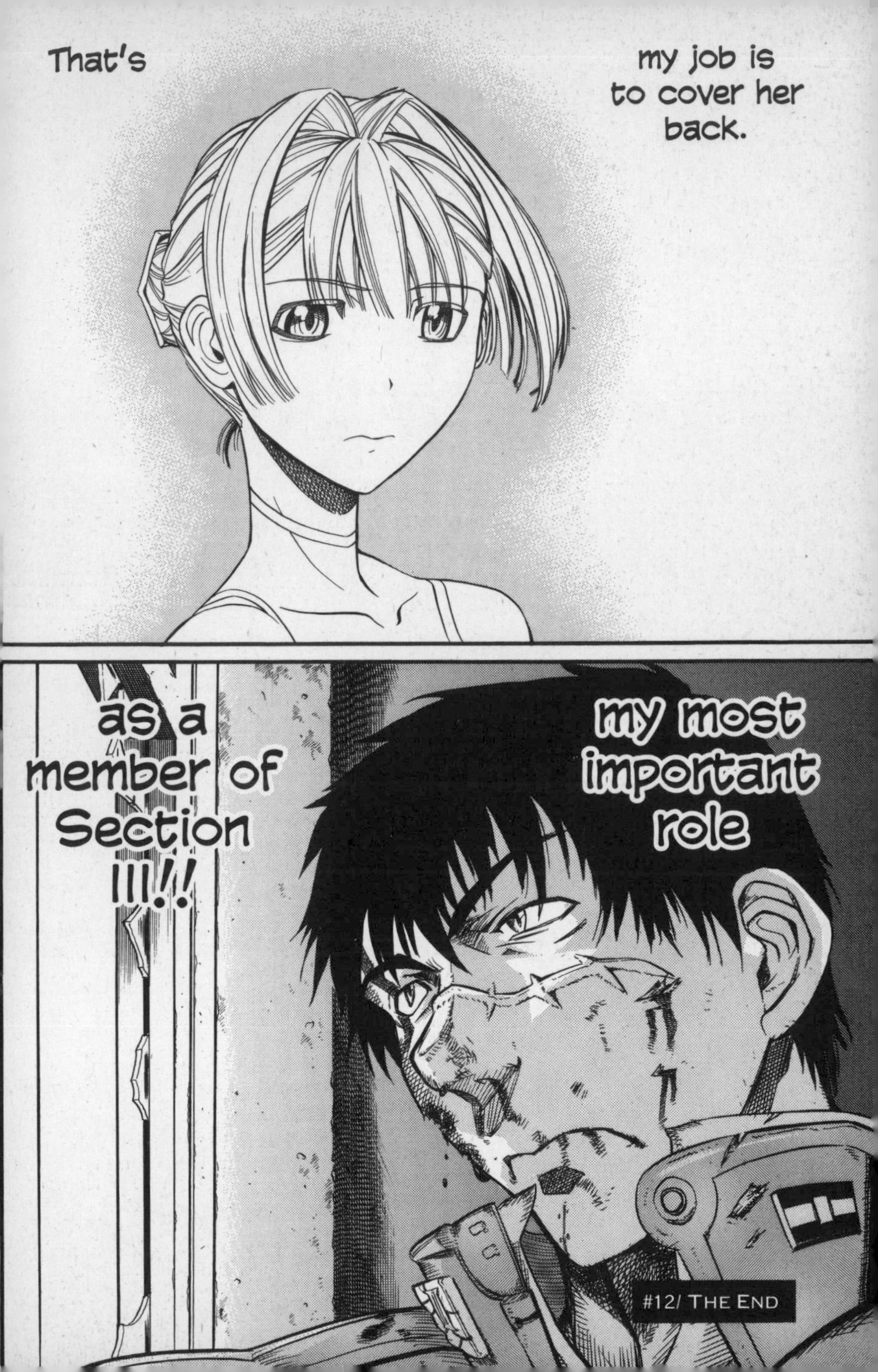
my job is to cover her back.
That's
my most important role
as a member of Section III!!
#12/ The End

PumpkinScissors

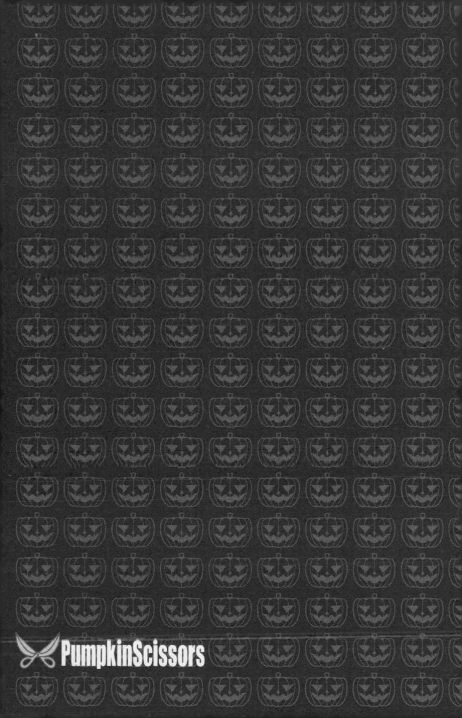

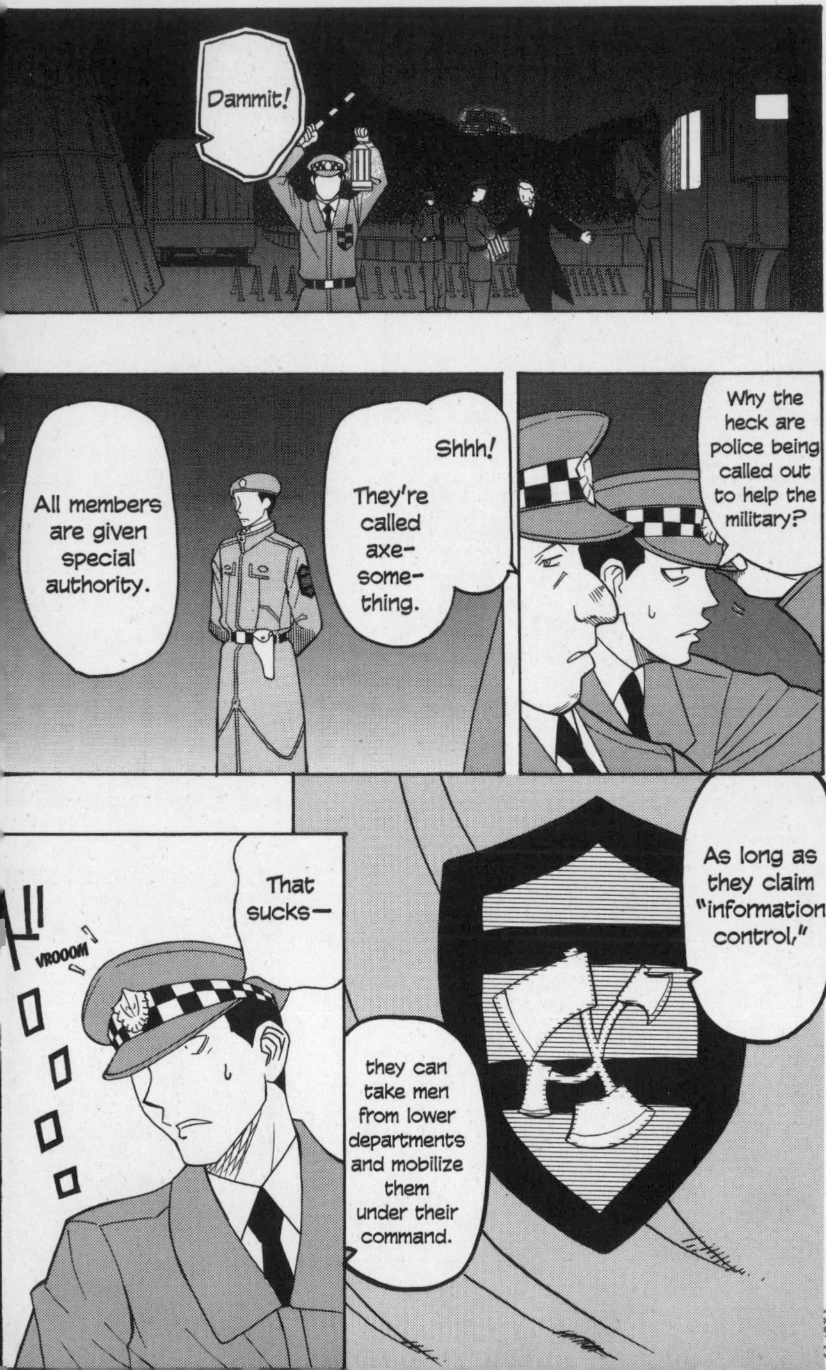
Dammit!
Why the heck are police being called out to help the military?
Shhh!
They're called axe-something.
All members are given special authority.
As long as they claim "information control,"
they can take men from lower departments and mobilize them under their command.
That sucks—
VROOOM

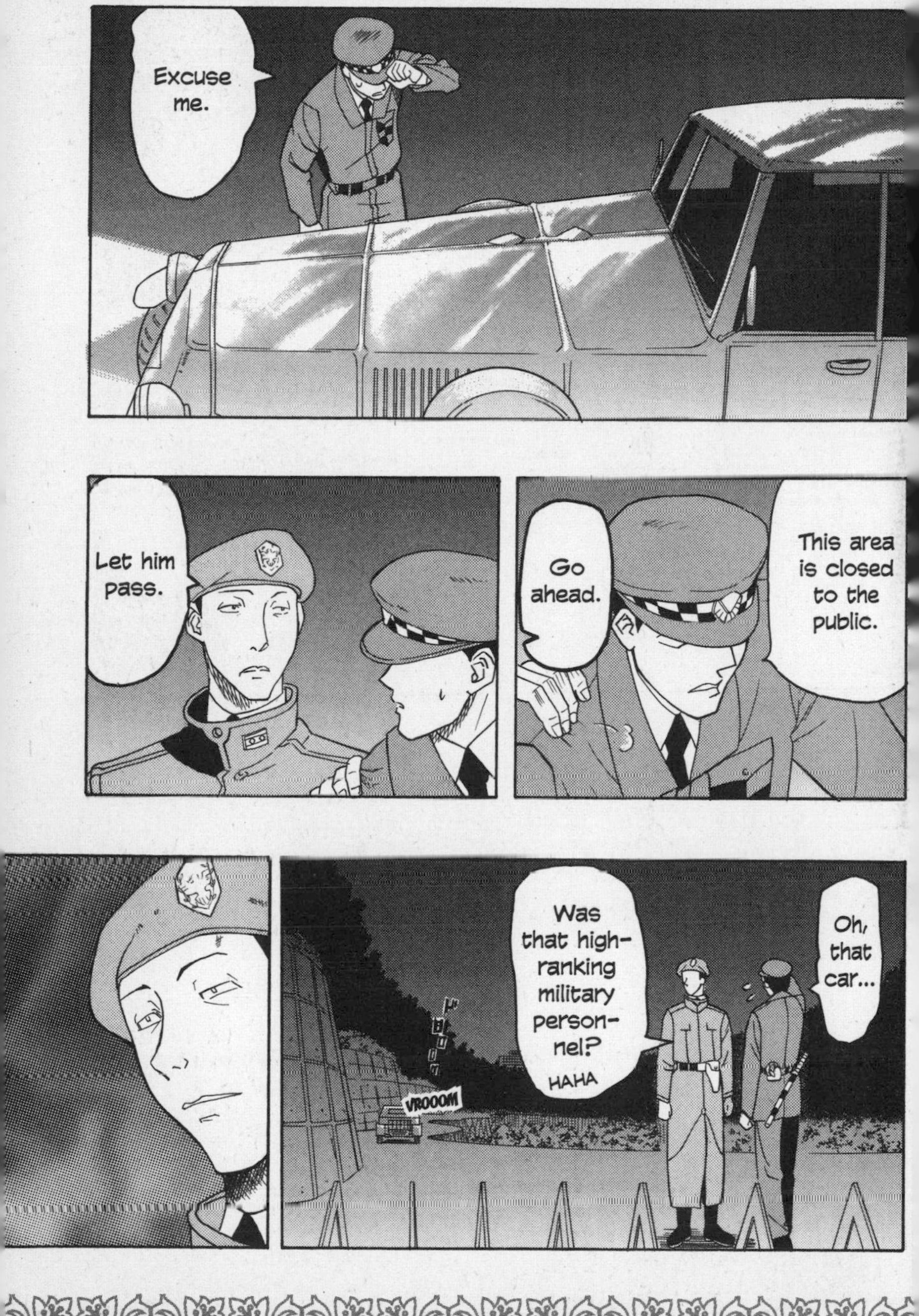
Excuse me.
This area is closed to the public.
Go ahead.
Let him pass.
Oh, that car...
Was that high-ranking military personnel?
HAHA
VROOOM

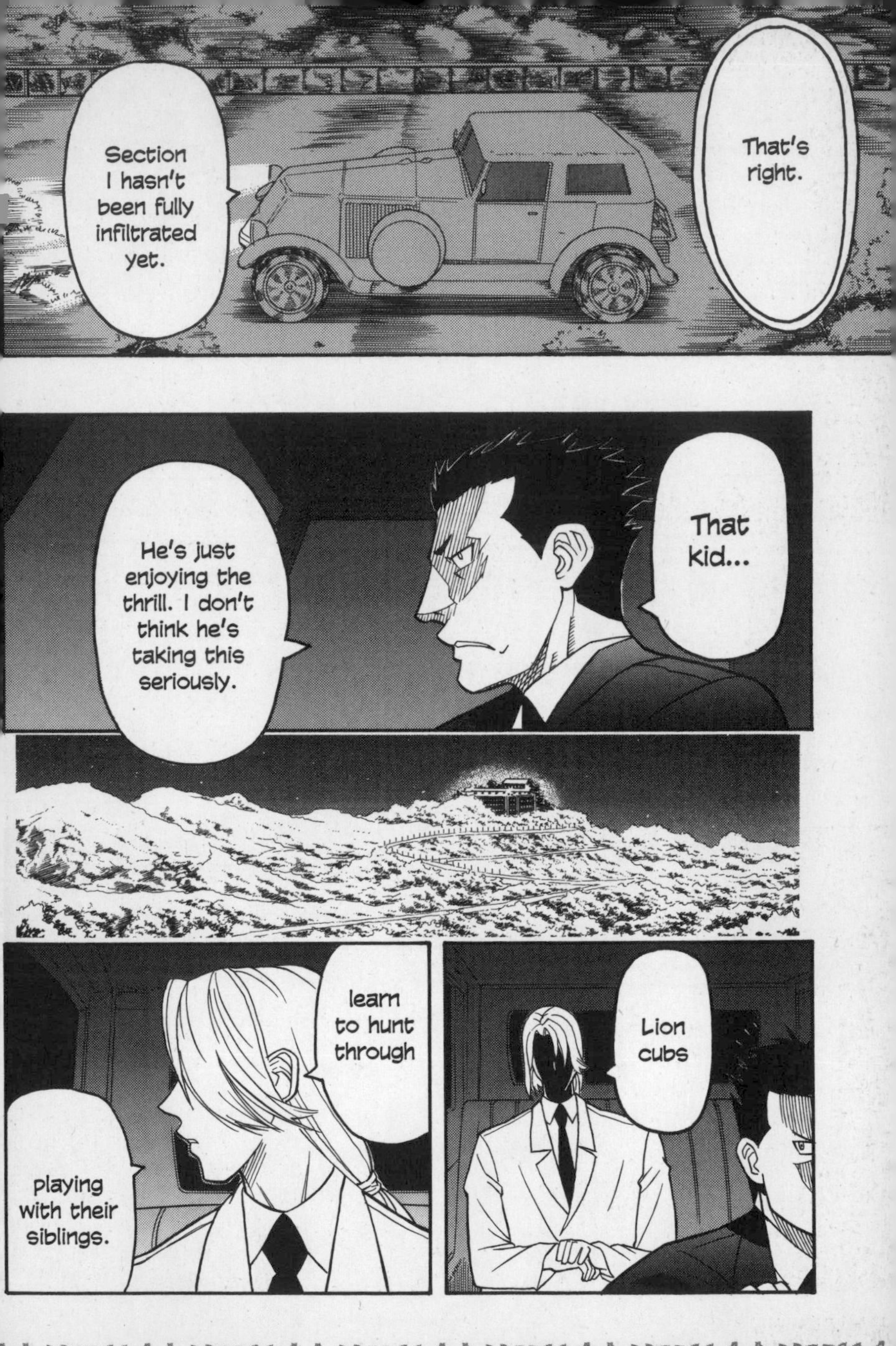
That's right.
Section I hasn't been fully infiltrated yet.
That kid...
He's just enjoying the thrill. I don't think he's taking this seriously.
Lion cubs
learn to hunt through
playing with their siblings.

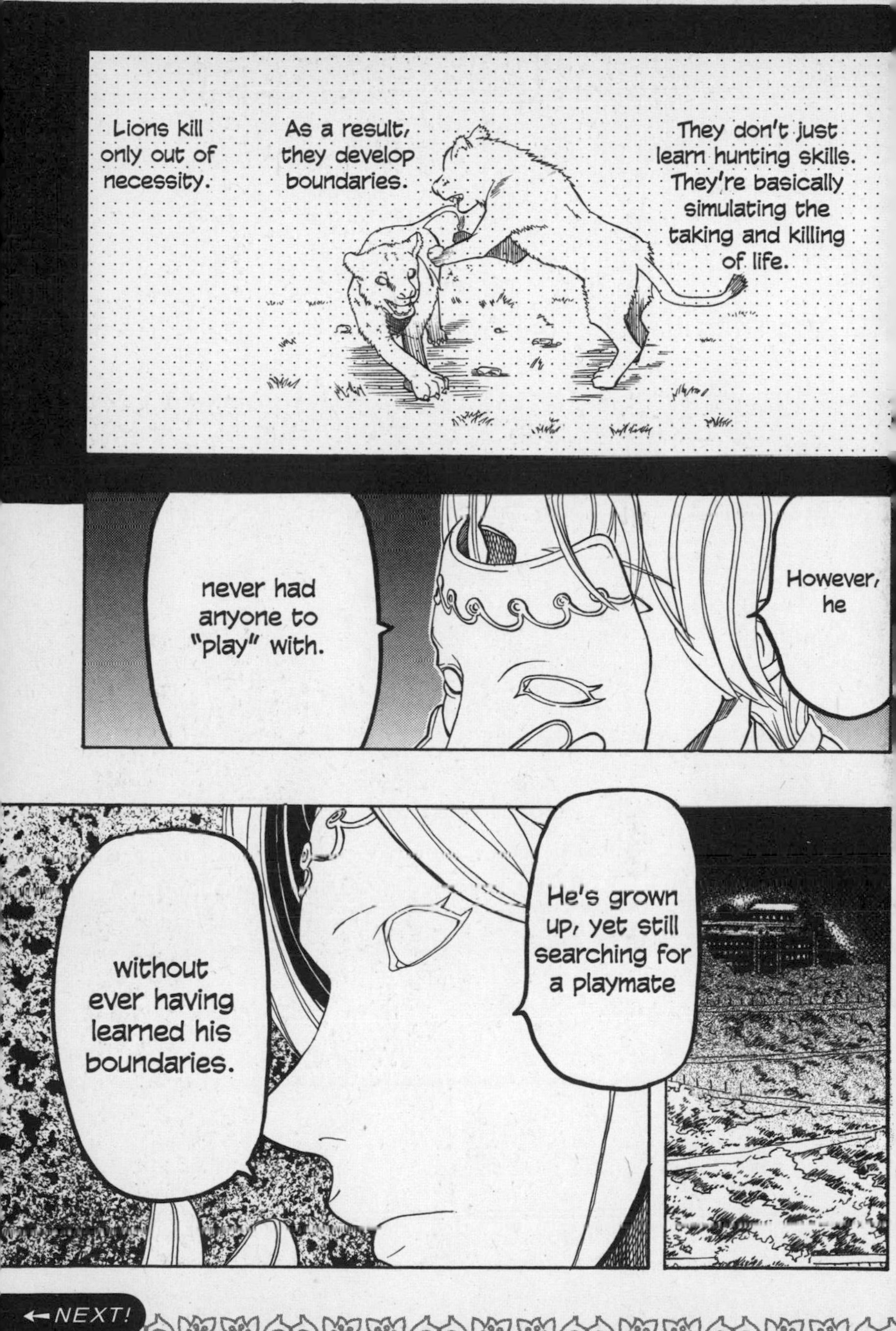
They don't just learn hunting skills. They're basically simulating the taking and killing of life.
As a result, they develop boundaries.
Lions kill only out of necessity.
However, he
never had anyone to "play" with.
He's grown up, yet still searching for a playmate
without ever having learned his boundaries.

← NEXT!

PumpkinScissors

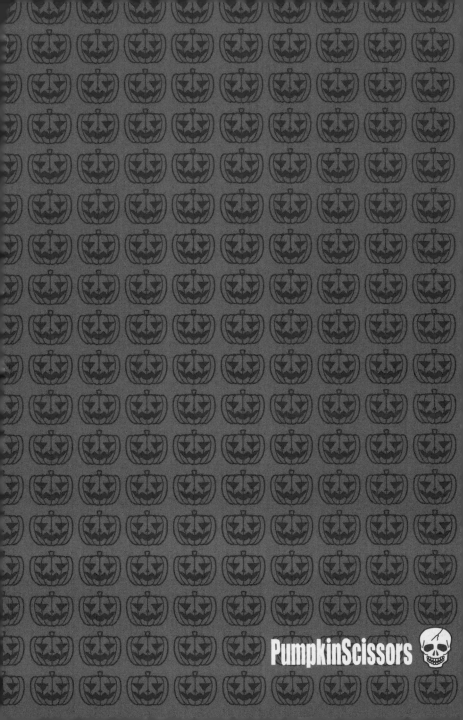

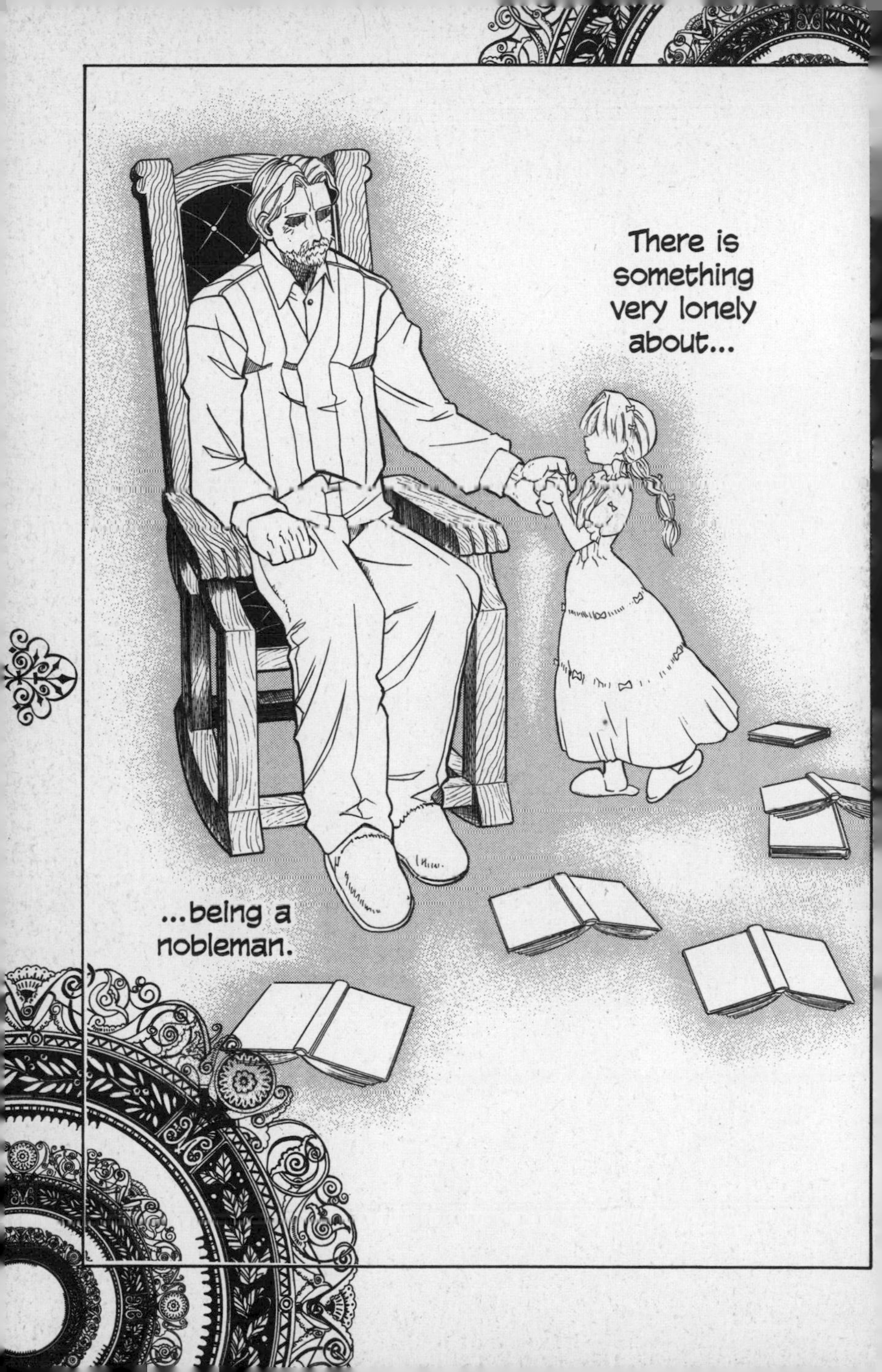
There is something very lonely about...
...being a nobleman.

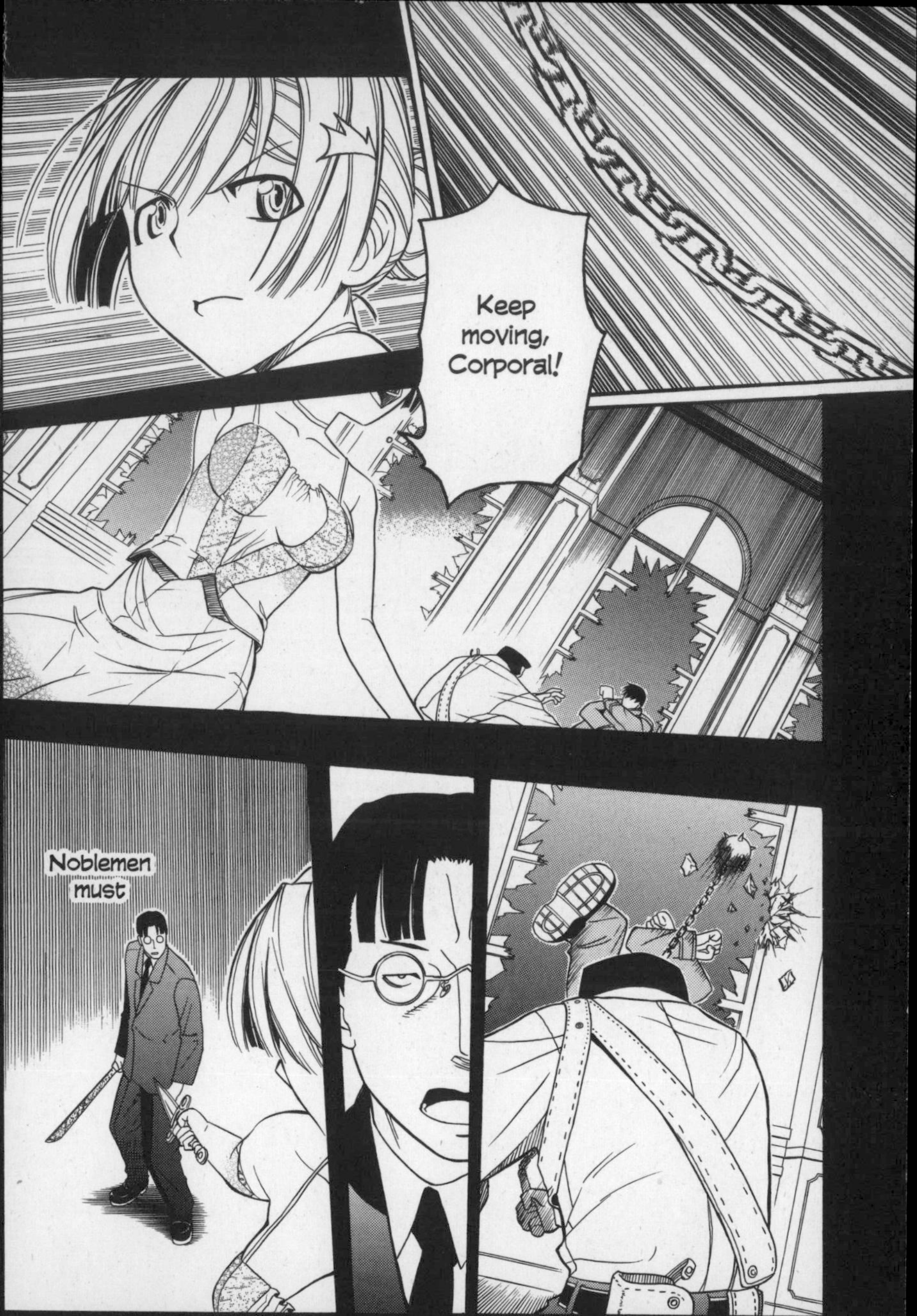
Keep moving, Corporal!
Noblemen must

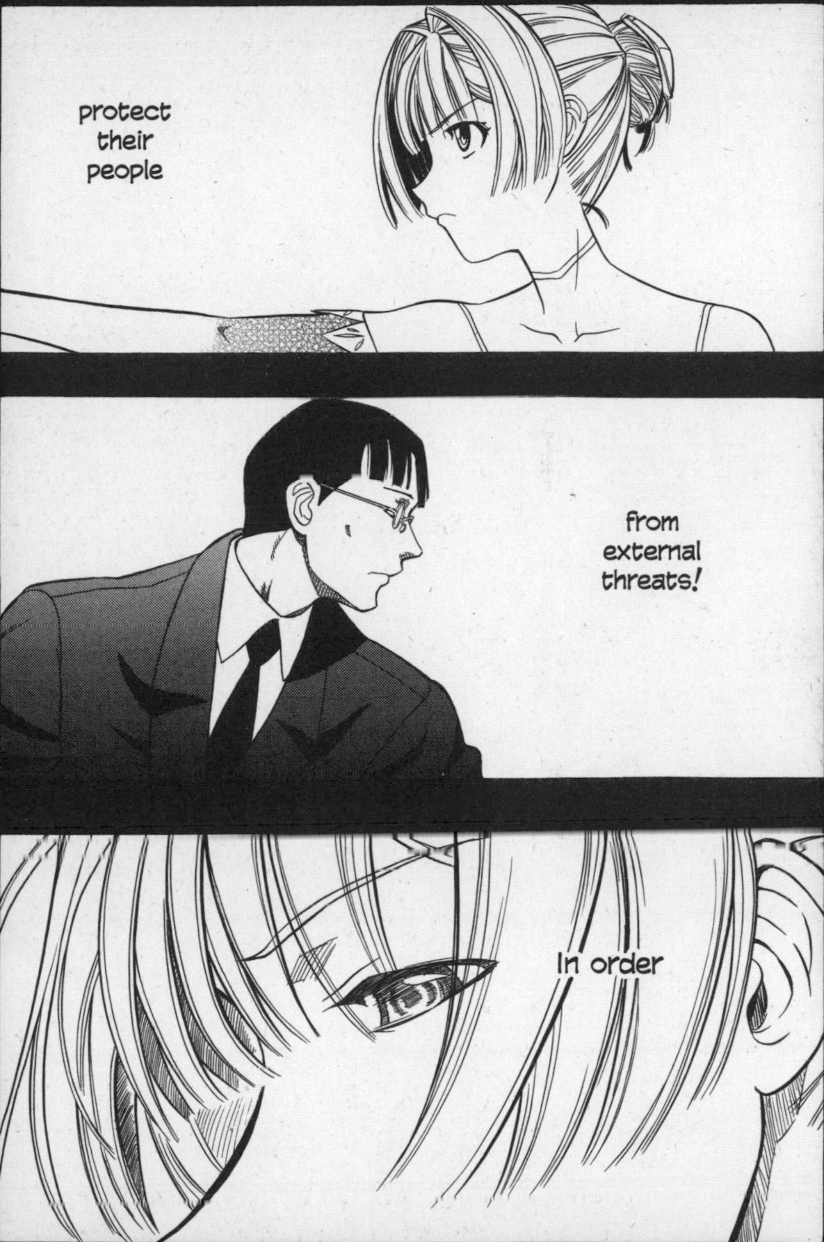
protect their people
from external threats!
In order

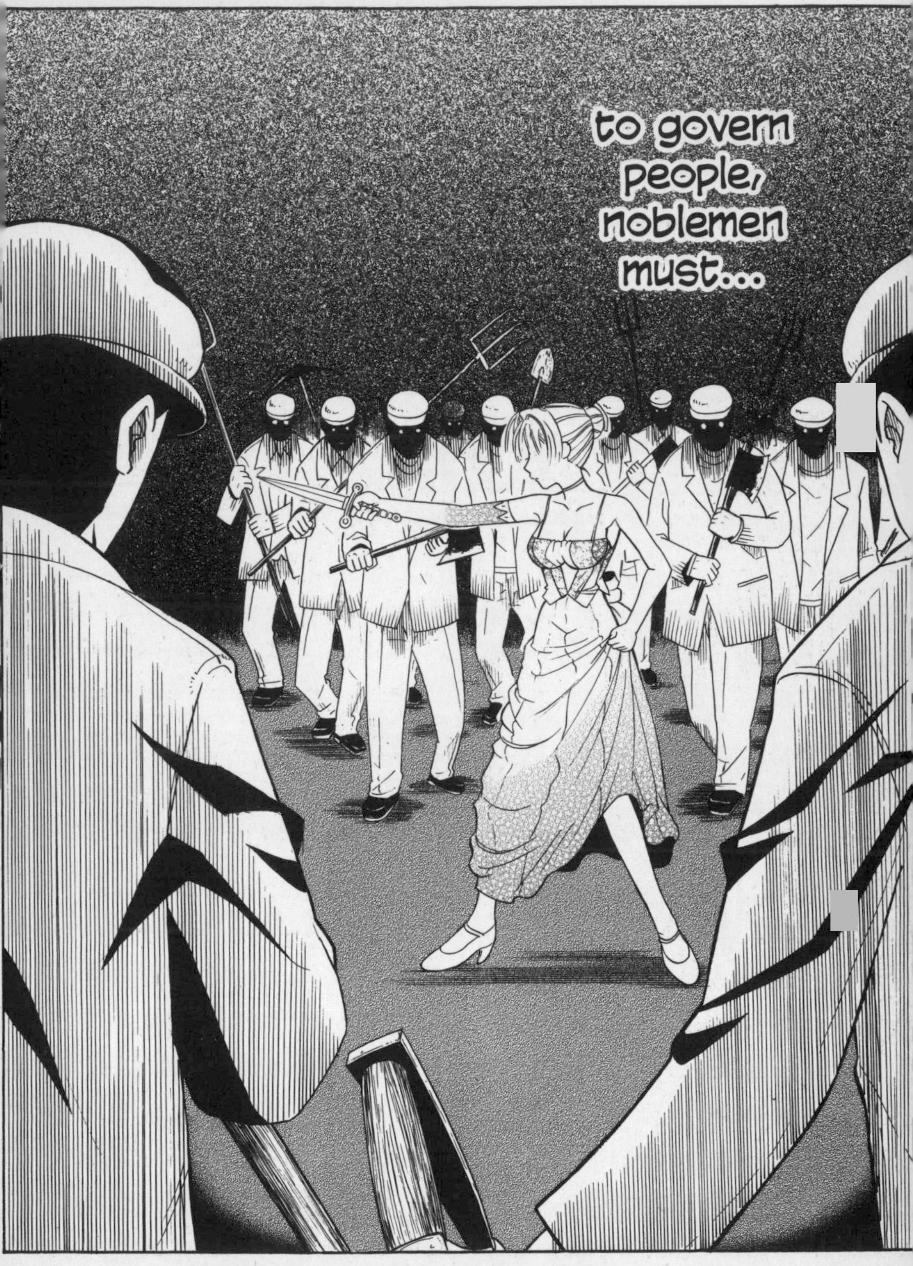
to govern people, noblemen must...

Episode 13 Trick in Treat ~ The Lonely Scale

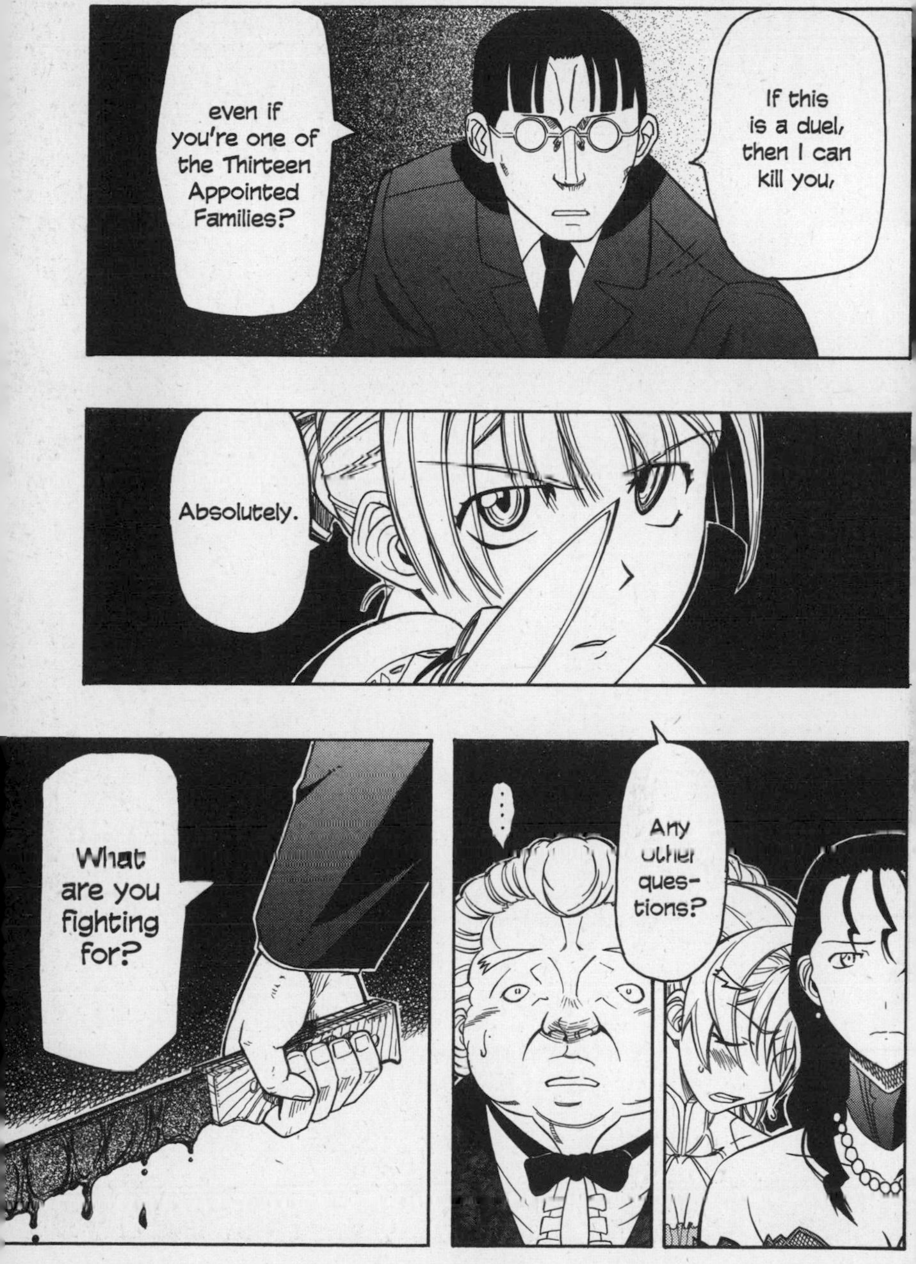
If this is a duel, then I can kill you,
even if you're one of the Thirteen Appointed Families?
Absolutely.
Any other questions?
...
What are you fighting for?

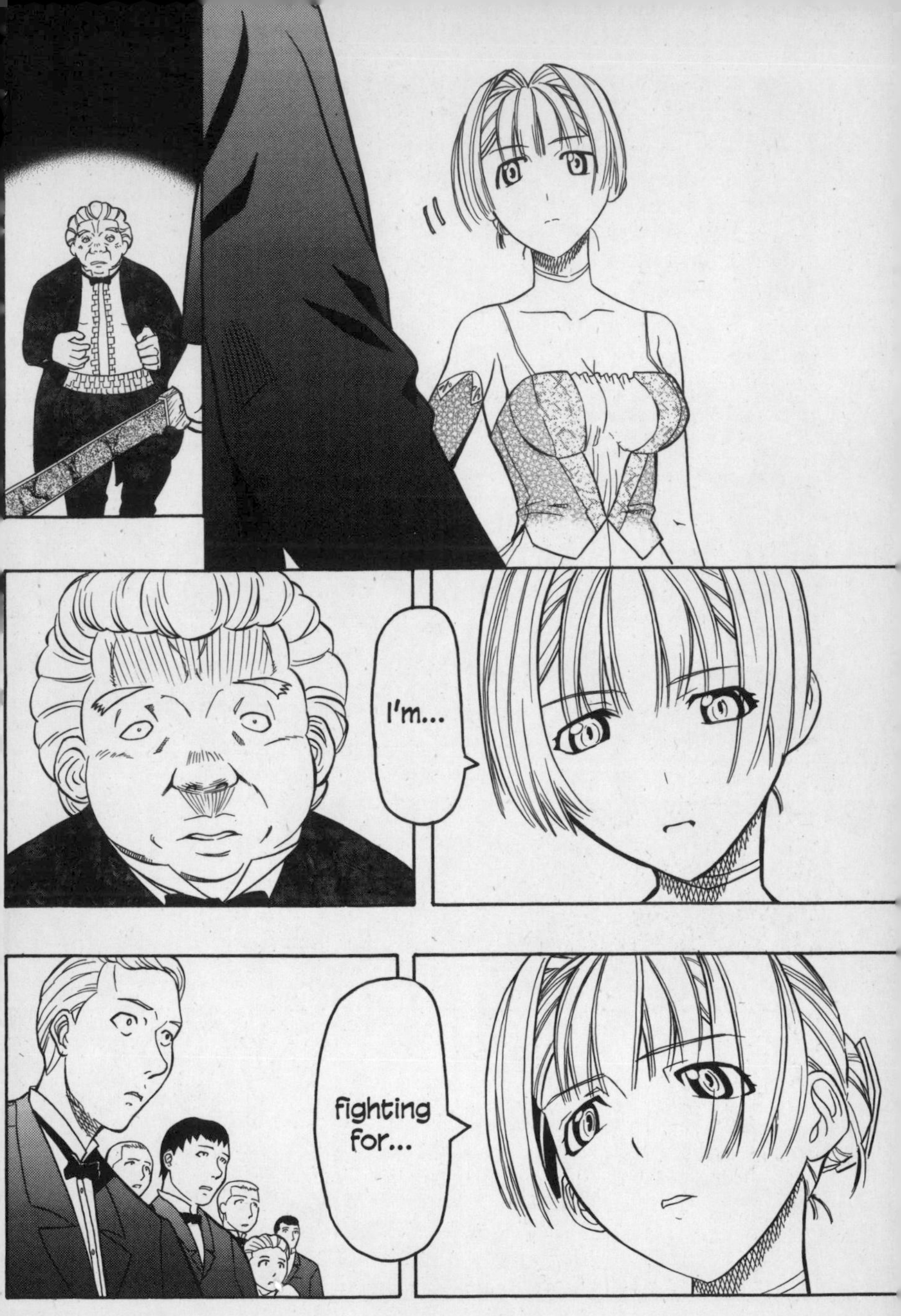
I'm...
fighting for...

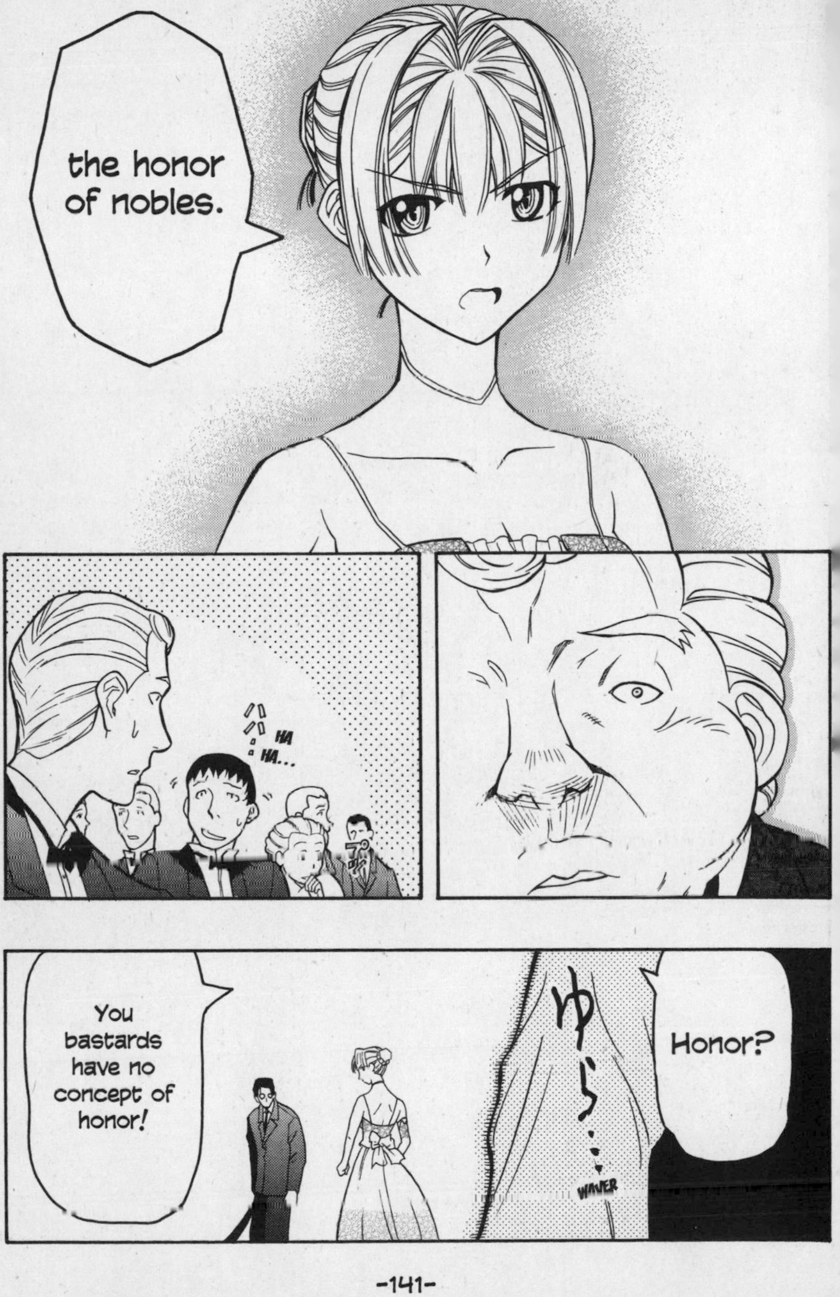
the honor of nobles.
HA HA...
Honor?
ゆら
WAVER
You bastards have no concept of honor!

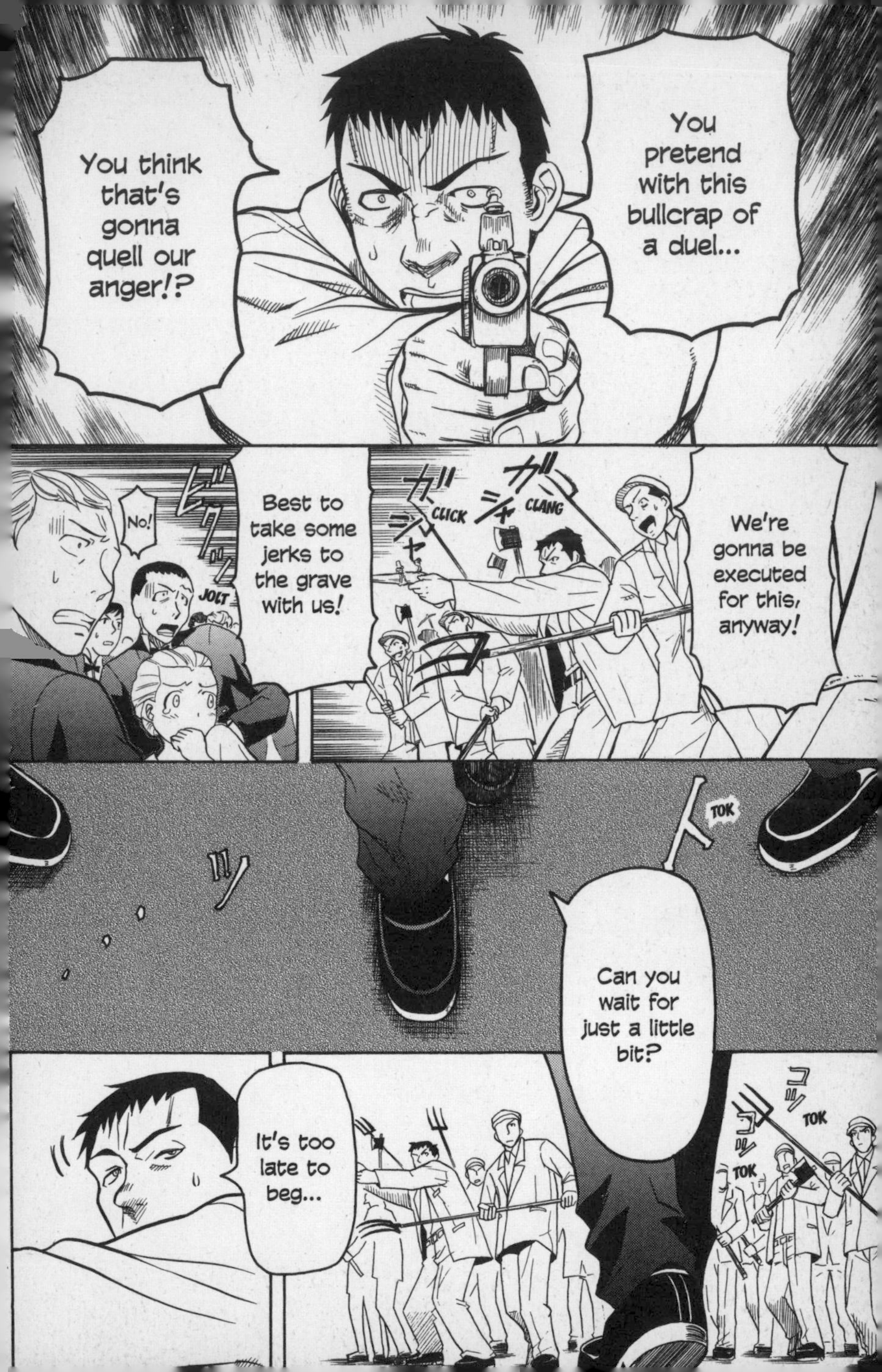
You pretend with this bullcrap of a duel...
You think that's gonna quell our anger!?
We're gonna be executed for this, anyway!
CLANG
CLICK
Best to take some jerks to the grave with us!
JOLT
No!
TOK
Can you wait for just a little bit?
TOK
TOK
It's too late to beg...

What?

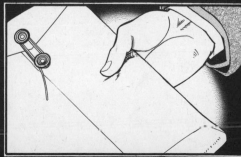

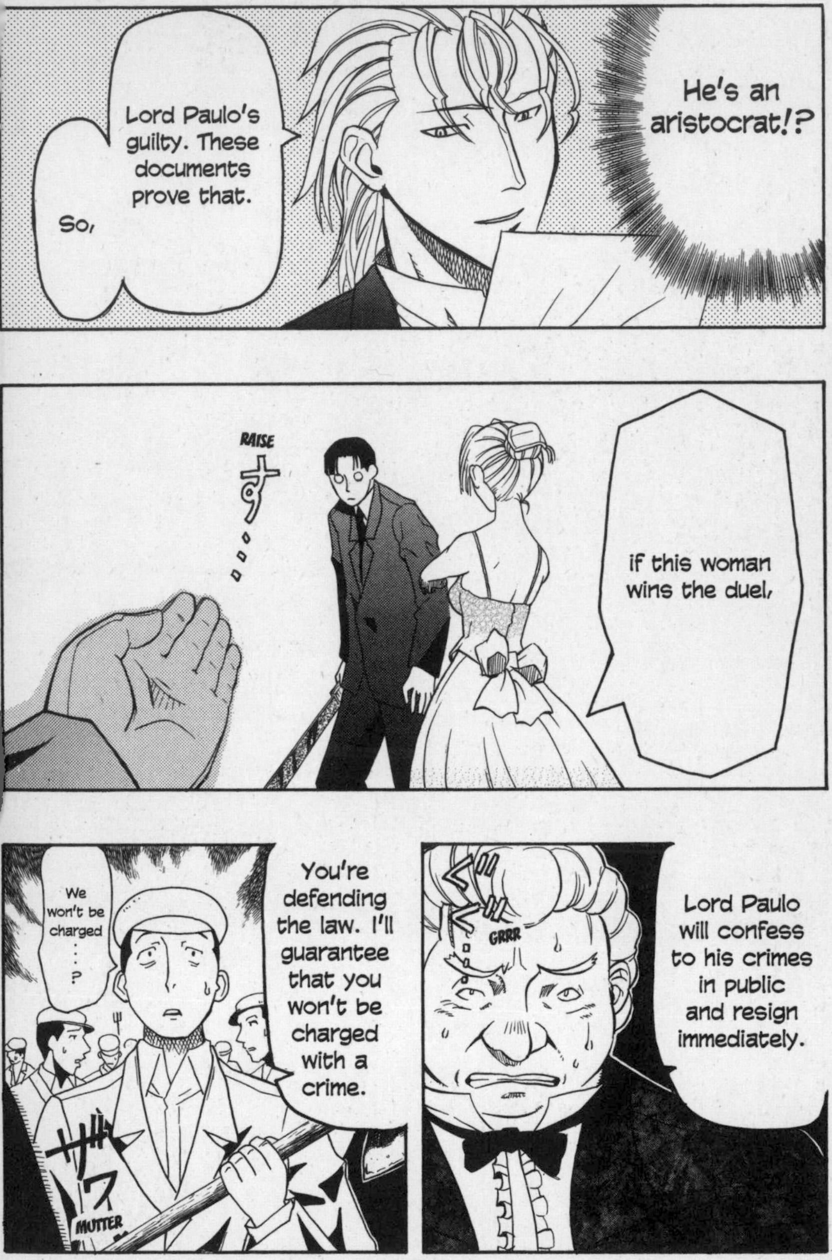
He's an aristocrat!?
Lord Paulo's guilty. These documents prove that.
So,
if this woman wins the duel,
RAISE
Lord Paulo will confess to his crimes in public and resign immediately.
GRRR
You're defending the law. I'll guarantee that you won't be charged with a crime.
We won't be charged...?
MUTTER

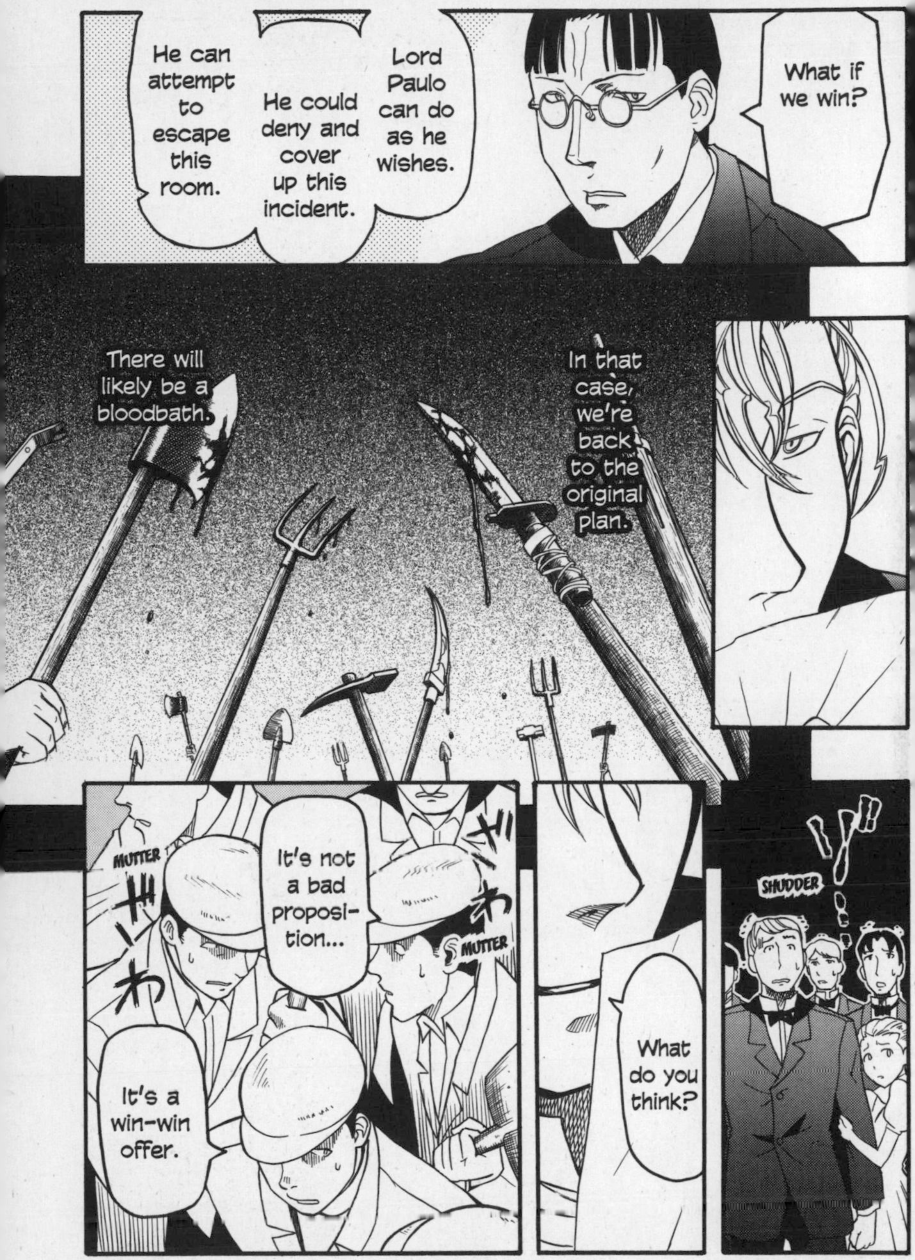
What if we win?
Lord Paulo can do as he wishes.
He could deny and cover up this incident.
He can attempt to escape this room.
In that case, we're back to the original plan.
There will likely be a bloodbath.
SHUDDER
What do you think?
MUTTER
It's not a bad proposition...
MUTTER
It's a win-win offer.

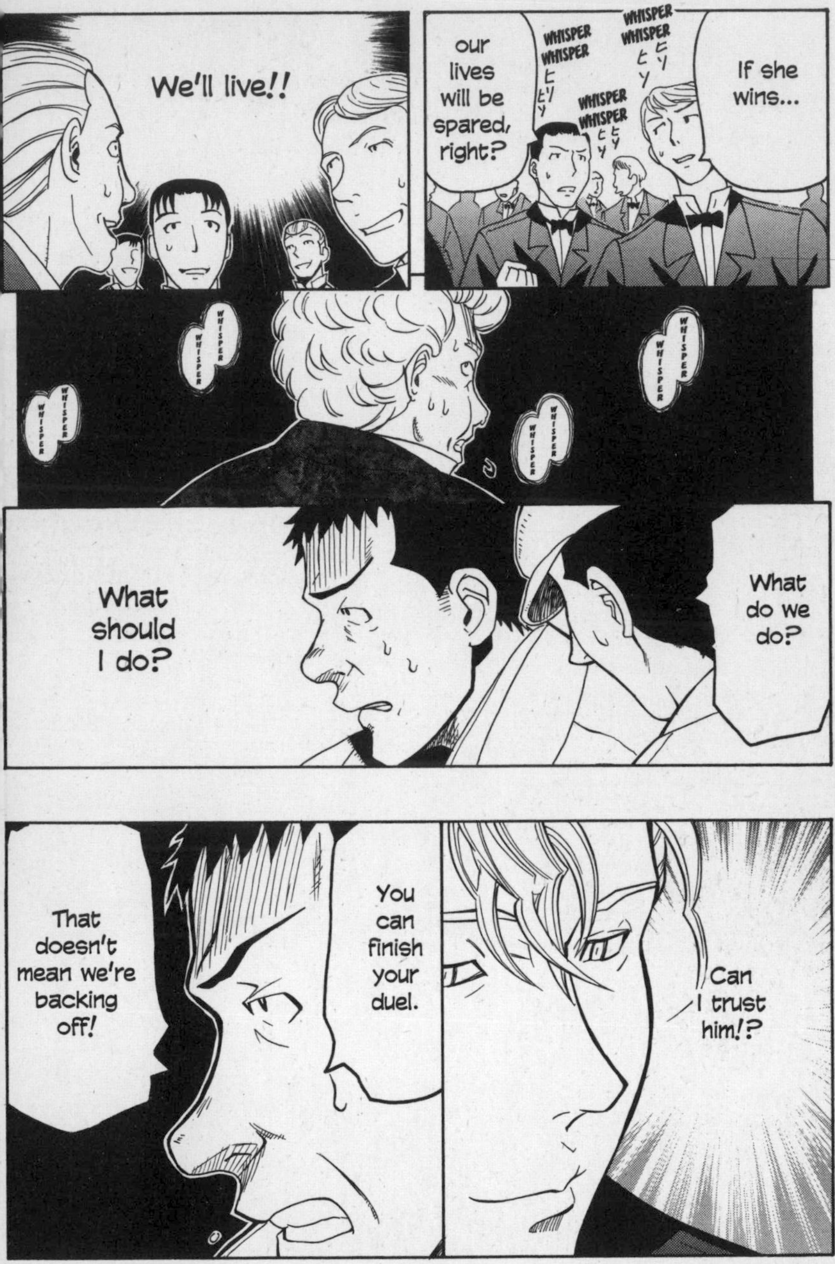
If she wins...
WHISPER WHISPER
WHISPER WHISPER
WHISPER WHISPER
our lives will be spared, right?
We'll live!!
WHISPER WHISPER
WHISPER WHISPER
WHISPER WHISPER
WHISPER WHISPER
What do we do?
What should I do?
Can I trust him!?
You can finish your duel.
That doesn't mean we're backing off!

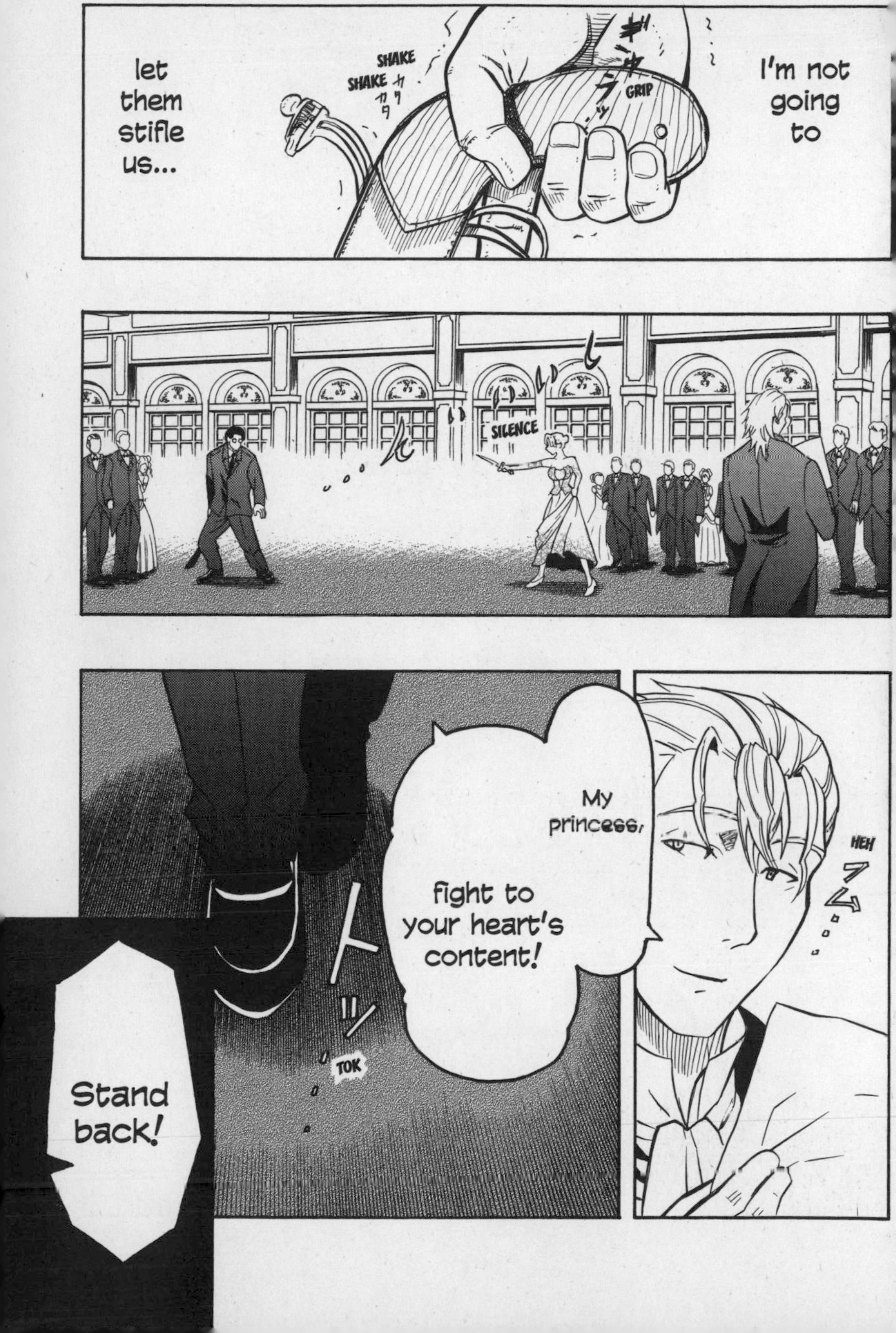
I'm not going to
GRIP
SHAKE
SHAKE
let them stifle us...
SILENCE
HEH
My princess, fight to your heart's content!
TOK
Stand back!

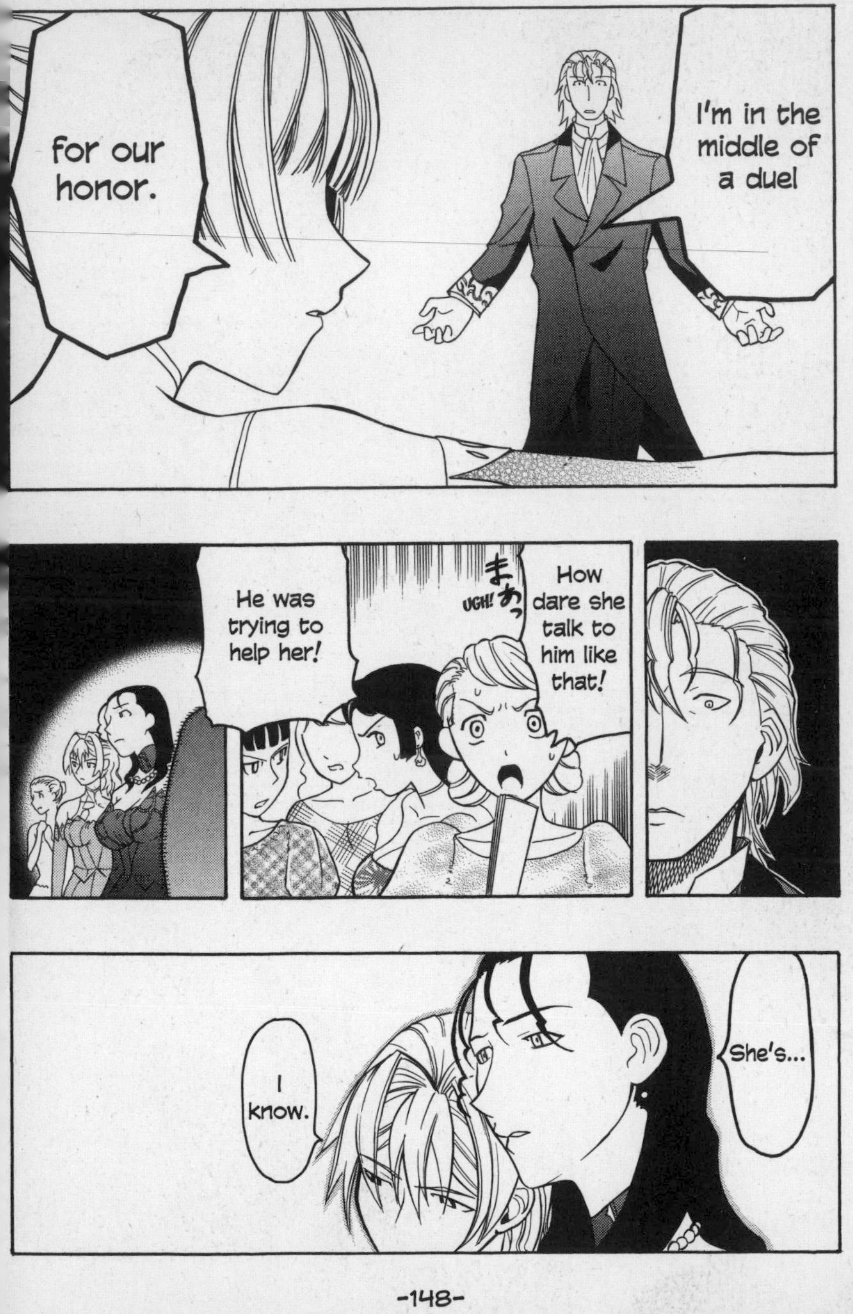
I'm in the middle of a duel
for our honor.
How dare she talk to him like that!
まあっ
UGH!
He was trying to help her!
She's...
I know.

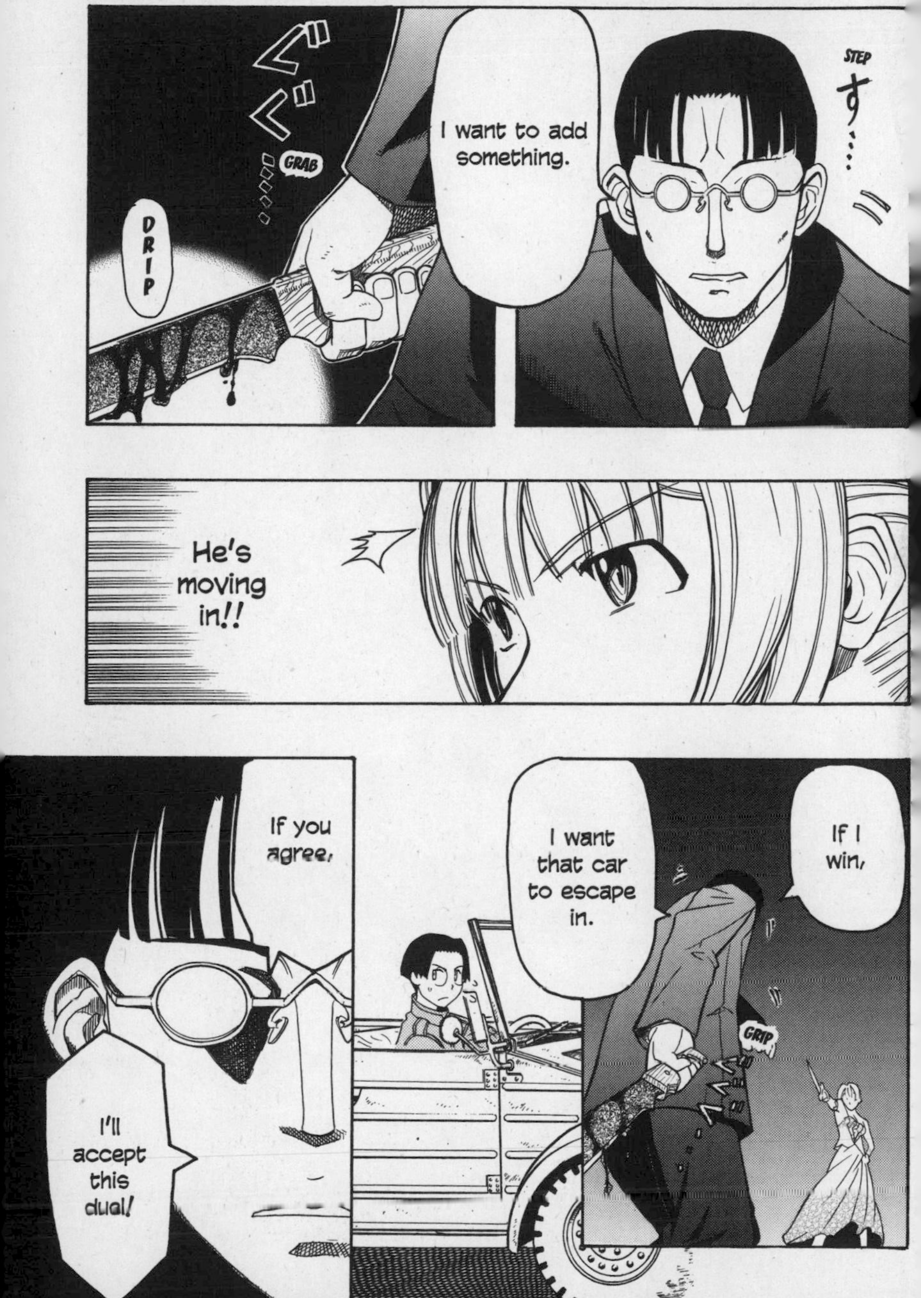
STEP
I want to add something.
GRAB
DRIP
He's moving in!!
If I win,
I want that car to escape in.
GRIP
If you agree,
I'll accept this dual!

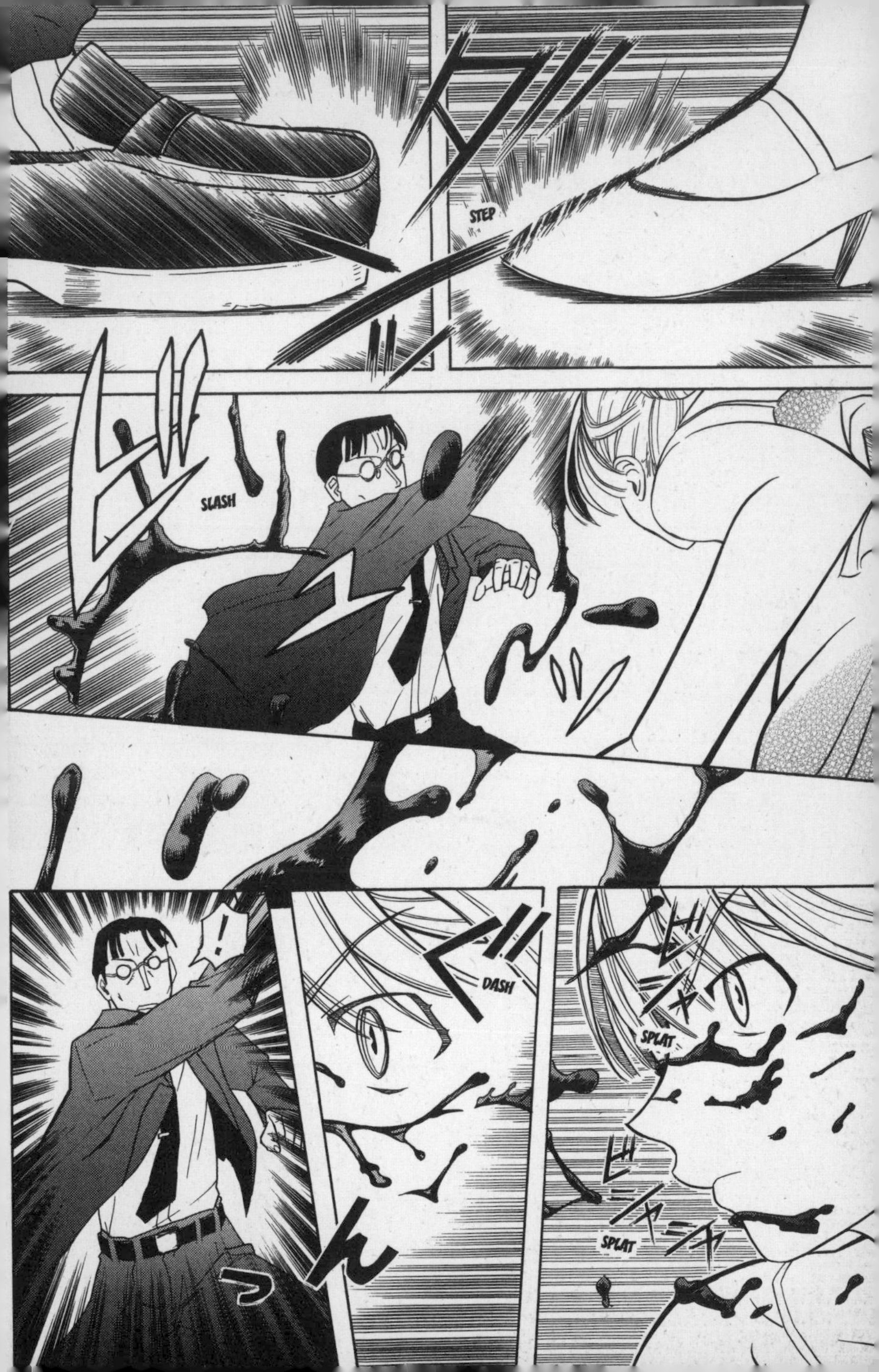
STEP
SLASH
SPLAT
SPLAT
DASH
!

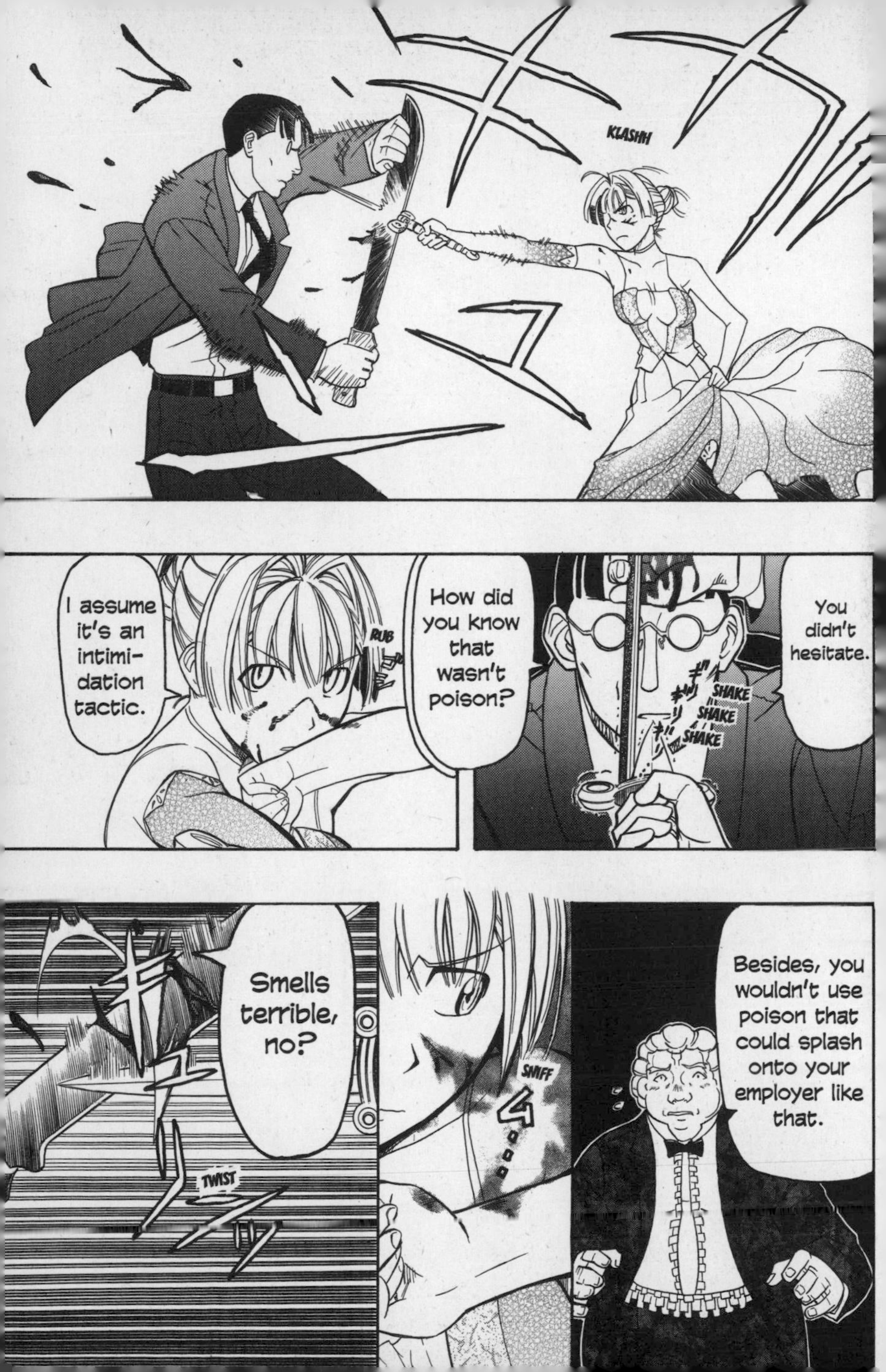
KLASHH
You didn't hesitate.
SHAKE
SHAKE
SHAKE
How did you know that wasn't poison?
RUB
I assume it's an intimi-dation tactic.
Besides, you wouldn't use poison that could splash onto your employer like that.
SNIFF
Smells terrible, no?
TWIST

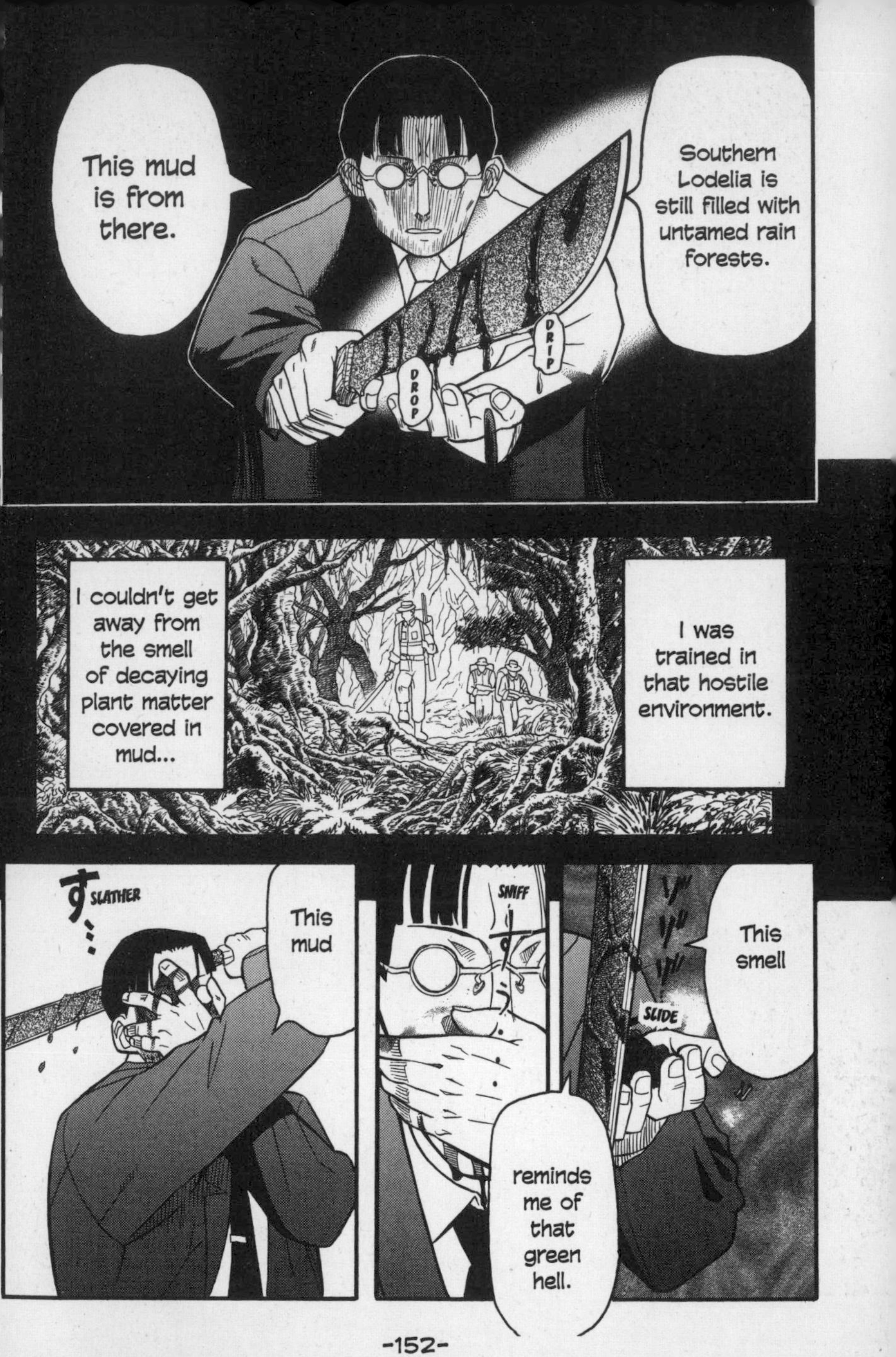
Southern Lodelia is still filled with untamed rain forests.
This mud is from there.
DRIP
DROP
I was trained in that hostile environment.
I couldn't get away from the smell of decaying plant matter covered in mud...
SLIDE
This smell
SNIFF
reminds me of that green hell.
す SLATHER
This mud

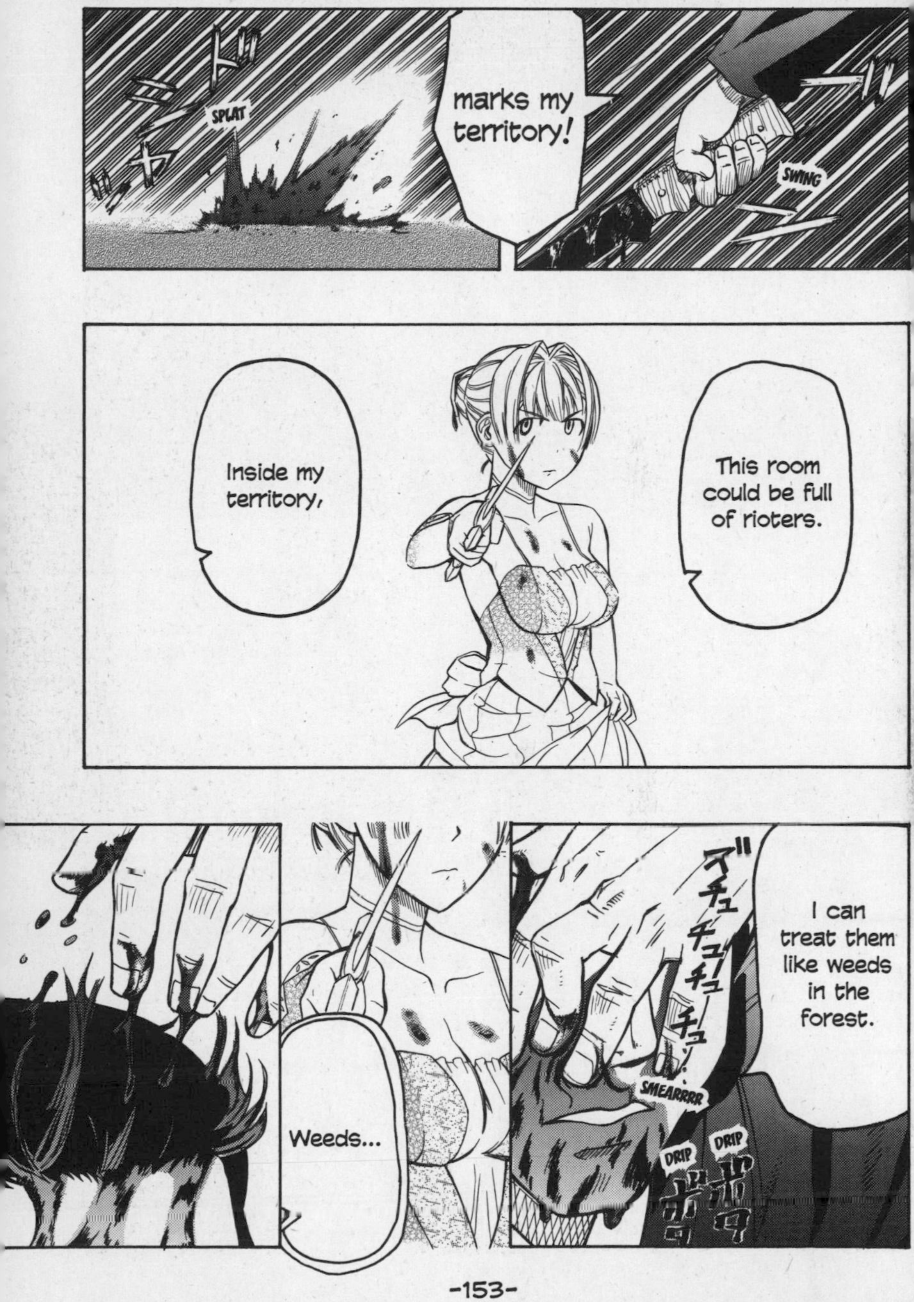
marks my territory!
SWING
SPLAT
This room could be full of rioters.
Inside my territory,
I can treat them like weeds in the forest.
SMEARRRR
DRIP
DRIP
Weeds...

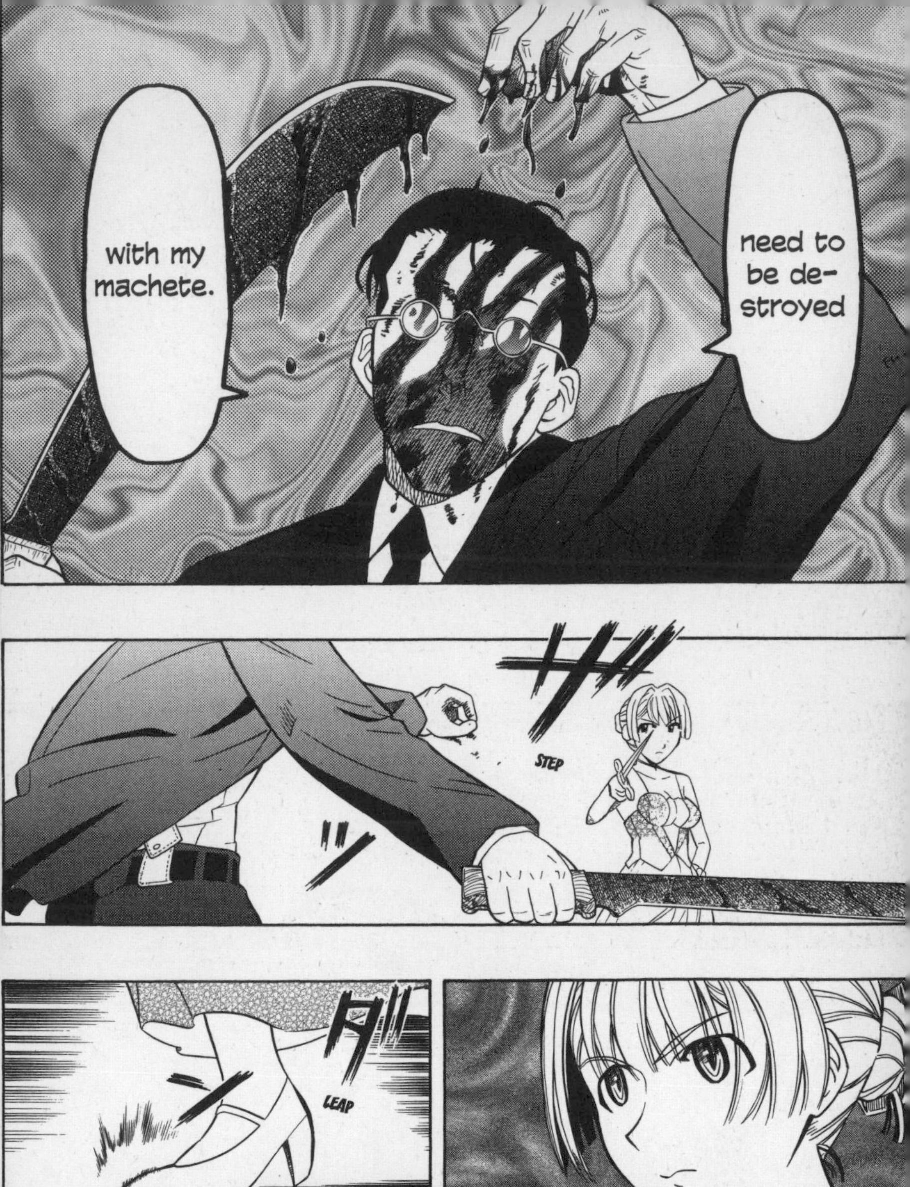
need to be de-stroyed
with my machete.
STEP
LEAP

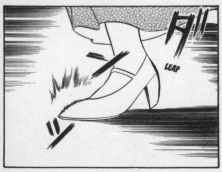

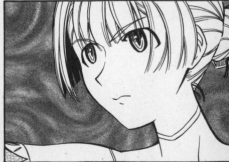

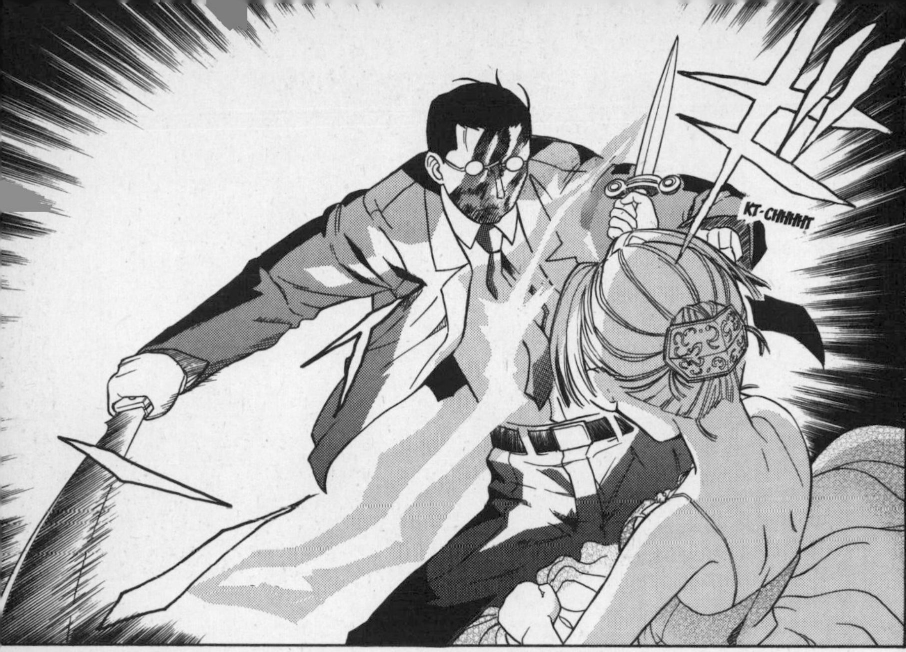
KT-CHHHHT

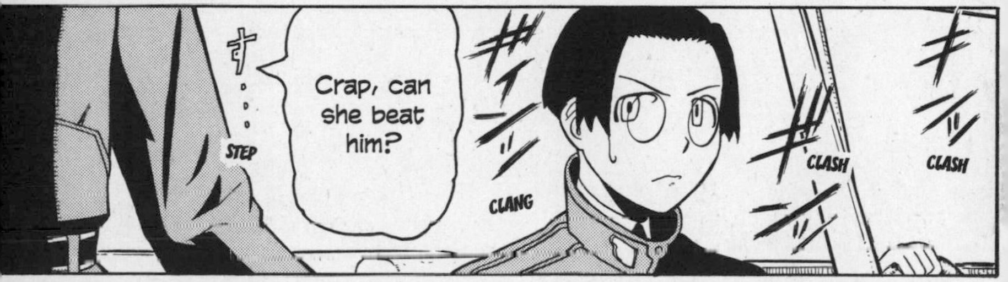
CLASH
CLASH
CLANG
Crap, can she beat him?
す...
STEP

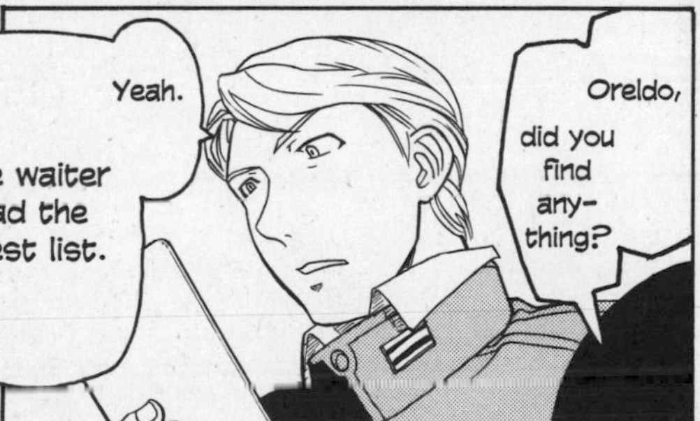
Oreldo, did you find any-thing?
Yeah.
The waiter had the guest list.

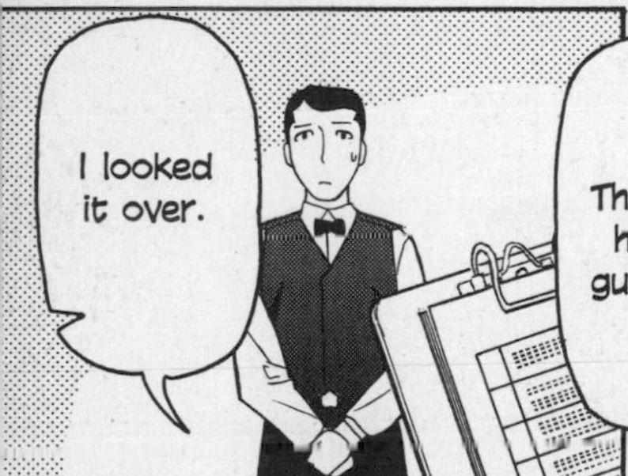
I looked it over.

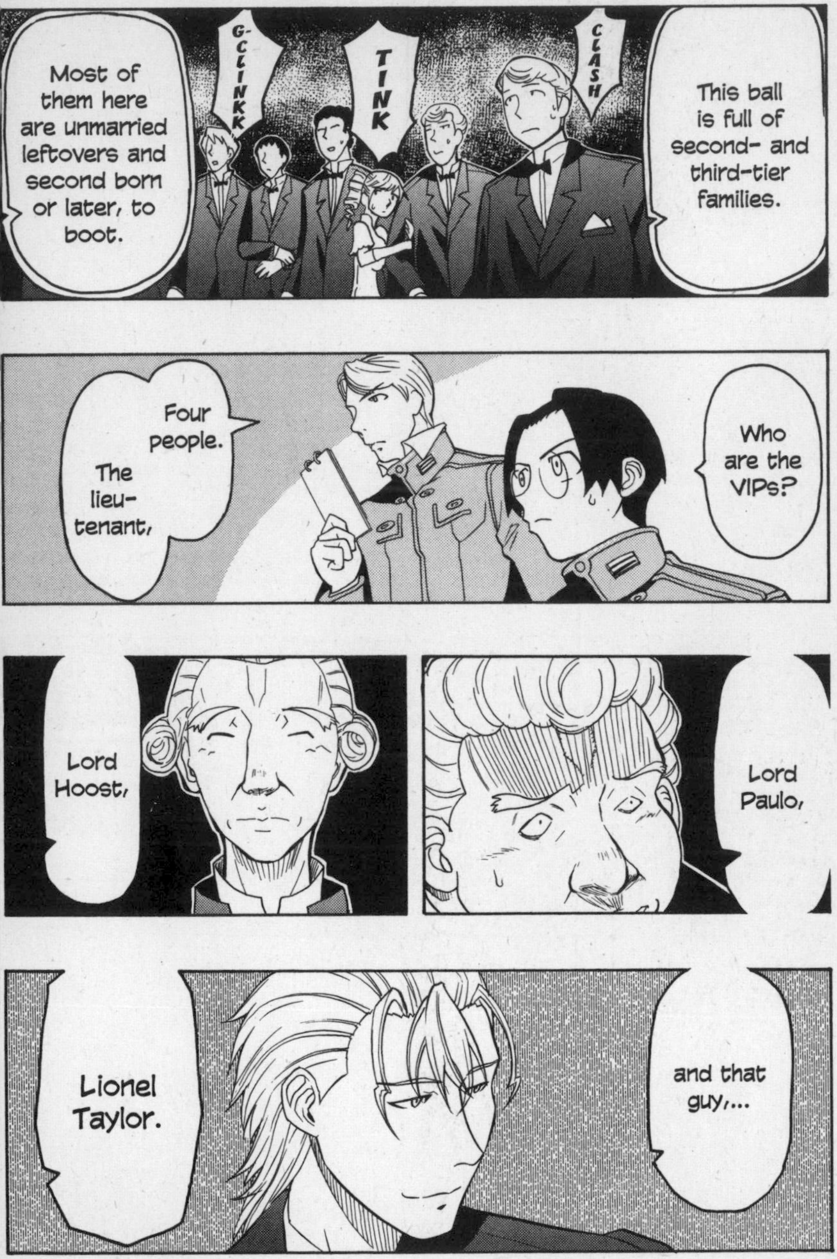
This ball is full of second- and third-tier families.
CLASH
TINK
G-CLINKK
Most of them here are unmarried leftovers and second born or later, to boot.
Who are the VIPs?
Four people.
The lieu-tenant,
Lord Paulo,
Lord Hoost,
and that guy,...
Lionel Taylor.

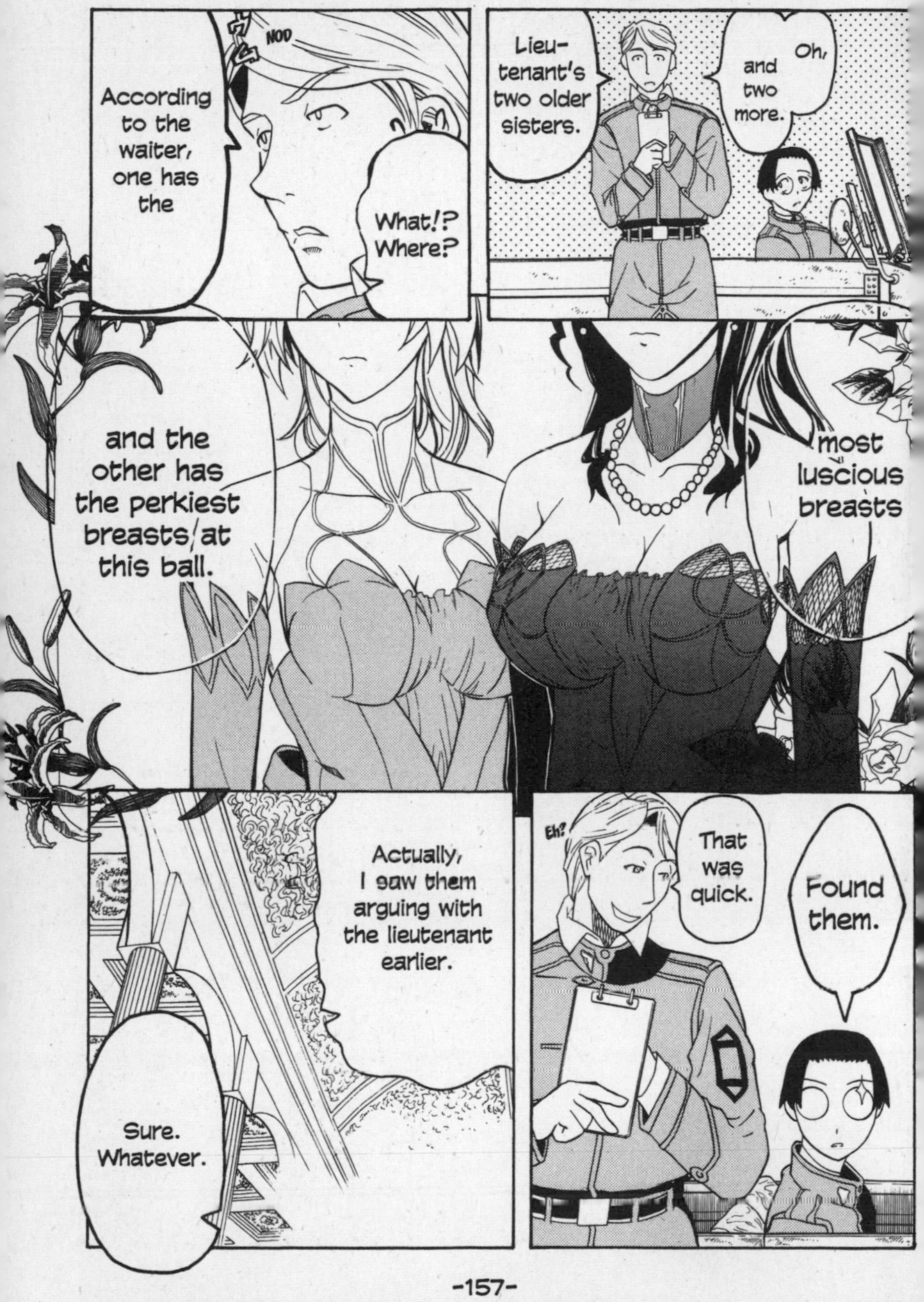
Oh, and two more.
Lieutenant's two older sisters.
NOD
What!? Where?
According to the waiter, one has the
most luscious breasts
and the other has the perkiest breasts at this ball.
Found them.
Eh?
That was quick.
Actually, I saw them arguing with the lieutenant earlier.
Sure. Whatever.

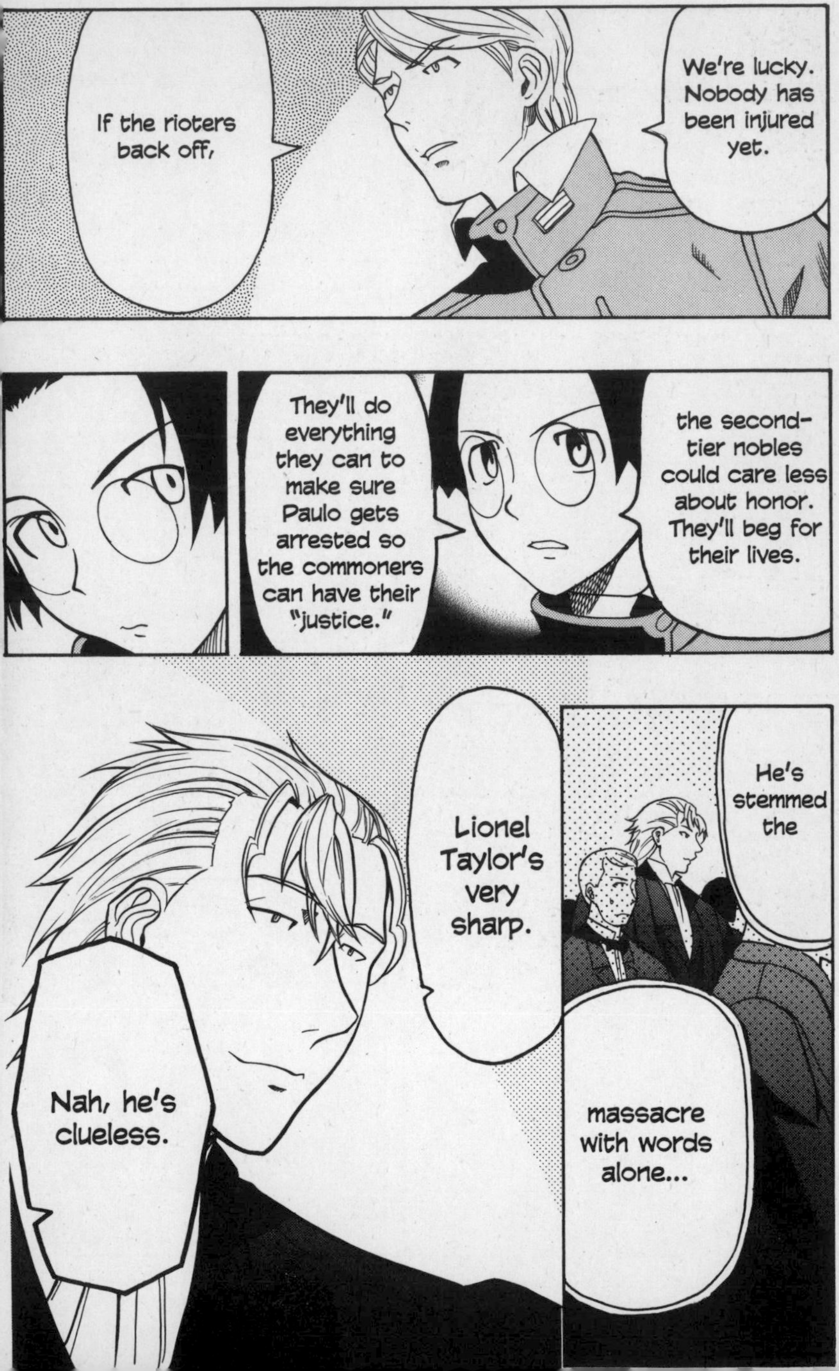
We're lucky. Nobody has been injured yet.
If the rioters back off,
the second-tier nobles could care less about honor. They'll beg for their lives.
They'll do everything they can to make sure Paulo gets arrested so the commoners can have their "justice."
He's stemmed the
massacre with words alone...
Lionel Taylor's very sharp.
Nah, he's clueless.

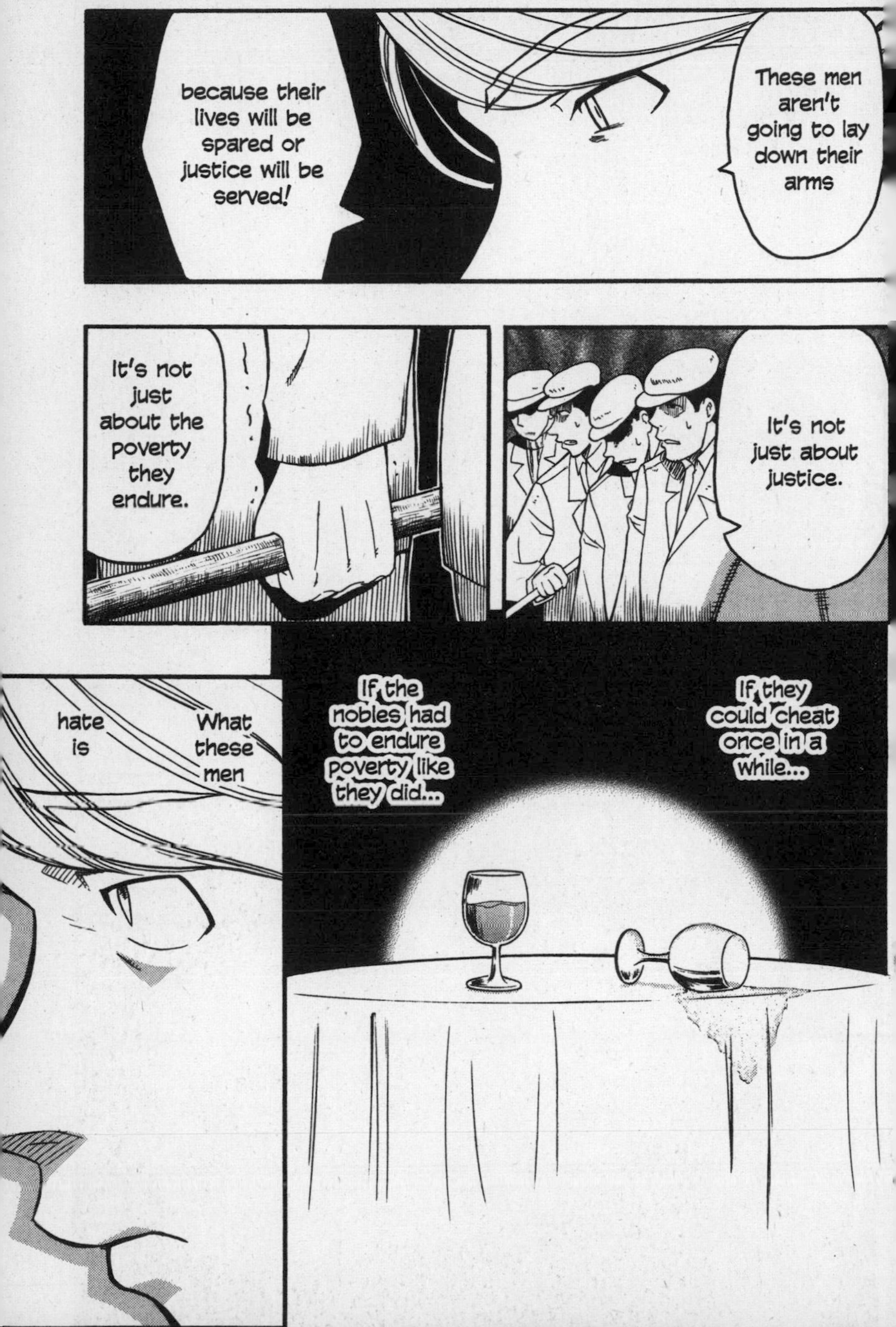
These men aren't going to lay down their arms
because their lives will be spared or justice will be served!
It's not just about justice.
It's not just about the poverty they endure.
If they could cheat once in a while...
If the nobles had to endure poverty like they did...
What these men
hate is

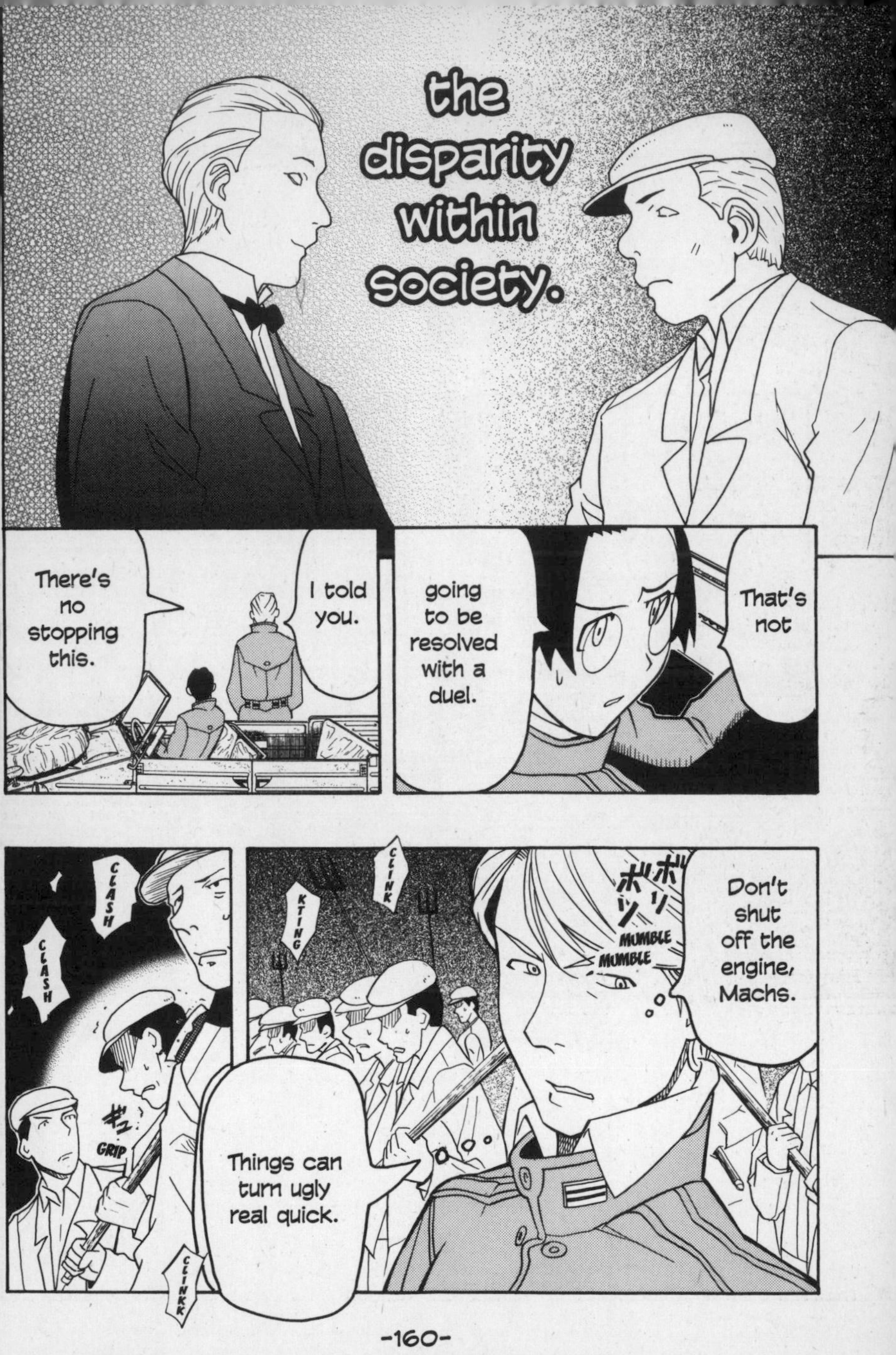

the disparity within society.
That's not
going to be resolved with a duel.
I told you.
There's no stopping this.
Don't shut off the engine, Machs.
MUMBLE
MUMBLE
CLINK
KTING
Things can turn ugly real quick.
CLASH
CLASH
GRIP
CLINKK

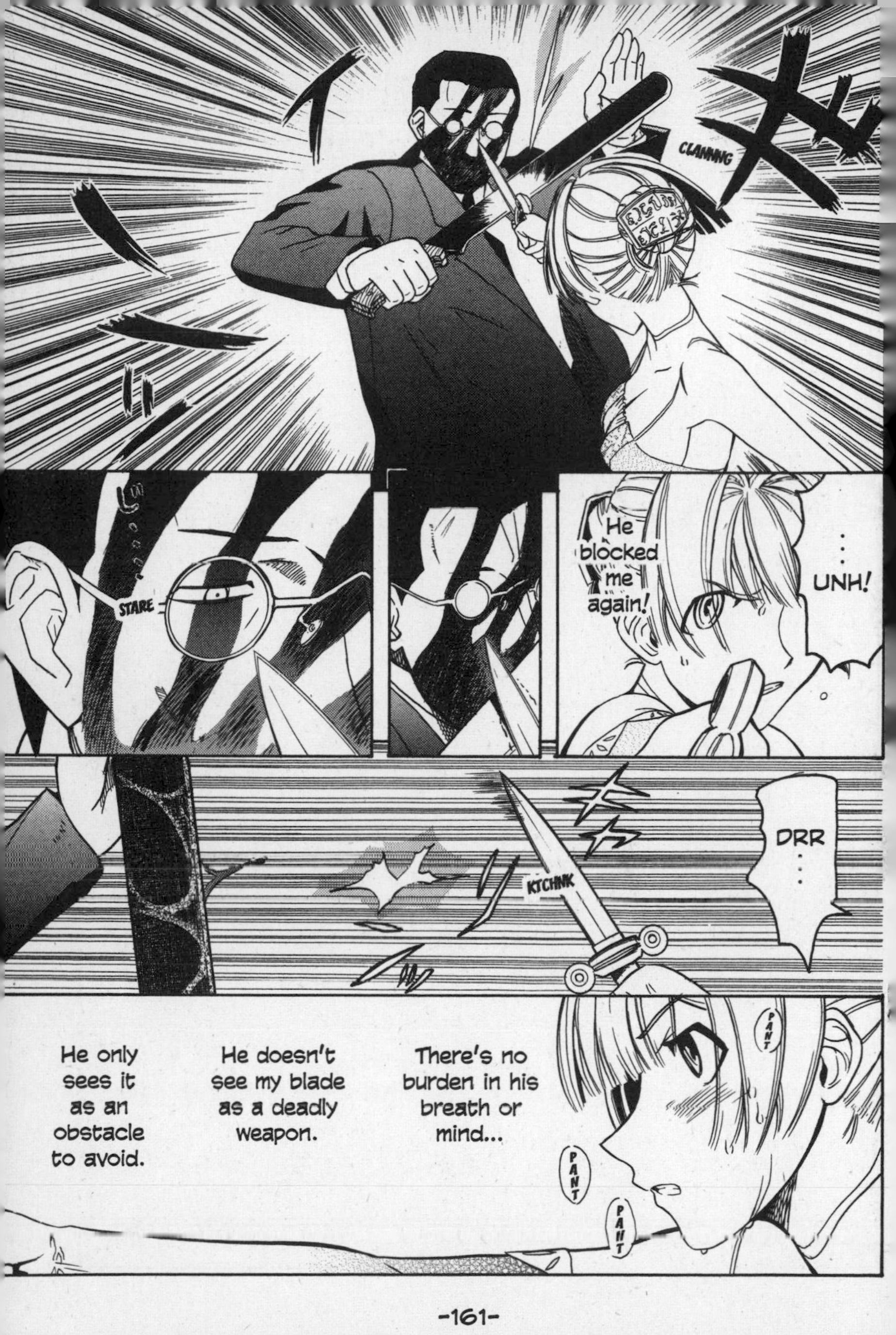
CLANNNG
...UNH!
He blocked me again!
STARE
DRR...
KTCHNK
PANT
There's no burden in his breath or mind...
He doesn't see my blade as a deadly weapon.
He only sees it as an obstacle to avoid.
PANT
PANT

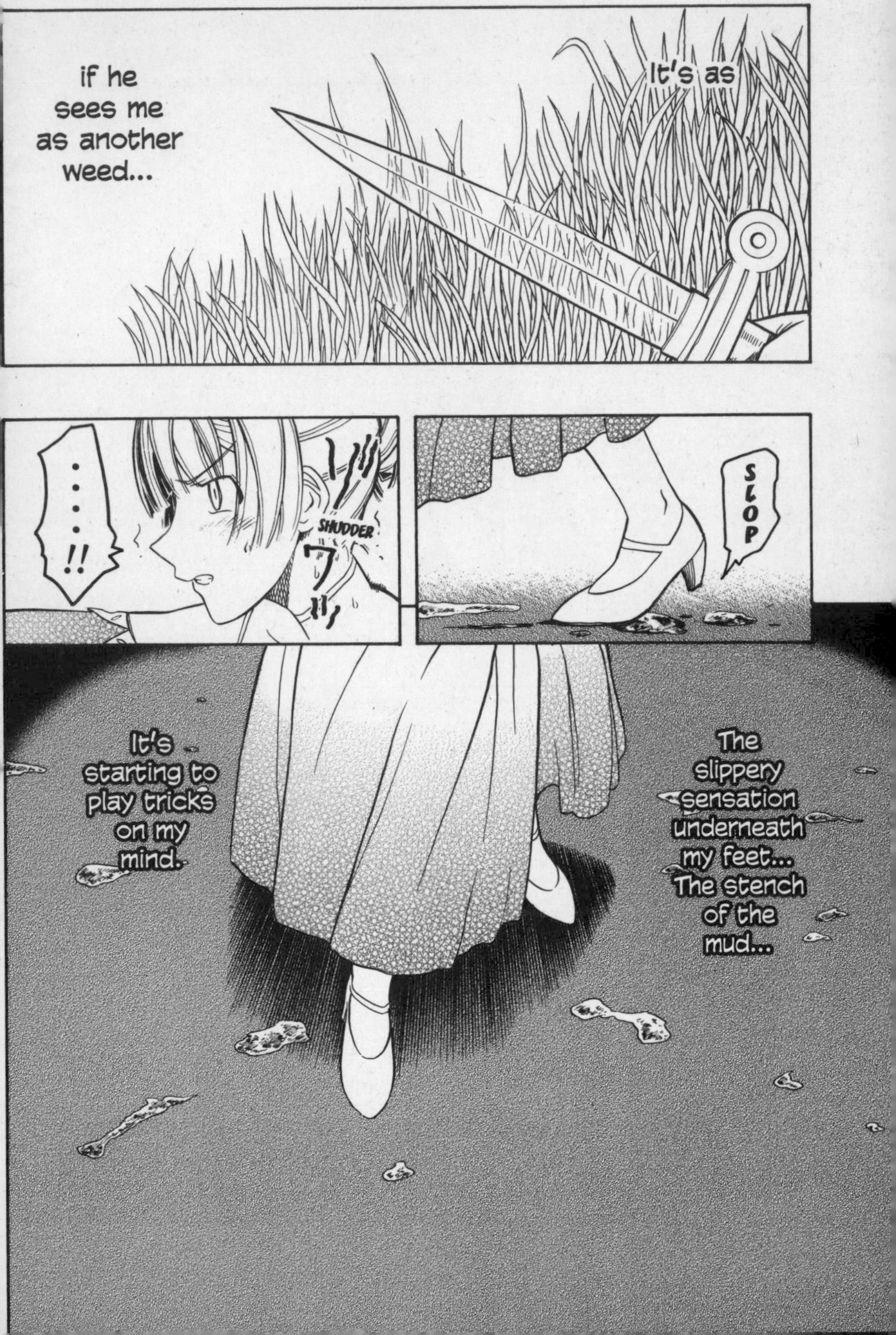
It's as
if he sees me as another weed...
SLOP
......!!
SHUDDER
The slippery sensation underneath my feet... The stench of the mud...
It's starting to play tricks on my mind.

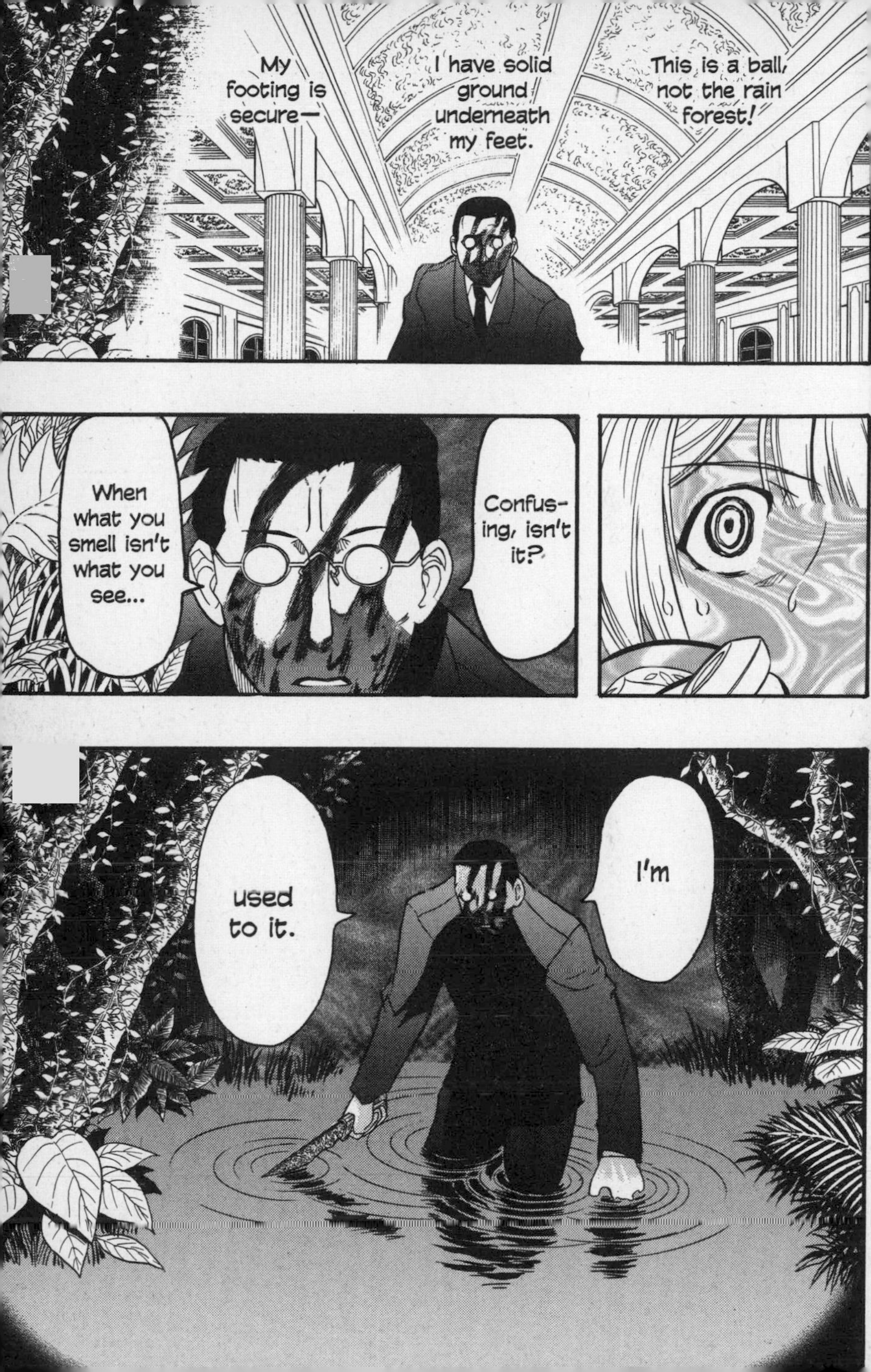
This is a ball, not the rain forest!
I have solid ground underneath my feet.
My footing is secure—
Confusing, isn't it?
When what you smell isn't what you see...
I'm
used to it.

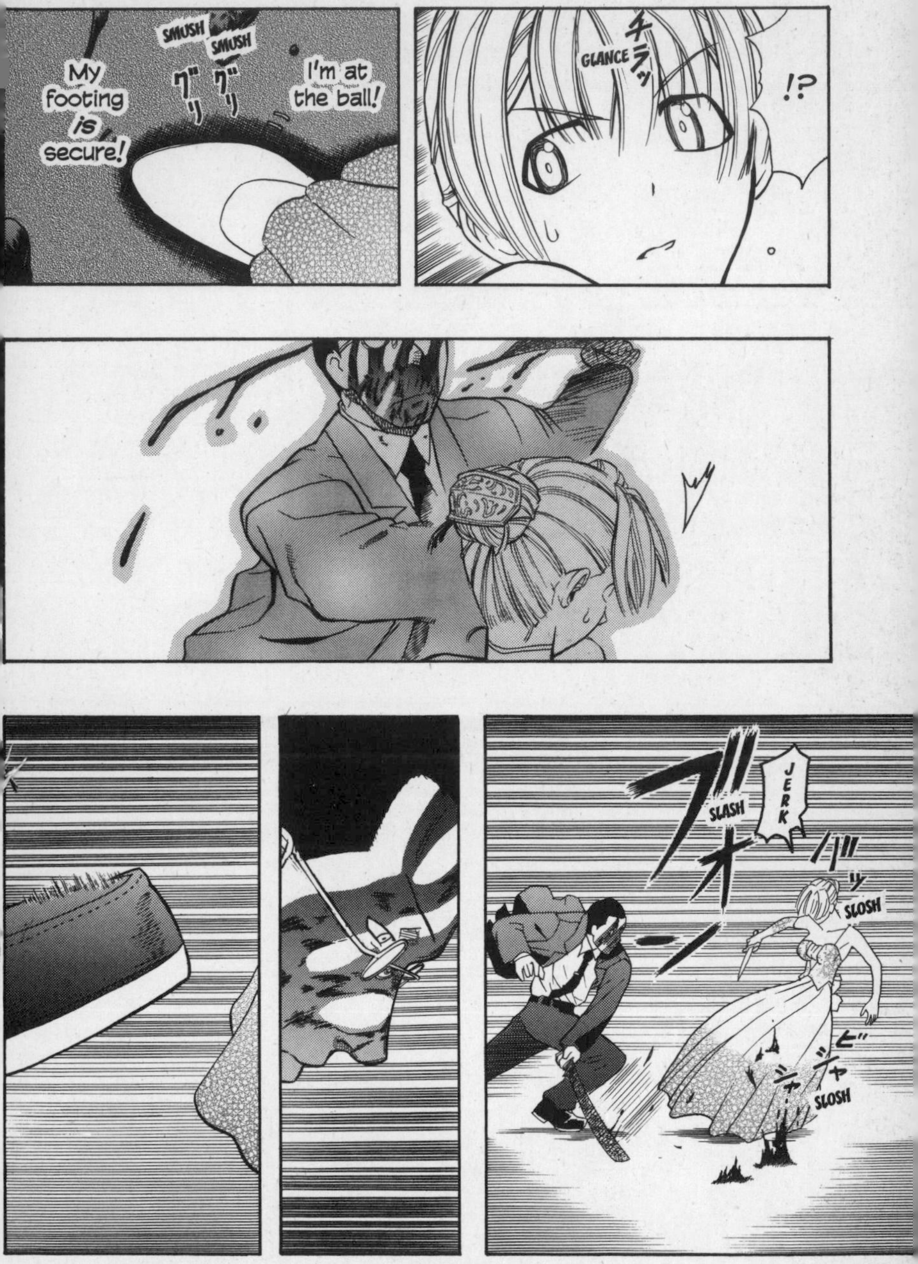
GLANCE
チラッ
!?
SMUSH
SMUSH
グリ
グリ
I'm at the ball!
My footing is secure!
JERK
SLASH
SLOSH
SLOSH

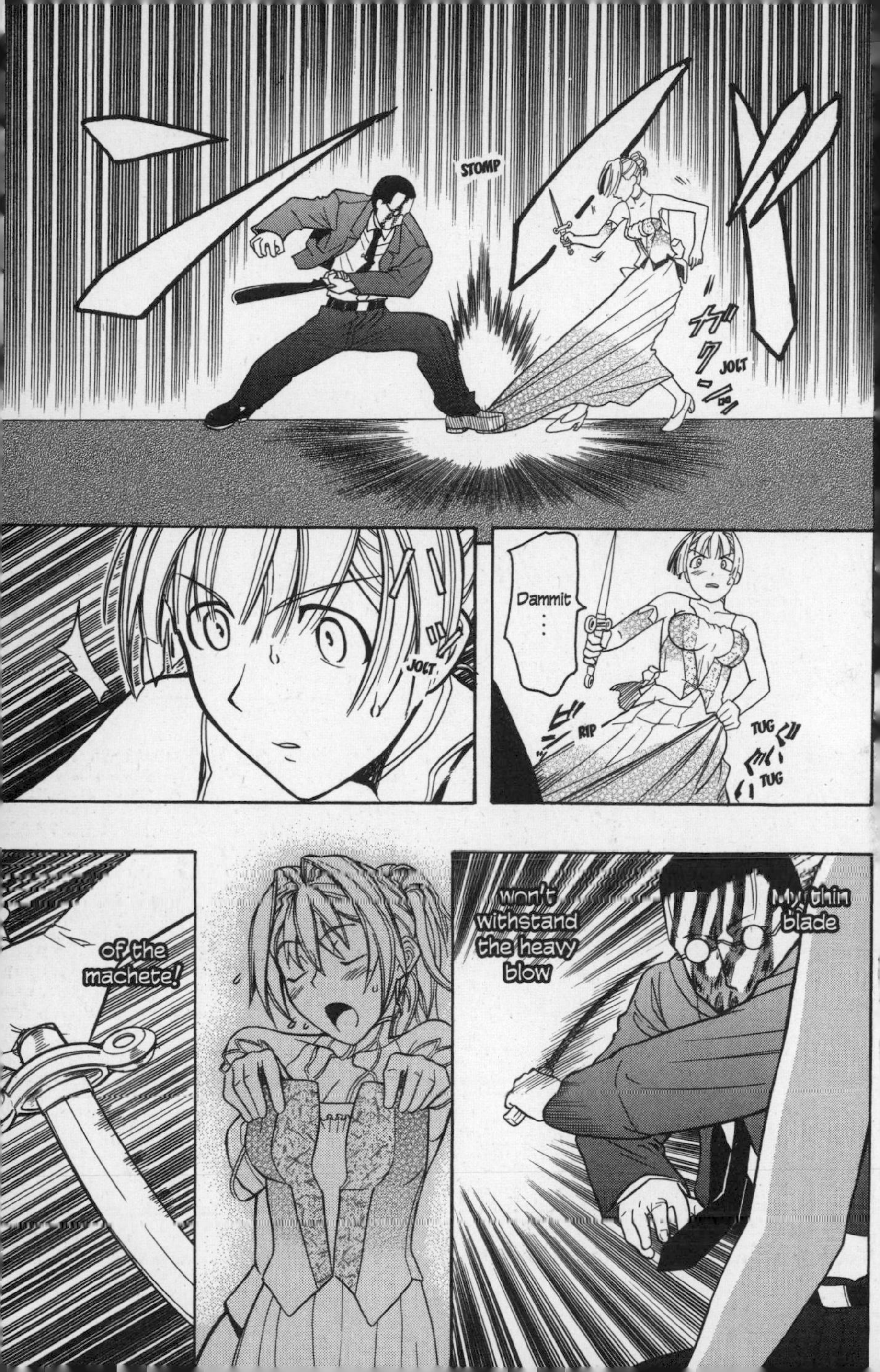
STOMP
JOLT
Dammit . . .
RIP
TUG
TUG
JOLT
My thin blade
won't withstand the heavy blow
of the machete!

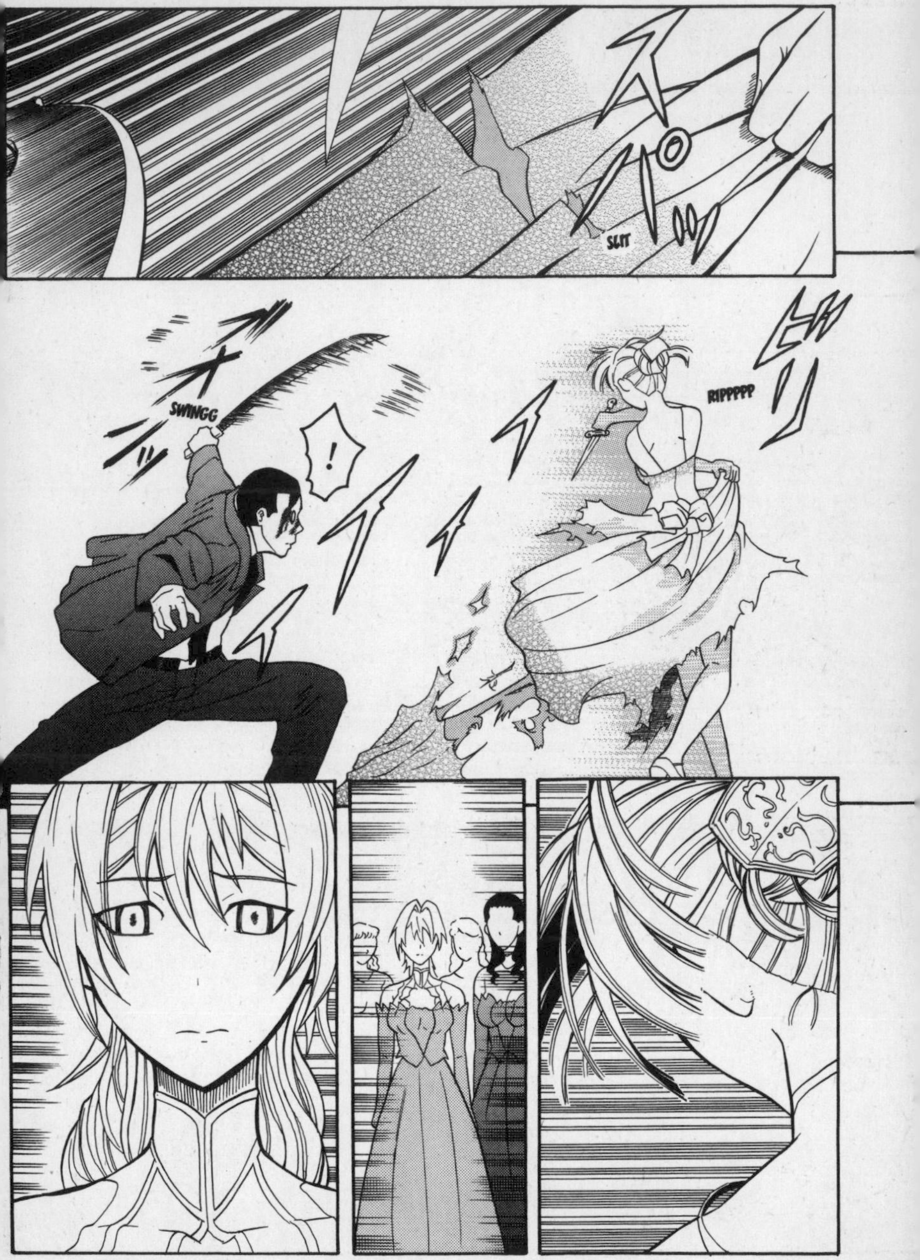
SLIT
RIPPPPP
!
SWINGG

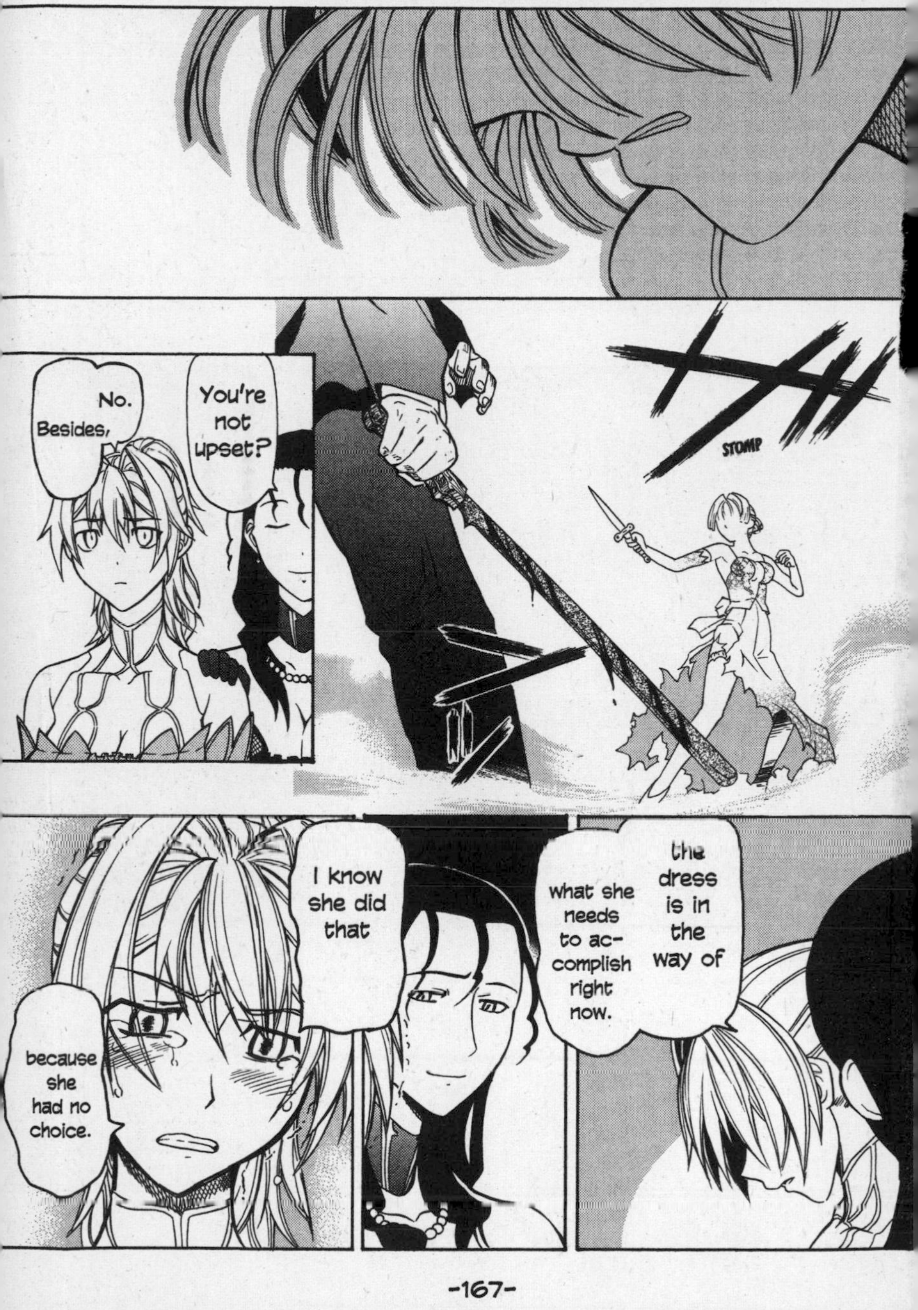
STOMP
You're not upset?
No. Besides,
the dress is in the way of
what she needs to accomplish right now.
I know she did that
because she had no choice.

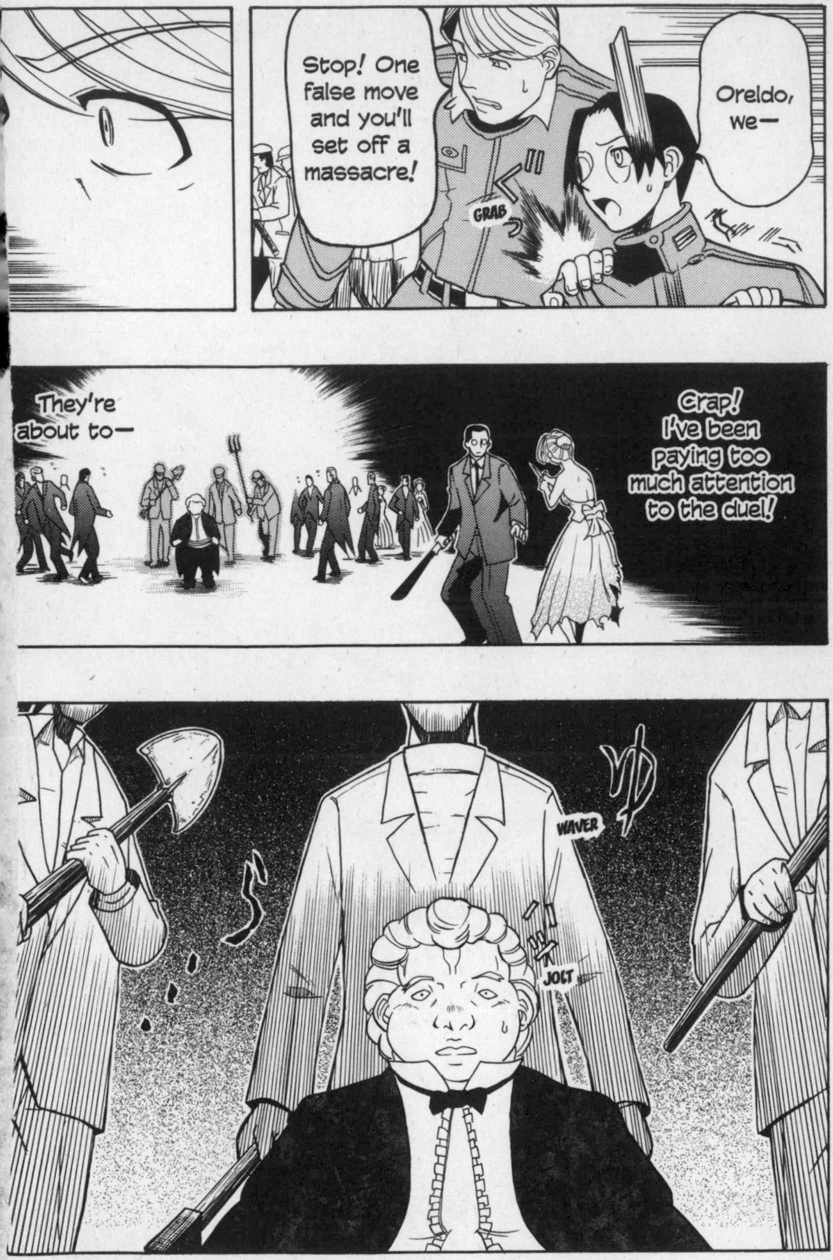
Oreldo, we—
Stop! One false move and you'll set off a massacre!
GRAB
Crap! I've been paying too much attention to the duel!
They're about to—
WAVER
JOLT

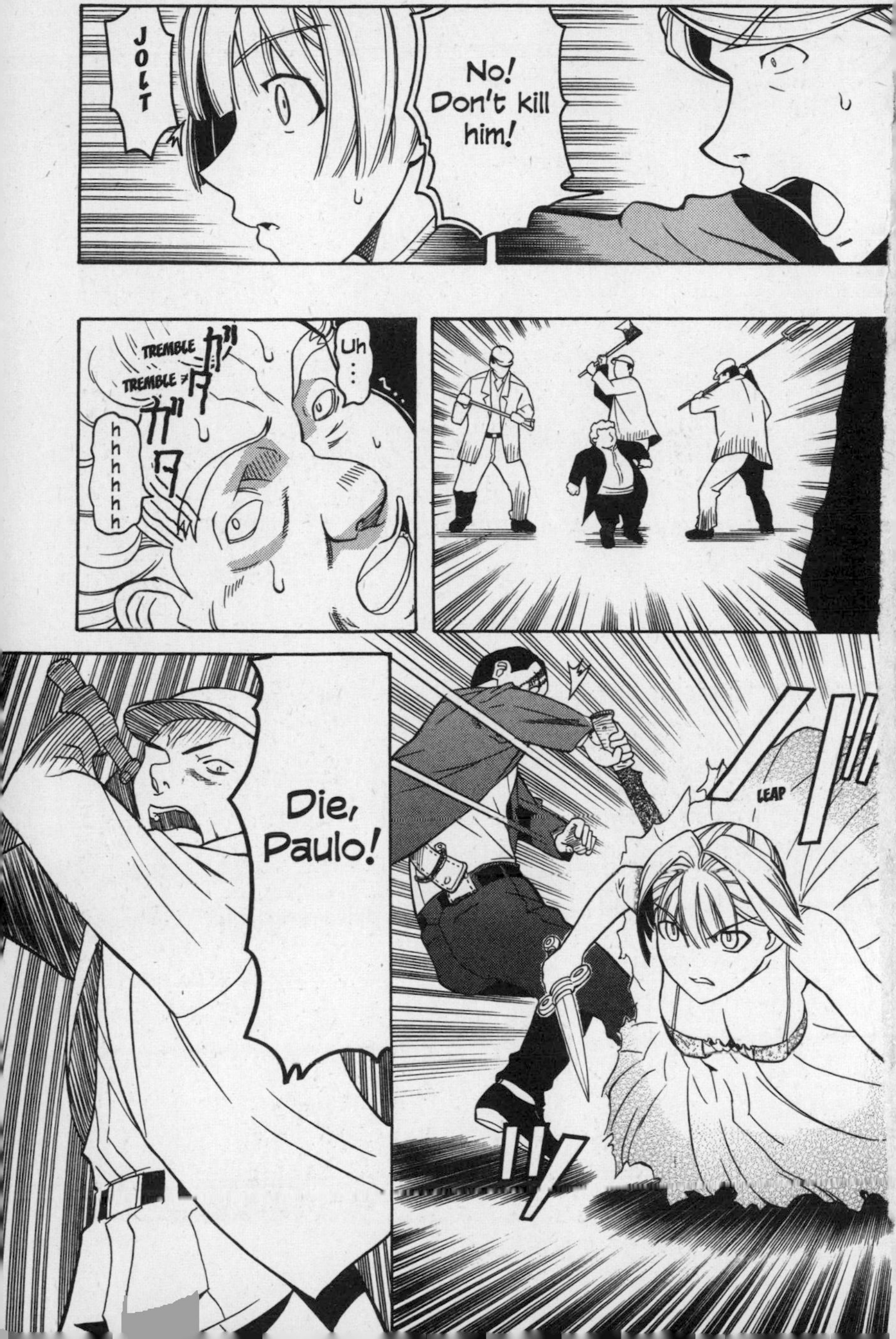
No! Don't kill him!
JOLT
Uh...
TREMBLE
TREMBLE
hhhhhh
LEAP
Die, Paulo!

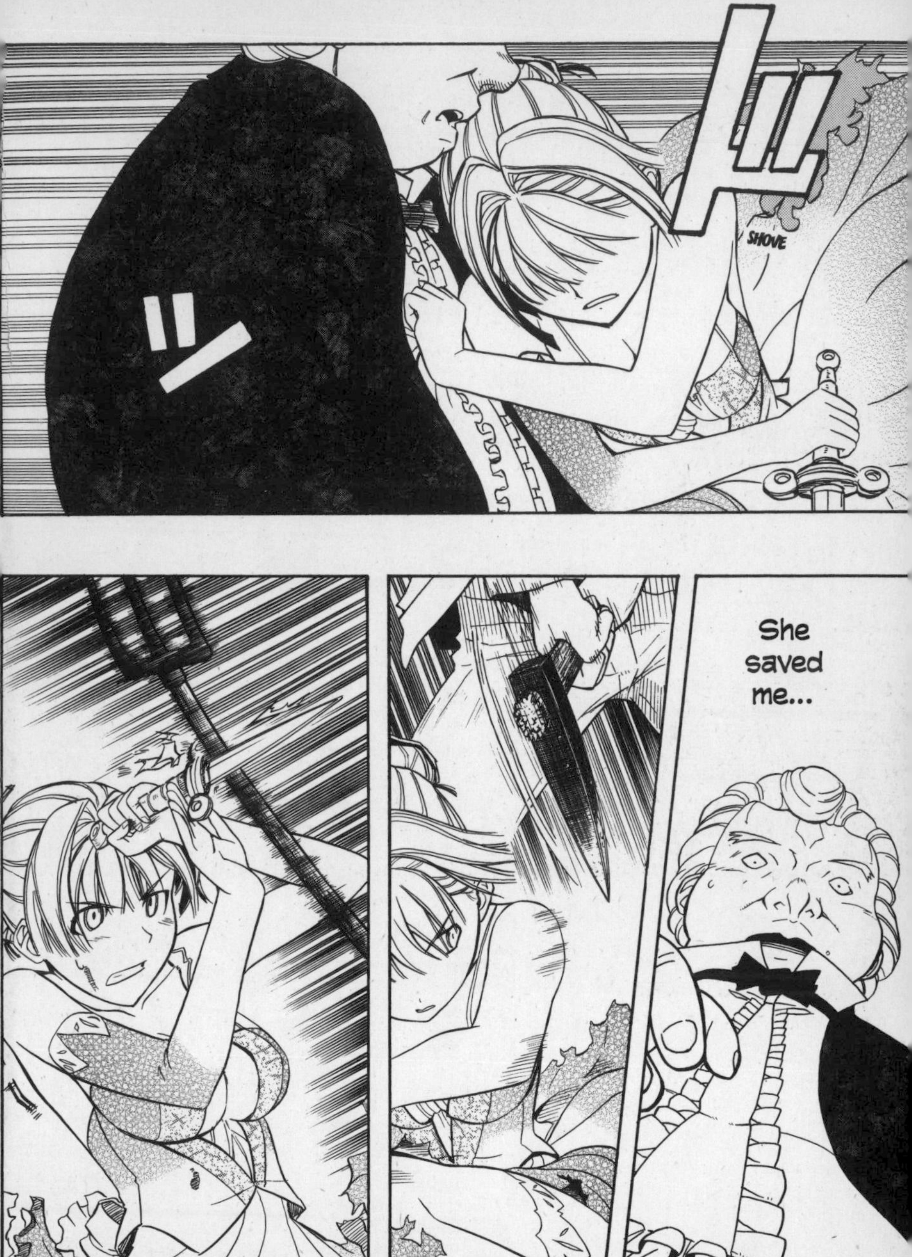
SHOVE
She saved me...

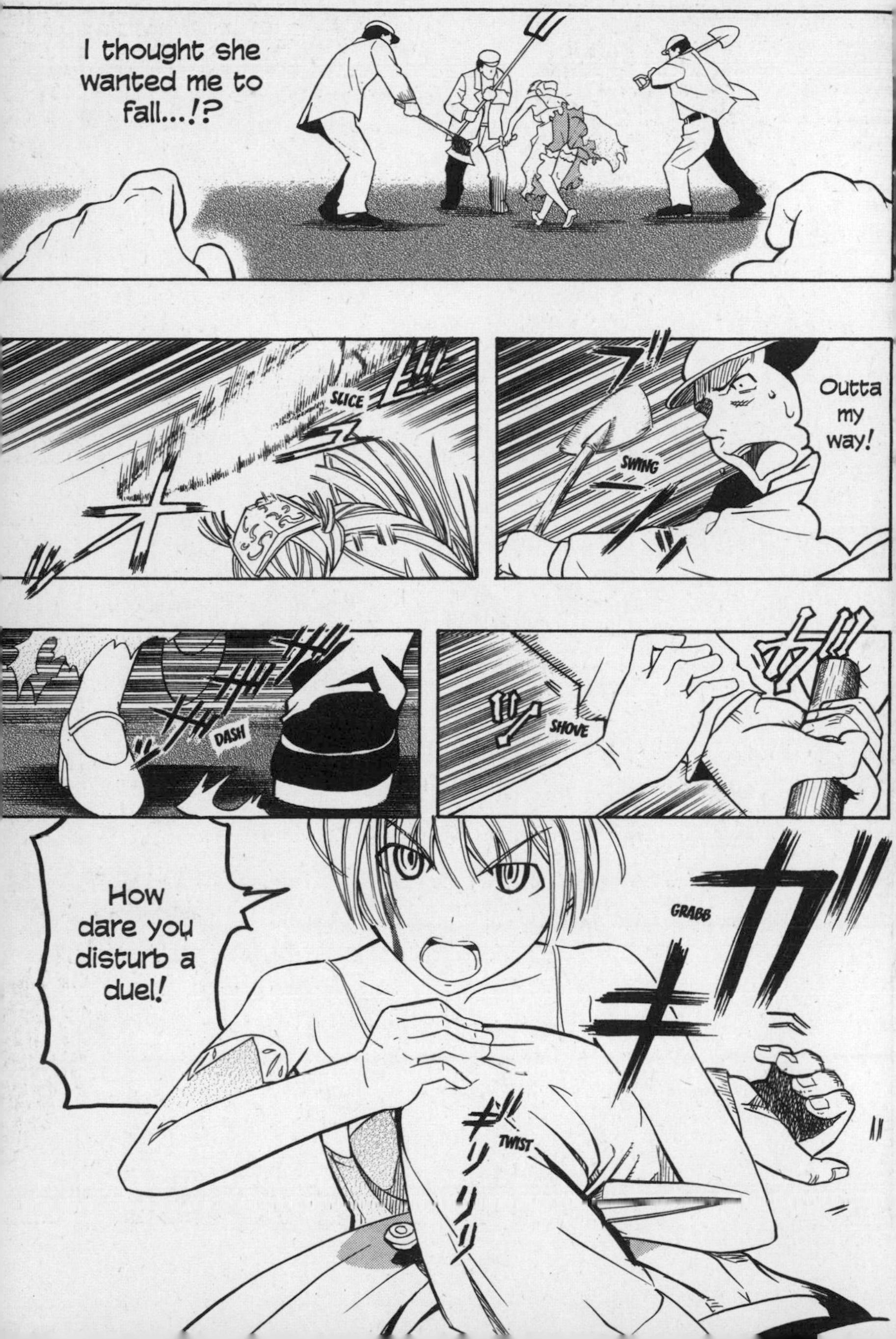
I thought she wanted me to fall...!?
Outta my way!
SWING
SLICE
SHOVE
DASH
How dare you disturb a duel!
GRABB
TWIST

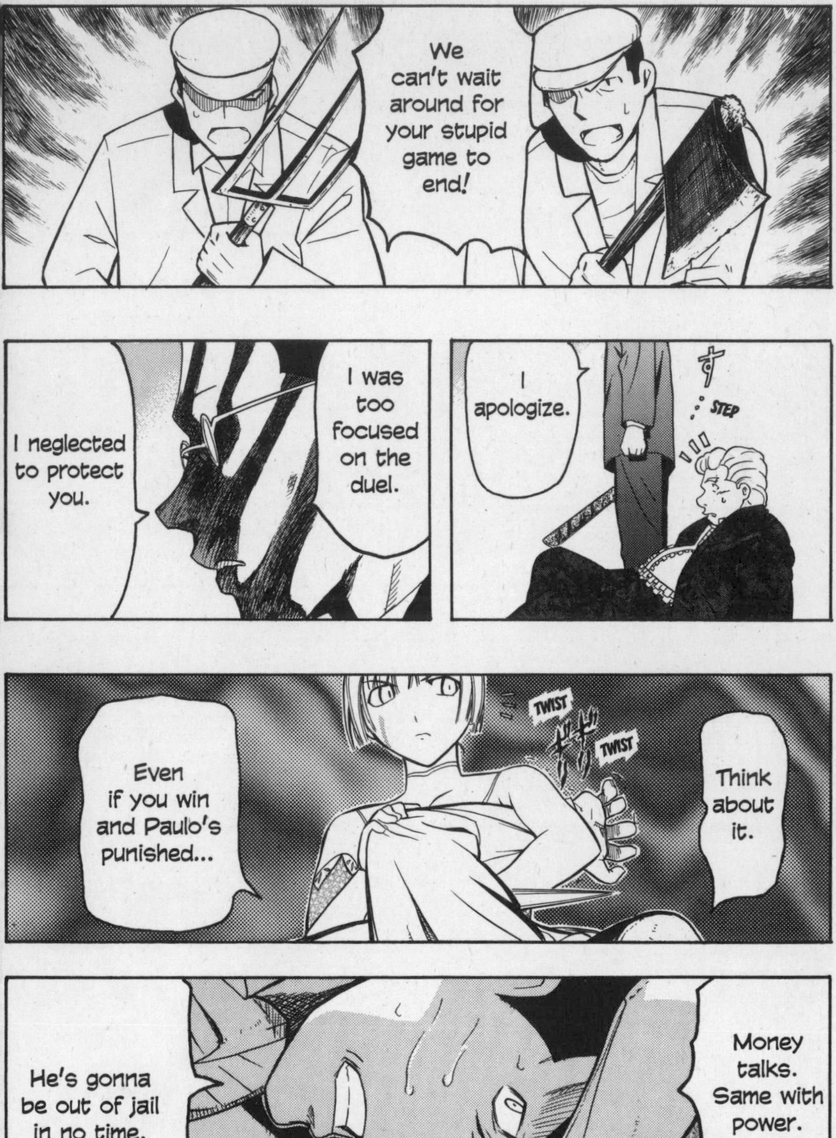
We can't wait around for your stupid game to end!
I apologize.
STEP
I was too focused on the duel.
I neglected to protect you.
Think about it.
TWIST
TWIST
Even if you win and Paulo's punished...
Money talks. Same with power.
He's gonna be out of jail in no time.

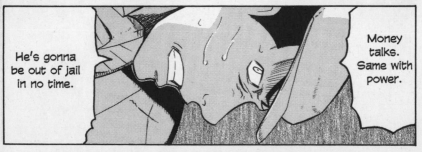

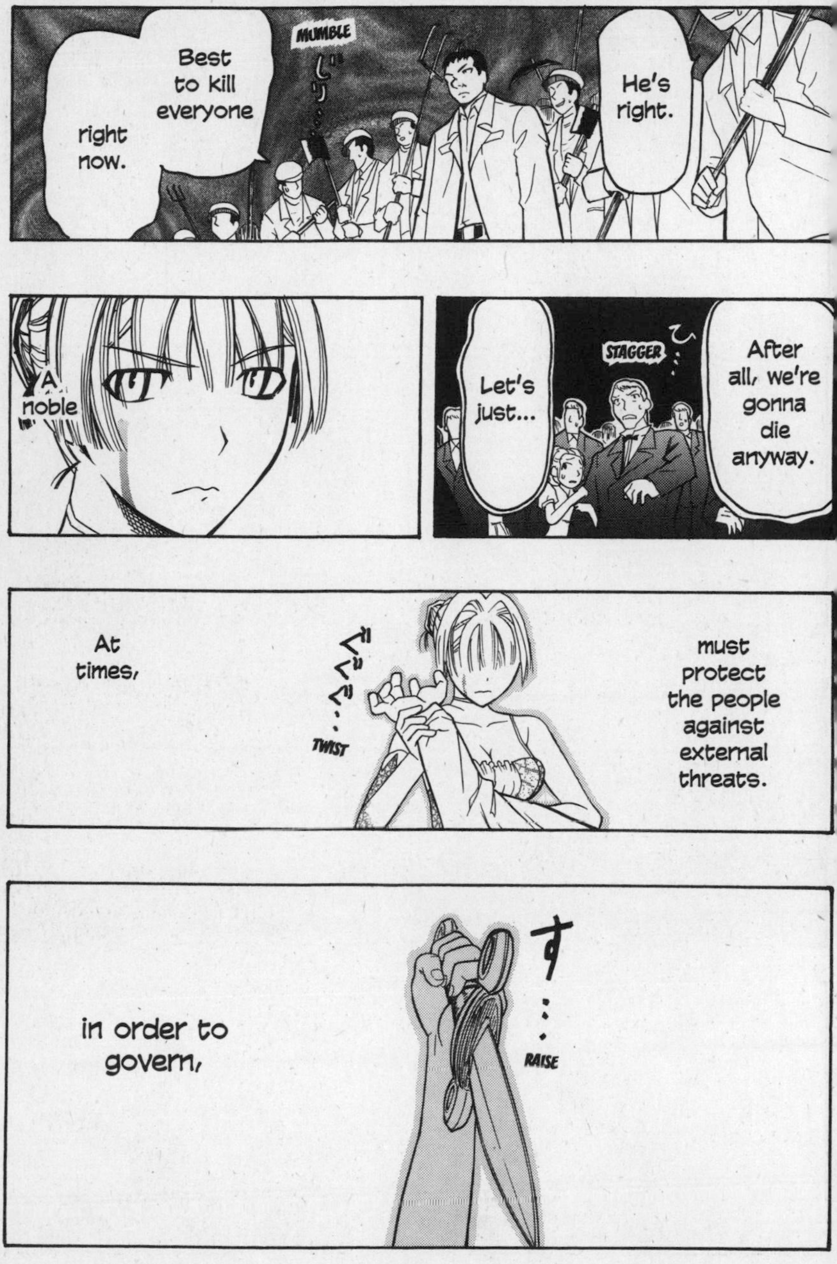
He's right.
MUMBLE
じり…
Best to kill everyone right now.
After all, we're gonna die anyway.
ひ…
STAGGER
Let's just...
A noble
must protect the people against external threats.
TWIST
At times,
す…
RAISE
in order to govern,

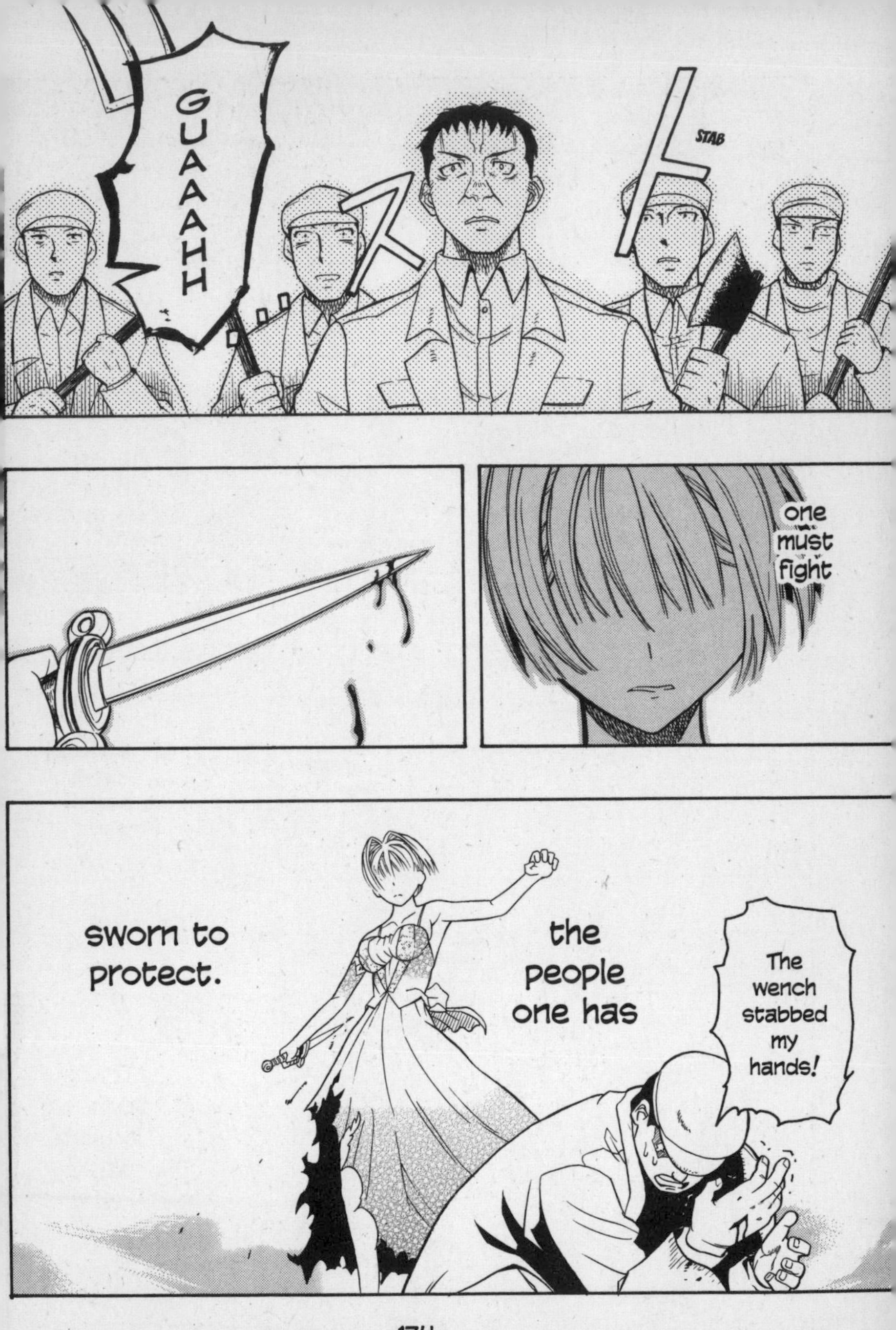
STAB
GUAAAHH
one must fight
The wench stabbed my hands!
the people one has
sworn to protect.

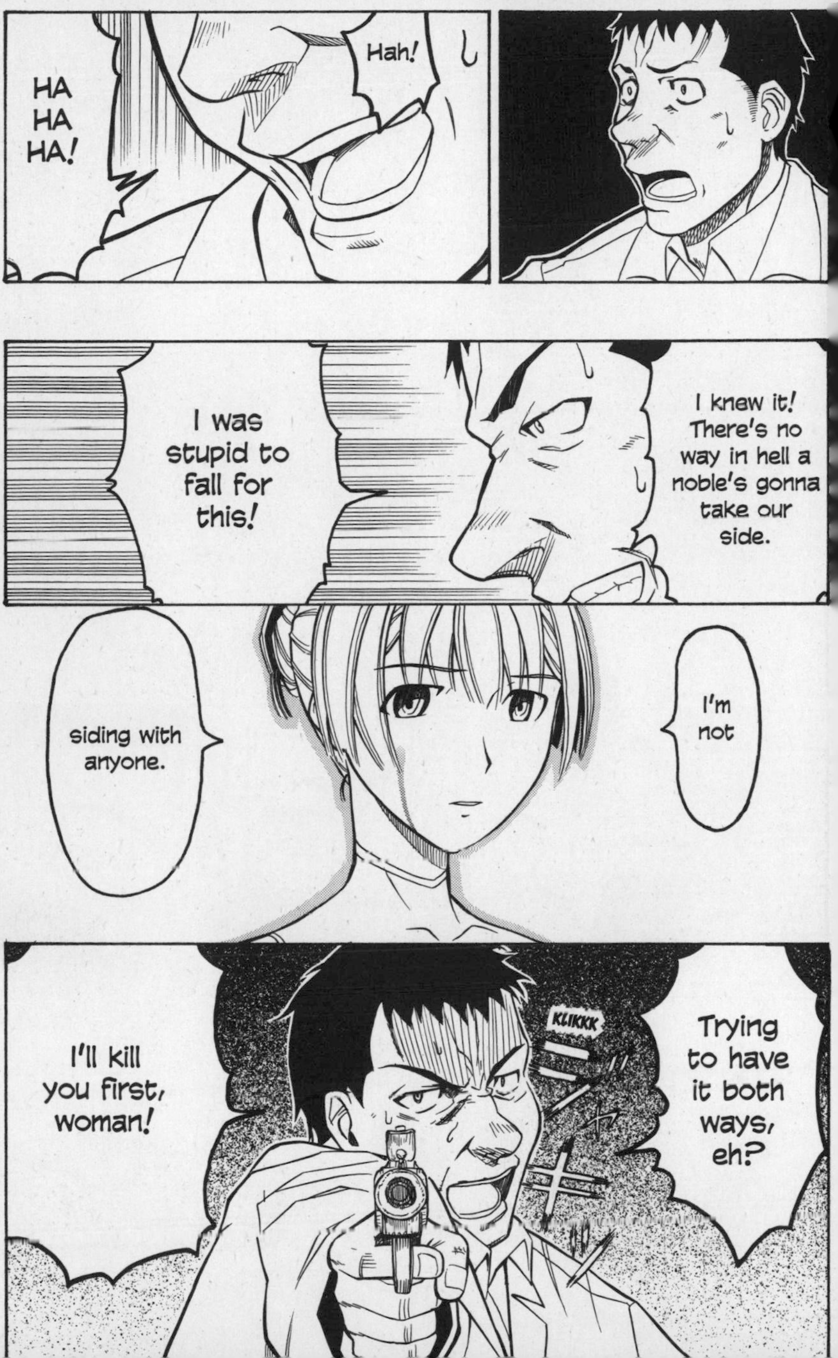
Hah!
HA HA HA!
I knew it! There's no way in hell a noble's gonna take our side.
I was stupid to fall for this!
I'm not
siding with anyone.
Trying to have it both ways, eh?
KLIKKK
I'll kill you first, woman!

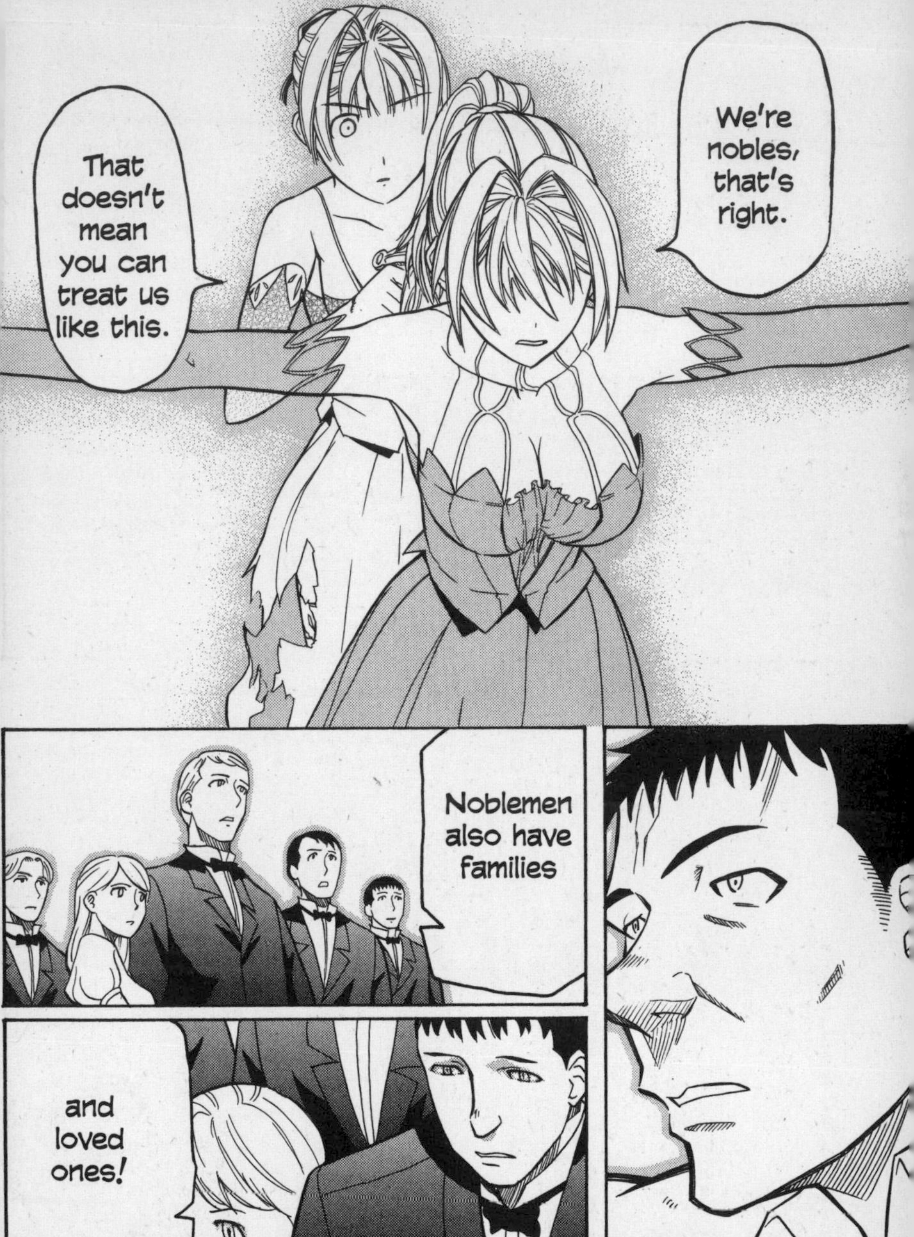
We're nobles, that's right.
That doesn't mean you can treat us like this.
Noblemen also have families
and loved ones!

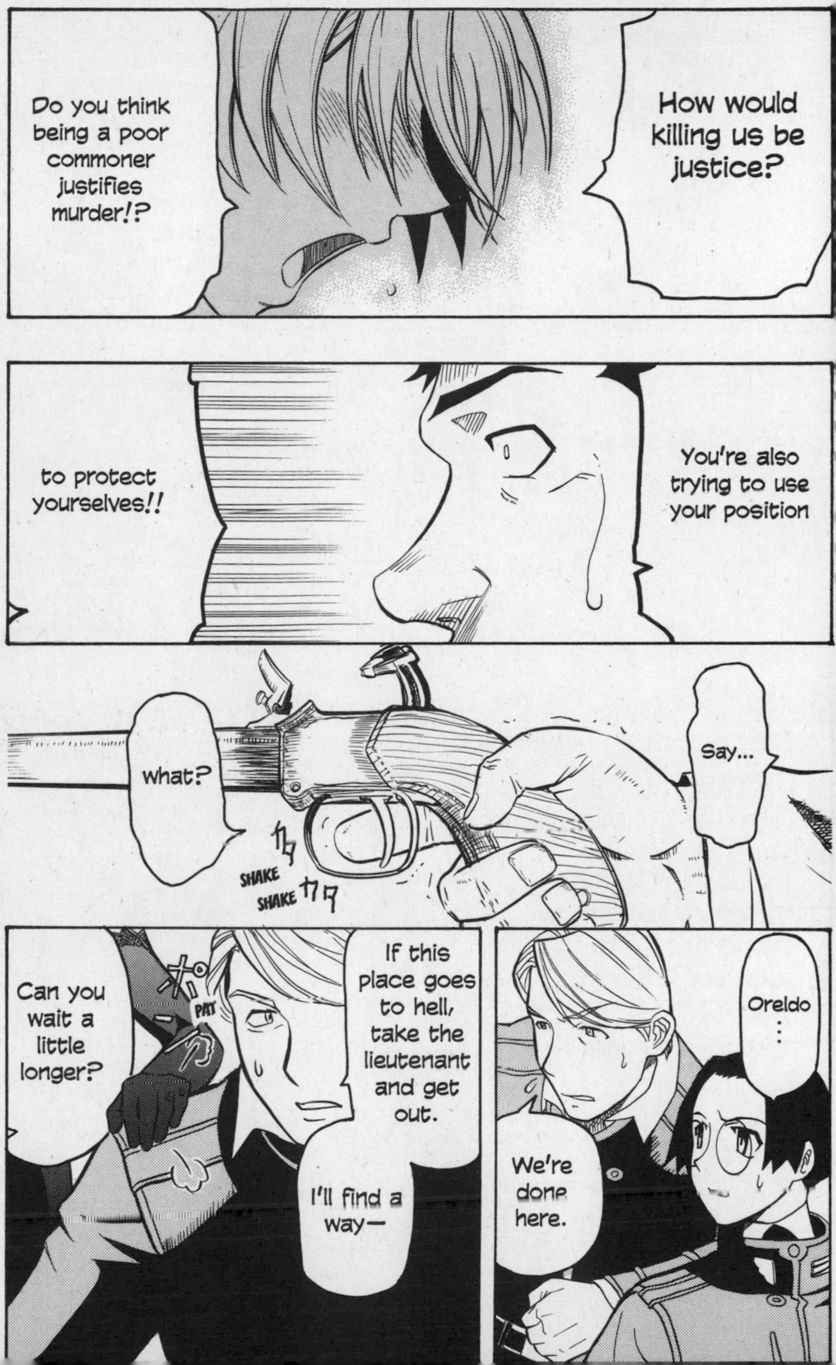
How would killing us be justice?
Do you think being a poor commoner justifies murder!?
You're also trying to use your position
to protect yourselves!!
Say...
what?
SHAKE SHAKE
Oreldo...
We're done here.
If this place goes to hell, take the lieutenant and get out.
I'll find a way—
PAT
Can you wait a little longer?

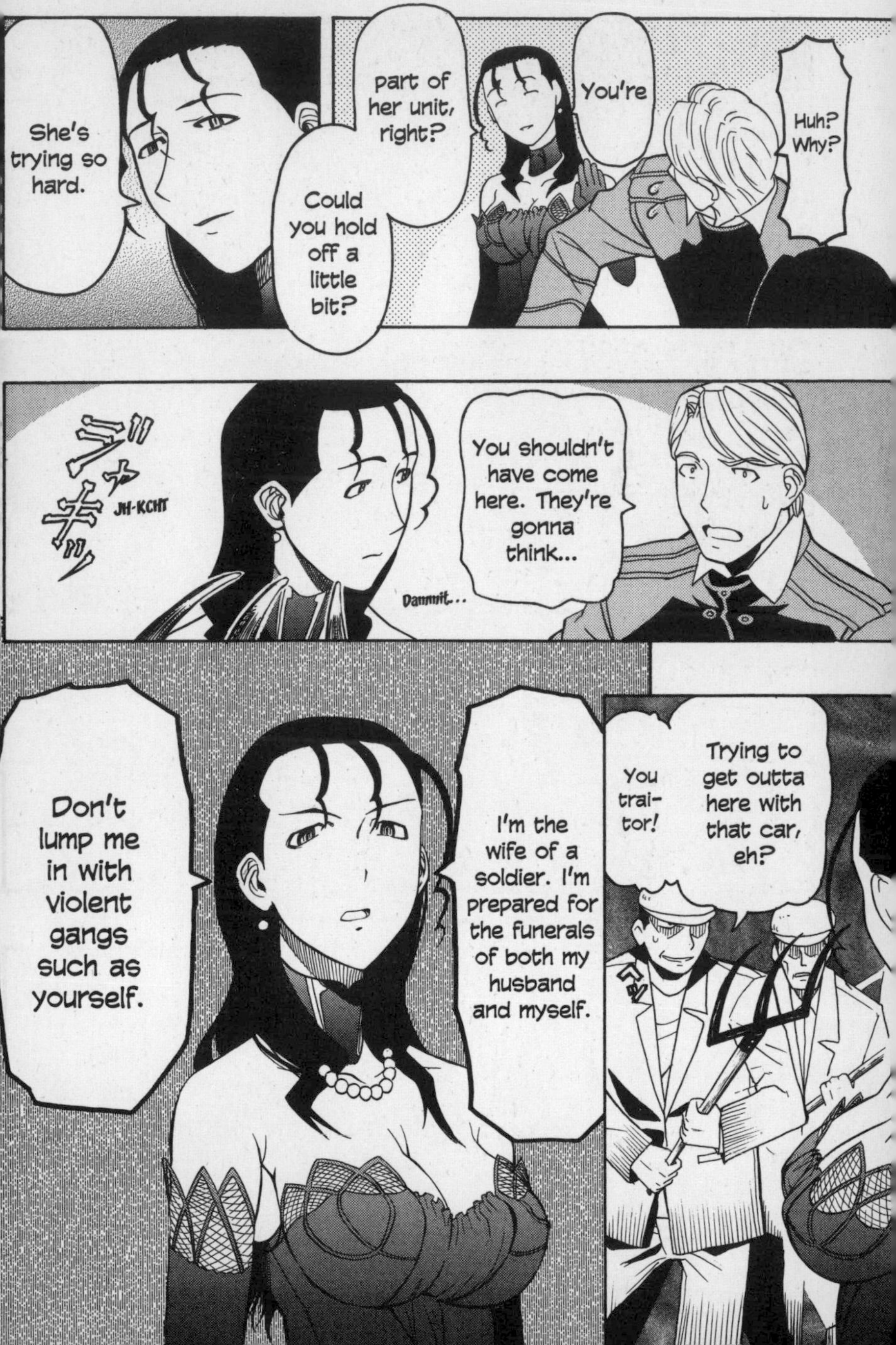
Huh? Why?
You're
part of her unit, right?
Could you hold off a little bit?
She's trying so hard.
You shouldn't have come here. They're gonna think...
Dammit...
JH-KCHT
Trying to get outta here with that car, eh?
You traitor!
I'm the wife of a soldier. I'm prepared for the funerals of both my husband and myself.
Don't lump me in with violent gangs such as yourself.

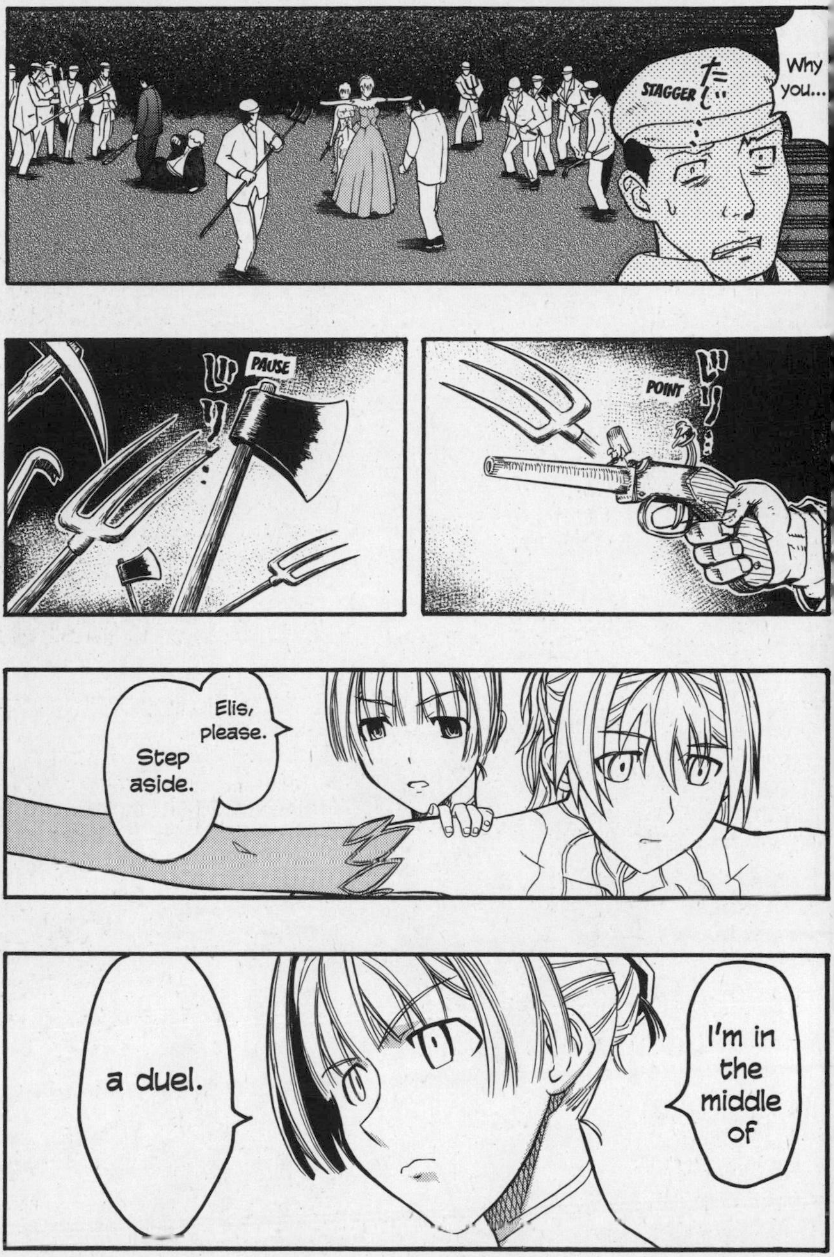
Why you...
STAGGER
POINT
PAUSE
Elis, please.
Step aside.
I'm in the middle of
a duel.

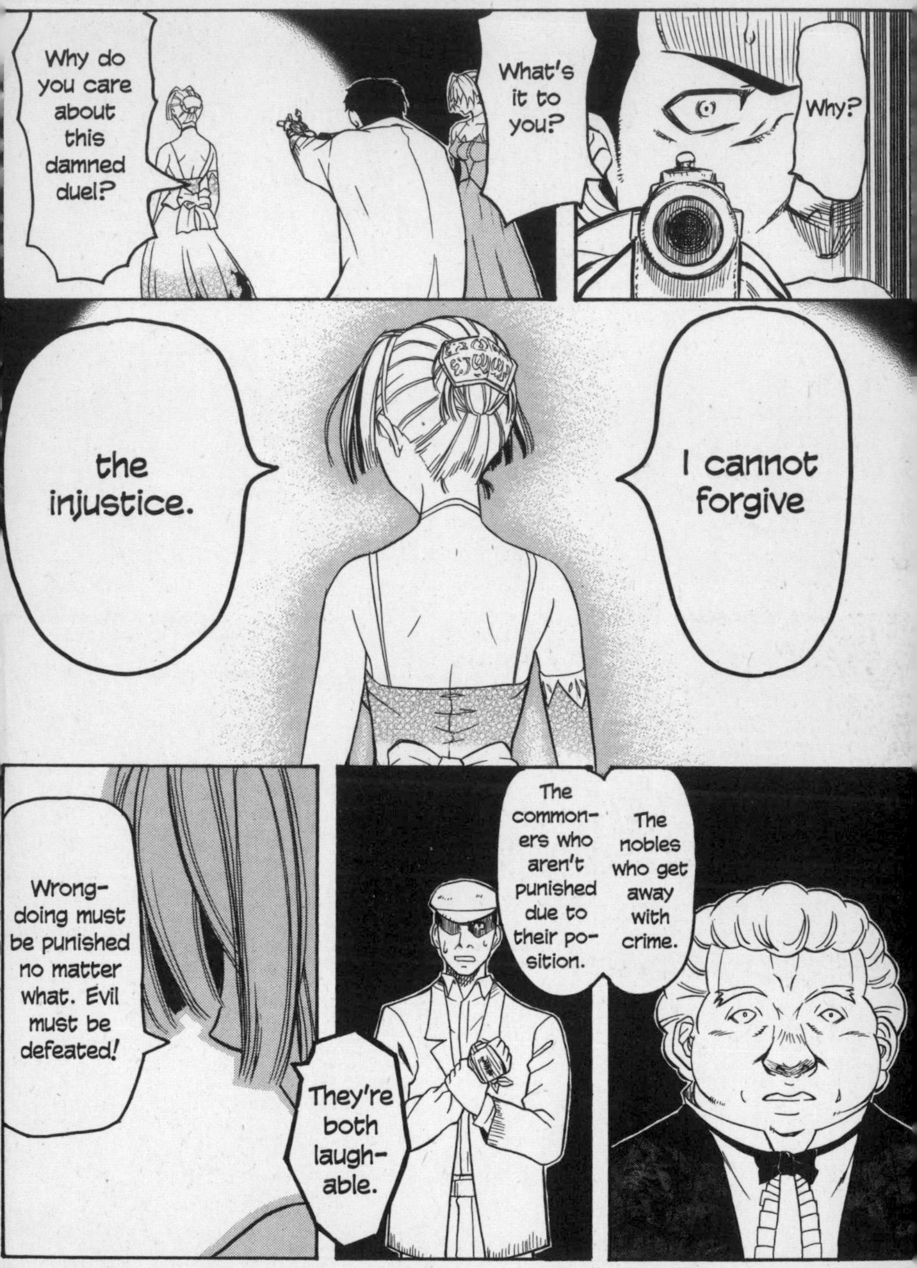

Why?
What's it to you?
Why do you care about this damned duel?
I cannot forgive
the injustice.
The nobles who get away with crime.
The commoners who aren't punished due to their position.
They're both laughable.
Wrong-doing must be punished no matter what. Evil must be defeated!

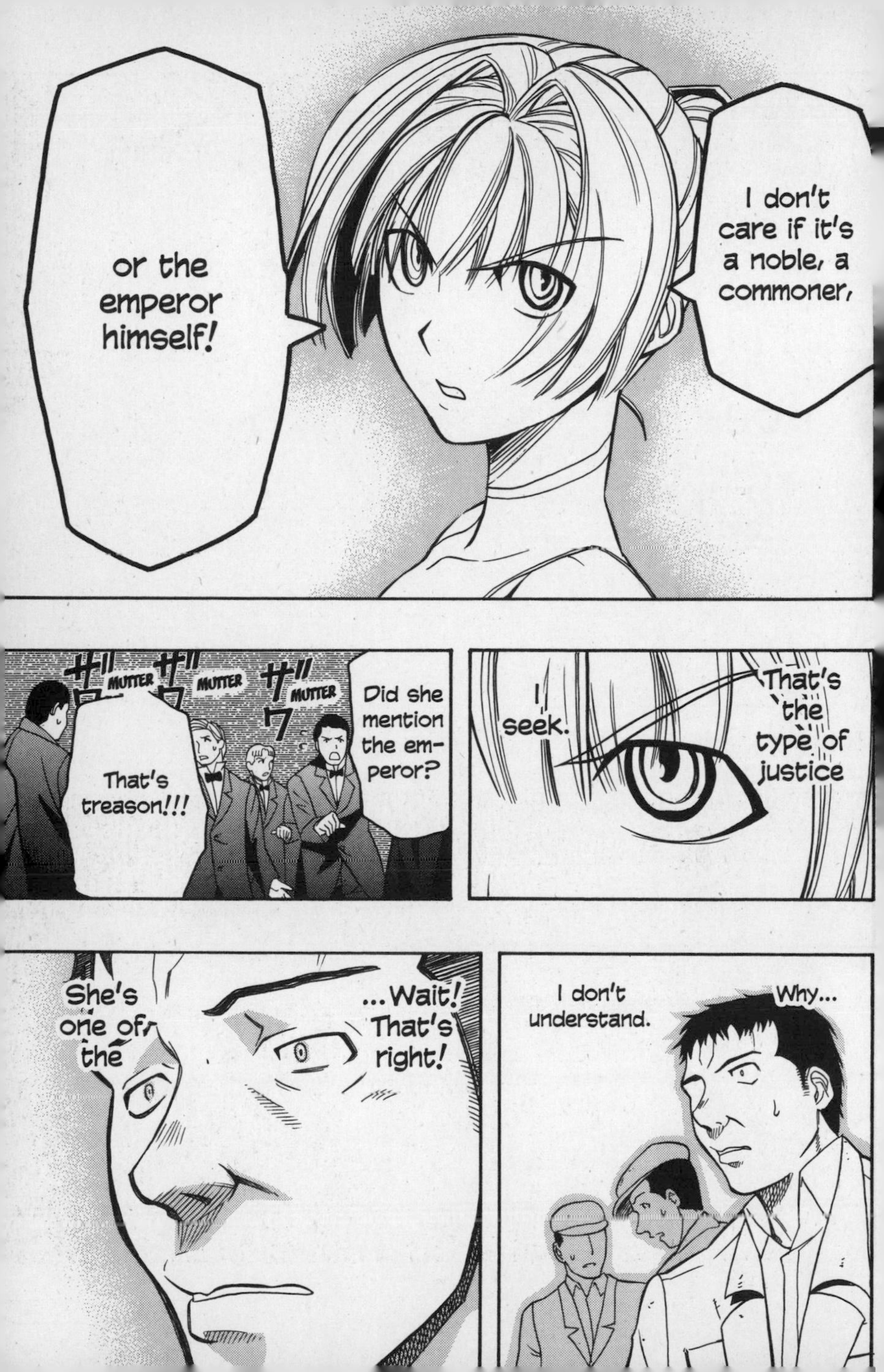
I don't care if it's a noble, a commoner,
or the emperor himself!
That's the type of justice
I seek.
MUTTER
MUTTER
MUTTER
Did she mention the emperor?
That's treason!!!
Why...
I don't understand.
...Wait! That's right!
She's one of the

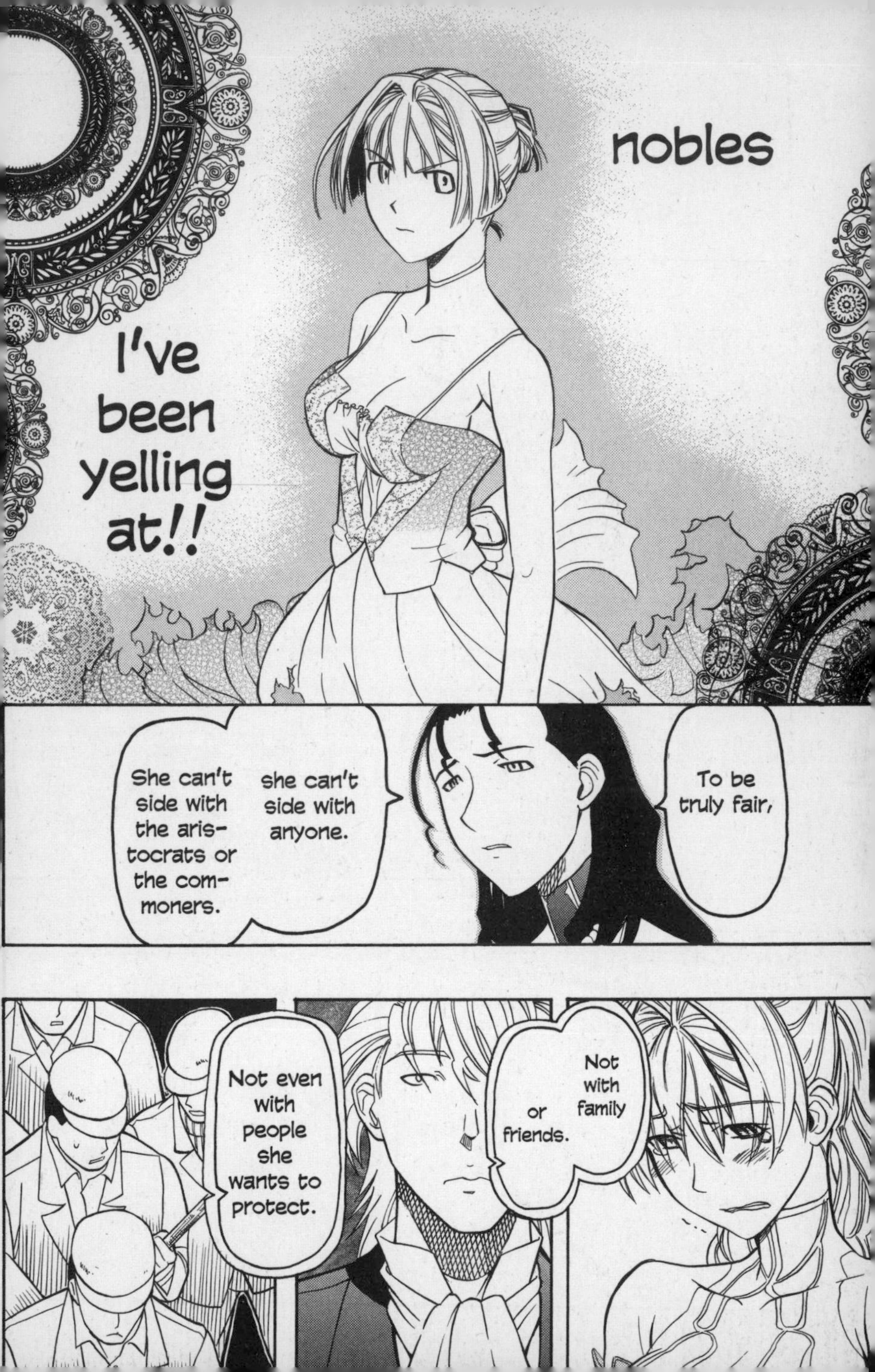
nobles
I've been yelling at!!
To be truly fair,
she can't side with anyone.
She can't side with the aristocrats or the commoners.
Not with family
or friends.
Not even with people she wants to protect.

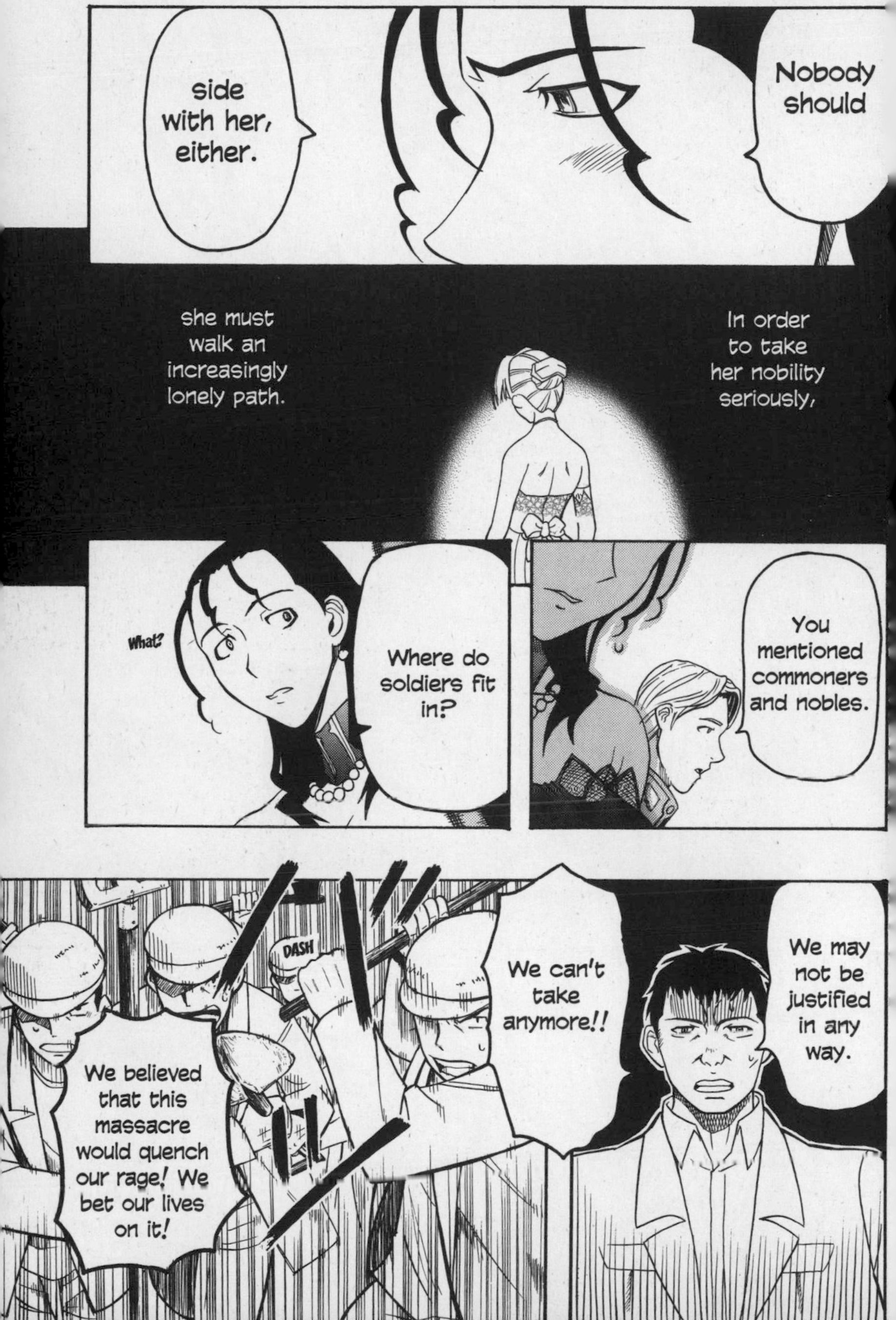
Nobody should
side with her, either.
In order to take her nobility seriously,
she must walk an increasingly lonely path.
You mentioned commoners and nobles.
Where do soldiers fit in?
What?
We may not be justified in any way.
We can't take anymore!!
DASH
We believed that this massacre would quench our rage! We bet our lives on it!

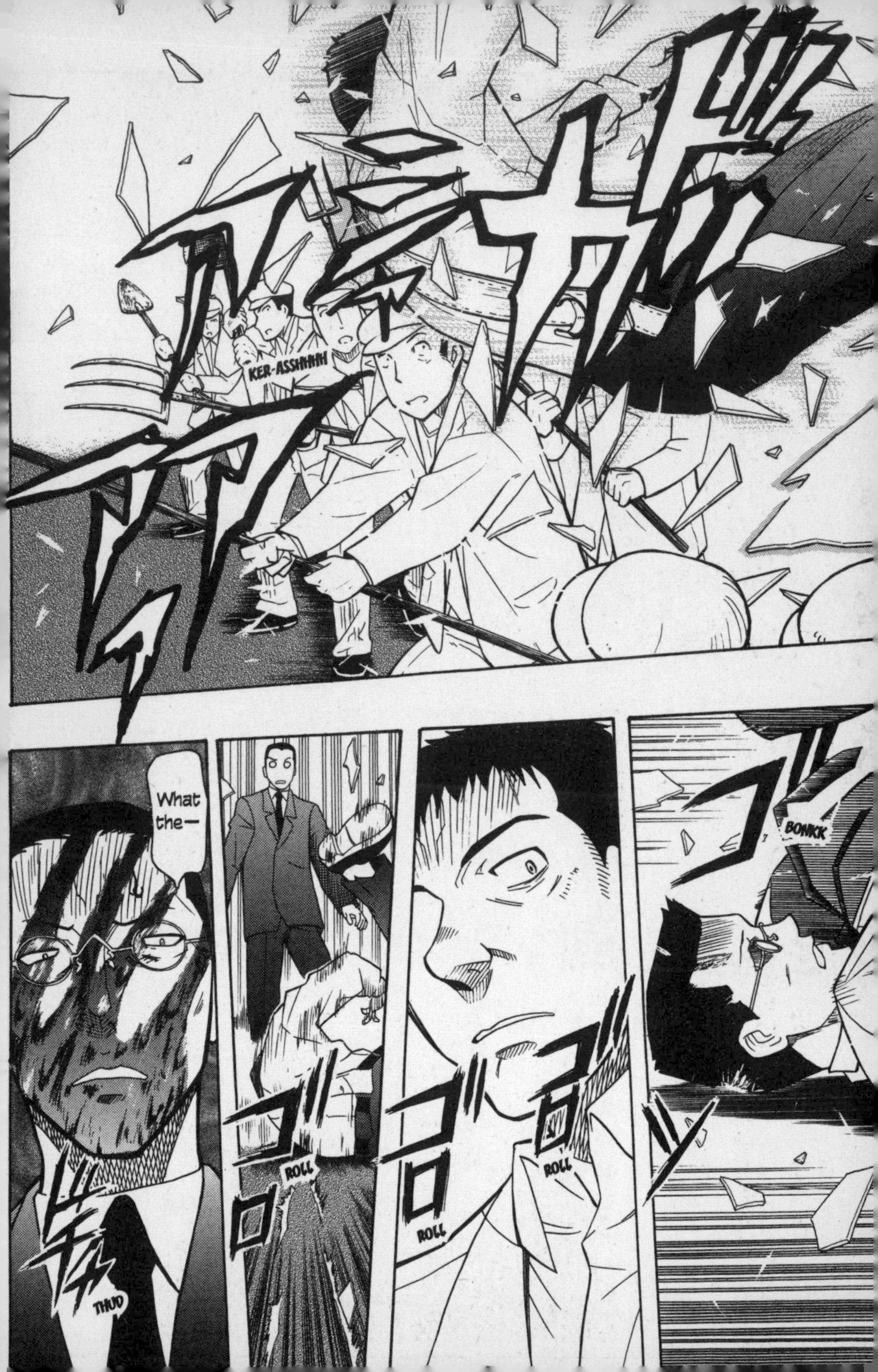
KER-ASSHHHH
BONKK
ROLL
ROLL
ROLL
What the—
THUD

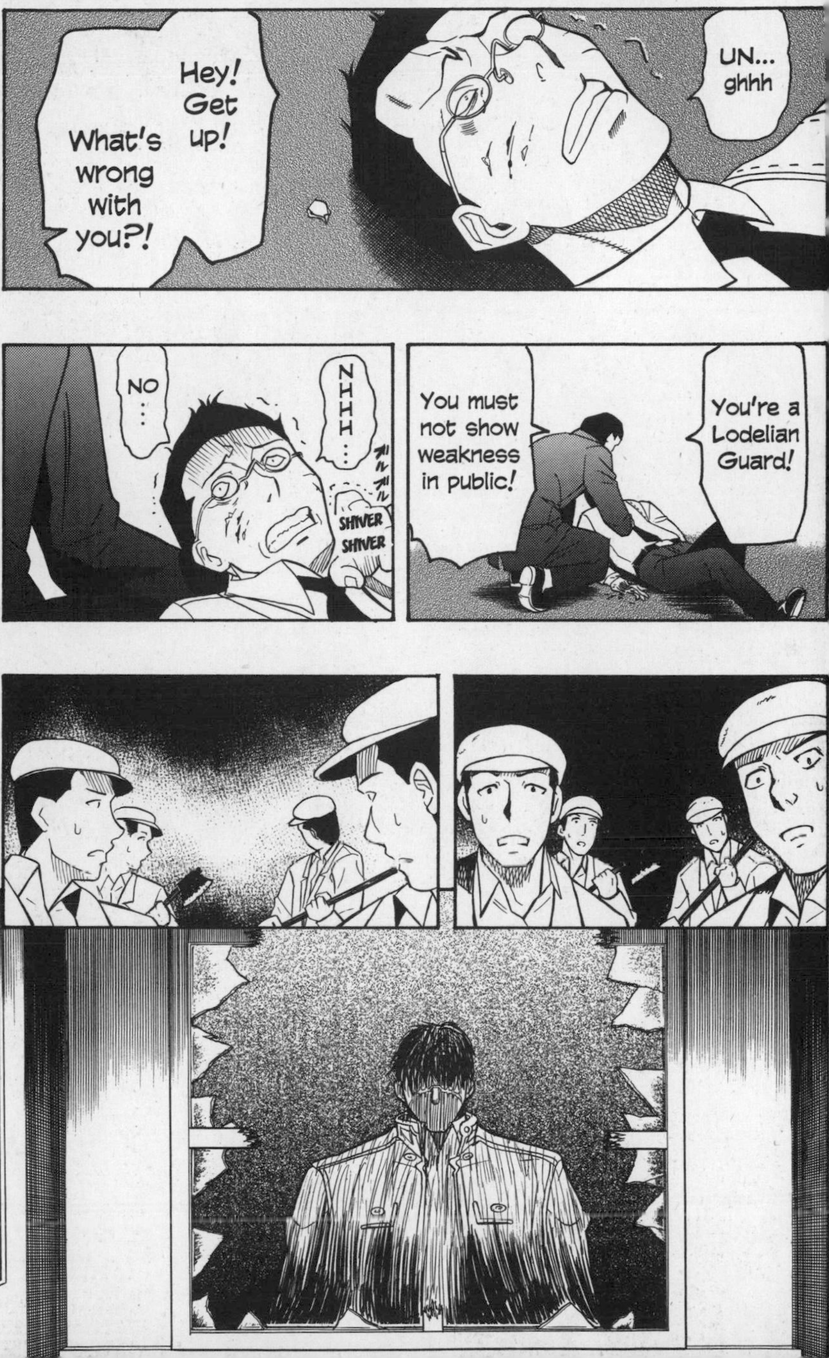
UN... ghhh
Hey! Get up!
What's wrong with you?!
You're a Lodelian Guard!
You must not show weakness in public!
NHHH...
ブルブル
SHIVER SHIVER
NO...

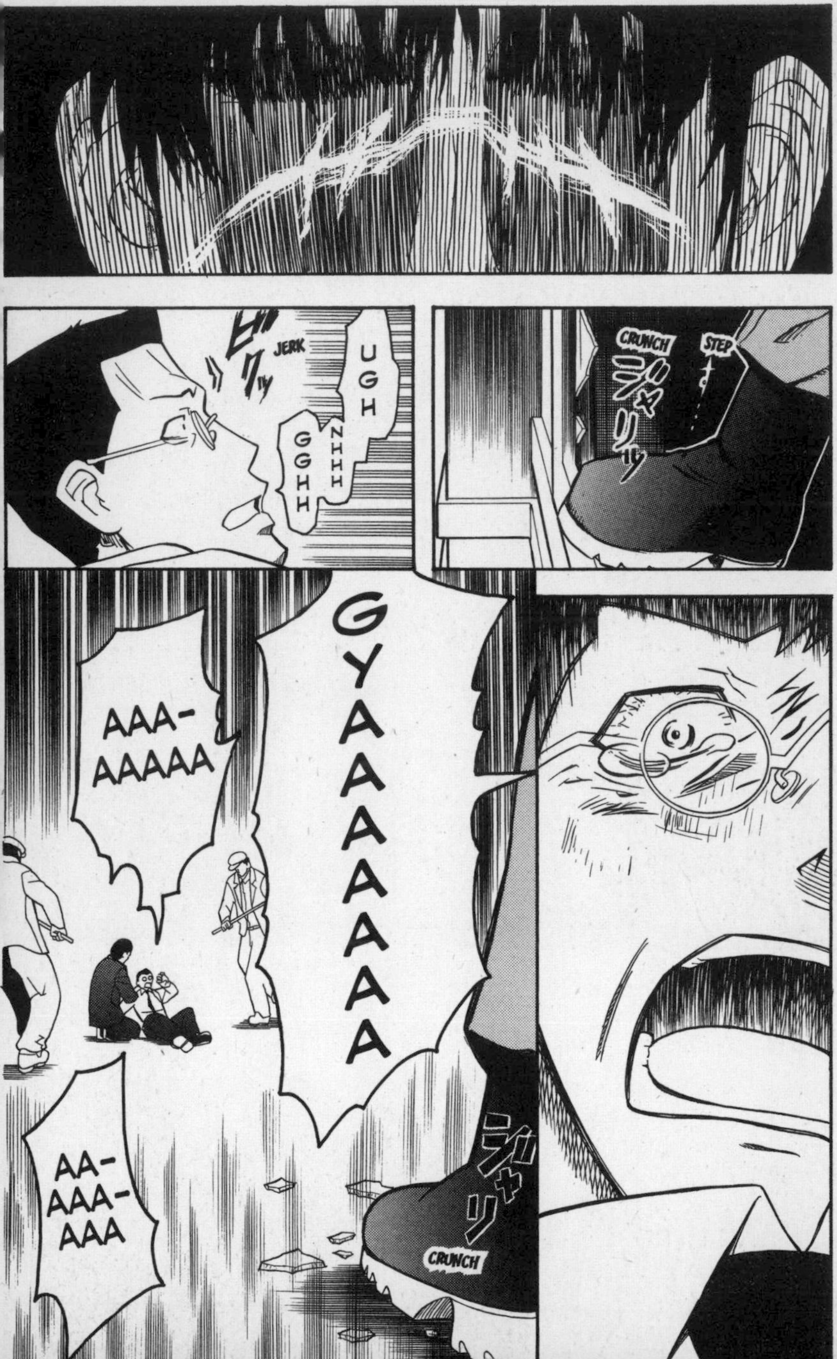
CRUNCH
STEP
JERK
UGH
GGHH NHHH
GYAAAAAAAA
AAA-AAAAA
AA-AAA-AAA
CRUNCH

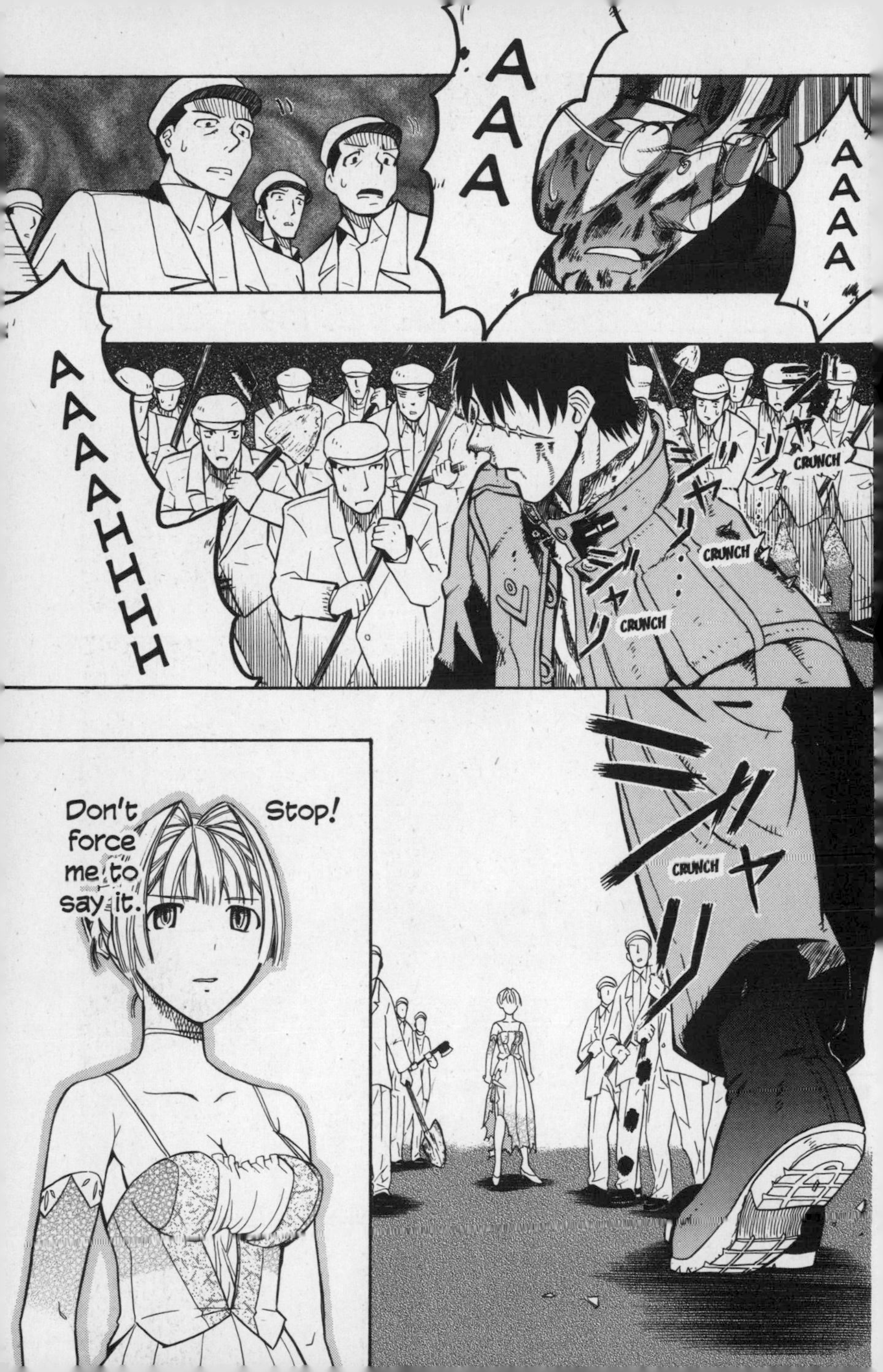
AAA
AAAA
AAAAHHHH
CRUNCH
CRUNCH
CRUNCH
CRUNCH
Stop!
Don't force me to say it.

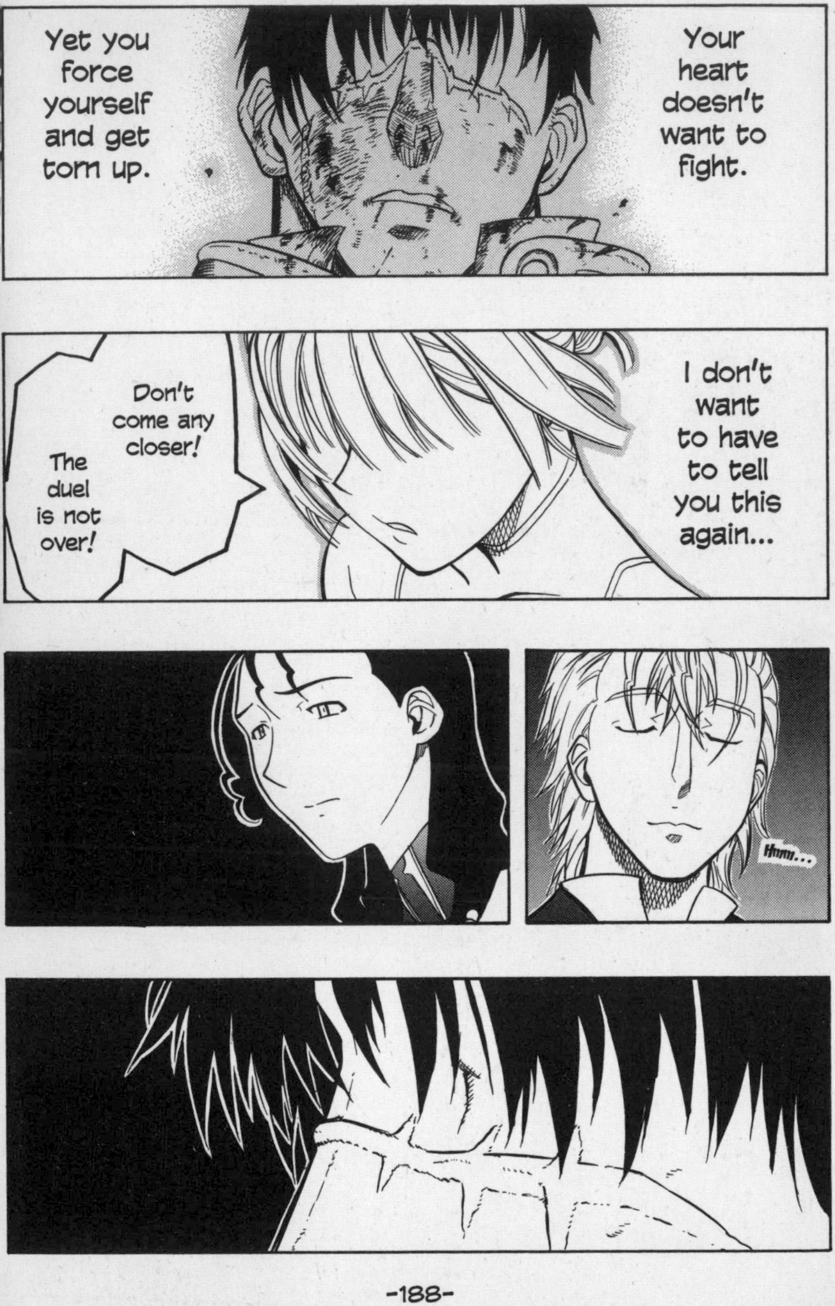
Your heart doesn't want to fight.
Yet you force yourself and get torn up.
I don't want to have to tell you this again...
Don't come any closer!
The duel is not over!
Hmm...

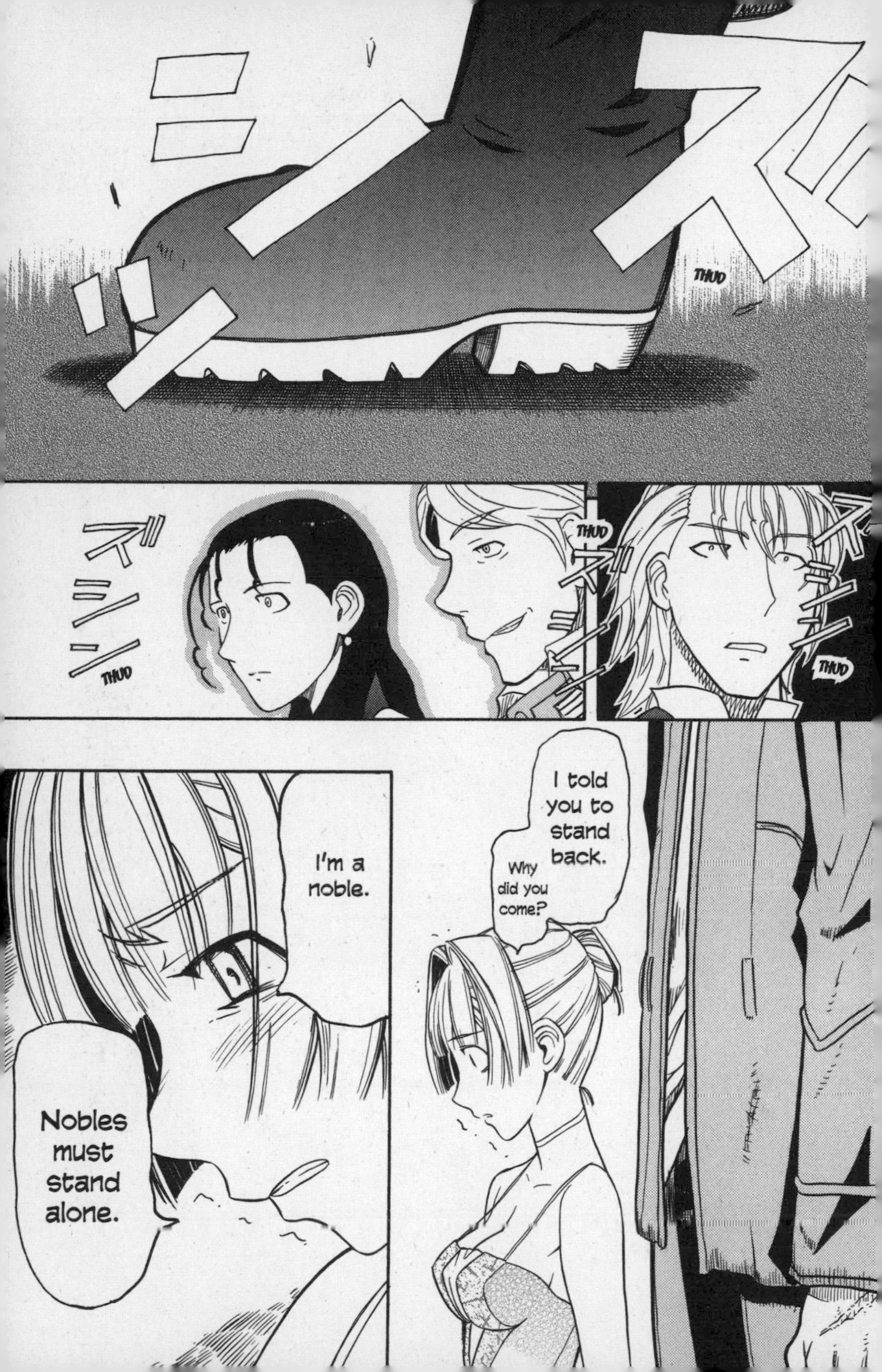
THUD
THUD
THUD
THUD
THUD
I told you to stand back.
Why did you come?
I'm a noble.
Nobles must stand alone.

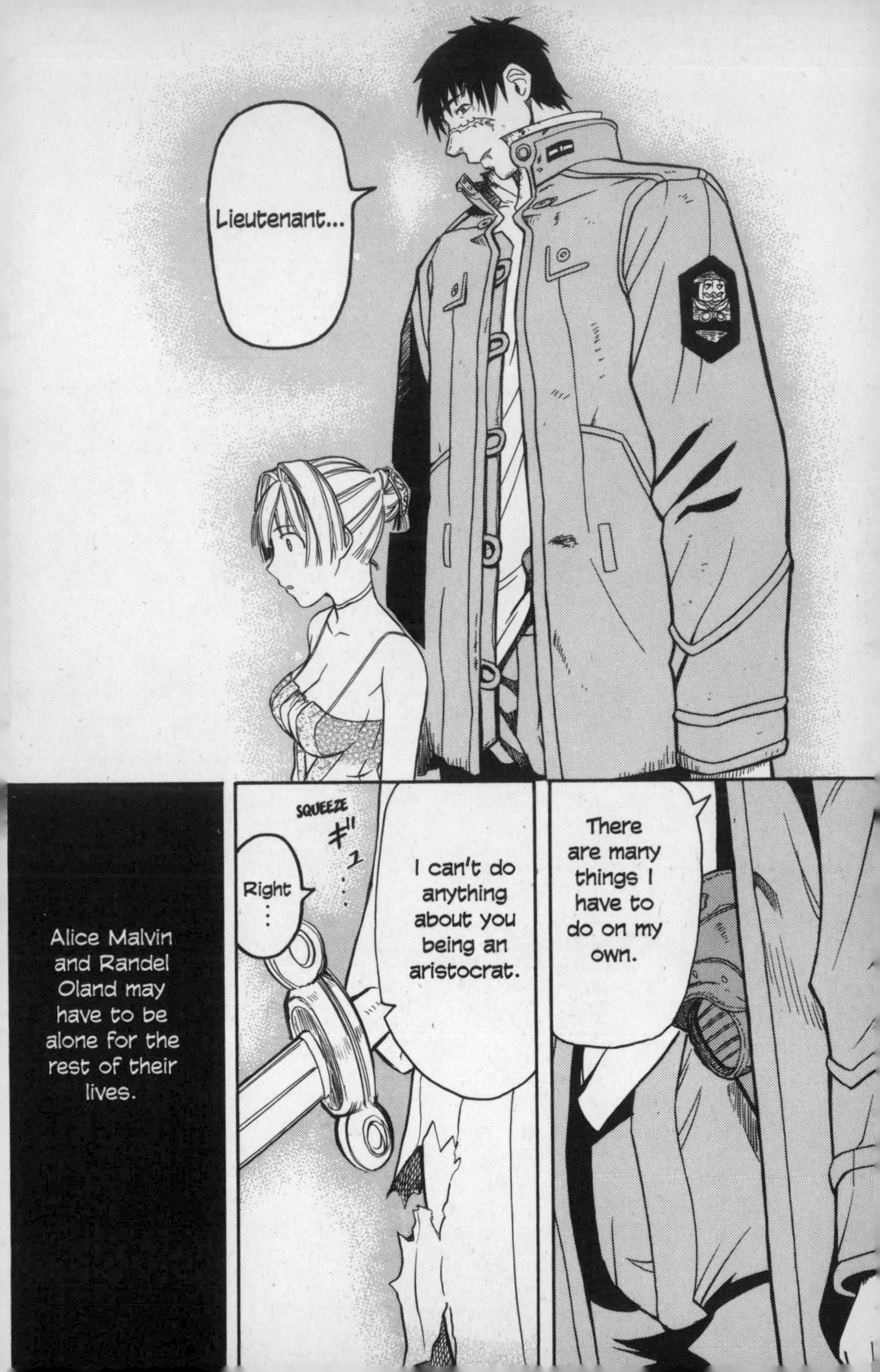
Lieutenant...
There are many things I have to do on my own.
I can't do anything about you being an aristocrat.
SQUEEZE
ギュ…
Right...
Alice Malvin and Randel Oland may have to be alone for the rest of their lives.

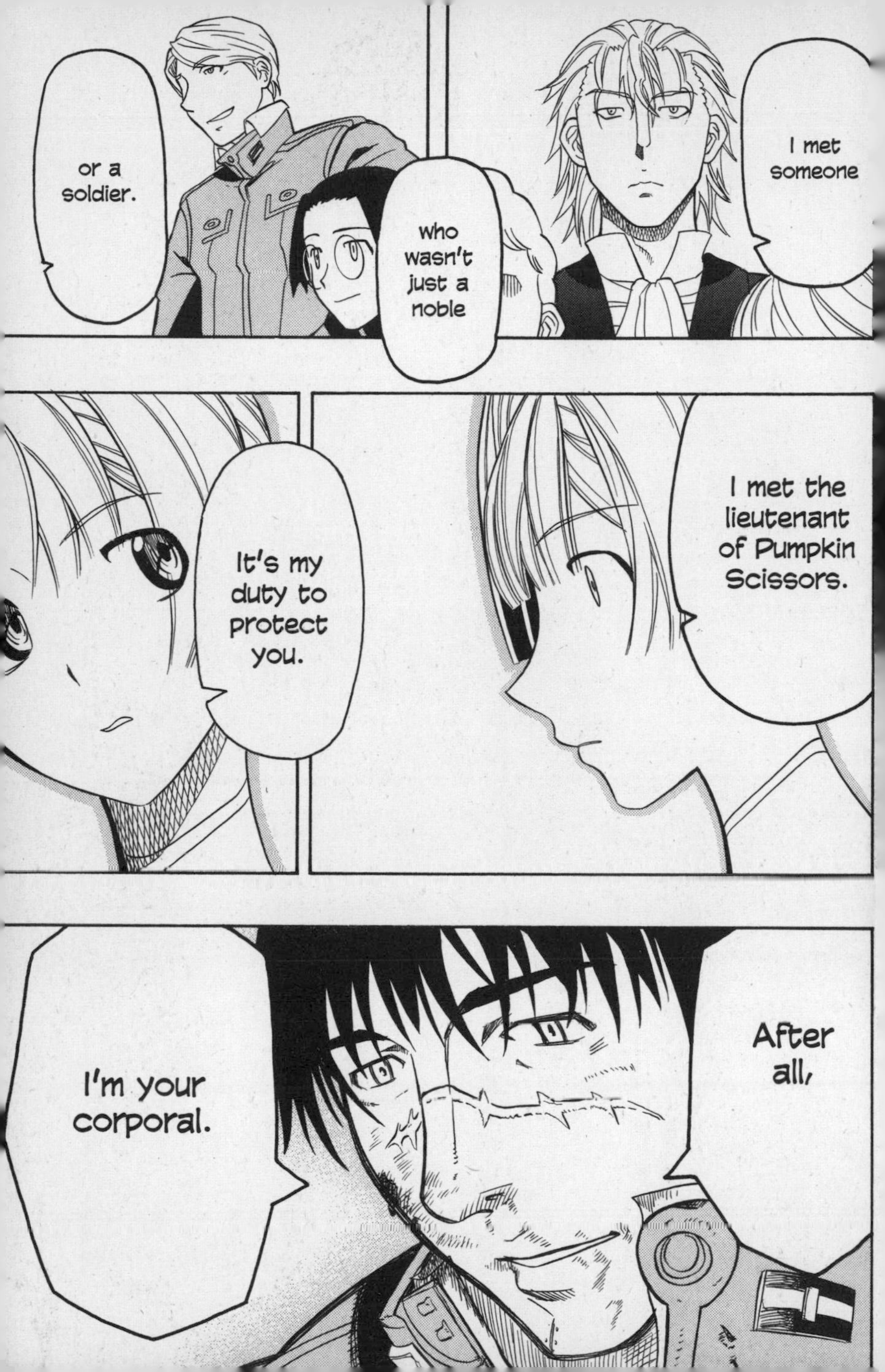
I met someone
who wasn't just a noble
or a soldier.
I met the lieutenant of Pumpkin Scissors.
It's my duty to protect you.
After all,
I'm your corporal.

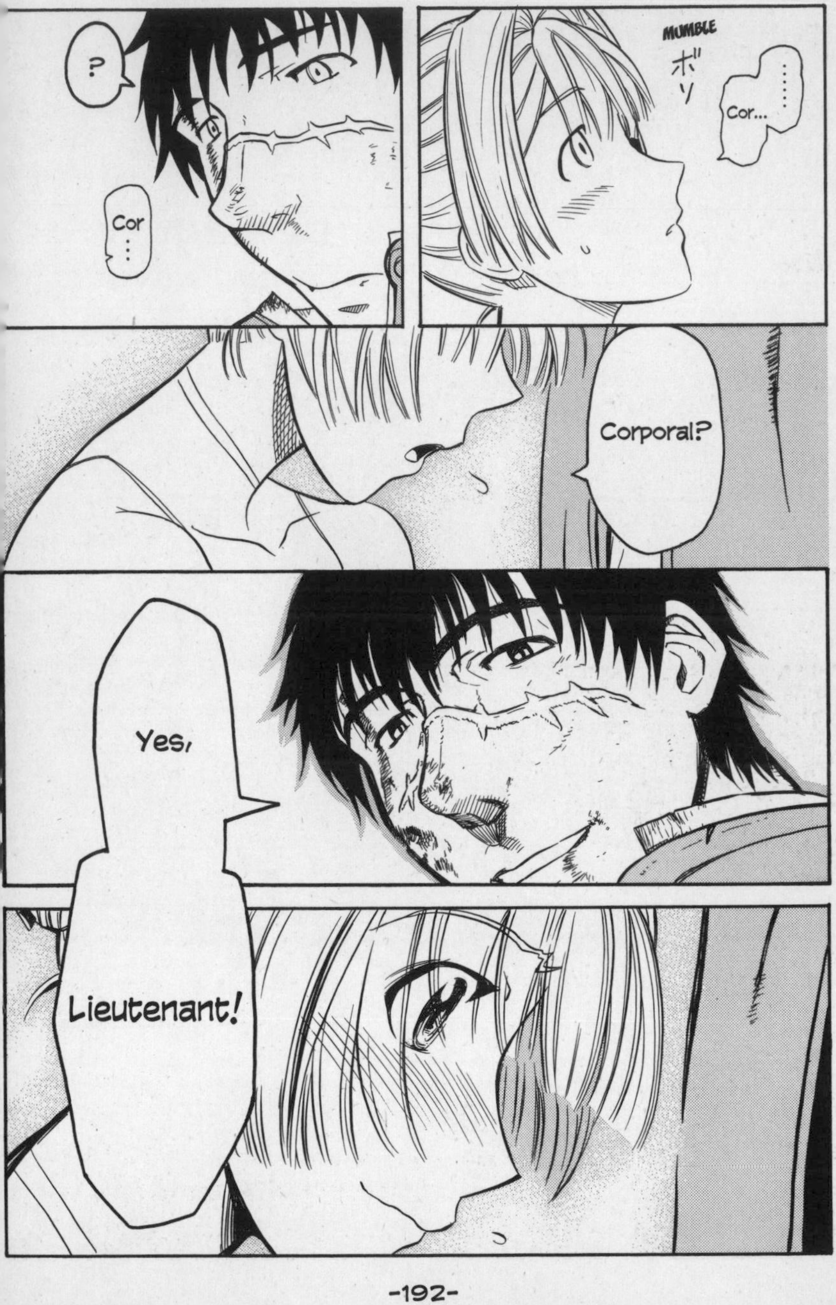
MUMBLE
ボソ
...... Cor...
?
Cor...
Corporal?
Yes, Lieutenant!

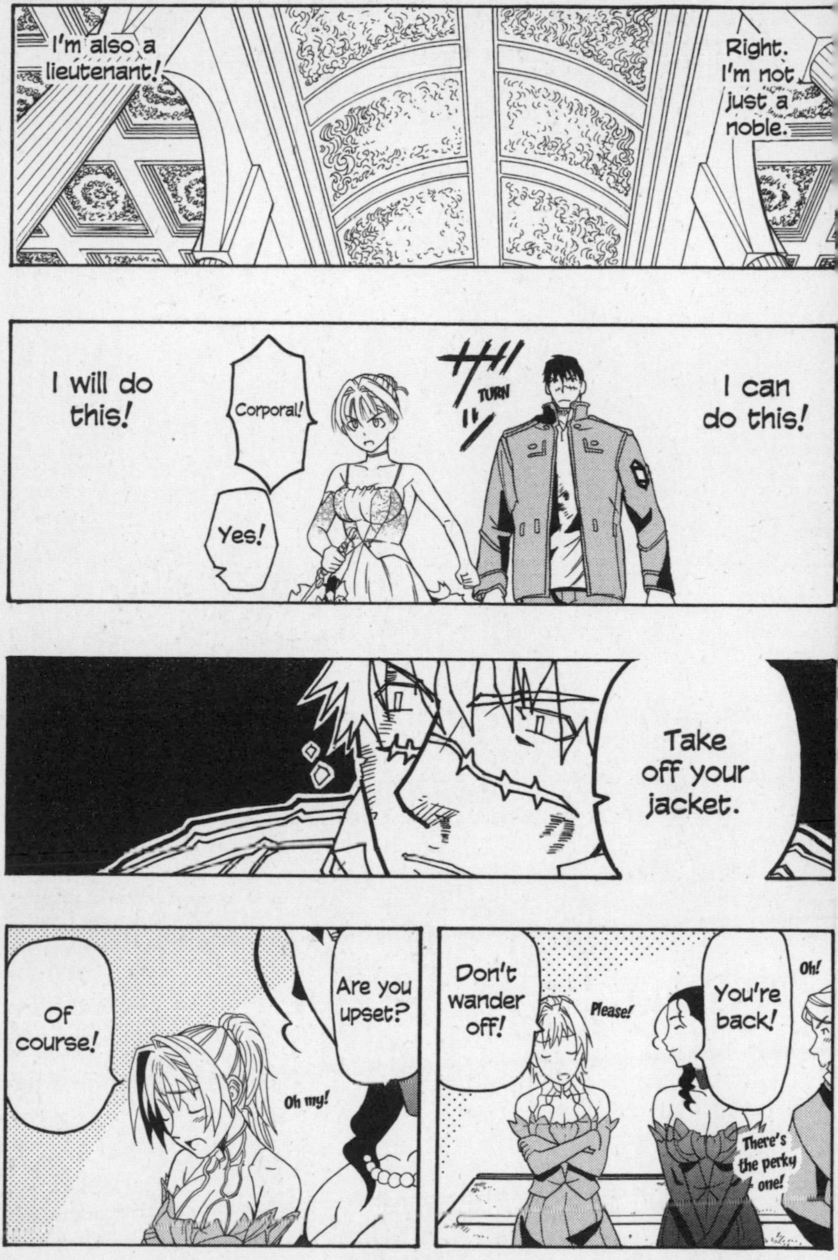
Right. I'm not just a noble.
I'm also a lieutenant!
I can do this!
TURN
Corporal!
Yes!
I will do this!
Take off your jacket.
Oh!
You're back!
There's the perky one!
Please!
Don't wander off!
Are you upset?
Oh my!
Of course!

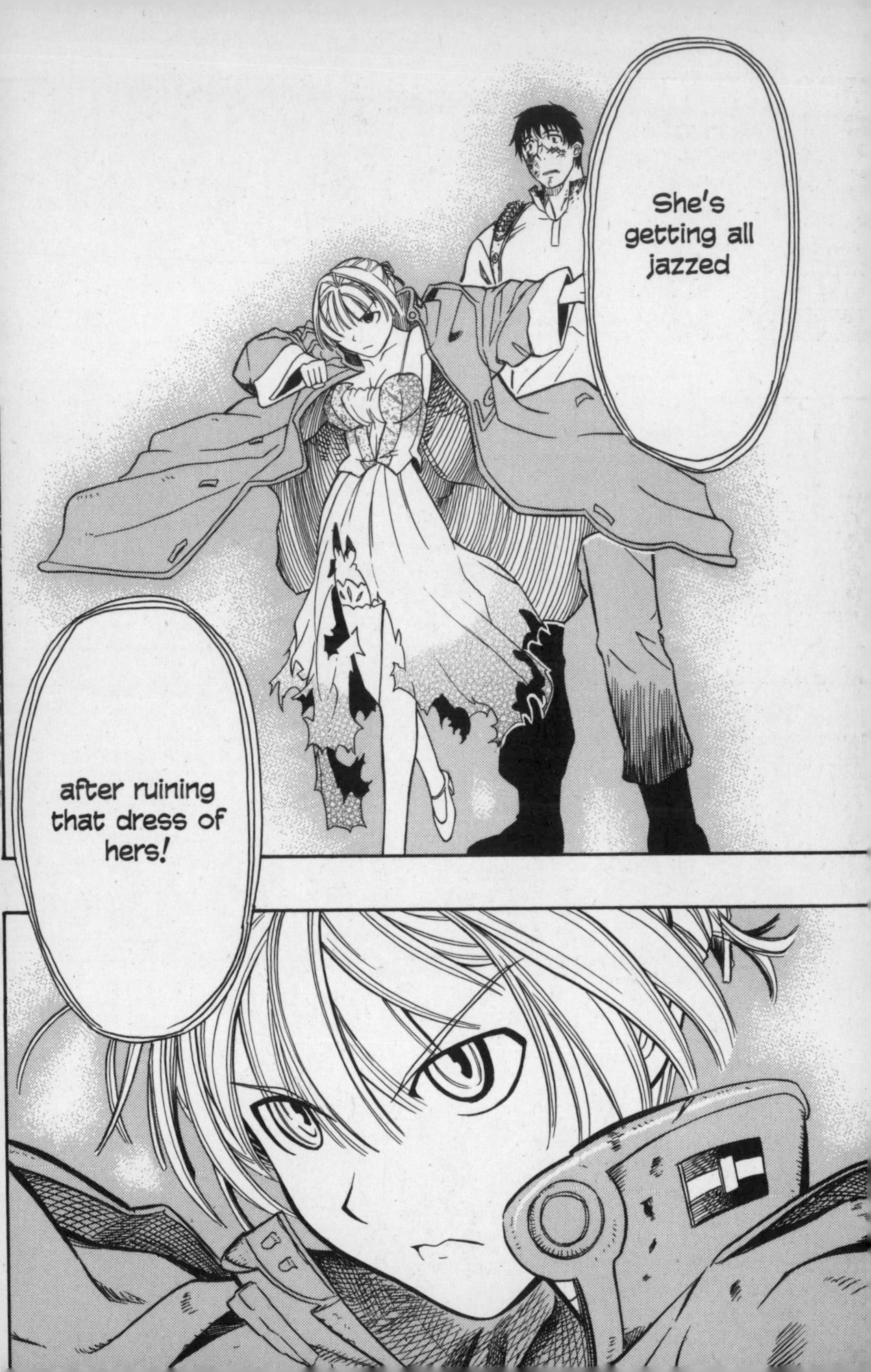
She's getting all jazzed
after ruining that dress of hers!

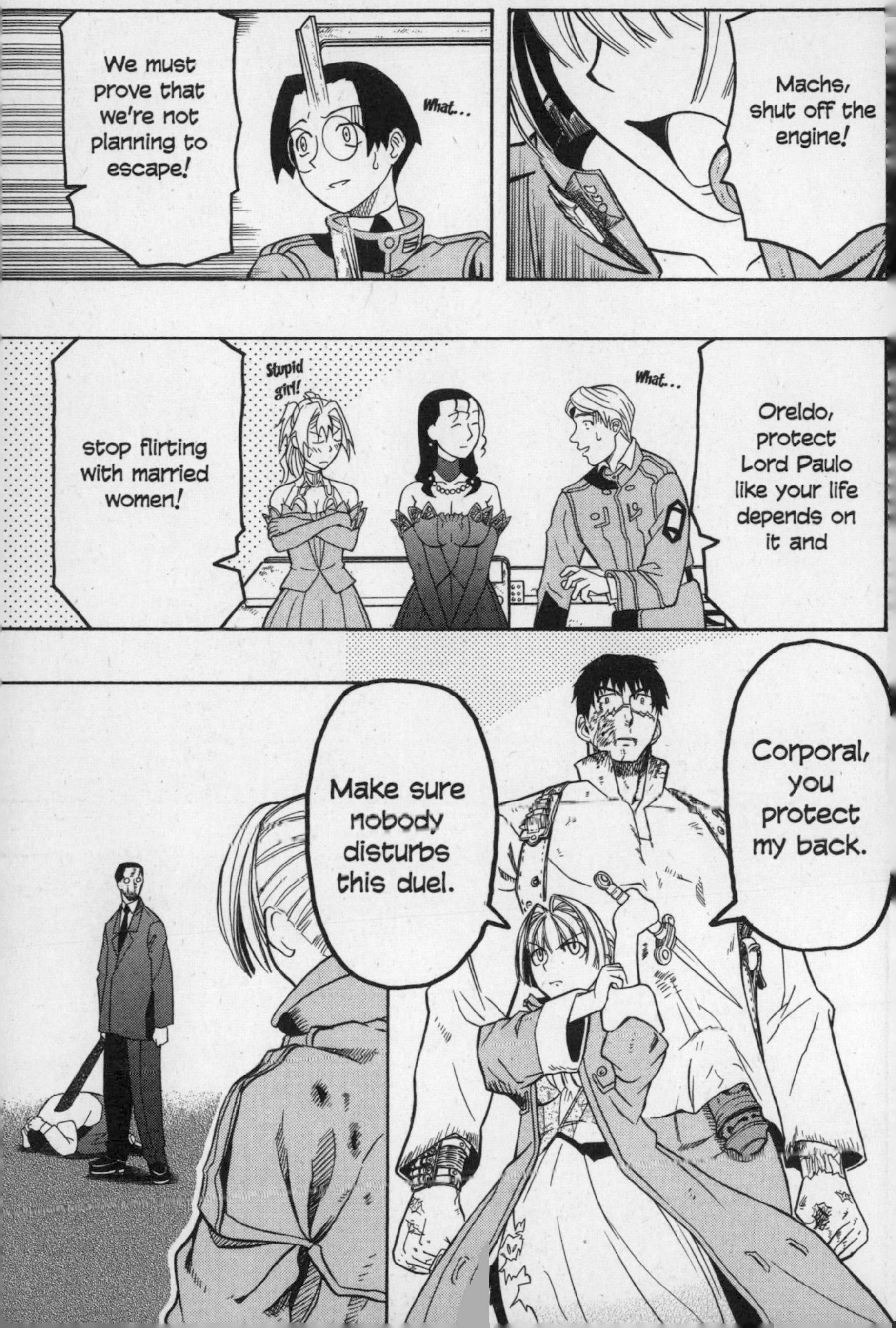
Machs, shut off the engine!
We must prove that we're not planning to escape!
What...
Oreldo, protect Lord Paulo like your life depends on it and
stop flirting with married women!
What...
Stupid girl!
Corporal, you protect my back.
Make sure nobody disturbs this duel.

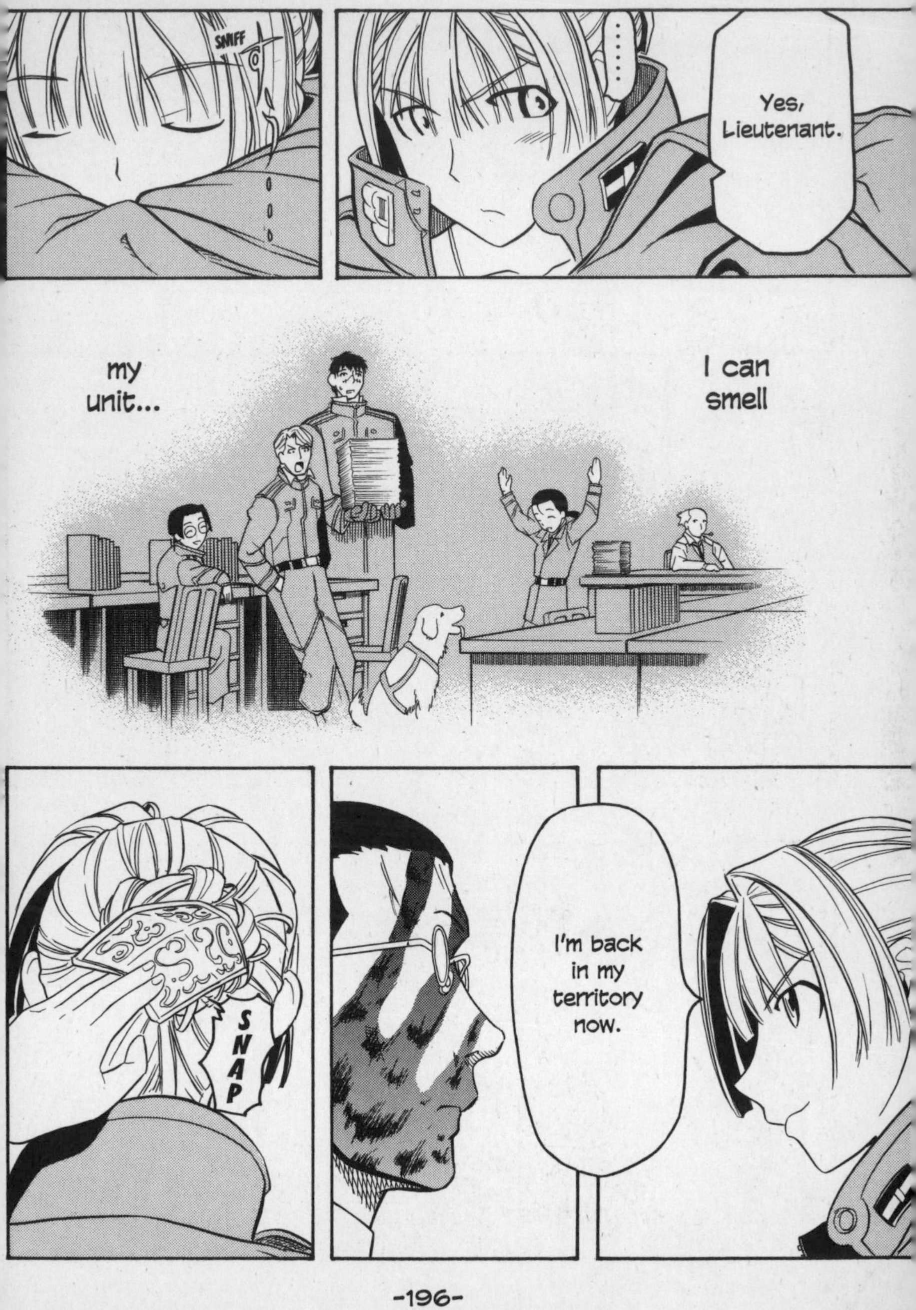
Yes, Lieutenant.
SNIFF
I can smell
my unit...
I'm back in my territory now.
SNAP

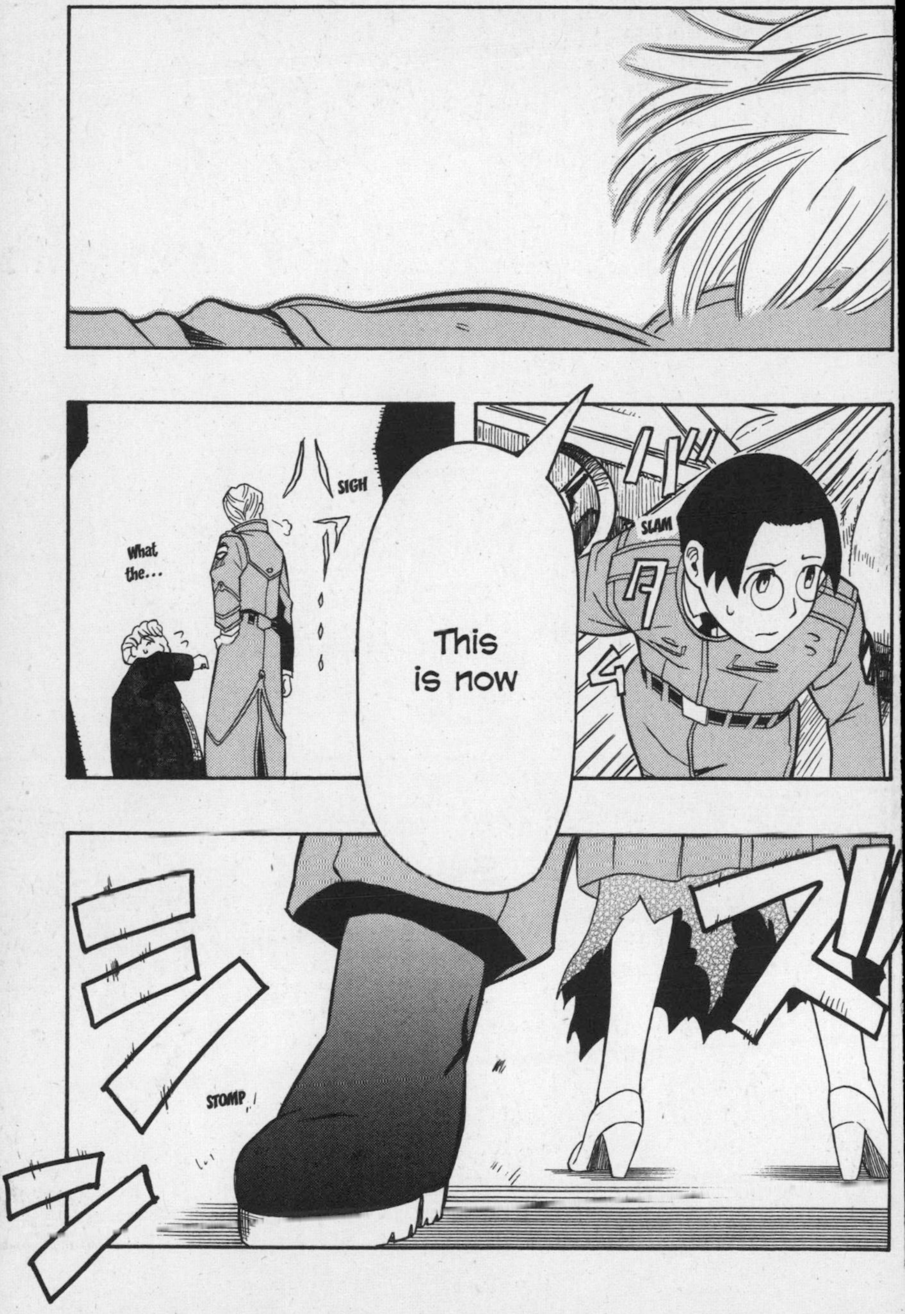
SLAM
This is now
SIGH
What the...
STOMP

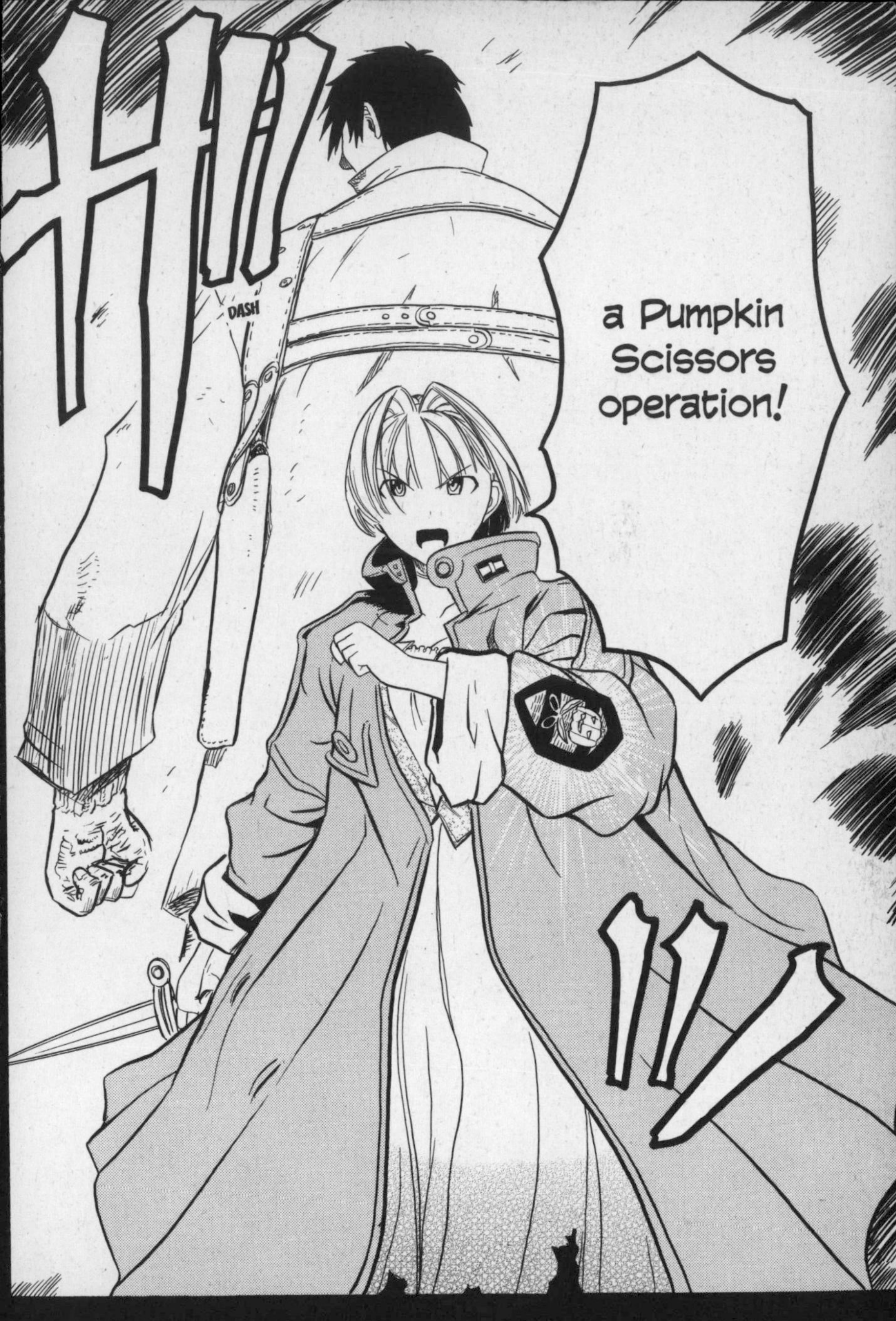
a Pumpkin Scissors operation!
DASH

#13/ The End

PumpkinScissors

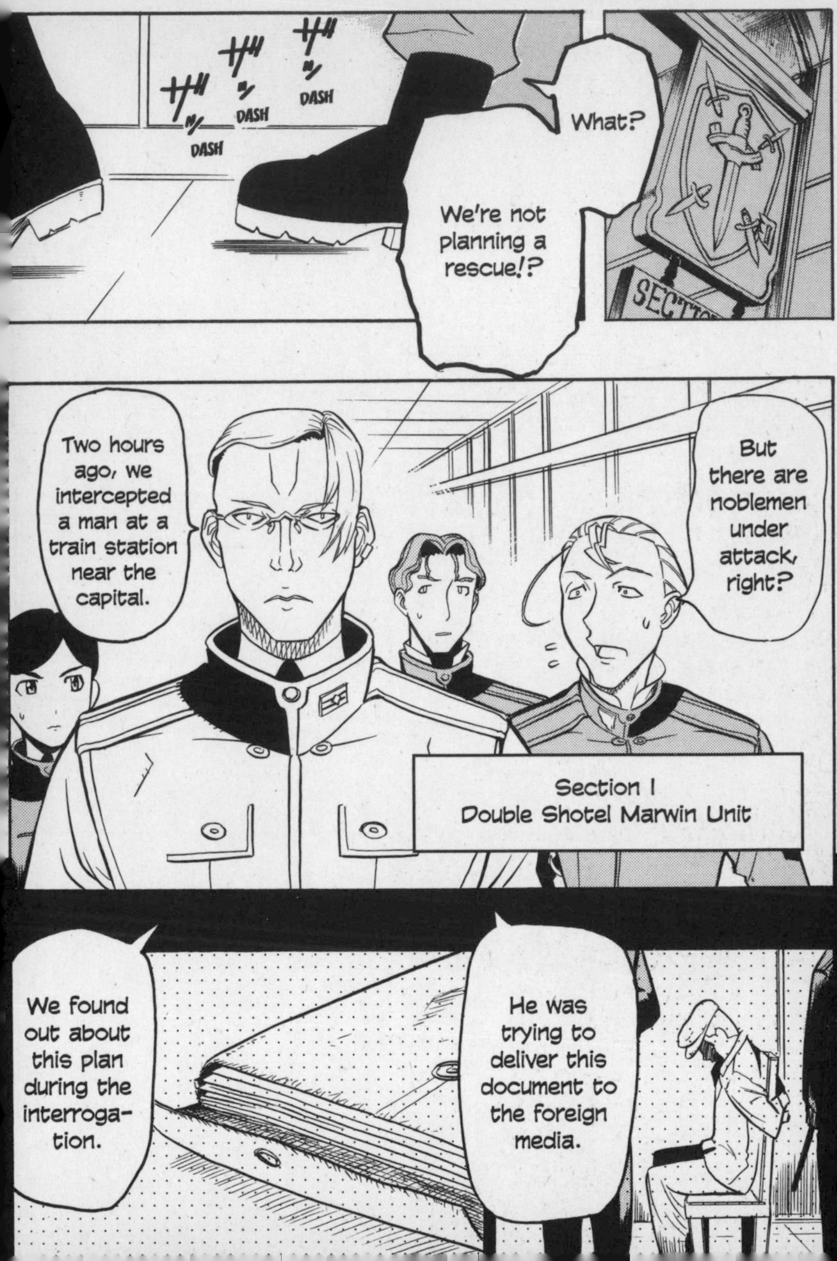
What?
We're not planning a rescue!?
DASH
DASH
DASH
But there are noblemen under attack, right?
Two hours ago, we intercepted a man at a train station near the capital.
Section 1
Double Shotel Marwin Unit
He was trying to deliver this document to the foreign media.
We found out about this plan during the interrogation.

We're too late.

By this time,

dozens of people are probably dead.

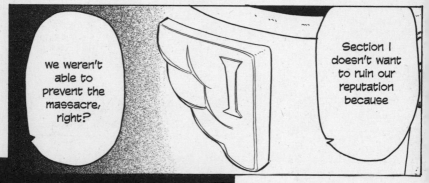

Section I doesn't want to ruin our reputation because

we weren't able to prevent the massacre, right?

We're blocking the path to the ball so we can

claim that we happened upon the rioters and arrested them.

GULP

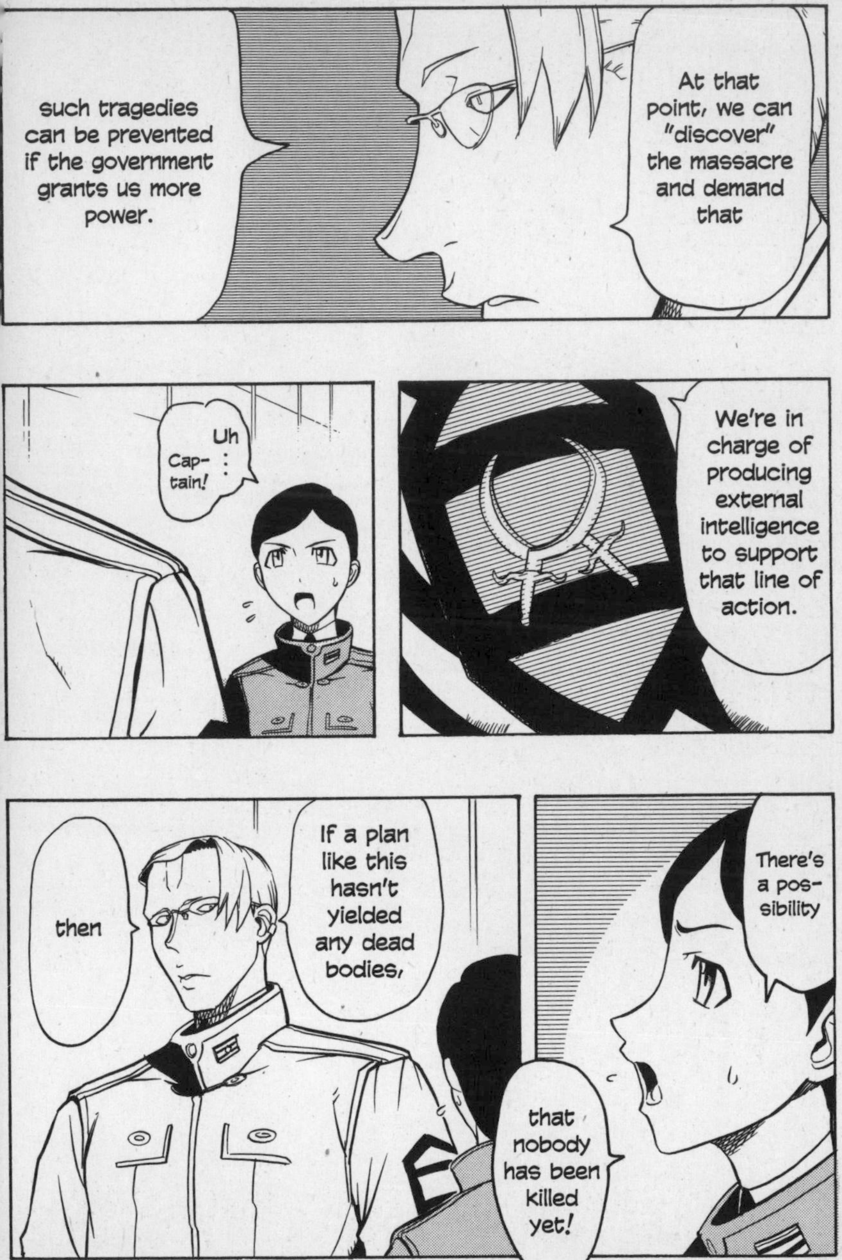
At that point, we can "discover" the massacre and demand that
such tragedies can be prevented if the government grants us more power.
We're in charge of producing external intelligence to support that line of action.
Uh... Cap-tain!
There's a pos-sibility
that nobody has been killed yet!
If a plan like this hasn't yielded any dead bodies,
then

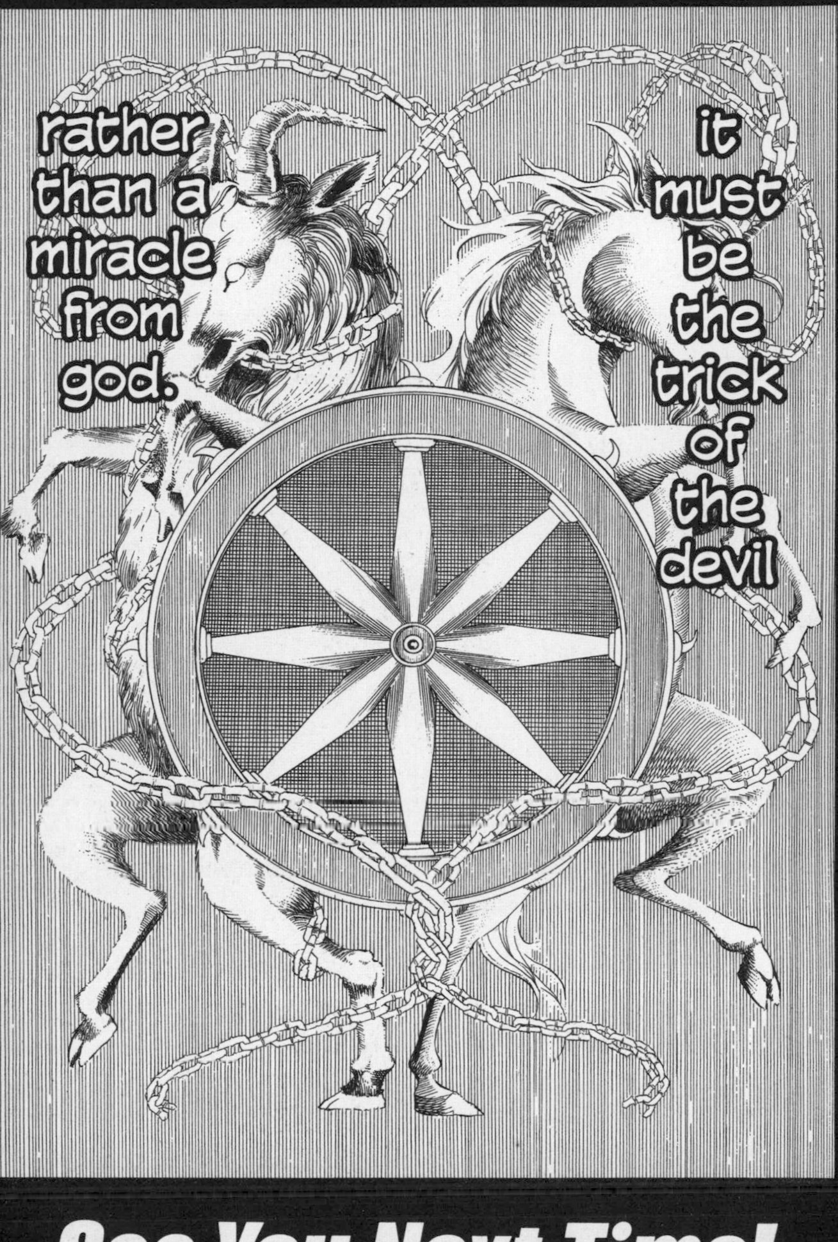
it must be the trick of the devil
rather than a miracle from god.

See You Next Time!

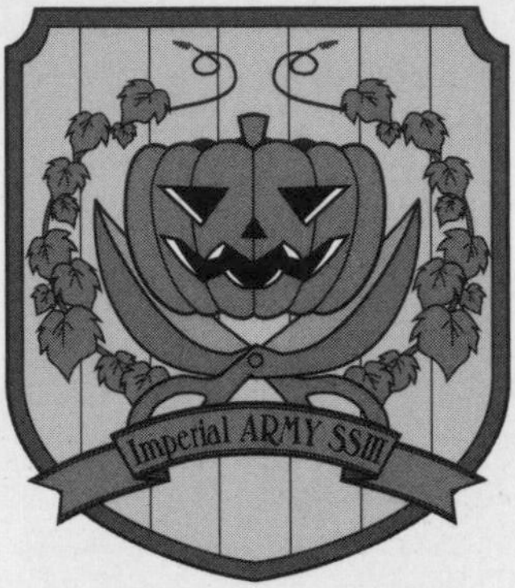
Imperial ARMY SSIII

Alice is soft!
I would have twisted the blade 90
degrees after stabbing his hand!
(Failed the Review)

Either way, the author's soft, too.
He didn't plan properly, hence I don't
make an appearance in this volume!
He didn't do his homework!
I need to twist his arm 90 degrees...
(Failed the Review)

Oh, who am I?

I don't have a name yet!!
(More details in volume 5)

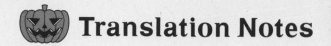 **Translation Notes**

Japanese is a tricky language for most Westerners, and translation is often more an art than a science. For your edification and reading pleasure, here are notes on some of the places where we could have gone in a different direction, or where a Japanese cultural reference is used.

We're at the ball, after all. Shall we dance, my princess?

BALLROOM DANCE, PAGE 5

Balls were one of the events associated with the aristocracy. As a result, balls appear frequently in Western fairy tales that involve aristocratic characters (examples include *Swan Lake, Sleeping Beauty,* and *Cinderella*). Ballroom dance is a Western form of dance that requires a partner. The male partner is most often the "leader" and the female is the "follower."

Ballroom dancing is now enjoyed all over the world for recreation as well as sport. It was officially recognized as a sport by the International Olympic Committee. However, it is not featured during the summer or winter Olympics at this time.

FLAIL, PAGE 85

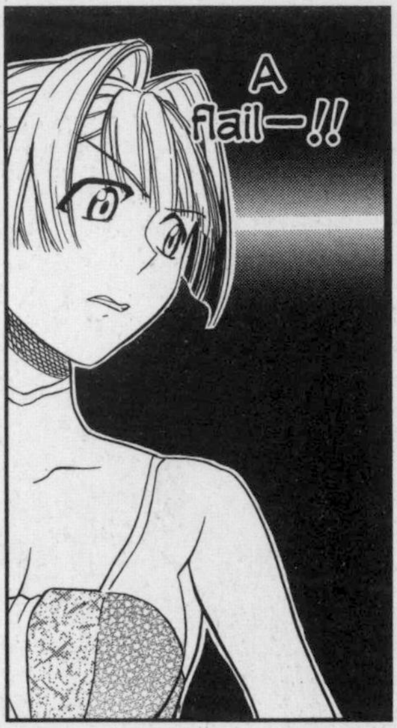
A flail—!!

A flail has one or multiple heavy objects secured to a chain, which is attached to a handle. The most common flail is a spiked sphere attached to a handle, one of which is shown in the book. There are also variations where the weight(s) are attached to the stick with a hinge instead. Other flails have multiple chains attached to the stick without weights. Developed during the Middle Ages, there are similar weapons across the globe, with the Asian nunchaku being one of the more recognizable ones.

There are several key advantages to using the flail. Aside from the weapon's ability to kill, it could also split armor and shields, making the opponent incredibly vulnerable to attack. It also had the ability to insulate the user from vibrations that can cause fatigue, unlike more rigid weapons such as the sword. The flail found favor with horsemen, who could gain momentum for their strikes on horseback through the speed of the horse without compromising their balance. It's also a difficult weapon to block because unlike rigid weapons, the flail can wrap and/or curve around objects.

On the other hand, there are disadvantages to this weapon. For one, it is not always effective in close quarters as the user requires room to swing the weapon. It's also much less accurate than rigid weapons, and an inexperienced user can injure himself quite easily with the weapon.

There is also a farming tool known as the flail.

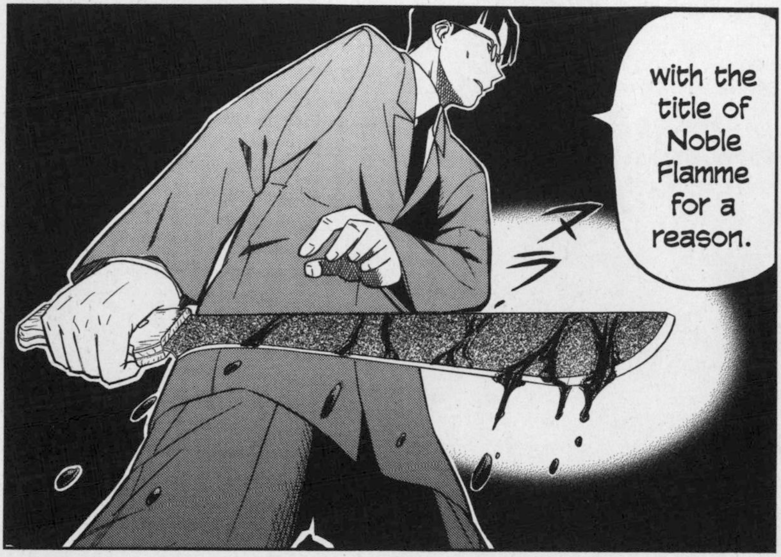
with the title of Noble Flamme for a reason.

MACHETE, PAGE 90

The machete is associated with jungles, which is reflected in this book. While it appears here as a formidable weapon, the main use for the machete is as a farming/gardening tool because of its ability to hack through difficult and persistent vegetation. It's even a useful kitchen tool due to the cleaverlike shape of the blade. People also use it as a simple woodworking tool. As a result, it's often considered an essential and versatile tool in many households throughout the globe.

Preview of Volume 5

We're pleased to present you a preview from *Pumpkin Scissors* volume 5. Please check our website (www.delreymanga.com) to see when this volume will be available in English. For now you'll have to make do with Japanese!

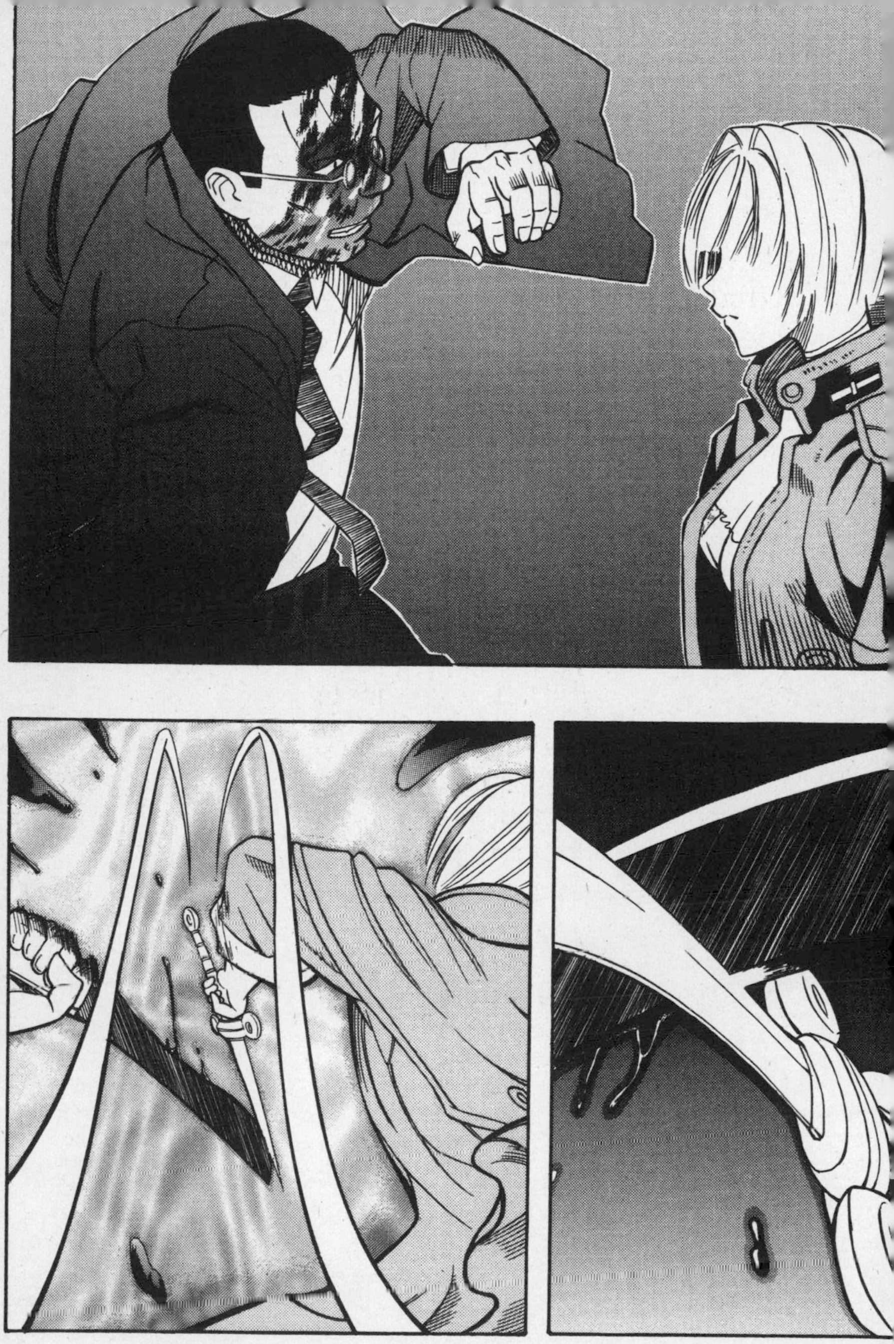

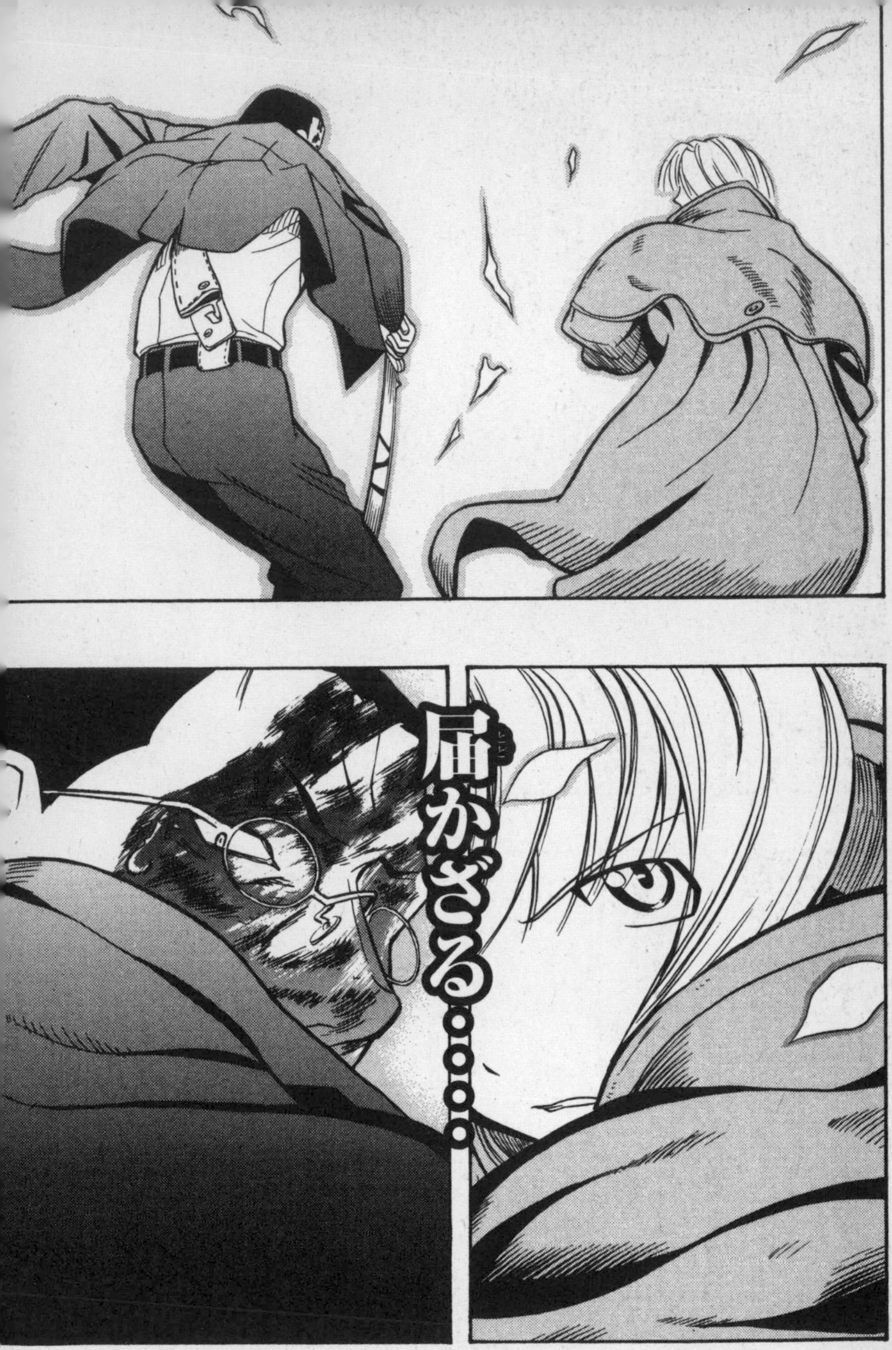
届かざる・・・・・

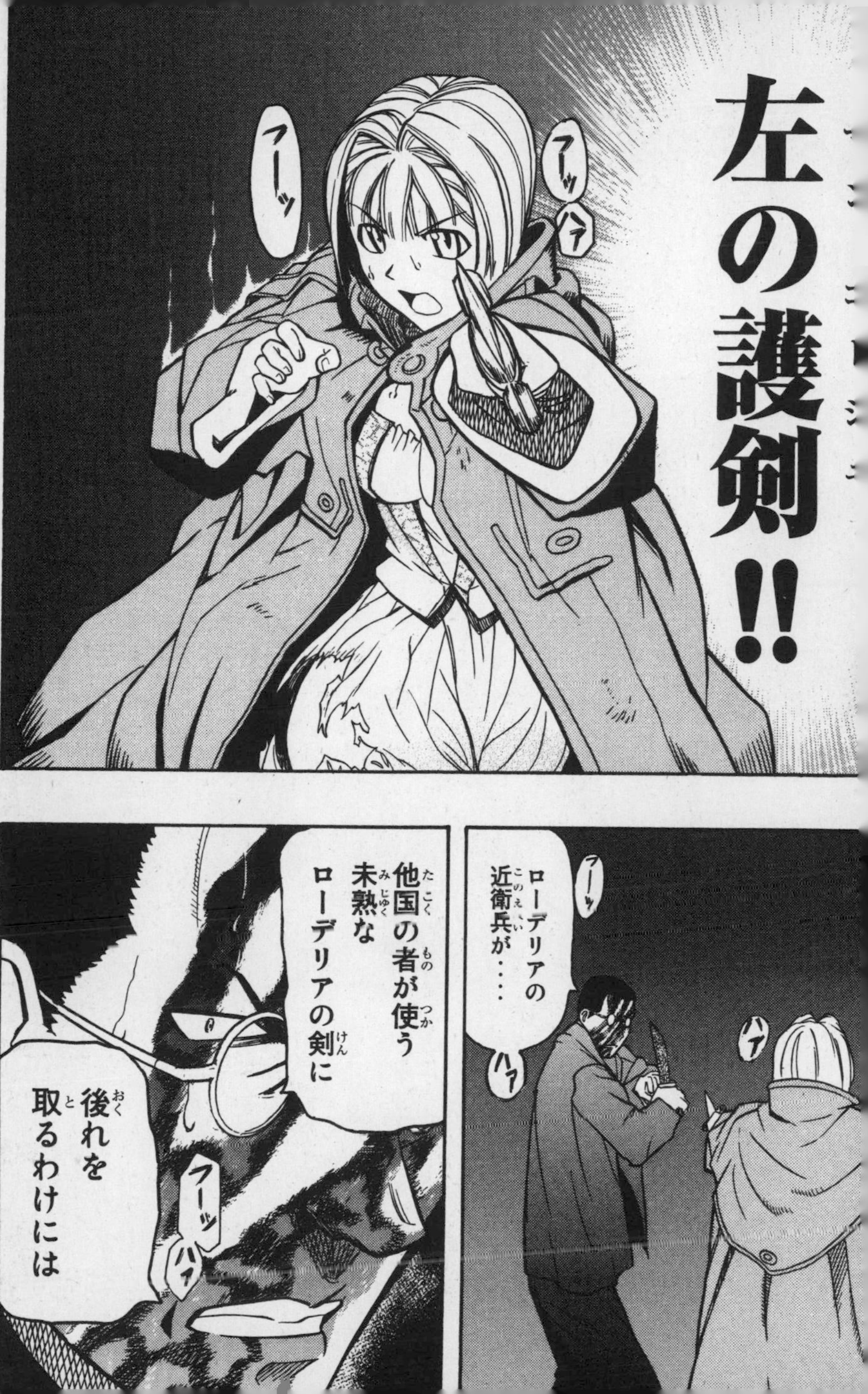
左の護剣!!
ファッ
ハァ
フーッ
フーッ
ローデリアの近衛兵が・・・・
ハァ
ハァ
他国の者が使う未熟なローデリアの剣に
後れを取るわけには
フーッ
ハァ

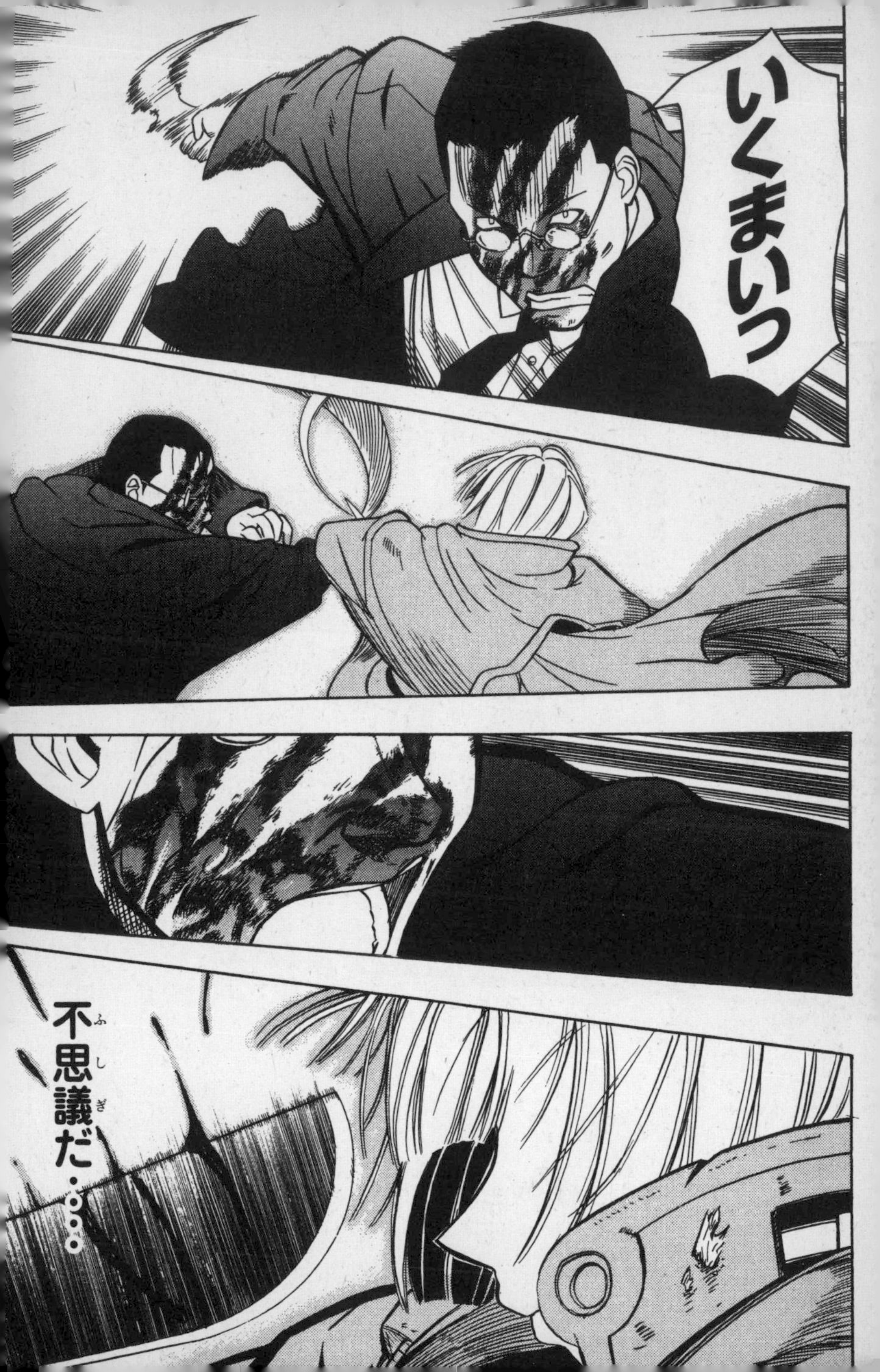
いくまいっ
不思議だ……

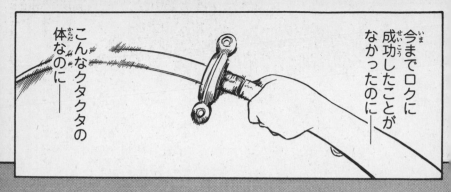

今までロクに成功したことがなかったのに——

こんなクタクタの体なのに——

こいつらの前だと・・・

こんなにも自在に動ける——

TOTO! THE WONDERFUL ADVENTURE

BY YUKO OSADA

SEE THE WORLD WITH ME!

Kakashi is a small-town boy with a big dream: to travel around the world. He's so determined to leave his little island home behind that he stows away onboard a marvelous zeppelin—one that just happens to be loaded with treasure and a gang of ruthless criminals!

Special extras in each volume! Read them all!

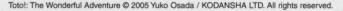

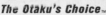

Yozakura Quartet

BY SUZUHITO YASUDA

A DIFFERENT SET OF SUPERTEENS!

Hime is a superheroine. Ao can read minds. Kotoha can conjure up anything with the right word. And Akina . . . well, he's just a regular guy, surrounded by three girls with superpowers! Together, they are the Hizumi Everyday Life Consultation Office, dedicated to protect the town of Sakurashin. And with demon dogs and supernatural threats around every corner, there's plenty to keep them busy!

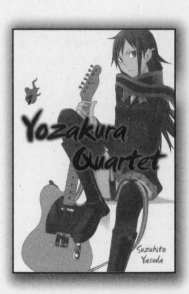

Special extras in each volume! Read them all!

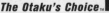

Psycho Busters

MANGA BY AKINARI NAO
STORY BY YUYA AOKI

PSYCHIC TEENS ON THE RUN!

Out of the blue, a beautiful girl asks Kakeru to run away with her. This could be any boy's dream come true, but there's something strange afoot.

It turns out that this girl is on the run from a shadowy government organization intent on using her psychic abilities for its own nefarious ends. But why does she need Kakeru's help? Could it be that he has secret powers, too?

- Story by Yuya Aoki, creator of *Get Backers*

Special extras in each volume! Read them all!

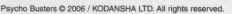